The Vauxhall File

AN ERIC DYMOCK MOTOR BOOK

The Vauxhall File
Model by Model

AN ERIC DYMOCK MOTOR BOOK

Second Edition

DOVE PUBLISHING LIMITED

First published in Great Britain in 1999 by
DOVE PUBLISHING

Second edition published 2007 by
DOVE PUBLISHING LIMITED
Old West Church Manse, Argyle Terrace, Rothesay, Isle of Bute PA20 0BD

Text copyright © Eric Dymock
Jacket design by Andrew Barron

British Library Cataloguing-in-Publication Data
A catalogue record for this book is available from the British Library

ISBN 978-0-9554909-0-3

Colour seperation by Colourwise, Goring-by-Sea, West Sussex

Printed in China by 1010 Printing International Limited

Foreword

Who would have known, back in 1903, that the first Vauxhall car we built would mark the birth of a company that would go on to be one of the world's most respected and best-loved car brands?

A brand that, in the UK alone, sells over 400,000 new vehicles a year, and is home to two of General Motors' most significant models – the Astra, built in Ellesmere Port, and the Vivaro van, built in Luton.

Vauxhall's history is a fascinating one. A story that includes some great engineers and some fantastic cars, and a brand that has touched the lives of millions of people in Britain, be it as owners, employees or simply those who have travelled in a Vauxhall car.

This book charts the history, model by model, of how Vauxhall grew as a company, became part of General Motors, and went on to become such a powerful brand. It takes an in-depth look at each individual model, from the very first 1903 5hp through to the very latest Antara and New Corsa – cars that continue to set new standards of design, just as Vauxhall cars always did in the past.

Today, as it always has been, Vauxhall is a British brand of which we should all be very proud. It is part of the very fabric of our society, and this book is a wonderful celebration of that fact. I, for one, find it hard to put down

Bill Parfitt
Managing Director, Vauxhall Motors Limited

Contents

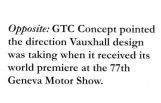

Opposite: **GTC Concept pointed the direction Vauxhall design was taking when it received its world premiere at the 77th Geneva Motor Show.**

From Vauxhall Gardens to Luton Hoo

Vauxhall was a familiar name in South London a hundred years before the first Vauxhall car in 1903. By the dawn of the 21st century Vauxhall Motors was part of British social and industrial history, having made limousines for Edwardian aristocracy and royalty, a dynasty of sports cars that gained international recognition, then spanning the distinctions of class and wealth for a wider public. Vauxhall came into General Motors' ownership in 1925, yet its founding principles held good. It adopted a marketing slogan that would have suited it following transformation from a purveyor of sporting cars for the nobility and gentry, to a mass-market manufacturer: "Quality is a right, not a privilege".

It was not an uninterrupted catalogue of achievement. The magnificent sporting Vauxhalls of the 1920s were commercially satisfactory yet, as with Bentley and Napier, Vauxhall would probably not have survived the Depression of the 1930s independently. Under GM the technical advances pioneered for popular cars included independent front suspension, synchromesh gearboxes, and unitary construction.

Left: **Vauxhall Heritage Centre.**

Yet GM was responsible for the styling hiatus of the first Victor, and could not avoid the industry's quality problems of the 1960s. Vauxhall's market share collapsed. It was a reverse only stemmed by a change of policy and the integration of Vauxhall into GM's European structure. This brought about the brilliantly successful Cavalier, followed by a series of cars that took it into the 21st century and drew together the two main strands of General Motors' European operations.

Vauxhall traced its roots back to the Middle Ages. A rather seamy mercenary to the unpopular Plantagenet King John (1167-1216) of Magna Carta fame, Fulk Le Bréant, was granted the Manor of Luton, made Sheriff of Oxford and Hertford and married by royal decree a rich heiress. Lady Margaret de Redvers was widow of Baldwin de Redvers, a member of the powerful Fitzgerold family, with a nice house at Lambeth up-river from London. After she married Fulk it was known as Fulk's Hall.

When Henry III succeeded King John, a desolate Le Bréant fled to France where he died in penury. The house's name was corrupted to Fulk's Hall then Fawke's Hall, Fox Hall and finally Vauxhall when the New Spring Gardens, a posh sort of private park, opened in 1661. Charles II and Nell Gwyn frequented it, and Samuel Pepys wrote about its rural charm. The Rt Hon George Canning featured the gardens in poetry and Thackeray described them in Vanity Fair. The Prince Regent liked to dine there, but by the latter part of the 19th century, the inhabitants included gamblers and ladies of the night. In 1836 English balloonist Charles Green flew from Vauxhall to Weilburg Germany 480 miles away, an 18-hour trip not matched until 1907.

Vauxhall's rustic attractions were in decline by 1857, when Scottish engineer Alexander Wilson set up an ironworks. This was coupled with Vauxhall Junction railway station, and the industrial smoke and grime of Wilson's works, which made compound twin and triple steam expansion engines for Thames River vessels plying between Westminster and Hampton Court finally did for the gardens. Wilson also made refrigeration plant, boilers, the Excelsior Steam Pump, and gained an Admiralty contract for high-pressure engines for naval pinnaces.

More of an engineer, less of a businessman, by 1894 Wilson was in financial difficulties. A receiver was called in, he went off to become a consulting engineer, and the firm became The Vauxhall Ironworks Company Ltd with a workforce of 150.

Following the reorganisation at the turn of the century,

one of Wilson's apprentice marine engineers, Frederick William Hodges, suggested making cars. One was bought, probably a Canstatt-Daimler, to see how it was done and two belt-driven prototypes were built. Hodges tried out all sorts of combustion engines, some ambitious like the opposed-piston design for his boat Jabberwock, yet it was 1902 before he and John Henry (Jack) Chambers, the 1896 receiver, designed the first production Vauxhall.

Chambers designed a second car, but resigned in 1904 taking his expertise with him back to the family business in Belfast, where a similar car to the first Vauxhall became the basis for generations of Chambers cars manufactured up to 1928. Harry Pratt, the engineer who bored-out that first engine, remained with Vauxhall following its move to Luton, retired in 1946, and died in 1964 aged 93.

Making cars was a gamble, so the pioneer partners stuck to straightforward principles. Their engineering was good and the cars well made, with a single cylinder and chain drive. A total of about 50 were sold the first year, so by the time the 3-cylinder 12/14, was ready for production, a bigger factory was needed. The old Ironworks lease was running out, car manufacture was crammed into four times the area of the former marine engine works, and there was no room to expand.

Vauxhall moved to Luton, by coincidence to Fulk's old country estate, and amalgamated with neighbouring West Hydraulic Engineering to form Vauxhall and West Hydraulic Ltd. Luton was expanding. It had just installed municipal

electricity; a seven-acre site was available, and there were plenty of skilled wood workers from Luton's hat-making industry.

The car business was separated from West Hydraulic in 1907, yet the variety of Vauxhall products looked like being its undoing, none was receiving the priority it deserved, so the car business was purchased for £17,000 by young director and shrewd merchant banker Leslie Walton. He and Percy Kidner became joint managing directors, and the former Wilson apprentice Frederick Hodges consultant engineer. A J Hancock joined as works organiser and the group was completed with the recruitment of gifted young engineer Laurence Henry Pomeroy. A premium apprentice with the North London Railway and former draughtsman with John Thornycroft at Basingstoke, Pomeroy was only 23 when he joined as drawing office assistant to Hodges, yet although he left in 1919 his work exerted a profound influence on Vauxhalls over two decades.

Fulk Le Bréant's enduring legacy was his heraldic emblem, a griffin or gryphon, half lion half eagle, that hung over the entrance to the old Vauxhall pleasure gardens and the ironworks kept it even following the move to Luton. Another distinguishing feature, the famous bonnet flutes, appeared on the engine cowling of the 1905 18HP, and remained on

Left: **Vauxhall Gardens.**

Vauxhalls for the following 50 years. The distinctive sculpted shape of the radiator and bonnet sides became an industrial icon that identified more than a make of car. On suburban driveways they were symbolic of an emerging British middle class. Just as the mock-Parthenon radiator of the Rolls-Royce identified the upper-class, or the Ford oval the blue-collar working-class, Vauxhall's mid-Atlantic style of the 1930s following GM's capture marked staunch, prosperous middle Britain.

Vauxhall's early years were notable for the performance of the 20HP in the RAC 2000 Miles (3219km) International Touring Car Trial of 1908. Competitions secured Edwardian reputations and Vauxhall had been keen to make its name. So was the ambitious Pomeroy. When the RAC published regulations for the Trial in the winter of 1907-1908, and the directors decided to develop a car for it, he was quick off the mark. The formidable F W Hodges was on holiday in Egypt, so Pomeroy started work on a radical new design. There was no chance of Hodges catching the next flight home, so the young designer worked without interference. The company entered a prototype known as the Y-type, and the subsequent A-types or 20HP cars made up to 1914, ensured Vauxhall's place among the great Edwardians.

Work cascaded from the drawing board of the talented Pomeroy. In 1910 a motoring competition once again marked a Vauxhall landmark. Kidner was eager to take part in the trial organized by Prince Heinrich of Prussia, car enthusiast brother of Kaiser Wilhelm II. The long-distance reliability test to which the Prince gave his name combined the prestige of a Monte Carlo Rally with the social cachet of Ascot. It followed a tortuous route to Munich from Berlin of 1150 miles (1850 km), and such aristocratic patronage amounted to a command performance for most of the 200 entrants. An archduke sponsored Ferdinand Porsche's Austro-Daimler.

For 1910 it was tougher than ever, with 17 special tests from Berlin to Bad Homburg via Braunschweig, Kassel, Nürnberg, Strasbourg and Metz. Road sections were interspersed with hill-climbs and speed tests, the cars had to be fully equipped, and all four seats occupied. Austro-Daimler entered three cars and finished first second and third.

It was a crushing defeat for Mercédès, and established

Right: **Cars of the works team, Prince Henry of Prussia tour 1910, photographed at Luton.**

another motor industry precept – that motor racing was not only useful for motivating customers, it also gave encouragement to management and engineers. Porsche had been determined that his production Austro-Daimler would meet Mercédès' challenge and it developed into one of the best sporting cars of the 1920s.

Pomeroy was an engineer in the Porsche mould, relishing the opportunity to design a great sporting car. Notable Vauxhalls came after the Y-type including some that competed with Porsche's Austro-Daimlers. Regulations for the Prince

Henry Trial encouraged long-stroke, large capacity engines, so Pomeroy adapted the 4-cylinder for a team of three cars. His 3.0-litre engine was no match for Porsche's 5.7-litre, yet they finished trouble-free and came back with finishers' awards. The 1911 production version introduced at the Olympia Motor Show in October was duly called the Prince Henry Vauxhall.

Company publicity stressed it was weight reductions that had made it such a strong performer, the body and chassis were narrow and tapered, and Pomeroy gave a great deal of thought to the precise curves and flutes on the radiator and bonnet. He aimed at good aerodynamics and adequate cooling, although his son Laurence Evelyn Pomeroy, distinguished technical editor of *The Motor* many years later was sceptical. "Unfortunately the 3-litre radiator had insufficient cooling area and was notorious for boiling if driven fast upon a summer's day. Nevertheless this small light car was tremendous fun to drive and I remember as a boy long journeys sitting in the dickey-seat of my father's two-seater."

The Prince Henry was by no means the only conspicuous sporting Vauxhall. In 1909 A J Hancock drove a single-seater known as KN up Shelsley Walsh hill climb at record speed and went on to break Brooklands class records at

Above: erecting shop, Luton.

88.6mph. Whimsical names were a Brooklands custom; KN was a punning allusion to Cayenne Pepper, advertised as "Hot Stuff". The following October a narrow-bodied single-seater with KN's engine became the first 20HP car officially timed at 100mph.

By 1909 Vauxhall was making nearly 200 chassis a year for the coach-building industry to construct bodies on. In 1910 nearly 250 were turned out, as well as speed-boat engines in commercial quantities. The cars were elegant and up-market and in 1911, after Kidner won his class in reliability trials, well thought-of by the Russian Imperial family. Vauxhall set up a workshop in St Petersburg staffed by British fitters, and printed catalogues in Russian.

Promoted to works manager in 1910, Pomeroy designed an ingenious overhead cam engine for the Prince Henry team cars, which was never alas used. With astonishing prescience he proposed moving the camshafts lengthways, bringing a second set of cams into play to alter valve timing and lift, effectively reconfiguring the engine. At slow speeds one set of cams provided smooth economical running, at high speeds others came into play enabling the valves to gulp a bigger charge of mixture and produce more power. Fixed valve openings could not manage both, Pomeroy's invention was a generation ahead of its time, but the materials and techniques to make it work were not yet available. Each cam had to be painstakingly shaped by hand. Variable valve timing was re-invented in the 1980s once metallurgy enabled steel tough enough.

Kidner had another success in February 1912 with the C-type Prince Henry in the Swedish winter trials. He constructed a canvas screen rather like the dodger on a ship's bridge to deflect snow, and drilled holes in the floor to draw in heat from the engine. He arrived at the finish in Stockholm but was excluded from the results for being too far ahead of the field.

Vauxhall raced in the Coupe de l'Auto voiturette races of 1911, 1912 and 1913, and in 1914 twin overhead cam engines were designed for the TT and the French Grand Prix, but the official competition programme was dogged by misfortune. Some of the cars only did well after they were disposed of to private owners. Pomeroy's influence was waning and although he spent much of the First World War experimenting with camshafts, he resigned soon after it ended. His successor Clarence King had an unconventional background for a senior engineer in the motor industry. Mystic and artist, he had been apprenticed as a mechanic and worked with the Adams

Manufacturing Company and the Société Lorraine. When he left France during the war he had been trying to earn a living as a painter. CEK, as he was known in company memos, was instrumental in the design of Vauxhalls for the next 30 years.

Among the individuals that influenced development at Vauxhall was Joseph Higginson of the Autovac company, who asked Pomeroy for a 4.5-litre engine in a small Prince Henry chassis. Higginson wanted it in time for the 1913 Shelsley Walsh hill-climb, leaving 13 weeks to do it. Pomeroy rose to the occasion. His first 30-98 (nobody really knew what the figures represented but the name stuck) had a narrow aluminium body and no doors. It also had a new rounded radiator unlike the V-shaped Prince Henry prow, and Higginson used it to great effect beating the latest Sunbeam and setting a record that would not be broken for 15 years.

Between 1914 and 1918 Vauxhalls acted as staff cars for British officers and a 25hp Vauxhall took King George V to Vimy Ridge. Another carried General Allenby on his conquering entry into Jerusalem and a Vauxhall was the first car across the Rhine into Germany following the Armistice. In the 1920s the 30-98 re-emerged as an 80mph sporting rival for the Bentley.

Vauxhalls were still not for the man in the street, and the 2.3-litre 14/40 of 1925, ostensibly at the cheaper end, cost a formidable £750. Yet it was a dwindling market, and even the splendid 4.2-litre-OE with overhead valves and four-wheel brakes was not enough to save the day. Despite its reputation as one of Britain's classic makes, Vauxhall was not making enough cars to keep in business. By 1924 it was selling only 1,400 a year, and although in 1925 sales held steady, price reductions were going to be essential in 1926. Vauxhall's last independent engineering decision was to bring in the extraordinary S-type, despite sleeve-valves being the ruin of many distinguished names in Britain and elsewhere. The sporting Vauxhalls were not selling in sufficiently large numbers even though advertised as *The Car of Grace that Sets the Pace*. The S-type (slogan, *Superexcellent*) was expected to compete with Daimler, Rolls-Royce, and Sunbeam.

It was not to be. General Motors was looking for production capacity in 1925 and rebuffed by Austin, went after Vauxhall, and in a deal encouraged by Alfred P Sloan Jnr president of GM, bought the ordinary shares for $2.5 million. By 1931 production was 5000 cars a year and a £500,000 expansion programme was undertaken to increase it, although it was still only a twentieth of what Austin and Morris were making. Luton was GM's first manufacturing plant outside North America, the next was Opel at Rüsselsheim in Germany, in January 1929 when the Opel family reorganised the company it had founded in 1898. Two months later GM purchased 80 per cent of the stock in Adam Opel AG, increasing to 100 per cent after two years.

Vauxhall stopped making expensive cars, ceased competing with Bentley and Sunbeam, and went over to

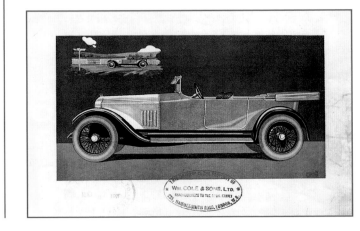

popular models. It did not neglect innovation however, beating Rolls-Royce to synchromesh gearchanging by several months in 1932, then pioneering unit body-chassis structures and the famous "knee-action" independent front suspension. GM established a spectacularly successful truck and van division, Bedford, gaining export sales and sustaining the passenger car business through hard times. A milestone came in 1933 when Vauxhall and Opel together made more cars than GM was exporting from North America.

Vauxhall's family cars, the Cadet, Light Six, Big Six, and later the Ten-Four, Twelve-Four, and Fourteen-Six were larger and more softly sprung than most of their contemporaries. They acquired a hint of Chevrolet or Buick style in 1937, with decorative grilles ahead of the radiator, yet the fluted bonnet survived. The 1930s finished with a flourish, the 25HP with a variety of bodies returning Vauxhall to its traditional classy clientele. By 1939 Luton was making 30,000 a year, one in ten of all the cars built in Britain, and far from being outsold five to

Left: **25HP D-type c 1920. Cole coachwork featured single door.**
Right: **23-60 OD-type c 1924.**

one, Vauxhall was now one of the Big Six together with Austin, Morris, Ford, Rootes (Hillman, Humber, Sunbeam), and Standard. It was also selling as many Bedford lorries and light commercials as it did Vauxhall cars.

In 1939 car production stopped. Vauxhall made a handful of 10HP saloons for the government, turning instead to making nearly a quarter of a million Bedford trucks. The QL was the company's first enterprise in four-wheel drive. Luton presses turned out five million jerricans; the spare fuel canisters proving so puncture-proof that they were copied without reference to their German designers. The presses also made 750,000 steel helmets. Luton made six-pounder armour-piercing shells, and the sheet-metal department not only did development work on Mosquito, Halifax, and Lancaster bombers, but also became involved with mines and radar equipment.

Vauxhall's secret war involved work on a batch of the first jet aircraft engines, but its grandest assignment was the design and manufacture of the Churchill tank. In 1940 the United Kingdom had only 100 tanks available for home defence, and Vauxhall took on the task of developing and putting a new one into production in the shortest time possible.

After 1945, obliged to export the bulk of its production to meet Britain's war debts, Vauxhalls were almost identical to the pre-war H, I, and J models. By the autumn of 1947, when horsepower was abandoned as the basis of car tax, there was little point in keeping the 10HP as a separate model and it was amalgamated with the 12HP. During the course of a £14 million factory expansion in 1948, the range was rationalised into the L-type Wyvern and Velox, with new frontage and boot but much the same middle. It was a practical way of introducing a new range, keeping it up to the mark in fashion, and preparing for the E-Series Velox and Wyvern in 1951. These were based on a 1949 Chevrolet although perhaps less well proportioned.

Nevertheless they were in for a long production run. In

Left: **Griffin or gryphon, unlikely heraldic beast attached to Vauxhall.**
Right: **Wrap-round window and** tailfins for the **PA Cresta. This 1959 one from the Heritage Collection had a one-piece rear window.**

the company's golden anniversary year of 1953, production exceeded 100,000 for the first time and the millionth Vauxhall was made. The Luton plant expanded to 80 acres (32 hectares), employed more than 13,000, and once again a major (£35 million) programme was put in hand to extend the car production building and move Bedford trucks to Dunstable. Within four years there were 22,000 employees and turnover was £76 million.

The first Victor in 1957 was in some respects another neo-Chevrolet although less successful than the first. Later Victors showed improvements but the indifferent quality of the stylish 1960s Crestas, despite their fashionable tail fins, set the firm on a roller-coaster of disappointment that lasted until the 1970s.

Vauxhall car sales peaked in 1964 at 342,873 following a vigorous new model strategy that included the small angular Viva HA. This brought Vauxhall back into the 1-litre class, and with a production run of over 321,000 in 1966 led to the stylish HB (556,752 made from 1966 to 1970), and a successful series of 26 models that survived in essentials until the Chevette of 1984. The millionth Viva came off the production line at Luton in July 1971 and the 1,000,001st from the new plant at Ellesmere Port on Merseyside. Vivas grew up so much that in the 1970s they became known as Magnums. The Firenza two-door coupe lent itself to motor sport and the distinctive droop-snoot racing Firenza enhanced Vauxhall's reputation among younger buyers.

The FD Victor with new overhead camshaft engines celebrated the diamond jubilee of the Luton plant in 1967. FD won the Don Safety Trophy and continued until 1971. The Chevette following the third generation Viva showed the shape

Above: **The GM T-car project was a success of the 1970s, and by 1983 when this Vauxhall Chevette was made was well into its stride not only as a practical small saloon, but also as a successful competition car.**

Right: **This 1994 car exemplified the third and final generation of the Cavalier, one of the most successful Vauxhalls ever, and the model that restored the make's reputation for quality and reliability.**

of things to come. It was European-engineered, like the essentially Opel-oriented Cavalier of 1975, which brought an end to the long-running series of Victors and derivatives such as the 6-cylinder Ventora. The Cavalier's exemplary reliability and improved quality kept the Luton home fires burning, and in 1978 Vauxhall moved up-market with the Carlton and Royale, signifying the strength of GM's design and development at Rüsselsheim in West Germany. But by the end of the 1970s sales were in decline throughout the industry, Vauxhall's share falling to 230,420. The workforce still stood at 33,000.

The Cavalier was a key to recovery. There were three saloons and a coupe based on the successful Opel Ascona, and it became one of Britain's most sought-after cars. The business community valued its reliability, and private buyers found it rewarding to drive. Its superior anti-corrosion treatment was particularly welcome in restoring Vauxhall's good name.

The revival of the 1980s saw the Astra, a wide range of C-sector saloons and hatchbacks and an affiliate model for the Opel Kadett, which in due course took the Astra name. GM's tentative steps to promote Opel in Britain in competition with Vauxhall were rebuffed, the sturdy heritage of Fulk Le Bréant showed that buyers were reluctant to relinquish a treasured name. By 1983 the

579 British Vauxhall and 224 Opel dealers had merged to become joint Vauxhall-Opel dealers, later simply reverting to Vauxhall.

Yet the confluence of Vauxhall and Opel marked the beginning of Vauxhall's recovery. In a vigorous endorsement of GM's UK manufacturing operations and the Astra operation at Ellesmere Port, Luton was given over to the J-car Cavalier. In 1981 and 1982 the Viceroy and Senator spread the range upwards until the last Viscount in 1972. A new-version Carlton and the splendid Senator with its boldly styled grille of 1987 set the seal on Vauxhall's up-market aspirations.

At the other end of the scale the Nova came in 1983, on GM's S-car platform like the Spanish-built Opel Corsa. The chunky Corsa was replaced in 1986 and later updated with a range that included Vauxhall's first 3-cylinder car since the 12/14 of 1904.

Losses were stemmed in 1984 to £1.1 million, Vauxhall/Opel sales recovering to over a quarter of a million, 22.6 per cent of the UK car market, encouraging Roger Smith then GM chairman, to put £100 million into upgrading both Luton and Ellesmere Port. A new £90 million paint plant was inaugurated at Luton in 1987, when the Carlton was voted Car of the Year, following its rival Ford Scorpio. Sales were up to

304,000, losses were things of the past with profits up to £31 million, and Cavalier passed a million. The 1988 Cavalier had 22 variants including a four-wheel drive 2.0-litre, and when its successor the Vectra was introduced Luton's reward was to be nominated host plant, exporting many cars badged as Opels to world markets. Ellesmere Port now matched the Luton paint plant on top of the £85 million spent on Merseyside inside four

years. At the dawn of the 1990s Vauxhall's profits stood at over £150 million a year.

In the 1990s Luton became not only the principal Vectra plant but also, following a £100 million investment with IBC Vehicles, a joint manufacturing facility between General Motors and Isuzu of Japan. It already produced the Rascal and Midi vans and now the plan was to double production to 60,000 a year. Engines and transmissions were imported but local content accelerated following the introduction of a new welding plant and an automated paintshop. On the threshold of the millennium the principal models were giving a good account of themselves. In the sport-utility market Frontera was in the European top ten ahead of Land Rover Discovery. The Astra was a firm third ahead of the Ford Escort in the lower medium category and among the superminis Corsa vied for the lead just behind the long established Fiat Punto.

A significant development for Vauxhall was the announcement in February 1999 by chairman and managing director Nick Reilly of the re-establishment of a UK engineering

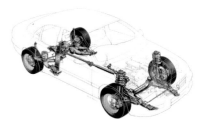

centre. Vauxhall once again took charge of a good deal of design and development. A £5m facility with an engineering staff of 75 at Millbrook became responsible for light commercial vehicles and recreational vehicles. Engineers were relocated from Europe and Japan to join up with the British team on a Technology Park close to the world-class Millbrook facilities.

In 2001 General Motors set up a joint venture with Fiat that had far-reaching consequences. Under the agreement the V6 engine plant at Ellesmere Port became Vauxhall Powertrain Ltd, a unit of Fiat-GM and the Vauxhall purchasing department was similarly subsumed into the new global strategy. A side-effect of the policy however meant addressing Europe's over-capacity for car-making, leading to the end of car production at Luton in the spring of 2002. After 97 years the 7,415,045th came off the line in March. The more welcome corollary was a

Left: **Controversial Carlton. Surprised perhaps that a Vauxhall could do 282kph**
(176mph) safety groups campaigned for its proscription, but were overruled by demand.

Above: **Omega dynamics. Front suspension had silicone-filled bushes to absorb vibration and**
eliminate steering wheel shake. Multi-link rear suspension limited response to torque reversals.

further £200 million investment at Ellesmere Port to allow production of the new Vectra together with Astra and Astravan under flexible production arrangements.

The alliance with Fiat was later unscrambled although doubts over Ellesmere Port persisted until 2007, when General Motors confirmed its prospects were secure. Vauxhall chairman Jon Browning, who was also head of GM's sales and marketing operations in Europe, said: "We went through a lot of pain at the plant last year and that is paying dividends. Ellesmere Port

is now able to put forward a competitive proposal to build the next generation Vauxhall Astra." The factory already produced the current Astra, but faced competition from GM plants worldwide to win the next generation due around 2010. Now a decision was made in order to start investment and tooling.

Vauxhall sales in the UK grew to 302,000 in 2006. Browning continued "We are particularly pleased because our sales to individual consumers were up eight per cent and that represents much better business for Vauxhall. We are consciously reducing the number of vehicles we sell into large fleets in order to make the business more profitable." And following the departure or collapse of a good deal of the indigenous car-building industry Vauxhall was once again among Britain's major producers.

Left: **VX Lightning, 2003 design study by Simon Cox and Martin Smith at GM Advanced Design in Coventry for Vauxhall's centenary celebrations, had a supercharged aluminium 2.2 engine producing 179kW (240bhp) and 305Nm (225lbft).**

Right: **Commitment to eco-friendliness exemplified by 2006 GM hydrogen fuel cell Zafira. Based on Sequel it had steer- and brake-by-wire controls, wheel hub motors as pioneered by Ferdinand Porsche in 1900, and lithium-ion batteries.**

1903-1905 5 and 6HP

F W Hodges and J H Chambers took no risks with the first Vauxhall. They gave it a slow-revving, horizontal single cylinder engine (4in bore x 4.75in stroke) and a chassis that was straightforward save in one important respect. Most cars of the time relied on know-how from the bicycle industry with brazed tubes, or from structural engineering with channel-section frames, and the body was traditionally a wood-framed structure bolted on top.

Not the Vauxhall. With surprising prescience it amalgamated the chassis and the lower part of the body into a composite steel and wood structure. Appropriately for a car built by marine engineers it had tiller steering, with a control on the tiller upright regulating engine speed by altering the tension of the automatic inlet valve return spring. There was a speed governor on the exhaust valve which could be overridden by a pedal. The first cars of 1903 had wire wheels. Artillery wheels, reverse gear and a steering wheel instead of a tiller were adopted later. On the few 4-seater models the passengers sat ahead of the driver, over the engine. Vauxhall's sporting debut was in October 1903, when the Wolverhampton & District Motor Club verified A G Price's time of 5min 46sec for Hermitage Hill in the ninth Vauxhall made.

BODY open 2-seater, 4-seater; 272kg (600lb), 6hp 323kg (712lb).
ENGINE governed single cylinder, front, horizontal, 101.6mm x 120.65mm; 978cc; 3.7kW (5bhp) @ 900rpm; 3.8kW/L (5.1bhp/L); from February 1904 6HP 101.6mm x 127mm; 1029cc 6bhp @ 900rpm.
ENGINE STRUCTURE side exhaust valve; automatic inlet valve; integrally cast cyl head and block; 2-bearing crank; Vauxhall spray carb; trembler coil ign; water-cooled with pump driven off exhaust camshaft.
TRANSMISSION Clutchless; 2-speed epicyclic gearbox, no reverse until cars made after February 1904, chain drive to rear axle.
CHASSIS DETAILS integral steel structure; beam axles; spiral springs front and rear; no dampers; brakes: drums on rear wheels. tiller steering; wheel steering from September 1904; 16L (3.5 Imp gal) fuel tank; 26 x 3 tyres, non-detachable wire wheels.
DIMENSIONS wheelbase 159cm (62.5in); front track 132cm (52in); rear 129.5cm (51in); length 249cm (98in);

width 160cm (63in); height 132cm (52in).
PERFORMANCE speed governed to 30kph (18mph); pedal overriding governor to allow 40kph (25mph); 28 mph @ 900rpm; fuel consumption on Glasgow to London trial 7.4L/100km (38.25mpg).
PRODUCTION probably 84 5HP 1903-1904; 44 6HP all made in 1904.
PRICE 130 guineas (5HP) £136-£150.

Percy Kidner and Frederick Hodges took part in London to Glasgow trial on 19/20 May 1905 with 6HP, the smallest car entered, losing only 7 minutes as a result of a plug change. It climbed Woodcock Hill, Barnet, Herts in 1min 29sec, an average speed of 3.3kph (2mph). Fore and aft axle location on early Vauxhalls was by tie-rods anchored in the middle of the chassis to a V-shaped hanger.

The 12/14 of 1904 and the modern Corsa were among the few Vauxhalls with three cylinders. Production in 1904 was running at around 60 cars a year, and in November the 12/14 was introduced to keep up the momentum. Bigger than its single-cylinder predecessor, its water-cooled T-head engine of 2.4 litres had each cylinder cast and jacketed separately. There was a 3-speed gearbox, twin chain drive to the rear wheels, and leaf springs replaced the earlier car's coils. It retained the 5HP's stylish pointed prow on the engine cover, apparently sweeping the airflow round the sides of the car clear of the occupants. It was a brave effort to provide a styling feature by imitating the air stream, although the optional tall windscreen and flowing mudguards of the open 2-seater cancelled out any aerodynamic advantage there might have been. Cooling was by a gilled-tube radiator low down at the front.

Alfred John Hancock (AJ or Joey, former Vauxhall Ironworks engineering apprentice and later to be general manager) competed in one in the Isle of Man Tourist Trophy race of 1905. In an effort to keep engine revs down his car had a 6-speed overdrive gearbox but Hancock was thrown out and injured when he crashed at Kirkmichael on the second lap.

BODY made to order. 4 seats, tonneau weight 813kg (1792lb).
ENGINE governed to 1300rpm; 3 cylinders, front; 95mm x 115mm; 2445cc; water-cooled by scuttle tank and gilled-tube radiator.
ENGINE STRUCTURE T-head side valves; two gear-driven side camshafts; integrally cast cylinder head and block; Vauxhall simple carburettor; Trembler coil ignition; 4-bearing crankshaft.
TRANSMISSION rear wheel drive; cone clutch; 3-speed gearbox; double chain drive to rear wheels.
CHASSIS DETAILS wooden initially with flitch plates; after November 1904 pressed steel; beam axles, half elliptic leaf springs front and rear; brakes: pedal to external contracting band on countershaft, lever to rear drums; steering by sector and pinion; 45.5L (10 Imp gallon) fuel tank; 810x90 tyres.
DIMENSIONS wheelbase 218cm (86in); track 127cm (50in); length 279cm (110in); width 125cm (49in).
PERFORMANCE maximum speed 58kph (36mph); 44kph (27.5mph) @ 1000rpm; fuel consumption 14.1L/100km (20mpg).
PRODUCTION 20 made in London, 12 in Luton, 32 in all.
PRICE £375.

Right: handsome Tonneau Tourer on long 12/14 chassis was well-furnished in the style of many Edwardian Vauxhalls. Twin levers operated rear drum brakes. Other body styles included a dignified Landaulette with fixed canopy for the chauffeur.

1905 7/9HP

Almost as soon as the 12/14 was on the road, F W Hodges, the chief designer and a director, followed it with an economy and cheaper alternative, the 7/9HP. Engine capacity was reduced to 1.3-litres, but unless specialist coachbuilders could be persuaded to construct lightweight bodies, it was desperately slow. Among the last cars to be produced in London before the factory moved, the 9HP made in Luton superseded it. The smaller-engined cars had the 12/14's shapely prow and oblong radiator matrix at the front. The T-head engine had three separately cast cylinders with individual exhaust pipes coming together in a large silencer. Cooling was by a scuttle header tank and the familiar corrugated copper gilled-tube radiator. There was only one ball-race on the car, for the clutch thrust, all other bearings being plain. Tufnol timing gears ran exposed and unlubricated with the tappets well concealed within the crankcase. The engine's weakness was a tendency to break its cylinder flanges. The body was hand-painted and varnished, as were all Vauxhall bodies until the middle 1920s.

BODY made to order: tonneau, 4 seats; chassis weight 737kg (1624lb).
ENGINE 3 cylinders, governed to 1300rpm; front; 76.2mm x 95.25mm; 1293cc; water-cooled by scuttle tank, and gilled-tube radiator.
ENGINE STRUCTURE side valves, T-head, 2 side camshafts; integrally cast cylinder head and block; simple carburettor, trembler coil ignition; 4-bearing crankshaft.
TRANSMISSION rear wheel drive; cone clutch; 3-speed gearbox; double chain final drive.
CHASSIS DETAILS pressed steel structure; beam axles, semi elliptic springs; external contracting brakes; sector and pinion steering; 36.4L (8 Imp gallon) fuel tank; 700x80 tyres.
DIMENSIONS wheelbase 175cm (69in); track 127cm (50in); length 269cm (106in); width 152cm (60in).
PERFORMANCE maximum 61kph (38mph); 73.7kph (29mph) @ 1000rpm; 11.8L/100km (24mpg).
PRODUCTION 52, all London built.
PRICE £350.

Tall windscreen of 7/9 had supporting stays to brace it when the hood was erect *(top)* which were not required, apparently, when it was furled *(left)*. Wavy rear mudguard enclosed chain drive to rear wheel. Cooling was effective with deeply gilled tubular radiator matrix ahead of the engine.

1906-1907 9HP

In an effort to improve the performance of the 1.3-litre version of the 7/9HP, a 1.7-litre known as the 9HP was built in Luton and introduced at the London Motor Show. Effectively an up-rated 7/9HP, it turned out to be little better than its predecessor. The model was heavier and still rather feeble.

One of the less successful body styles that appeared for it was the Motor Hansom. Following a suggestion by the Earl of Ranfurly, who was apparently inspired by the popular Hansom cab, it had an engine in place of the horse and was intended to exploit the flourishing London taxi market. The driver occupied his traditional lofty perch at the rear of the cab where instead of reins he had a steering wheel. Long on logic but short on practicality, the passengers sat where they were accustomed to in the enclosed rear portion of the cab with half-doors ahead of their knees. The cabby had an unrivalled view of the traffic, but the long control shafts and rods between the driver and the engine, gearbox and front wheels proved problematical and the idea was abandoned.

BODY made to order: 4-seater, Hansom, chassis weight 610kg (1344lb).
ENGINE 3 cylinders, governed to 1400rpm; in-line, front, 81mm x 108mm; 1669cc.
ENGINE STRUCTURE side valves; T-head 2 side cams; integrally cast cylinder heads with blocks; 2-bearing crankshaft; simple carburettor; trembler coil ignition; water-cooled, scuttle tank and gilled tube radiator.
TRANSMISSION rear wheel drive; cone clutch; 3-speed gearbox; final drive: chains to rear wheels.
CHASSIS DETAILS pressed steel structure; beam axles, semi-elliptic springs; external contracting brakes; rack and pinion steering; 36L (8 gal) fuel tank; 700 x 80 tyres.
DIMENSIONS wheelbase 205cm (80.5in); front track 122cm (48in); length 295cm (116in); width 147cm (58in).
PERFORMANCE maximum speed 67kph (42 mph); 48kph (30mph) @ 1000rpm; fuel consumption 11.8L/100km (24mpg).

PRODUCTION approximately 27 cars built.
PRICE £375.

Sherlock Holmes might have hailed one to take him back to Baker Street following his exile. Then again perhaps not. Earl Ranfurly's creation was not a success and the 9HP was but a stepping-stone to the first 4-cylinder Vauxhall.

Production of the 7/9HP at London ended, leaving Vauxhall with a three-car range built at Luton. The 9HP and 12/14 3-cylinder cars were joined in late 1905 by the much larger 18HP, the first 4-cylinder and first production Vauxhall that could be equipped with substantial four-seat bodywork.

Its features included an efficient honeycomb radiator and a separate steel chassis, yet its most enduring characteristic was not a technical innovation. It had scooped-out corners, the famous flutes, on the engine cover. Their origins are obscure. Vauxhall folklore is full of explanations; some say they were patterned on the mouldings of a director's desk furniture. Perhaps they were incorporated to ease the construction of the bonnet hinges; at any rate they remained a Vauxhall feature for the next 50 years. Consigning the valves to each side of the T-head meant they could be large and the cylinders were still cast separately.

All 18HP cars had chain drive, and the last of the few made was sold in November 1907. Car production led to the creation of Vauxhall Motors Ltd in 1907, with Percy Kidner joint managing director, and F W Hodges consulting engineer.

BODY made to order: tonneau, landaulette; chassis weight 914kg (2016lb).

ENGINE governed 4 cyls, in-line, front, 95 mm x 120 mm; 3402cc; 13.4kW (18bhp) @ 950rpm; 3.9kW/L (5.3bhp/L), or 4kW/L (5.4bhp/L).
ENGINE STRUCTURE side valve; T-head, 2 side camshafts; cast iron cylinders and crankcase; 5-bearing crankshaft; simple carb; Simms HT magneto; water-cooled.
TRANSMISSION rear wheel drive by side chains to the rear wheels; 4-speed gearbox; top gear ratio 3.6:1.
CHASSIS DETAILS steel; half-elliptic leaf springs front and rear; external contracting brakes; worm and sector steering; 54.5L (12 Imp gal) fuel tank; 870x90 tyres.
DIMENSIONS wheelbase 279cm (110 in); track 132cm (52in); length 376cm (148in); width 168cm (66in).
PRODUCTION approximately 10.
PRICE £475.

Replacing the 18HP, the 12/16 also had a T-head engine with five main bearings and four separate cylinders, but reduced to 2.4 litres. Small and efficient, it had near-square cylinder dimensions and produced 3.7kW (5bhp) more than its predecessor at nearly twice the engine speed. Control was achieved by varying the advance of the trembler coil ignition, and a system of wedges under the inlet valves moved in and out by a lever to alter the valve opening.

This was among the first Vauxhalls completed after Laurence Pomeroy joined the company. It is not known how much he influenced it as Hodges was still chief designer, but he raised the compression so that the mixture pre-ignited if the engine was stationary for more than a few minutes. For 1908 it was revised as the 12/16 'X'-type, replacing the archaic valve wedge governor system with a conventional foot throttle.

The first Vauxhall built in large production batches of perhaps 20 cars, the 12/16 remained in production for more than three years. An experimental X-type 85mm x 95mm 2156cc engine drawn up for the 1908 RAC 2000 Mile and the Scottish Trials developed 17.5kW (23.5bhp) @ 1800rpm. Pomeroy's 20HP development, known as the Y-type, was adopted as the Trial car.

BODY made to order: 4-seat tourer; weight 962kg (2120lb).
ENGINE 4 cylinders, in-line, front, 90 mm x 95 mm; 2417 cc, (later 92mm x95mm, 2526cc); 13.4kW (18bhp) @ 950rpm; 5.3kW/L (7.6bhp/L); early cars 17kW (23bhp) @ 1800rpm, later cars 19kW (26bhp).
ENGINE STRUCTURE side valves; T-head 2 side camshafts; cast iron cylinder head and block; 5-bearing crankshaft; White & Poppe carburettor; trembler coil ignition, later HT magneto; water-cooled.
TRANSMISSION rear wheel drive; cone clutch; 3-speed gearbox; shaft drive; straight bevel final drive; ratio 4.1:1.
CHASSIS DETAILS pressed steel ladder structure; semi-elliptic springs front and rear; rear wheel and transmission external contracting drum brakes, later internal expanding; worm and sector steering; 50L (11 Imp gallon) fuel tank; 810x90 tyres.
DIMENSIONS wheelbase 248cm later 259cm (98in, later 102in); track 124.5cm (49in); length 350.5cm (138in); width 152cm (60in).
PERFORMANCE maximum speed 76kph (47.5mph); 43kph (27mph) @ 1000rpm; 71.8kg/kW (53.4kg/bhp); fuel consumption 11.3L/100km (25 mpg).
PRODUCTION 85.
PRICE chassis £375, 4 seat tourer £417.

Pomeroy was a theorist who believed that high compression ratios and large valves were the keys to power and speed. A student of Heirman's *L'Automobile à l'Essence: Principes de Construction et Calcul*, he was determined to apply his ideas to the 12/16, which he believed could produce 30kW (40bhp). *Right:* Vauxhall managing director W G Gardner occupies the rearmost seat of a 12/16 designed by W F Hodges.

1908 RAC 2000 Mile Trial Y-type prototypes

Laurence Pomeroy worked quickly on the 3-litre car for Percy Kidner to drive in the1908 International Touring Car Trial, consisting of the RAC 2000 Mile Trial and the Scottish Trial run concurrently. The result was a crucially important car in Vauxhall's development. It was basically a 12/16 with a monobloc cylinder block and head with large valves and ports, and a new crankcase. There was full pressure lubrication to main and big end bearings, and the 12/16 gearbox had a fourth gear added where reverse had been. An ingenious extra gear operated by a separate lever gave reverse. The rear axle was completely redesigned, and plain bearings were replaced with ball bearings. The Trial started in London, and underwent timed hill-climbs in the Lake District before reaching Glasgow, where it joined up with the Scottish Reliability Trial. After more timed speed events it finished with a 200-mile speed test at the newly opened Brooklands track *(see far right)*. Kidner was principally concerned with reliability, yet contrived to be 37sec faster on aggregate than any other car in his class. By Brooklands he had a useful margin in hand, and reckoned his cautious 74kph (46mph) average was 16kph (10mph) below the Y-type's potential. It won the event overall from a 40-50 Rolls-Royce laying the foundations of a dynasty of sporting Vauxhalls.

BODY open 4-seater.
ENGINE 4 cylinders, in-line, front; 3in x 4¾in (92mm x 120.6mm); 3139cc; 28.3kW (38bhp) @ 2500rpm; 9.3kW/L (12.4bhp/L).
ENGINE STRUCTURE side valves; L-head; side camshaft; iron cylinder head and block cast in one piece; 5-bearing crankshaft; White & Poppe carburettor; Bosch high tension magneto ignition; water-cooled.
TRANSMISSION rear wheel drive; metal to metal cone clutch; 4-speed gearbox; straight bevel final drive; ratio 2.95:1.
CHASSIS DETAILS pressed steel ladder frame; semi-elliptic spring front suspension; semi-elliptic spring rear suspension, torque arm control on rear axle; no dampers; pedal to rear drums, lever to transmission drum brakes; worm and sector steering; 72.7L (16 Imp gallon) fuel tank; 875x105 tyres.
DIMENSIONS wheelbase 38.5cm (98in); front and rear track 124.5cm (49in); ground clearance 23cm (9in); length 350.5cm (138in); width 152cm (60in); height 166cm (65.5in).
PERFORMANCE maximum speed 97kph (65mph); 55kph (34mph) @ 1000rpm; fuel consumption 10.9L/100km (26mpg).
PRODUCTION 2.
PRICE Not sold on open market.

The second of the two Y-types made went to W J Scott, Vauxhall agent in New Zealand. It won a gold medal in a 4-day trial run by the AA of Canterbury, recorded 109kph (68mph) in 1912 after engine modifications enabled it to reach 3000rpm, and survived as "Old Blue".
Top: **A later racy 20HP with knobbly rear tyres was made for a Mr Carter.**

The 1908 Trials Car was such a success that it seemed all Vauxhall had to do to secure commercial prosperity was reproduce it in great numbers. The long-running A-type had the virtues of the 1908 Trial car, and was made in steadily developing form until 1914. It comprised four distinct models. Three were designated 20HP, the A09, A11, and A12. Fourth was the 16/20 A-type, which remained in production until 1915. A few A12 cars were built with an engine bored out an extra 5mm in 1912. The numerical sequence related approximately to the first full year of production, so the A09 was introduced in 1908 for the 1909 and 1910 season, the A11 in 1910 for 1911, and the A12 in 1912. A wide variety of coachwork was built on this chassis, formal, touring and sporting.

The A09 was developed directly from the Trials Car, with a heavier chassis and a newly designed 4-speed gearbox. Cooling of the monobloc-cast forced lubrication engine was by fan and thermosyphon, and a 30mm White & Poppe carburettor supplied the mixture. Vauxhall boasted in 1910 that of 36 sporting events in which its cars took part, they won 24, came second 8 times, and third on four occasions.

BODY made to order: 4-seater tourer, landaulette, phaeton, cabriolet; chassis weight 889kg (1960lb).

ENGINE 4 cylinders, in-line; front, 90mm x 120mm; 3054cc; compr ratios optional to suit fuel; 28.3kW (38bhp) @ 2,500 rpm, 9.3kW/L (12.4bhp/L).

ENGINE STRUCTURE side valves; gear-driven side camshaft; cast iron cylinder head and block; 5-bearing crankshaft; White & Poppe 30mm carburettor; HT magneto ignition; forced lubrication; water-cooled.

TRANSMISSION rear wheel drive; cone clutch; 4-speed gearbox; straight bevel final drive; ratio 3.3:1, 3.9:1 optional.

CHASSIS DETAILS parallel channel section longerons; 3in x 1.5in U-section steel sub-frame; semi-elliptic springs front and rear; rear wheel 12in drum brakes operated by lever, foot-operated transmission brake; 54.5L (12 Imp gallon) fuel tank; tyres 815 x 105.

DIMENSIONS wheelbase 292cm (115in) or 312cm (123in); track 137cm (54in); ground clearance 22.8cm (9in); length 399cm (157in); width 168cm (66in).

PERFORMANCE maximum speed 80kph (50mph); 42kph (26mph) @ 1000rpm; 31.4kg/kW (23.4kg/bhp); fuel consumption 11.3L/100km (25mpg).

PRODUCTION 253 (1908, 18; 1909, 123; 1910, 111; 1911, 1).

PRICE £420 chassis only, £425 for lwb; semi-racer £35, cabriolet £200.

1909-1912 Brooklands A-types, KN, O'Gorman Trophy cars

Vauxhall's first big track success came at Easter 1909 when a stripped 20HP A-type driven by Rudolph Selz won at Brooklands. Hancock won the O'Gorman Trophy in August with a similar car. Also in 1909 an A-type with a streamlined body conceived by Hodges and named KN, did 88.6mph for the flying half-mile, going on for ten laps of Brooklands at 81.33mph. In 1910 Pomeroy obtained 44.7kW (60bhp) from a second, even narrower, KN, and on 7 October it reached 97.15mph. It returned a fortnight later for a frustrating 98.1mph, so the gearbox and back axle were drained to reduce oil drag, and on 26 October it did 100.8mph.

In 1911 a freak long-stroke 16HP engine was constructed with 80x200mm cylinders of 4021cc capacity, yet it only measured 15.87HP on the old RAC Rating. With the top of the engine sticking out of its tall bonnet the car tackled 16HP records, raising the half-mile from 90.04mph to 97.67mph, the kilometre from 88.24mph to 96.67mph, the mile from 86.37mph to 94.91mph and ten laps from 81mph to 91.46mph. An attempt on the flying half-mile ended with a piston ejected from the crankcase probably on account of the high piston speeds resulting from the eccentric cylinder dimensions. A-type Vauxhalls won the O'Gorman Trophy in 1910 and 1912.

BODY single-seat streamlined narrow racer, weight 862kg (1900lb).
ENGINE (late 1909) 4 cylinders, front, 90mm x 120mm; 3054cc; 39kW (52.6bhp) @ 2400 rpm; 12.8kW/L (17.2bhp/L).
ENGINE STRUCTURE side valves; gear driven side camshaft; integrally cast cylinder head and block; White & Poppe carb; HT magneto ignition; 5-bearing crank; forced lubrication.
TRANSMISSION rear wheel drive; cone clutch; 4-speed gearbox; live axle final drive.
CHASSIS DETAILS (late 1909) Parallel channel section side members; semi-elliptic springs front and rear; no dampers; worm and sector steering; tyres 875x105.
DIMENSIONS wheelbase 292cm (115in); track 137cm (54in); length 488cm (192in); width 162.5cm (64in).
PERFORMANCE max 160.5kph (100mph) (1910); 22.1kg/kW (16.4kg/bhp).
PRODUCTION n/a.
PRICE n/a.

The O'Gorman Trophy races started as long-distance events at Brooklands. By 1910 there were only three entries, all Vauxhalls, and the winning average speed rose from 71mph in 1909 to over 92mph in 1912 as a result of weight reduction, more power, and streamlining. Mervyn O'Gorman's statuette was later presented to the RAC and until 1972 was awarded to the winner of the British Grand Prix.

Right: first 20hp car in the world to exceed 100mph.
Left: silver salver detailing 42 major wins by the official Vauxhall works team 1908-1924, made by melting down most of the team trophies.

1909-1912 B-type 16HP B09

Confusingly there were two Vauxhalls designated B-types in the early years, one in effect a 6-cylinder development of this 4-cylinder. The 16HP was in most respects a small A-type, with a 4-cylinder 2324cc engine, the other was the 27HP, later the 30 and 35hp 6-cylinder range sometimes associated with the Russian Imperial family.

The speed range of the 4-cylinder was between 300rpm idling to 2700rpm (even though the power peak was much lower) and the maximum piston speed, something of an obsession with engineers of the time, was 1810 ft/min. Valve servicing was still by means of screwed-in valve caps in the non-detachable cylinder head. Among the optional equipment offered was a windscreen, hood, Lodge coil ignition or Bosch dual ignition, nickel plated brightwork instead of brass, lamp brackets, head, side, and tail lamps, luggage carrier, waterproof seat covers, a sprag for bracing the car on a hill, bulb horn and Stepney spare wheel. The ride was notably smooth on well-surfaced roads, but on rough going the absence of shock absorbers resulted in a rather bouncy time for the two occupants of the popular semi-racer body. Among the many alternatives to the sketchy semi racer with its luggage box behind the seats was a handsome 4/5 seat Touring Phaeton.

BODY 2-seater, tourer, cabriolet, limousine, landaulette; chassis weight 686kg (1512lb); typically 1067kg (2352lb) with body.
ENGINE 4-cylinders, in-line, front, 80mm x 100mm, 2011cc, later 86mm x 100mm; 2324cc; 11.9kW (16bhp) @ 1000rpm; 5.9kW/L (8bhp/L).
ENGINE STRUCTURE side valves; side camshaft; integral cast iron cylinder head and block; aluminium crankcase; 5-bearing crank; White and Poppe 30mm updraught carburettor with gravity fuel feed; magneto with manual ignition timing control, dual ignition optional; water-cooled.
TRANSMISSION rear wheel drive; metal-faced cone clutch integral with flywheel; 3-speed; bevel gear final drive, fully-floating axle; ratio 4.1:1.
CHASSIS DETAILS pressed steel chassis frame; semi-elliptic springs front & rear; foot transmission brake; handbrake on rear; worm and segment steering, one turn lock to lock; 43L (9.5 Imp gal) fuel tank; 815 x 105 tyres; wooden artillery wheels, Rudge Whitworth wire wheels opt.

DIMENSIONS wheelbase 269cm (106in); track 129.5cm (51in) front, 124.5cm (49in) rear; ground clearance 20.9cm (8.25in); turning circle left 12.49m (41ft) right 12m (39.5ft); length 376cm (148in); width 162.5cm (64in); height 188cm (74in) screen up, 168cm (66in) screen down.
PERFORMANCE maximum 80kph (50mph); 37.8kph (23.5mph) @ 1000rpm; 0-64kph (40mph) 29.1sec; 57.6kg/kW (43kg/bhp), 90kg/kW (67kg/bhp); fuel consumption 15.9L/100km (17.75mpg).
PRODUCTION 130.
PRICE £365, chassis £330.

Top right: **specially made on long wheelbase for a customer in Cornwall, Baggage Car exemplified the variety of bodywork to be found on Edwardian Vauxhalls.**
Right: **smart semi-racer exploited Vauxhall's flourishing reputation for cars with a sporting flavour.**

The A11 and A12 designs were straightforward developments of the successful A09 3-litre car. The first A11 was delivered in October 1910 and, to the buying public, was no more than the normal 20HP car with a few improvements.

Production continued throughout 1911 with many detail developments incorporated as they were designed. Significant among these was the introduction of the Vauxhall multiplate clutch, similar in its operating principle to the Hele-Shaw but different in detail. Its design remained in production until after the GM takeover in 1925. Other improvements were thanks to racing development and included redesigned camshafts and lighter moving parts.

The first A12 appeared in June 1912, and after a few cars with 95mm bore engines had been produced production ended. The last A12 was built in December 1912. The 3-litre cars designated as Prince Henry models were taken as required from the A11 and A12 production lines and built to the more sporting specification.

BODY made to order, tourer, landaulette, limousine.
ENGINE 4 cylinders, in-line, 90mm x 120mm; 3054 cc; 36kW (48bhp) @ 2500rpm; (a few 95mm x120mm; 3403cc in 1912).
ENGINE STRUCTURE side valves; side camshaft; cast iron cylinder head and block; 5-bearing crankshaft; White and Poppe or Zenith carburettor; HT magneto ignition; water-cooled.
TRANSMISSION rear wheel drive; cone, later Vauxhall multiplate clutch; four-speed gearbox; straight pinion final drive, ratio 3.6:1, (3.9:1 optional).
CHASSIS DETAILS pressed steel structure; semi-elliptic leaf springs front and rear; brakes: pedal on transmission, lever on rear drums; worm and wheel steering; 54.5L (12 gal) fuel tank; 875x105 tyres.
DIMENSIONS wheelbase 292cm (115in), 312cm (123in) optional; front and rear track 137cm (54in); ground clearance 20.3cm (8in); length 399cm (157in), 419cm (165in) optional; width 168cm (66in).

PERFORMANCE maximum speed 80kph (50mph); 41.7kph (26mph) @ 1000rpm; fuel consumption 11.3L/100km (25 mpg).
PRODUCTION Total 718 of which 70 were A12.
PRICE £525 (1910).

Right: page from 1912 Vauxhall catalogue showing coachwork on 20HP chassis, most common version being the Norfolk (top).

Examples of coachwork

The " Norfolk " Torpedo

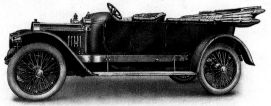

The " Norfolk " four-seated torpedo type body, with divided front seat, fitted to a 20 h.p.
four-cylindered chassis, wheelbase 10-ft. 3-in.

Price of body, £85

The rear seats can be made to accommodate three persons comfortably, for £5 extra.
(Hood not included. Quotations on page 36).

The " Stoneleigh " Torpedo-de-Luxe

The " Stoneleigh " four-seated torpedo-de-luxe type body, with divided front seat, fitted
to a 20 h.p. four-cylindered chassis, wheelbase 10-ft. 3-in.

The tops of the front doors are lined with polished mahogany, useful mahogany cup-
boards are fitted in the corners of the scuttle dash, metal or patent leather valances are fitted
between the steps and frame. Price of body, £105

(Hood, screen, etc.. not included. Quotations on page 36).

1910-1912 27HP B10 6-cylinder

The first production 6-cylinder Vauxhall was introduced for the 1910 model year. It was in practice simply a lengthened 20HP chassis fitted with a B09 engine with two extra cylinders. Its first attempt to produce a car capable of carrying heavy luxurious coachwork, Vauxhall freely admitted that it had conducted extensive tests on a 6-cylinder Napier before setting out the design. The model's publicity claimed that there had been no prejudice regarding the choice of four or six cylinders, each having advantages in power, lightness and smoothness. Only 23 were built, mostly with formal coachwork, an expensive option with Landaulette or Cabriolet bodywork costing more than £200.

BODY made to order; chassis weight 915kg (2016lb).

ENGINE 6 cylinders, in-line, front; 85mm x 102 mm; 3473cc; 34kW (45bhp) @ 2500rpm; 9.6kW/L (12.9bhp/L).

ENGINE STRUCTURE side valves; side camshaft; integral cast iron cylinder block and head; 7-bearing crankshaft; White and Poppe carburettor; Trembler coil, later HT magneto ignition; water cooled.

TRANSMISSION rear wheel drive; metal to metal cone clutch; 4-speed gearbox; final drive ratio 3.3:1, 3.9:1optional.

CHASSIS DETAILS pressed steel frame; semi elliptic leaf spring front suspension; Semi elliptic leaf spring rear suspension; brakes on rear wheels and transmission; worm and segment steering; 52L (11.5 Imp gal) fuel tank; 880x120 tyres.

DIMENSIONS wheelbase 312cm (123in) or 335cm (132in); track 137cm (54in); ground clearance 22.9cm (9in); length 419cm (165in); width 168cm (66in).

PERFORMANCE maximum speed 83.5kph (52mph); 48kph (30mph) @ 1000rpm; 26.9kg/kW (20.3kg/bhp); fuel consumption 14.1L/100km (20mpg).

PRODUCTION 23.

PRICE Chassis: £535, Tourer:£595.

1910-1913 C10 Prince Henry 3.0 and 3.5-litre

Vauxhalls maintained their sporting prowess in 1909 when A J Hancock and F W Hodges came first and second in the Irish and Scottish Trials. In 1911 Percy Kidner competed in the Russian Reliability Trial from St Petersburg to Sevastopol without loss of marks. The company's sporting laurels gave the confidence for the development of the most famous Edwardian Vauxhall of all. This was the Prince Henry, with its distinctive pointed radiator, built for the 1910 Trial sponsored by Prinz Heinrich of Prussia. Production Prince Henrys were delivered to customers from the spring of 1911 and were catalogued for sale for the 1912 model year.

These fast cars were built up from standard A11 and A12 chassis drawn from the main production and finished to a higher specification. Early cars carried both A and C chassis numbers. Handsome Prince Henrys with their distinctive prow and sporting disposition were enjoyed by wealthy Edwardians who regarded sporting motoring as something of an adventure coupled with an interest in new technology. The combination was a mark of a well bred gentleman who did not even have to enter in races although many did. According to *The Daily Telegraph* of 6 October 1910 it was "The most remarkable Twenty in the motor car world."

BODY made to order: tourer, 4 seats; weight 1067kg (2352lb).
ENGINE 4 cylinders, in-line, front, 90 mm x 120 mm; 3054 cc; (final 12 cars were 95x120; 3402cc); 44.7kW (60bhp) @ 2700rpm; 14.6kW/L (19.6bhp/L).
ENGINE STRUCTURE side valves; side cam; integrally cast iron cylinder block and head; 5-bearing crank; White and Poppe or Zenith carb; HT magneto ignition; water cooled.
TRANSMISSION rear wheel drive; cone, later Vauxhall multiplate clutch; 4-speed; final drive; ratio 3.0:1.
CHASSIS DETAILS pressed steel structure; semi elliptic leaf spring front and rear suspension; footbrake on transmission, handlever on rear drums. worm and wheel steering; 54.5L (12 Imp gal) fuel tank; 875x105 tyres.
DIMENSIONS wheelbase 290cm (114 in); track 132cm (52in); ground clearance 22.9cm (9in); length 386cm (152in); width 163cm (64in).
PERFORMANCE maximum speed 104kph (65mph); 45kph (28mph) @ 1000rpm; 23.8kg/kW (17.8kg/bhp); 14.1L/100km (25mpg).
PRODUCTION 58.
PRICE: Fast light touring car £565.

Right: epic journeys, epic car. Dignified with touring bodywork or stripped for racing, the Prince Henry was the epitome of sporting motoring.
Below: Laurence Pomeroy with friends and prototype Prince Henry outside the hotel in Lynmouth where he designed the 1914 racing engines.

1911-1913 Coupe de l'Auto racing cars

Vauxhall contested the Coupe de l'Auto Voiturette races for 3-litre cars three years in succession. In 1911 one car made little impression and retired early with a broken connecting rod. The 1912 race at Dieppe took place over two days on a 47-mile course at the same time as the Grand Prix de l'Automobile Club de France. Three Vauxhalls were specially constructed with short Prince Henry radiators and bob-tails. They were light, had the rear springs shackled at both ends, and extra radius rods controlled the rear axle. Unfortunately, while they had the speed of the 4-valves-per-cylinder twin ohc Peugeot, they lacked the reliability of the side-valve Sunbeams, which won handsomely. Vauxhall and Sunbeam believed that contemporary racing cars were the production sports cars of the future and their design should reflect that. Yet both makes were up against stiff competition. In the 1913 race held at Boulogne two Peugeots won from a Sunbeam, with a Vauxhall fourth over 50 minutes in arrears after six hours' racing. As the cars crossed the finishing line Laurence Pomeroy famously agreed with his opposite number at Sunbeam, Louis Coatalen, that they would need to 'get some old drawings off the shelf', resurrect experiments with overhead valves, and abandon production-based engines.

1912 Cars:
BODY open 2-seater, no doors, weight 889kg (1960lb).
ENGINE 4 cylinders, in-line, front, 89.7mm x 118mm; 2983 cc; compr 5:1; 52kW (70bhp) @ 2780 rpm; 17.5kW/L (23.5bhp/L).
ENGINE STRUCTURE side valves; integrally cast cylinder head and block; 5-bearing crank; Claudel carb; HT magneto ignition; water-cooled.
TRANSMISSION rear wheel drive; Vauxhall multiplate clutch; 4-speed; straight bevel final drive; ratio 2.8:1.
CHASSIS DETAILS pressed steel ladder frame; semi elliptic leaf spring front and rear suspension; Derihon dampers; footbrake on transmission, lever to rear drums; worm and wheel steering; 820x120 tyres.
DIMENSIONS wheelbase 274cm (108in); front and rear track 137cm (54 in); length 371cm (146in); width 168cm (66in).
PERFORMANCE maximum speed 141kph (88mph); 47kph (29mph) @ 1000rpm; 17.1kg/kW (12.7kg/bhp); 14.1L/100km (20 mpg).

PRODUCTION 5.
PRICE not sold on open market.

The 1912 cars were pointed-radiator Prince Henrys. A J Hancock's car *(below)* pauses for consultation. *Right:* reconstructed team car V1019 (chassis C13 engine D13) auctioned by Coys of Kensington, 1999. *Centre & far right:* No 14, 1913 entry of Willie Watson and mechanic Jack Payne with flat radiator and curiously nautical steering wheel. Watson's car finished with a broken back axle on last lap, Hancock finished 4th.

1911-1915 30HP and 35HP 6-cylinder, B11 and B12

Vauxhall's first production 6-cylinder car, the 27HP of 1910 suffered from various shortcomings. The one-piece cylinder block proved difficult to handle in manufacturing and the revised B11, introduced for the 1911 model year, was cast in two blocks of three cylinders on a new crankcase instead. The cylinder dimensions were the same as the 20HP 4-cylinder car giving an RAC rating of 30HP, although six cars were built with enlarged engines of 35HP. The B12 design delivered from June 1912 for a year were 30HP with 35HP cars continuing until early 1915. The final 15 cars were delivered after the start of hostilities.

The chassis was popular with outside coachbuilders, and 6-cylinder Vauxhalls could be found on many bespoke coachbuilder's stands at motor exhibitions of the time. They were large and powerful enough to be fitted with elegant coachbuilt bodies that had not only plenty of headroom but lots of hat-room for formal dress.

Following Vauxhall's success with fur-wrapped but nonetheless frozen drivers in the 1911 Russian trial, 6-cylinder formal limousines proved popular in Russia, with cars supplied from Vauxhall's St. Petersburg depot to the Romanoffs, last of the Czars, as well as other wealthy customers.

BODY made to order: tourer, landaulette, cabriolet, limousine, 2 seats; chassis 1067kg (2352lb).
ENGINE 6 cylinders, in-line, front, 90mm x 120mm, 4579cc; later 95x120, 5013cc; 44.7kW (60bhp) @ 2500 rpm; 9.8kW/L (13.1bhp/L).
ENGINE STRUCTURE side valves; side camshaft; cast iron cylinder head and block; 7-bearing crank; Zenith or White and Poppe carburettor; HT magneto ignition; water-cooled.
TRANSMISSION rear wheel drive; Vauxhall multiplate clutch; 4-speed gearbox; straight bevel final drive; ratio 3.3:1.
CHASSIS DETAILS pressed steel frame; semi elliptic leaf springs front and rear; no dampers; footbrake on transmission, lever to rear drums; worm and wheel steering; 54.5L (12 Imp gal) fuel tank; tyres 880 x 120.
DIMENSIONS wheelbase 343cm (135in) or 366cm (144in); track 137cm (54in); ground clearance 20.3cm (8in); length 445cm (175in) or 470cm (185in); width 163cm (64in).
PERFORMANCE maximum speed 104kph (65mph); 48kph (30mph) @ 1000rpm; 23.9kg/kW (17.8kg/bhp); fuel consumption 15.7L/100km (18mpg).
PRODUCTION 83.
PRICE: Chassis: £725.

Exporting to Russia could be problematical, and more than one car was stolen during the journey. Optional bodyguard's seat on the running-board could be folded and stored away in the scuttle behind a detachable panel. Electric lighting was standard on the B-type and later cars had the back of the bonnet line raised so that it tapered down towards the radiator. *Right:* **elegant open tourer in city street scene, and** *(top right)* **upright landaulette of the sort favoured by the Czar.**

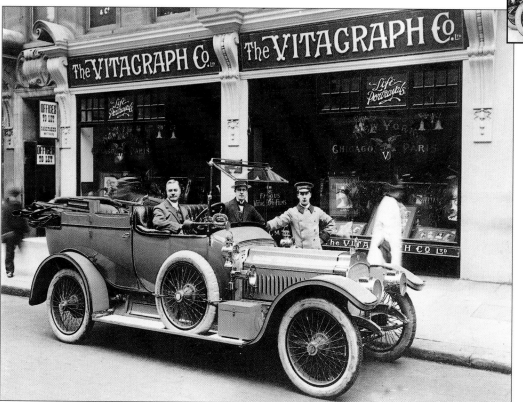

A heavily built car with a wide 91cm (36in) chassis, the engine followed the broad lines of the A-type except that an internal toothed 'silent' chain drove the camshaft. The aim was quietness and reliability rather than sheer power, and the result was great top-gear flexibility. For 1914 it had electric lighting, and could do over 96kph (60mph). Pre-war D-types had a flat radiator like the A-type's, which continued until 1915 when it was replaced by a revised design first seen in 1913 on the inaugural 30-98.

In 1913 and 1914 there was a choice of axle ratio, the 3.3:1 was standard, but the 3.6:1 described as suitable for "heavy use" was adopted for all cars including the War Department staff cars produced at the rate of eight per week. Nearly 2000 were made and, while they saw service, experimental work took place in Luton.

The design was developed continually during the war often thanks to ideas from Matthew Park, a Vauxhall racing mechanic commissioned in the Royal Engineers, who commanded a maintenance depot for staff cars in France. After the war the *Morning Post* correspondent H Massac Buist said that 'The four-cylinder Vauxhall cars have proved to be the most generally satisfactory of any British make for Staff service'.

BODY made to order: tourer, all-weather landaulette, limousine; weight with landaulette body, 1778kg (3920lb).

ENGINE 4 cyls, in-line, front, 95mm x 140mm; 3969cc; 45kW (60bhp) @ 2000rpm; 11.3kW/L (15.1bhp/L).

ENGINE STRUCTURE side valves; side cam; cast iron integral cyl head and block; 5-bearing crank; Zenith carburettor; magneto ignition; water-cooled; mounted in steel sub-frame.

TRANSMISSION rear wheel drive; multi-plate clutch; 4-speed gearbox; fully-floating back axle spiral bevel final drive; ratio 3.3, later 3.6:1.

CHASSIS DETAILS pressed steel frame; semi-elliptic suspension front and rear; friction dampers; lever-operated drum rear brakes, foot-operated transmission brake; worm and wheel steering; 54.5L (12 Imp gal, 14.4 US gal) fuel tank; 880 x 120 tyres.

DIMENSIONS wheelbase 322.6cm (127in); front track 160cm (63in), rear 155cm (61in); ground clearance 22.9cm (9in); length 457cm (180in); width 168cm (66in).

PERFORMANCE maximum speed 104kph (65mph); 45kph (28mph) @ 1000rpm; 39.5kg/kW (29.6kg/bhp); 14.1L/100km (20mpg).

PRODUCTION the last military chassis built was D2319, indicating some 322 civilian cars produced before the war.

PRICE £1600.

Far right: **General Allenby's triumphant entry into Jerusalem in a Vauxhall staff car.**
Left: **British officers in the first car across the Rhine following Armistice at end of First World War.**

For 1913 the Prince Henry model was revised and fitted with the new D-type 4-litre engine. Although heavier, the 25HP car was considerably quicker than the earlier model and quickly established itself as one of the fastest cars available for sale in England. Vauxhall built many of the stylish open bodies fitted to these cars, but a number carried coachwork built by outside firms. Hardly any two Prince Henrys were the same. The larger engine underlined the cooling limitations of the stylish radiator under extreme conditions and by later standards Prince Henry brakes were derisory. In its day, however, the car was considered quite outstanding.

BODY made to order: usually sporting; weight Fast Tourer 1243kg (2740lb).

ENGINE 4 cylinders, in-line, front, 95mm x 140mm; 3969cc; compr 5:1; 48kW (86bhp) @ 3300 rpm; 12.1kW/L (21.7bhp/L).

ENGINE STRUCTURE side valves; side camshaft ; cast iron integral head and block; 3-bearing crankshaft; White and Poppe or Zenith carburettor; HT magneto ignition; water cooled.

TRANSMISSION rear wheel drive; Vauxhall Multiplate clutch; 4-speed gearbox; straight bevel final drive, ratio 3.0:1.

CHASSIS DETAILS pressed steel frame; semi elliptic leaf springs front and rear; no dampers; footbrake to transmission drum, handbrake on rear wheels; worm and wheel steering; 54.5L (12 Imp gal, 14.4 US gal) fuel tank; 815x105 (later 820x120) tyres.

DIMENSIONS wheelbase 305cm (120in); track 137cm (54in) front and rear; ground clearance 20cm (8in); length 409cm (161in); width 168cm (66in).

PERFORMANCE maximum speed 120kph (75mph); 48kph (30mph) @ 1000rpm; 25.9kg/kW (14.5kg/bhp); fuel consumption 12.8L/100km (22mpg).

PRODUCTION 133.

PRICE chassis £580.

How Prince Henry got its name. Cars 104 and 105 were two of the three team cars in the 1910 Trial promoted by Prince Heinrich of Prussia. Timed at 112.6kph (70mph), they proved their speed and reliability. The long-tailed Prince Henry was used by the factory for racing and record breaking with A J Hancock at the wheel. *Right:* **Laurence Pomeroy Junior at Prescott.**

The final evolution of the A-type, the 16/20HP was built with a revised engine, having the camshaft driven by an internal tooth 'silent' chain, in appearance looking like a miniature 'D' type unit. There was a new cylinder block and the bonnet, which sloped upwards towards the rear, carried tapering flutes for the first time. The model sold well in England and Australia, and a 16/20HP saloon was exhibited in Russia in May 1913. The model was popular, and would have continued in the range had the War Department not taken over all Vauxhall's capacity for D-type Staff Car production.

BODY made to order: chassis weight 927kg (2044lb).
ENGINE 4 cylinders, in-line, front, 90mm x 120mm; 3053cc; 37kW (50bhp) @ 2500 rpm; 12.2kW/L (16.4bhp/L).
ENGINE STRUCTURE side valves; side camshaft; cast iron cylinder head and block; 5-bearing crankshaft; White & Poppe, Zenith or Claudel-Hobson carburettor; HT magneto ignition; water-cooled, pumped circulation.
TRANSMISSION rear wheel drive; Vauxhall multiplate clutch; 4-speed gearbox; straight bevel final drive; ratio 3.9:1.
CHASSIS DETAILS pressed steel frame; semi-elliptic springs front and rear, no dampers; rear wheel and transmission brakes; worm and wheel steering; 54.5L (12 Imp gal, 14.4 US gal) fuel tank; 815 x 105 tyres.
DIMENSIONS wheelbase 297cm (117in); front and rear track 137cm (54in); ground clearance 20.3cm (8in); length 406cm (160in); width 168cm (66in).

PERFORMANCE maximum speed 88kph (55mph); 41.7kph (26mph) @ 1000rpm; 25.1kg/kW (18.5kg/bhp); fuel consumption 11.8/100km (24mpg).
PRODUCTION 271.
PRICE chassis £395.

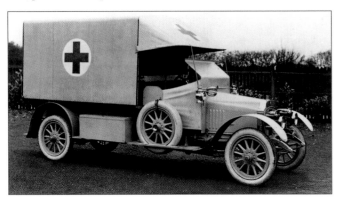

Left: A-types went to war as field ambulances and also to Australia, where in 1916 this one *(far right)* with sketchy bodywork set up a record 16 hours 55 minutes for the 570 miles between Melbourne and Sydney. Intrepid driver Boyd Edkins knocked 3.5 hours off the record the following year in a 25HP.

1913-1914 E-type 30-98

Pomeroy's masterpiece, the 30-98 (the origins of the title are obscure) became a benchmark not only for great sporting Vauxhalls, but also for a later Vintage generation that included Bentley, Talbot, Sunbeam and Alvis. It remained old-fashioned in many ways – mounting the engine in a rolled steel sub-frame was scarcely the last word in 1914 – yet it remained one of the most celebrated cars of its time. The basic design was a straightforward development of the 1908 Trials Car and a speed of 137kph (85mph) was possible in standard road equipped form, quite outstanding for 1913. A streamlined version lapped Brooklands at 173kph (108mph).

Only a dozen cars were built and sold to favoured customers before the Great War at £900 for the chassis, when a complete Prince Henry was catalogued at £580. The 30-98 only became a catalogued model in 1919.

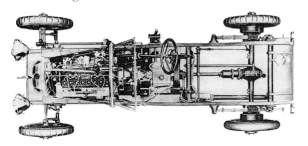

BODY open tourer, 4 seats; chassis weight 1118kg (2464lb), complete car 1219kg (2688lb).
ENGINE 4 cylinders, in-line, front, 98mm x 150mm; 4525cc; compr: 5:1; 67kW (90bhp) @ 2800rpm; 14.8kW/L (19.9bhp/L); RAC rating 23.8HP.
ENGINE STRUCTURE side valves; 3-bearing chain-driven side camshaft; roller cam-followers; cast iron monobloc, fixed cylinder head; steel connecting rods; 5-bearing crank; White & Poppe carburettor pre-war, Zenith later; Watford magneto ignition; water-cooled, honeycomb radiator, cast alloy fan, impeller.
TRANSMISSION rear wheel drive; Vauxhall dry multi-plate graphite lubricated clutch; 4-speed gearbox; open propellor shaft; straight bevel final drive; ratio 3.0:1.
CHASSIS DETAILS pressed steel chassis; half elliptic springs front and rear; foot transmission brake, handbrake rear drums; worm and wheel steering; 45.5L (12 Imp gal, 14.4 US gal) pressured fuel tank; 820 x 120BE tyres, centre-lock Rudge wheels.
DIMENSIONS wheelbase 264cm (104in); track 137cm (54in); ground clearance 6in; length 422cm (166in); width 168cm (66in).
PERFORMANCE maximum speed 128-136.5kph (80-85mph), 160kph (100mph) in race trim; 18.2kg/kW (13.5kg/bhp); fuel consumption 14.1/100km (20mpg).
PRODUCTION 12.
PRICE Chassis £900.

Right: 26 July 1913, Joseph Higginson, inspiration for the 30-98, competing in speed event on Beacon Hill with three passengers. *Left:* later production chassis shows sturdy side-members, cowled fan and separate gearbox.

1914 Tourist Trophy and Grand Prix racing cars

Laurence Pomeroy and Louis Coatalen of Sunbeam both had experience of radical engine design years before the Isle of Man Tourist Trophy in June and the Grand Prix de l'Automobile Club de France in July 1914. Both men produced classic twin-cam 16-valve racing engines for these events.

Pomeroy and his chief draughtsman locked themselves away at the Bevans Hotel in Lynmouth to create the new racing engine. It had two gear driven camshafts in tunnels cast integrally with the cylinder block and heads, operating tungsten alloy valves through rockers with exposed springs. A crankshaft with bolted-on counterweights reduced main bearing loads. A novel two-speed transmission giving the driver eight gears was abandoned for the races. The rear suspension was a novel cantilever arrangement that had a torque tube transmission which included the gearbox, with a spherical anchorage at the front.

In the TT one car broke its crankshaft four miles from the start, another lost its oil, the third was a long way behind the winning Sunbeam and crashed on the second day. They fared little better in the Grand Prix at Lyon, for which they were fitted with 4½-litre engines, but were rehabilitated with revised semi-elliptic rear springs after the war with successes at Brooklands and Shelsley Walsh.

BODY open, 2 seats, weight 1043kg (2300lb) ballasted to 1092kg (2408lb) for TT.
ENGINE 4 cylinders, in-line, front mounted. TT engine: 90mm x 130mm, 3307cc; 67kW (90bhp) @ 3600rpm; 20.3kW/L (27.2bhp/L). French GP engine: 101mm x 140mm; 4487cc; compr: 6:1; 97kW (130bhp) @ 3300rpm; 21.4kW/L (28.7bhp/L).
ENGINE STRUCTURE 2 overhead camshafts driven by bevel and worm gears, 4 valves per cylinder; cast iron integral cylinder head and block, aluminium crankcase; 5-bearing counterbalanced crankcase; vertical Zenith carburretor; front cross-shaft to oil and water pumps; water-heated manifold: HT magneto driven from inlet cam; water-cooled; wet sump.
TRANSMISSION rear wheel drive; cone clutch on flywheel made from boiler plate, friction material riveted to flywheel; 4-speed cast aluminium gearbox built in unit with torque tube; straight bevel gear final drive; ratio 3.0:1, aluminium rear axle.
CHASSIS DETAILS steel frame; front suspension beam axle with semi-elliptic springs passing through it; cantilever rear, (1921 car semi-elliptic springs); Houdaille vane-type dampers; drum rear brakes operated by outside lever, drum transmission foot brake; worm and wheel steering, cast aluminium 6-spoke steering wheel; 136L (30 Imp gal, 36 US gal) pressurised fuel tank; front tyres 875 x 105, rear 880 x 120, Rudge-Whitworth detachable wheels with knock-on hubs.
DIMENSIONS wheelbase 282cm (111in); track 137cm (54in); 1.2sq metres (13sq ft) frontal area; length 366cm (144in); width 157.5cm (62in).
PERFORMANCE maximum speed 185-193kph (115-120mph); 28.6mph @ 1000rpm; TT 16.3kg/kW (12.1kg/bhp); GP 10.8kg/kW (8kg/bhp); fuel consumption 14.1L/100km (20mpg) (touring).
PRODUCTION 3.

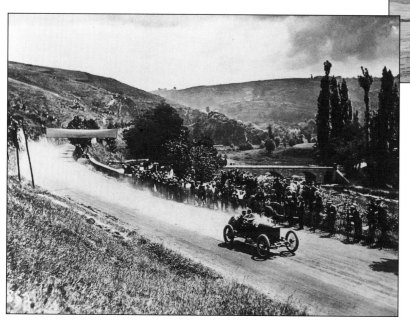

Left: Often called the Greatest Grand Prix, the Vauxhalls may have been the fastest cars in the 1914 French Grand Prix. It proved to be a curtain-raiser for a more serious Franco-German conflict erupting a month later, in August.

Top: Car No 6, A J Hancock's 3.3-litre in the Isle of Man. The driver escaped in an ensuing crash but his mechanic Gibbs was badly hurt.

1919-1922 D-type 25HP

In 1912 Laurence Pomeroy was made chief engineer and the D-type 25hp introduced. Its roots lay in the long-lived A-type with a chain-driven camshaft for the 4.0 litre engine. The 25hp was strongly built, aimed at the luxury limousine market with refinement and reliability enhanced in the light of experience gained in building some 2000 for the War Department. Electric lights and starter motor were added for the civilian version.

Five cars had maintained the King's Messenger Service between Paris and Boulogne throughout the war, and in 1919 *The Times* described it as "the most successful of staff vehicles. The *Morning Post* correspondent H Massac Buist said that, "the four cylinder Vauxhall cars have proved the most generally satisfactory of any British make for staff service".

The 4.0-litre engine found its way into a modified Prince Henry chassis of which 130 were made. Another bonus of the war was Vauxhall's acquisition of Clarence E King. He had been trying to make a living as a painter in France but when the war intervened he had to leave or be interned. He asked Vauxhall for a job, succeeded Laurence Pomeroy, and remained with the company until 1954.

BODY to order: Kington tourer, weight 1550kg (3416lb).
ENGINE 4 cylinders, in-line, front, 95mm x 140mm; 3969cc; compr: 4.2:1; 44.7kW (60bhp) @ 2300 rpm; 11.3kW/L (15.1bhp/L).
ENGINE STRUCTURE side valves; side camshaft; cast iron integral cylinder head and block; 5-bearing crankshaft; Zenith carburettor; magneto ignition; water-cooled; mounted in steel sub-frame.
TRANSMISSION rear wheel drive; multi-plate clutch; 4-speed gearbox right hand change; fully-floating back axle spiral bevel final drive; ratio 3.6:1.
CHASSIS DETAILS pressed steel frame; semi-elliptic springs all round; friction dampers; lever-operated rear wheel brakes, foot-operated transmission brake; worm and wheel steering; 54.5L (12 Imp gal, 14.4 US gal) fuel tank; 880-120 tyres.
DIMENSIONS wheelbase 330cm (130in); front and rear track 142cm (56in); ground clearance 23cm (9in); length 467cm (184in); width 178cm (70in); height hood up 201cm (79in),

hood down 175cm (69in).
PERFORMANCE maximum speed 104kph (65mph); 45kph (28mph) @ 1000rpm; 34.7kg/kW (25.9kg/bhp); fuel consumption 15.7L/100km (18mpg).
PRODUCTION approx 1,590.
PRICE Kington Tourer £1450; Windsor Saloon £1875.

Civilian cars had a variety of coachwork including the standard Grosvenor Warwick landaulette. The Grosvenor Carriage Co Ltd became a subsidiary of Shaw & Kilburn, the main London Vauxhall dealer, and made formal Vauxhall bodies until long after WW2. Other notable D-type bodywork builders included Arthur Mulliner of Northampton, and Salmons (later Tickford) of Newport Pagnell.
***Top right:* 1925 D-type.**
***Far right:* 1920 D-type.**

Immediately after the Great War Armistice, Vauxhall was able to sell as many D-type cars as it could produce and its evolution into the 30-98 began. The E-type was essentially a revision of it in detail for quantity production, benefiting from Vauxhall's wartime experience. It had electric lighting and starter as standard equipment, and inherited all the 25HP's trustworthiness and fine reputation. A more robust cylinder block and improvements to the exhaust valves came in and the White & Poppe carburettor was replaced by a Zenith 48RA updraught instrument. Every chassis was subjected to a half-hour road test before being passed as satisfactory for body mounting. Demand was already strong when the first Velox coachwork was shown at the 1919 Olympia show. It was an instant success and Vauxhall produced the complete car, unchanged, until the OE arrived for 1923. A number of 30-98s appeared with other coachwork. The Grosvenor 2-seaters were popular and even a few saloons were built, although the flexible nature of the chassis frame discouraged anything but lightweight open bodywork. The 30-98 was widely regarded as the finest all round sporting car it was possible to own in the early 1920s, after one attained 145kph (90mph) in the 1919 Westcliffe-on-Sea speed trials standing kilometre.

BODY to order: Velox fast tourer; weight 1359kg (2996lb).
ENGINE 4 cylinders, in-line, 98mm x150mm; 4526 cc; compr: 5.5:1; 73kW (98bhp) @ 2750 rpm; 16.1kW/L (21.7bhp/L).
ENGINE STRUCTURE side valves; side camshaft; Monobloc cast iron cylinders and head; 5-bearing crankshaft; Zenith carburettor; HT magneto ignition; water-cooled.
TRANSMISSION rear wheel drive; Vauxhall multi plate clutch; 4-speed gearbox; straight bevel final drive; ratio 3.0:1.
CHASSIS DETAIL pressed steel frame; semi elliptic leaf springs front and rear; Derihon dampers; footbrake on transmission, hand lever to rear drums; Worm and wheel steering; 56.5L (12 Imp gal, 14.4 US gal) fuel tank; 820x120 tyres.
DIMENSIONS wheelbase 290cm (114in); front and rear track 137cm (54in); ground clearance 15cm (6in); length 422cm (166in); width 168cm (66in).
PERFORMANCE maximum speed 137kph (85mph); 48kph (30mph) @ 1000rpm; acceleration 0-96kph (60mph) 17sec; 18.6kg/kW (13.9kg/bhp); fuel consumption 14.1L/100km (20mpg).
PRODUCTION 274.
PRICE £1675 Velox fast tourer.

Classic profile. The 30-98 gradually grew longer, making the E-type in 2- or 4-seater form appear almost truncated.

Far right: 1921 motor show 4-seater photographed on 2 November.

Although by no means fast or sporting, the M-type (later 14/40) was a progressive design with the clutch and gearbox in unit with the engine. Ready for the 1921 motor show at Olympia, the Fourteen was the first Vauxhall with a detachable cylinder head (making valve maintenance and the regular chore of decarbonising easier), cantilever rear springs, Autovac fuel feed and spiral bevel final drive. The inclusion of Autovac, which used the engine manifold depression to draw fuel to a header tank above the carburettor, was perhaps in deference to Joseph Higginson, successful Vauxhall racing driver and proprietor of Autovac Ltd. Yet the engine was reduced from Vauxhall's customary five main bearings to three. Gone too was the engine sub-frame, there were only three gears and the transmission brake was abandoned, probably a wise move for a car aimed at the non-sporting owner-driver who often equipped it with rather grand closed bodywork. Yet it was a modern light car with contemporary weight and cost-saving amenities such as extensive use of aluminium, and disc wheels (wires remained an option). It retained magneto ignition and right hand gearshift lever. Supremely successful, production went on until 1924, mostly with Princeton 4-door touring bodywork, the left front door containing the comprehensive tool kit.

BODY to order, Princeton Tourer; weight 1105kg (2435lb).
ENGINE 4 cylinders, in-line, front, 75mm x 130mm; 2297cc; compr: 4.8:1; 32kW (43bhp) @ 2400 rpm; 14kW/L (18.7bhp/L).
ENGINE STRUCTURE side valves; side camshaft; detachable aluminium cylinder head; cast iron block, aluminium crankcase in unit with clutch; 3-bearing crankshaft; Zenith 30F carburettor; Autovac fuel feed; magneto ignition; water-cooled.
TRANSMISSION rear wheel drive; single-plate clutch; integral 3-speed gearbox with right hand change; torque tube; spiral bevel final drive; ratio 4.5:1.
CHASSIS DETAILS pressed steel frame; half-elliptic spring front suspension; cantilever rear suspension; friction dampers; rear wheel brakes; worm and sector steering; 41L (9 Imp gal, 10.8 US gal) fuel tank; 815 x 105 beaded edge tyres, six-stud disc wheels.
DIMENSIONS wheelbase 289.5cm (114in); track 127cm (50in); ground clearance 15cm (6in); length 414cm (163in); width 168cm (66in).
PERFORMANCE maximum speed 88.5kph (55mph); 33.7kph (21mph) @ 1000rpm; 34.5kg/kW (25.7kg/bhp); fuel consumption 11.8-12.8L/100km (22-24mpg).
PRODUCTION 1848.
PRICE 1922 £650, 1924 tourer £595.

Right: The 14/40 Princeton tourer was better-proportioned thanks to a 297.2cm (117in) wheelbase, wider track, and wire wheels instead of resonating discs. A 4th gear was added and more sporting rations provided giving 53kph (33mph) in 2nd, 72 kph (45mph) in 3rd, and 96kph (60mph) in top. Taller radiator improved appearance.

1922 TT Vauxhall

The ignominy of the 1914 TT lingered until 1922, when three 3.0-litre racing cars were ordered from Pomeroy's successor C E King, with engines designed by H R (later Sir Harry) Ricardo. Vauxhall wanted to contest the RAC TT once again, yet while the formidable Bentleys were based on catalogued production models just as pre-1914 side valve Vauxhalls had been, in 1922 Luton wanted out and out racing cars. Losing to lightweight overhead camshaft Peugeots in 1914 had taught Vauxhall a lesson. Accordingly although no production Vauxhalls had overhead camshafts, Ricardo's expensive experiment had two, driven by gears, with four valves per cylinder. It also had roller bearing big-ends, a central flywheel, and wet cylinder liners in the aluminium block. A diligent researcher into the combustion process, Ricardo specified three spark plugs per cylinder and wet sump lubrication, two pumps supplying each half of the engine. The Perrot brakes had a balancing arrangement to distribute braking effort front to rear by means of a lever on the steering column applying compressed air to a Westinghouse servo. The race result was little better than in 1914 however, with only one car finishing fourth. Successes came later with Jack Barclay, Humphrey Cook, John Cobb, Malcolm Campbell, Raymond Mays, H F Clay, and Parry Thomas.

BODY racing, 2 seats, weight 1021kg (2520lb).
ENGINE 4 cylinders, in-line front, 85mm x 132mm; 2996cc; compr: 5.8:1; 96kW (129bhp) @ 4500rpm; 32.1kW/L (43.1bhp/L).
ENGINE STRUCTURE 2 overhead camshafts; 4-valve bronze cylinder heads, aluminium wet liner block; 6-bearing crankshaft; air pump driven off timing case; pressure fuel feed to dual-choke Zenith carburettor; 12-volt coil ignition, twin distributors; water-cooled.
TRANSMISSION rear wheel drive; multi-plate clutch in unit with engine; 4-speed gearbox; bevel final drive, no differential; ratio 3.75:1.
CHASSIS DETAILS pressed steel chassis; semi-elliptic suspension front and rear; Hartford friction dampers; Perrot 4 wheel brakes, pedal working on 30.5cm (12in) drums at front, lever on 40.6cm (16in) at rear, air pump servo; worm and wheel steering 1.5 turns lock to lock; 136L (30 Imp gal, 36 US gal) fuel tank; front tyres 810x90, rear tyres 820x120.

DIMENSIONS wheelbase 272cm (107in); front and rear track 135cm (53in); length 389cm (153in); width 160cm (63in); height 119cm (47in).
PERFORMANCE maximum speed 180kph (112mph); 42kph (26mph) @ 1000rpm; 10.6kg/kW (7.9kg/bhp); fuel consumption 8.3L/100km (34mpg) at steady 72-80kph (45-50mph).
PRODUCTION 3.

Matthew Park, Vauxhall repair shop foreman, and Ernie Swain, road test department foreman, both retired their works cars in the 1922 TT, but Jock Payne, running shop foreman in the third team car, finished third.

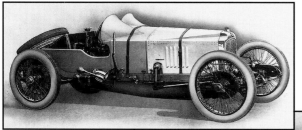

1922-1927 OD-type 23/60

Among C E King's first post-war tasks was to bring the D-type up to scratch. He equipped the OD with a Lanchester harmonic balancer to improve quietness and refinement, overhead valves to improve efficiency, and a detachable cylinder head to improve accessibility and maintenance (engines still had to undergo frequent decarbonisation), but left the brakes alone. Even by the standards of the 1920s Vauxhalls were not accomplished at stopping, and although two notches on the ratchet could lock up the rear wheels, this did not do much to slow the car.

The extra wheelbase and wider track against the 30-98 OE made the OD comfortable at the expense of greater weight but provided the stability necessary for tall bodywork. The gearbox was still separate from the engine, clutch and flywheel. Starting was effected by pumping up a pound or so of pressure in the fuel tank, flooding the carburettor, moving the dashboard mixture control to Start, the ignition lever on the steering wheel to Retard and the throttle five or six notches open. After switching on the magneto the starter motor turned the crankshaft over five or six revolutions before the engine fired with a deep *basso profundo* rumble in the large exhaust pipe.

BODY 5-seat tourer, 7-seat tourer limousine, landaulette; weight 1575kg (3472lb).
ENGINE 4 cylinders, in-line, front, 95mm x 140mm; 3969cc; 45kW (60bhp) @ 2000rpm; 11.3kW/L (15.1bhp/L); compression ratio 4.2:1; 22.4 rated horse power.
ENGINE STRUCTURE pushrod overhead valves; chain driven camshaft; detachable cast iron cylinder head; cast iron block; 5-bearing crankshaft; Zenith 42KA triple diffuser carb, (later SU) pressurised fuel feed, (later Autovac); magneto ignition; water-cooled.
TRANSMISSION rear wheel drive; Vauxhall multi-plate clutch; 4-speed; bevel final drive; ratio 3.6:1.
CHASSIS DETAILS pressed steel chassis; suspension half-elliptic all round; no dampers; handbrake operated rear wheel drum brakes, transmission footbrake; worm and wheel steering; 54.5L (12 Imp gal, 14.4US gal) fuel tank; 880x120 beaded edge tyres.
DIMENSIONS wheelbase 330cm (130in); track 142cm (56in); ground clearance 23cm (9in); length 457cm (180in); width 170cm (67in).
PERFORMANCE maximum speed 104kph (65mph); 45.8kph (28.5mph) @ 1000rpm; 35kg/kW (26.3kg/bhp); fuel consumption 15.7L/100km (18mpg).
PRODUCTION 1297 approx.
PRICE Kington Tourer £925 in 1924.

Far right: OD-type 23/60 Kington Tourer.

1923-1927 30-98 OE-type

An overhead valve 30-98 had been in Laurence Pomeroy's mind in 1919. His departure was a loss, not only to Vauxhall but also to the indigenous motor industry, for he had all the makings of a British Ferdinand Porsche. His successor C E King developed pushrod overhead valve engines for the D-type 25HP and the E-type 30-98 in 1923, making it the fastest catalogued car in Britain. Almost every 30-98 was sold as a fast tourer.

The new engine had much the same robust lower half as before but with a redesigned block and new overhead valves so large they needed rockers on offset pedestals. Their seats extended to the edge of the combustion spaces. Double valve springs and substantial four-bolt Duralumin connecting rods were necessary for an engine that revved freely to 3400rpm. The result was greater refinement but not, at first, a great deal more speed, although in racing trim and with a high axle ratio 30-98s were guaranteed for 100mph. Later cars had a balanced crank and good hydraulic brakes. The elegant 4-seat open 3-door tourer Velox was handsome and well-proportioned, but the most dramatic was the nautical-looking "boat-tailed" Wensum with no doors, no hood, flared wings, polished wood panelling V windscreen, and £150 premium. Mulliner and Grosvenor also catalogued 2-seaters.

BODY to order, Velox fast tourer 1423kg (3136lb). Wensum sports 4-seater weight complete car 1473kg (3248lb), chassis 1245kg (2744lb).
ENGINE 4 cylinders, in-line, front, 98mm x 140mm; 4224cc; compr: 5.2:1; 83.5kW (112bhp) @ 3400rpm; 19.8kW/L (26.5bhp/L); rated horse power 23.8. Later cars 89.5kW (120bhp) @ 3500rpm.
ENGINE STRUCTURE pushrod ohv; chain driven cam; detachable cast iron cyl head; cast iron block; 5-bearing crank; Zenith 48RA carb, pressurised fuel feed until 1923, then Autovac; Watford magneto ignition; water-cooled, honeycomb radiator, cast alloy fan.
TRANSMISSION rwd; Vauxhall multi-plate clutch; 4-speed; ENV spiral bevel final drive; ratio 3.3:1.
CHASSIS DETAILS pressed steel chassis, engine sub-frame channel pressed steel section; half-elliptic suspension all round; Hartford friction dampers; 4 wheel brakes from 1923, hydraulic in front from 1926; worm and wheel steering; 54.5L (12 Imp gal, 14.4 US gal) fuel tank; 820x120 beaded edge tyres till 1925, then 32x4.5SS rims; centre-lock Rudge wheels.
DIMENSIONS wheelbase 299cm (117.5in); track 137cm (54in); ground clearance 6in; length 429cm (169in); width 170cm (67in).
PERFORMANCE maximum speed 144.5kph (90mph), 160kph (100mph) guaranteed when stripped for racing; 44.9kph (28mph) @ 1000rpm; 0-96kph (60mph) 17sec; 19kg/kW (14kg/bhp); 15.7L/100km (18mpg).
PRODUCTION 312.
PRICE chassis 1923 £1020, later £950.

Left: **E-type chassis.**
Right: **1924 30-98, first owner Maharajah of Kashmir.**

1923 Vauxhall motorcycle prototype

The only mid-engined, air-cooled Vauxhall was a radical prototype motorcycle. It was drawn up by Ricardo's Frank B Halford, who enjoyed a distinguished career in aero-engineering at Farnborough, then with Beardmore and Arroll-Johnston was the "H" in the BHP aero-engine consortium, and created the Cirrus engine for de Havilland in 1924. He was also responsible for the flat-H liquid-cooled Napier Sabre and worked with Sir Frank Whittle in jet engines. Vauxhall believed in recruiting the best brains. Major Halford's motorcycle would have been expensive to make however, since it incorporated advanced technology to which he might have been accustomed in aero-engines but would have been uneconomical. Motorbikes after all were still largely the transport of the working class, with girder forks, single cylinders, and belt drive. Sports motorcycles with four cylinders and shaft drive had not yet been invented. The cylinder dimensions were "square" and wick lubrication was provided for the rockers on the vertical overhead valves. Bottom-end lubrication was by dippers on the ends of the H-section connecting rods, and the clutch was constructed of alternate steel and bronze plates. Two machines were completed and components for a further four frames and ten engines made before the project was sold off.

BODY single-seat motorcycle, weight 193kg (425lb).
ENGINE 4 cylinders, in-line, mid; 67mm x 67mm; 945cc; 22.4kW (30bhp) @ 3500 rpm; 23.7kW/L (31.7bhp/L).
ENGINE STRUCTURE pushrod overhead valves; side camshaft; cast iron integral cylinder heads and

barrels; aluminium crankcase; 3-bearing 2-piece crankshaft; single carburettor; magneto ignition; 6-volt electrics; air-cooled.
TRANSMISSION rear wheel drive; 15cm (6in) multi-plate clutch; 3-speed gearbox; shaft drive; worm final drive; ratio 3.5:1.
CHASSIS DETAILS duplex cradle frame; coil-sprung twin forks front suspension; no rear suspension; no dampers; 17.8cm (7in) drum brakes; 20.5L (4.5 Imp gal, 5.4US gal) fuel tank; 700x80 tyres.
DIMENSIONS wheelbase 147cm (58in); length 229cm (90in); height 99cm (39in).
PERFORMANCE maximum speed 132kph (82mph); 38.5kph (24mph) @ 1000rpm; fuel consumption 4L/100km (70mpg) @ 80kph (50mph).
PRODUCTION 2, see text.

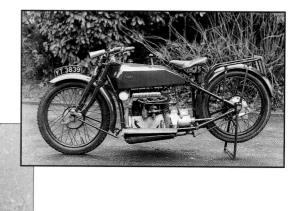

In 1924 the M-type was selling well. Typical of the wide range of coachwork options was a coupe-cabriolet, and a cumbersome all-weather car with a hood picturesquely described by historian Michael Sedgwick as "… of surpassing weight and clumsiness." Grosvenor made both. The revised LM14/40 boasted a taller radiator, balloon tyres, wire-spoked wheels, and 7.6cm (3in) extra on the wheelbase which improved the appearance and allowed even more upright and luxurious formal bodywork. An extra gear with more sporting ratios gave 72kph (45mph) in third and 53kph (33mph) in second. Seats on the Norfolk 4-door saloon folded down to form a bed. One painted red and yellow was supplied to the King of Siam.

With the help of such good quality if unsporting and relatively slow cars, Vauxhall sales reached 637 in 1921, and more than doubled in 1923 to 1462. By 1925 they were 1388 enabling the 14/40 to be reduced by £100. The following year they went up to 1516, the majority 14/40s. Its final fling was to have a number equipped with Wilson pre-selector gearboxes whose experimental nature would continue "until a number of 14HP (still the official name) cars fitted with this gearbox have covered many thousands of miles in the hands of certain selected drivers who are not actual members of the Vauxhall company".

BODY to order, all-weather tourer, dh coupe, saloon; 2 seats; weight 1925 saloon 1194kg (2632lb). Chassis weight 2100lb.
ENGINE 4 cylinders, in-line, front, 75mm x 130mm; 2297cc; 32kW (43bhp) @ 3000 rpm; 14kW/L (18.7bhp/L).
ENGINE STRUCTURE side valves; side camshaft; detachable aluminium cylinder head; cast iron block, aluminium crankcase; 3-bearing crankshaft; Zenith triple diffuser carburettor; Autovac fuel feed; magneto ignition; water-cooled.
TRANSMISSION rear wheel drive; single-plate clutch; 4-speed gearbox with right hand change; spiral bevel final drive; ratio 4.5:1.
CHASSIS DETAILS pressed steel frame; half-elliptic spring front suspension; cantilever rear suspension; friction dampers; rear wheel brakes until 1925 thereafter 4-wheel brakes; worm and sector steering; 45L (10 Imp gal, 12 US gal) fuel tank; 31 x 5.25 balloon tyres, wire-spoked wheels.

DIMENSIONS wheelbase 297.2cm (117in); track 141cm (55.5in); ground clearance 15cm (6in); length 422cm (166in); width 168cm (66in).
PERFORMANCE maximum speed 101.4kph (63mph); 32.9kph (20.5mph) @ 1000rpm; 11.8-12.8L/ 100km (22-24mpg).
PRODUCTION 3497 approx.
PRICE £495 1925.

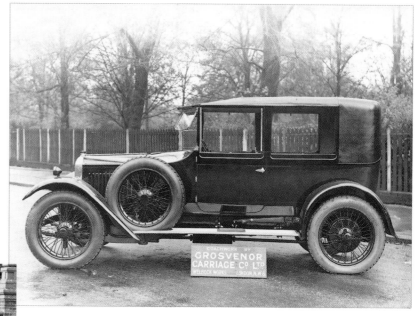

81

Burt-McCollum sleeve-valve engines turned out to be something of an engineering aberration for Vauxhall. Sleeve-valves were by no means new in 1928 and proved equally disastrous for Argyll and Arroll-Johnston in Scotland, and Picard-Pictet in Geneva. Daimler of Coventry and Minerva in Belgium adopted double sleeve valve engines designed by C Y Knight but although they were quiet and refined they were smoky, heavy, and complicated. Vauxhall's attempt to banish the poppet valve was a Ricardo design under patents of Glasgow engineer Peter Burt and Canadian JHK McCollum with single sleeve valves, which absorbed less power and promised 25,000 or 30,000 miles instead of 10,000 before decarbonising. Hydraulic front brakes did little to attract customers and the new General Motors management, which had altogether different sorts of Vauxhall in mind, mercifully quashed the pioneering effort. A 4-seater Morris Cowley stood at £341, an Austin 20 £695, a Crossley £895 and the Sunbeam Big Six £1295. Pomeroy had drawn up a V12 and an overhead camshaft version of the 30-98 but Vauxhall was making losses, £50,000 in 1922, and such extravagance was no longer a commercial proposition. A month after the introduction of the S-type when General Motors had failed to buy Austin, it bought Vauxhall.

BODY limousine, 6 seats, 4 doors weight 1981kg (4368lb), chassis alone 1600kg (3527lb).

ENGINE 6 cylinders, in-line, front, 81.5mm x 124mm; 3881cc; 52kW (70bhp) @ 2700 rpm;13.4kW/L (18bhp/L).

ENGINE STRUCTURE single sleeve valves; detachable cast iron cylinder head and block; Dural pistons and connecting rods 10-bearing balanced crankshaft with central flywheel; updraught SU carburettor, Autovac fuel supply; HT Magneto ignition; water-cooled.

TRANSMISSION rear wheel drive; Vauxhall multi-plate clutch; 4-speed gearbox; spiral bevel final drive; ratio 4.0:1.

CHASSIS DETAILS pressed steel chassis, 15cm (6in) deep side members; half-elliptic springs all round; friction dampers; hydraulic front brakes, mechanical rear, non-coupled; worm and wheel steering; 73L (16 Imp gal, 19.2US gal) fuel tank; 33x6.75 balloon tyres.

DIMENSIONS wheelbase 345cm (136in); front track 144cm (56.5in); rear track 142cm (56in); length 457cm (180in); width 185cm (73in).

PERFORMANCE maximum speed 104kph (65mph); 38.5kph (24mph) @ 1000rpm; 38.1kg/kW (28.3kg/bhp); fuel consumption 14.1-15.7L/100km (18-20mpg).

PRODUCTION 50 approx.

PRICE £1350 Royton 5-seat tourer, £1675 formal limousine.

1928-1929 R-type 20/60

The first Vauxhall made under General Motors was a short wheelbase 21HP, which became the staple Vauxhall for three whole seasons while the new management was feeling its way. By the time production came to an end in 1930 it was the only Vauxhall being made at all. It acquired some of the style of a contemporary Buick, and was equipped with 12 volt electrics, central gearshift, and a single-plate clutch replaced the fine multi-plate Vauxhall had used for 15 years. Gone too was the traditional Vauxhall worm and wheel steering, replaced by Marles gears, and plain artillery wheels were used instead of the Rudge wire wheels. The brakes were an improvement however. Vauxhalls had never been good at stopping, and although the R-type kept the generously sized transmission drum brake (Vauxhall persevered with it until 1932) its rod and cable arrangement gave good results. *The Motor* managed a stop of 12.2m (40ft) from 48kph (30mph) in 1928.

    The Autocar generously rated it "absolutely and completely British as far as its performance and appearance is concerned; it in no way suggests the American car in general or in particular." *Motor Sport* was more guarded although Vauxhall insisted that it had been conceived before the take-over.

BODY tourer, drophead, saloon, fabric saloon, landaulette, limousine, town car; 2 seats; weight 1575kg (3472lb).
ENGINE 6 cylinders, in-line, front; 73mm x 110mm; 2762cc; from 1929 75mm x 110mm, 2916cc.
ENGINE STRUCTURE pushrod overhead valves; side camshaft; detachable cast iron cylinder head and block, cast iron pistons, aluminium from 1929; 7-bearing crankshaft; Autovac fuel feed; Delco-Remy coil ignition; water-cooled.
TRANSMISSION rear wheel drive; Borg & Beck single-plate clutch; 4-speed gearbox; ratio 4.73:1. 5:1 from 1929.
CHASSIS DETAILS pressed steel chassis; half-elliptic springs all round; from 1929 Hartford dampers; 4 wheel brakes, handbrake on transmission; Marles gear steering; 5.25x21 tyres, artillery wheels, from 1929 30x5.50
DIMENSIONS wheelbase 312cm (123in) from 1929 Westminster 339cm (130in).

PERFORMANCE maximum speed 108kph (67mph); acceleration 0-80kph (50mph) 25sec; fuel consumption 15.3L/100km (18.5mpg)
PRODUCTION perhaps 4228.
PRICE Grafton 2-seater dh coupe £630, Wyndham 4-light Weymann £665, Kimberley £695, Town car £735, Westminster £705.

Right: Identical in almost every respect to the R-type in appearance, by 1930 the T-type was being used on official duties, here delivering the Prince of Wales to a civic function.

1930 Vauxhall Villiers Supercharge

The team cars from the 1922 TT became known as Vauxhalls I, II, and III. Vauxhall I was owned and driven by Jack Barclay and Dan Higgin, scoring many successes before being owned by Tim Carson in 1928, who suffered a catastrophic engine blow-up.

Vauxhall III was run by Humphrey Cook, the founder of ERA, at Brooklands, Kop, Aston Clinton, Shelsley Walsh and other venues and took world speed records. It was sold to the great Welsh engineer Parry Thomas for racing and record-breaking, then to David Brown (later Sir David, the DB of Aston Martin) who fitted a supercharger designed by Amherst Villiers. This car was broken up, but Vauxhall II had a long career that began with ftd at Colwyn Bay in 1923 driven by W Watson, and Raymond Mays eventually bought it from Jack Barclay in 1928 for £275. He wanted a sprint car, so fitted twin rear wheels, and the Amherst Villiers blower. With a replacement chassis and remodelled engine Mays took honours at Shelsley Walsh many times, finally climbing in late 1933 in 42.4 seconds beating the previous hill record which had stood for three years. Mays sold the car shortly afterwards but it was never quite the same again, although the engine was reputedly capable of 6000rpm.

BODY 2-seat racing, original weight 1143kg (2520lb) later 1497kg (3300lb).
ENGINE 4 cylinders, supercharged, in-line front, 85mm x 132mm, 2996cc; compression ratio 8.5:1; 224kW (300bhp) @ 6000rpm; 74.7kW/L (100bhp/L).
ENGINE STRUCTURE 2 overhead camshafts; 4-valve bronze cylinder heads, aluminium wet liner block; 5-bearing crankshaft; 3 x Zenith aircraft carburettors and 16psi later 20psi boost Villiers supercharger; twin BTH magneto ignition, twin distributors; water-cooled.
TRANSMISSION rear wheel drive; multi-plate clutch in unit with engine; 4-speed gearbox; bevel final drive, no differential; ratio 3.75:1.
CHASSIS DETAILS fabricated steel structure; semi-elliptic springs front and rear; Hartford friction dampers; 4 wheel brakes Clayton-Dewandre servo; worm and wheel steering 1.5 turns lock to lock; 182L (40 Imp gal, 48 US gal) fuel tank; 500x19 tyres, twin rear wheels.
DIMENSIONS wheelbase 272cm (107in); front and rear track 135cm (53in); length 389cm (153in); width 160cm (63in); height 114cm (45in).
PERFORMANCE maximum speed approx 241kph (150mph); 40.1kph (25mph) @ 1000rpm; 5.1kg/kW (3.8kg/bhp).
PRODUCTION 1.

Right: **Raymond Mays in driving seat and Peter Berthon at front of car survey their handiwork. Finned intercooler casing on right of engine.**
Far right: **Mays in 1926 with Berthon in the passenger seat tackling Shelsley Walsh with a TT Vauxhall in pre-supercharger form.**

1930-1932 T and T80

Introduced as a derivative of R-type but with taller radiator and on some versions chrome flutes, the big T-type 20.9HP and 23HP, sole Vauxhall at the beginning of 1930, was known by the end of the year as the Silent 80. A change of pricing policy brought the chassis under £300, and it had a stiffer frame, hydraulic shock absorbers and a mechanical fuel pump replaced the Autovac. In 1931 the larger-engined T80 had wire wheels as standard.

The stylish Hurlingham was an echo of the Wensum, a rakish 2-seater with a V-shaped windscreen and small dickey seat capable of 112kph (70mph), although *Motor Sport* was unsure of its appeal. "Third gear enables an excellent average to be put up as it gives excellent acceleration and one gets into the habit of spending a good deal of time in this gear on anything like a twisty road." But 88kph (55mph) remained about the maximum and the steering was too low geared. *Motor Sport* contrasted the Hurlingham's thoroughly gentlemanly behaviour with what it called the roughness of the old school Vauxhall.

Company records suggest production of the 20/60 T-type did not continue much after 1930, but the expensive (£750 for a 1931 saloon) Silent 80 (T80) sold for a further season.

BODY Hurlingham sports, Kington fixed-head coupe, drophead, fabric saloon, sports saloon, limousine, landaulette; 2 seats.
ENGINE 6 cylinders, in-line, front, 75mm x 110mm; 2916cc. T80 80mm x 110mm, 3317cc. Rubber engine mountings from 1931.
ENGINE STRUCTURE pushrod ohv; side cam; detachable cast iron cylinder head and block, aluminium pistons; 7-bearing crankshaft; Autovac fuel feed; Delco-Remy coil ignition; water-cooled; engine and gearbox in unitary structure.
TRANSMISSION rear wheel drive; single plate clutch; 4-speed gearbox; central change; spiral bevel final drive; ratio 5.1:1.

CHASSIS DETAILS pressed steel chassis; semi-elliptic springs; Luvax hydraulic dampers; 4 wheel cable brakes; Marles & Weller steering; wire wheels optional.
DIMENSIONS wheelbase 312cm (123in) or 330cm (130in).
PERFORMANCE maximum speed 112kph (70mph); 0-50mph 30sec; fuel consumption 14L/100km (20mpg).
PRODUCTION 1172 T; 624 T80.
PRICE £1930 saloon £750.

Left: Velox fabric saloon.
Top: Kington sportsman's coupe.
Right: Melton Golfer's coupe.

The new policy of widening Vauxhall production took effect with the introduction of the Cadet at the 1930 motor show. It was good value, with no sporting or luxury-car legacy, but it had leather upholstery, a smooth 6-cylinder engine with a 4-bearing pressure-lubricated crankshaft, and brought synchromesh to the British market for the first time in 1932. The engine was rubber-mounted, it had vacuum-operated windscreen wipers, and the brakes were modified American Bendix. In 1932 the 6-volt electric system was replaced by 12-volt and a wide variety of body styles was available from outside coachbuilders.

Motor Sport found the Cadet set new standards of smoothness and quietness, noting "American influence in the flexibility of the engine… it is meant to be driven by lazy people with a long way to go. This is apt to prove a disappointment to 100% sports car enthusiasts, but it has its points, certainly for anyone out to cover the ground with the least possible trouble."

Sales showed that there were more lazy people with a long way to go than there ever were sports car enthusiasts. GM's commercial objectives were changing Vauxhall, ties were being forged with its world wide family, in particular Opel. The results were happily embraced by a new generation of drivers.

BODY tourer, saloon, 2 seats; 2-and 4-light fixed-head coupe; drophead coupe, convertible, saloon, 2/4 seats; weight 1270kg (2800lb).
ENGINE 6 cylinders, in-line, front, 67.5mm x 95.2mm; 2048cc; compr: 5.5:1; 31.3kW (42bhp) @ 3300rpm; 15.3kW/L (20.5bhp/L); RAC Rating 16.9hp tax £17.
ENGINE STRUCTURE pushrod overhead valves; side camshaft; detachable cast iron cylinder head and block, aluminium pistons; 4-bearing crankshaft; downdraught Zenith carburettor; coil ignition; water-cooled by thermo-syphon and fan.
TRANSMISSION rear wheel drive; single plate clutch; 3-speed gearbox; synchromesh on 2nd and 3rd from 1932, central ball change; final drive ratio 5.1:1.
CHASSIS DETAILS pressed steel frame; half-elliptic springs all round; hydraulic dampers; 4-wheel servo-assisted brakes; Bishop (from 1932 Marles-Weller) cam and lever steering; 54.5L (12 Imp gal, 14.4 US gal) fuel tank; 5.25x18tyres.

DIMENSIONS wheelbase 272cm (107in); track 144cm (56.5in); ground clearance 20cm (8in); length 409cm (161in); width 169cm (66.5in); height…in.
PERFORMANCE maximum speed 100kph (62mph); acceleration 0-80kph (50mph) 29sec; 40.6kg/kW (30.2kg/bhp); fuel consumption 13.5L/100km (21mpg).
PRODUCTION 5932.
PRICE chassis £185, saloon £280, Sportsman's Coupe £298, open 2-seater £295, Tourer £275, Saloon de luxe £295, Tickford Saloon £335.

Far right: **Upright, practical, roomy, and stylish enough at the time, the Cadet standard saloon exemplified the growing demand for "family" cars. This early version has divided bumper and exposed wheelnuts.**

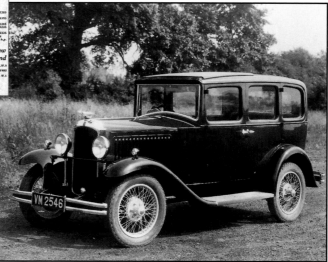

The 3.2-litre VX Cadet was rated at 26.33hp, so it carried an annual tax burden of £26. Accordingly two Cadets were introduced in 1931, the 2048cc VY for the home market and the VX for export. In 1932 both benefited from the introduction of synchromesh, which brought gears into mesh by means of synchronising cones, a development that revolutionised gear changing for the rising numbers of drivers not prepared to master the double declutching skills of which their sporting counterparts were so proud. The Cadet was not an instant sales success, production remaining at less than 4000 a year at first, but it became the basis for the subsequent range of Vauxhall Light Sixes which ensured Vauxhall Motors' long term prosperity. Synchromesh had been introduced on 1929 Cadillacs and drew on a 1922 patent of Earl Thompson. The VX engine was based on a Cast Iron Wonder American Chevrolet with a four instead of three-bearing crank. A variety of body styles were introduced, some by outside coachbuilders such as Martin Walter, Duple, Grose of Northampton, Salmons, Tickford, and Hoyal, while others were fully catalogued Vauxhall models. Luton also made a few Chevrolets, but more important in 1931 was the introduction of Chevrolet-based Bedford lorries and light commercials.

BODY 2-seat, tourer, saloon, 2- and 4-light fixed-head coupe, 2- and 4-seat drophead coupe, convertible, saloon, weight 1315kg (2900lb).
ENGINE 6 cylinders, in-line, front, 84mm x 95.25mm; 3180cc; compr: 5.5:1; 33kW (44bhp) @ 3400rpm; 10.3kW/L (13.8bhp/L). RAC Rating 26.33hp, tax £26.
ENGINE STRUCTURE pushrod overhead valves; side camshaft; detachable cast iron cylinder head and block, aluminium pistons; 4-bearing crankshaft; downdraught Zenith carburettor; coil ignition; water-cooled by thermo-syphon and fan.
TRANSMISSION rear wheel drive; single plate clutch; 3-speed gearbox; synchromesh on 2nd and 3rd from 1932, central ball change; final drive ratio 5.1:1.
CHASSIS DETAILS pressed steel frame; half-elliptic springs all round; hydraulic dampers; 4-wheel cable brakes; Bishop (from 1932 Marles-Weller) cam and lever steering; 54.5L (12 Imp gal, 14.4 US gal) fuel tank; 5.25x18tyres.
DIMENSIONS wheelbase 272cm (107in); track 144cm (56.5in); length 409cm (161in); width 169cm (66.5in).
PERFORMANCE maximum speed 112kph (70mph); 40kg/kW (30kg/bhp).
PRODUCTION 3759.
PRICE n/a.

Left: 1931 Bedford WHG 2-ton truck.
Right: Martin Walter Denton drophead 4-seater with 26HP engine.

1933-1934 Light Six ASX Fourteen

Identical save in engine to the 1.5-litre 12HP ASY, the 14HP Light Six was launched in May 1933 and shown at Olympia that autumn for the 1934 model year. The 12HP 1.5-litre with no frills cost £195, and the de luxe £215. The 14HP sold only as a de luxe and, with commendable logic, at the same price of £215. No-draught ventilation on the de luxe saloon comprised swivelling portions of the front and rear windows operated by winding handles, and it had two windscreen wipers.

New drivers, soon to undergo tests under the 1934 Road Traffic Act, found the small smooth-running 6-cylinder engines with a flexible top gear much to their liking. Vauxhall's pioneering synchromesh featured on third and top, maximum speeds of which were about 48kph (30mph) and 74kph (46mph). Springing was firm, and rear-seat occupants over the back axle suffered a certain amount of pitching on rough roads. The cable brakes had what was known perhaps optimistically as servo shoes, to keep pedal pressure down, and proved capable of a 1g stop at low speeds and 0.88g at higher speeds.

Standard equipment included a sunroof, leather upholstery, safety glass, and a bench seat. Adjustable bucket seats cost extra.

BODY 4-door, 6-light, 5-seat saloon, fixed head coupe, drophead, 4-door cabriolet, coachbuilt specials; weight saloon 1016kg (2240lb).
ENGINE 6 cylinders, in-line, front, 61.5mm x 100mm; 1782cc; compr: 5.5:1; 31.3kW (42bhp) @ 3500rpm; 17.6kW/L (23.6bhp/L).
ENGINE STRUCTURE pushrod overhead valves; side camshaft; cast iron cylinder head; chromidium iron cylinder block; 4-bearing crankshaft; Zenith downdraught carburettor, AC mechanical fuel pump; Lucas coil ignition; water-cooled, thermo-syphon and fan.
TRANSMISSION rear wheel drive; single-plate clutch; 4-speed gearbox; synchromesh top and 3rd; spiral bevel final drive; ratio 4.77:1; semi-floating rear axle.
CHASSIS DETAILS steel X-braced chassis; semi-elliptic springs front and rear; Lovejoy hydraulic dampers; semi-servo mechanical drum brakes; worm and sector steering; 40.9L (9 Imp gal, 10.8 US gal) fuel tank; AC fuel pump 4.75in tyres, 17in rims.

DIMENSIONS wheelbase 256.5cm (101in); track 127cm (50in); ground clearance 19.7cm (7.75in); turning circle 10.7m (35ft); length 392cm (154.5in); width 157.5cm (62in); height 168cm (66in).
PERFORMANCE maximum speed 112.6kph (70mph); 26kph (16mph) @ 1000rpm; acceleration to 80kph (50mph) 20sec; 32.5kg/kW (24.2kg/bhp); fuel consumption 10.5L/100km (27mpg) at steady 64kph (40mph); average 10.9L/100km (26mpg).
PRODUCTION 23,294 total ASY, ASX.
PRICE de luxe only £215 with extra screen wiper, sunroof, armrests, and GM Fisher no-draft ventilation.

Top: **Standard saloon exhibits growing sense of style.**
Right: **Coupe is 1934 Tickford drophead by Salmons.**

1933-1934 Light Six ASY Twelve

Rated at a mere 12.8hp by the Treasury, and sharing most things with the 1782cc ASX, the Light Six ASY kept pace with the Wolseley and Triumph small sixes, which added two more cylinders to existing 8HP fours to provide their customers with less of what they disliked most, namely gearchanging. Vauxhall had no 8HP and was more serious about the Fourteen than the Twelve, sales confirming its view that provided the price was about the same (and there was little reason for it not to be) most customers would go for the bigger engine. By the end of the production run of the AS-series the ratio of Fourteens to Twelves was around 10 to 1. The engines were derived from the pressure-lubricated Cadet.

The AS had much that its rivals did not. It provided contemporary styling, slightly American-derived with the headlights attached to the radiator shell. It had well-chosen gear ratios and accelerated well right up the speed range. There was a range of factory-approved special bodies that included an Abbey fastback coupe with the spare wheel concealed in a sort of tail fin.

There was even an equivalent Bedford van although commercial clients generally went for more workmanlike four-cylinder cars.

BODY 4-door, 6-light 5-seat saloon, fixed head coupe, drophead, 4-door cabriolet, coachbuilt specials; weight saloon 1016kg (2240lb). chassis weight 711kg (1568lb).
ENGINE 6 cylinders, in-line, front; 57mm x 100mm; 1531cc; compr: 5.5:1; 27kW (36bhp) @ 4000rpm; 17.5kW/L (23.5bhp/L).
ENGINE STRUCTURE pushrod overhead valves; side camshaft; cast iron cylinder head; chromidium iron cylinder block; 4-bearing crankshaft; Zenith downdraught carburettor; AC mechanical fuel pump; Lucas coil ignition; water-cooled, thermo-syphon and fan.
TRANSMISSION rear wheel drive; single-plate clutch; 4-speed gearbox; synchromesh top and 3rd; spiral bevel final drive; ratio 4.77:1; semi-floating rear axle.
CHASSIS DETAILS steel X-braced chassis; semi-elliptic springs front and rear; Lovejoy hydraulic dampers; semi-servo mechanical drum brakes; worm and sector steering; 40.9L (9 Imp gal, 10.8 US gal) fuel tank; AC fuel pump 4.75in tyres, 17in rims.
DIMENSIONS wheelbase 135cm (53in); track 127cm (50in); length 391cm (154in); width 157.5cm (62in).
PERFORMANCE maximum speed 104kph (65mph); acceleration 0-80kph (50mph) 21.6sec; 38kg/kW (28kg/bhp); fuel consumption 10.5L/100km (27mpg).
PRODUCTION 23, 294 total ASY and ASX.
PRICE £195; de luxe £215 with extra screen wiper, sunroof, armrests, and GM Fisher no-draft ventilation.

Right: **Rear passengers in the 1933 Stratford Sports 4-seater by Whittingham & Mitchell enjoyed privacy but not much of a view when the top was up.**

1934-1936 Big Six 20HP BX, BXL

By 1934 transatlantic influence was making itself felt, the Big Six bearing a strong resemblance to the Chevrolet Master sedan, with distinctive chrome mesh grille, prominent headlights, flowing wings, and on expensive models side-mounted spare wheels. Luggage boots were flush on saloons, gently rounded on convertibles, and with the engine mounted well forward in the frame, there was lots of room inside.

Among the innovations were Luvax-Bijur automatic chassis lubrication, and self-cancelling trafficators. There was also a foot-operated starter known as "pedomatic", which engaged the starter when the accelerator was pressed. As soon as the engine fired the vacuum in the inlet manifold disengaged the starter. For 1936 there were changes to the grille and the "Body Conformity" front bucket seats were redesigned for greater comfort.

Prices were the same with 20hp and 27hp engines and the 1935 tax rate promised an annual Road Fund licence of only £15. Advertising the cheapest model at £325 in 1934, Vauxhall advertising carried a cheerful assurance that "You would have been happy to pay £450 to £500 for this type of car previously." There were six models including the Wingham Convertible Cabriolet ("Saloon to Tourer at a touch").

BODY sports saloon, 7-seat saloon, limousine, 4-door cabriolet; weight 1524kg (3360lb).
ENGINE 6 cylinders, in-line, front, 73mm x 95.25mm; 2392cc; compr 5.6:1; fiscal rating 19.8hp.
ENGINE STRUCTURE pushrod overhead valves; side camshaft; cast iron cylinder head and block; 4-bearing crankshaft; downdraught carburettor; coil ignition; water-cooled.
TRANSMISSION rear wheel drive; single plate clutch; 4-speed gearbox; synchromesh; ratio 4.11:1.
CHASSIS DETAILS pressed steel X-braced chassis structure; semi-elliptic springs all round; mechanical brakes; 2.25 turns lock to lock steering; 54.5L (12 Imp gal, 14.4 US gal) fuel tank; 5.50 x 17in tyres, bolt-on wire wheels, automatic chassis lubrication.
DIMENSIONS wheelbase 282cm (111in) and 330cm (130in); front track 144cm (56.5in), rear 146cm (57.5in); ground clearance 20cm (8in); turning circle 11.6m (38ft); length 434cm (171in); width 149cm (58.75in); height 173cm (68in).
PERFORMANCE maximum speed 112kph (70mph); acceleration to 80kph (50mph) 22sec; max speed in 2nd approx 64kph (40mph), 3rd approx 80kph (50mph); fuel consumption 14.1L/100km (19-20mpg).
PRODUCTION 4584 all BY, BX, BXL.
PRICE £325 with 20hp or 27hp engines; Wingham convertible cabriolet £395; Romney 2 seater drophead £360; Tickford foursome drophead £365; 7-passenger Grosvenor on 27hp Big Six long chassis £550.

Right: **Later grille, changed from chequer pattern to vertical bars, distinguished 1936 BXL limousine.**

1934-1936 Big Six 27HP BX

A variety of coachbuilt bodies was available on the large 6-cylinder Vauxhall. A good deal of the old aristocratic flavour remained, even though Luton was now dedicated, under its American tutelage, to the production of large numbers of middle-class cars. The Royal Dukes of Kent and Gloucester favoured the Wingham tourer body built by Martin Walter, which caught just the faintest whiff of the parade cars used by government hierarchy in Germany. The close-grained mesh of the Vauxhall radiator even echoed the Teutonic dignity adopted by Mercedes-Benz. There was ample room for seven passengers on the 48cm (19in) extra wheelbase Regent 27hp limousine that became a feature plying for hire by the railway stations and steamer terminals of British resorts throughout the 1930s and 1940s. Municipalities and large corporations became customers for VIP transport that did not have the extravagance associated with Rolls-Royces or Daimlers, in an era dominated by unemployment and the great depression. The engine was rubber-mounted, a concession to the growing demand for improvements in quietness, an area in which GM had more experience than many European designers. It also had combustion chambers more closely approaching the classic hemispherical than many of its bathtub-shaped contemporaries.

BODY sports saloon, 7-seat saloon, limousine, 4-door cabriolet; weight 1524kg (3360lb).
ENGINE 6 cylinders, in-line, front, 84.14mm x 95.25mm; 3180cc; compr 5.6:1; fiscal rating 26.3hp.
ENGINE STRUCTURE pushrod overhead valves; side camshaft; cast iron cylinder head and block; 4-bearing crankshaft; downdraught carburettor; coil ignition; water-cooled.
TRANSMISSION rear wheel drive; single plate clutch; 4-speed gearbox; synchromesh 3rd and top; final drive ratio 4.78:1.
CHASSIS DETAILS pressed steel chassis structure; semi-elliptic springs all round; mechanical brakes; 2.25 turns lock to lock steering; 54.5L (12 Imp gal, 14.4 US gal) fuel tank; 5.50 x 17in tyres, bolt-on wire wheels; automatic chassis lubrication.
DIMENSIONS wheelbase 282cm (111in); front track 143.5cm (56.5in), rear 146cm (57.5in); ground clearance 20cm (8in); turning circle 11.6m (38ft); length 434cm (171in); width 149cm (58.75in).
PERFORMANCE maximum speed 116kph (72mph); max in 3rd 84kph (52mph); acceleration to 80kph (50mph) 18.5sec, to 96kph (60mph) 28sec; fuel consumption 14.5L/100km (19.5mpg).
PRODUCTION 4584 all BY, BX, BXL.
PRICE £325 with 20hp or 27hp engines; Wingham convertible cabriolet £395; Romney 2-seater drophead £360; Tickford foursome drophead £365; Newmarket 5/6 seat sports saloon on 25hp Regent Chassis with Grosvenor coachwork £550.

Right: Transatlantic as well as European influence on standard BX saloon.
Far right: Connaught catches the 1930s flavour with sweeping tails.

CONNAUGHT *present two distinguished New Models on the* VAUXHALL Big Six . . .

THE CONTINENTAL TOURING SALOON

FOR many years CONNAUGHT have specialised in the design of high-class coachwork on the Vauxhall chassis. In these two new models on the new Vauxhall Big Six Regent Chassis Connaught craftsmen have excelled themselves. For the moment of discriminating taste they offer true Connaught distinction of line and fine quality finish at a more modest price. Your local Vauxhall dealer will gladly supply full particulars. You can inspect these cars together with a wide range of the 1936 Vauxhall models in the Connaught Showrooms at 45, Stratton Street, Piccadilly, London, W.1.

THE CONNAUGHT FOURDOOR ALL-WEATHER

See these new models on the Connaught Stand No. 24 *at Olympia.*

HOWARD GODFREY & CONNAUGHT COACHWORK LTD.

45, STRATTON STREET, PICCADILLY, LONDON, W.1

1935-1936 Light Six DX Fourteen

The advent of Dubonnet independent front suspension in October 1934 "...changes riding into gliding" according to Vauxhall publicity. It was a major event in the evolution of the popular car and a notable initiative for Vauxhall. It may not have transformed country by-ways into arterial roads or enabled passengers to read newspapers while the speedometer needle flickered round the mile-a-minute mark as the advertisements suggested, yet it represented an improvement in comfort even though the corollary was a disagreeable nose-dive under braking. The chassis was redesigned with cross bracing to provide the stiffness the novel suspension demanded. The entire steering mechanism was mounted on the chassis, stiffened by tubular cross members, not only reducing unsprung weight, but also reducing the reaction felt by the driver through the wheel, a welcome advance on rough roads.

Named after the aperitif manufacturer who sponsored the inventor Gustave Chedru's research, the Dubonnet system hung the wheel on an arm pivoted to a cylinder containing a coil spring and hydraulic shock absorber. The engine was moved 10cm (4in) forward to provide more interior space and the boot lid could be folded flat to carry luggage. Special bodied cars abounded, including a stylish 4-window 2-door coupe at £245.

BODY 6-light saloon; fixed head coupe, drophead, cabriolet, coachbuilt specials; 4 doors; saloon weight saloon 1194kg (2632lb.)
ENGINE 6 cylinders, in-line, front, 61.5mm x 100mm; 1782cc; compr: 6.25:1; 31kW (42bhp) @ 3500rpm; 17.4kW/L (23.6bhp/L);.
ENGINE STRUCTURE pushrod overhead valves; chain-driven side camshaft; cast iron cylinder head; chromidium iron cylinder block; 4-bearing crankshaft; Zenith downdraught 30V carburettor; Lucas coil ignition, timing by combined vacuum and governor; water-cooled by pump, fan, and thermostat.
TRANSMISSION rear wheel drive; single-plate clutch; 4-speed gearbox; synchromesh top and 3rd; spiral bevel final drive; ratio 4.77:1; semi-floating rear axle.
CHASSIS DETAILS steel X-braced box-section chassis; Dubonnet independent front suspension with coil springs and hydraulic dampers; semi-elliptic leaf springs at rear; hydraulic Lovejoy dampers; rear anti-roll bar; semi-servo mechanical drum brakes; worm and sector steering; 41L (9 Imp gal, 10.8 US gal) fuel tank; AC fuel pump 4.75in tyres, 17in rims.
DIMENSIONS wheelbase 256.5cm (101in); track 127cm (50in); ground clearance 19.7cm (7.75in); turning circle 10.7m (35ft); length 392cm (154.5in); width 157.5cm (62in); height 168cm (66in).
PERFORMANCE (from ASX) maximum speed 104.3kph (65mph); 25.7kph (16mph) @ 1000rpm; acceleration to 80kph (50mph) 20sec; 38.5kg/kW (28.4kg/bhp); fuel consumption 10.5L/100km (27 mpg) at steady 64kph (40mph); average 10.9L/100km (26mpg).
PRODUCTION 20,026 DY, DX.
PRICE £205 standard saloon, £225 de luxe. Stratford sports tourer £250; Suffolk saloon £280; Tickford foursome coupe £285; Duple 2-seater £235; Duple tourer £240; Airline convertible 2-4-seater £257.10s.

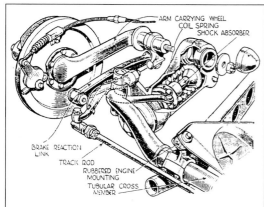

ARM CARRYING WHEEL
COIL SPRING
SHOCK ABSORBER

BRAKE REACTION
LINK

TRACK ROD
RUBBERED ENGINE
MOUNTING
TUBULAR CROSS
MEMBER

1935-1936 Light Six DY Twelve

The Light Six 12 echoed the Big Six, but with a 1530cc engine rated by the quaint treasury fiscal horsepower formula HP= $D^2 n/2.5$, where D represented the cylinder bore in inches and n the number of cylinders at 12.08 horse power. Car tax was consequently £12 per year against the 2.0-litre Cadet at £17 and the 3.2 litre 26.3 horsepower Big Six at £27.

Compared with the 1933-1934 AS range, the new suspension put 136kg (300lb) more on the front wheels and the engine was 10cm (4in) further forward, allowing the occupants to be accommodated within the wheelbase for a gentler ride.

Vauxhall made its own bodies for the standard range with pressed steel panels and traditional wooden frame. Cellulose paintwork was dried in huge ovens before the bodywork was mounted on the chassis. Following American practice, annual changes began to be introduced and for 1936 there were two-colour schemes with the flowing wings painted black. The windscreen wipers were now driven off the engine camshaft so they tended to slow when the car slowed. The object was to take some of the strain off the battery, by now quite heavily loaded and poorly re-charged in dark or foggy weather by a slow-turning dynamo.

BODY 6-light saloon; fixed head coupe, drophead, cabriolet, coachbuilt specials; 4 doors; saloon weight 1194kg (2632lb).
ENGINE 6 cylinders, in-line, front, 57mm x 100mm; 1530cc; compr: 6.25:1; 26.9kW (36bhp) @ 4000rpm; 17.5kW/L (23.5bhp/L).
ENGINE STRUCTURE pushrod ohv; chain-driven cam; c.i. cyl head; chromidium iron cyl block; 4-bearing steel crank; Zenith 30V downdraught carb; Lucas coil ignition by combined vacuum and governor; water-cooled by pump, fan, and thermostat.
TRANSMISSION rear wheel drive; single-plate clutch; 4-speed; sync top and 3rd; spiral bevel final drive; 4.77:1; semi-floating rear axle.
CHASSIS DETAILS steel X-braced box-section chassis; Dubonnet ifs with coil springs and hydraulic dampers; semi-elliptic leaf springs at rear; hydraulic Lovejoy dampers; rear anti-roll bar; semi-servo mechanical drum brakes; worm and sector steering; 41L (9 Imp gal, 10.8 US gal) fuel tank; AC fuel pump 4.75in tyres, 17in rims.
DIMENSIONS wheelbase 256.5cm (101in); track 127cm (50in); ground clearance 19.7cm (7.75in); turning circle 10.7m (35ft); length 392cm (154.5in); width 157.5cm (62in); height 167.6cm (66in).
PERFORMANCE (ASX) maximum speed 104kph (65mph); 25.7kph (16mph) @ 1000rpm; 0-80kph (50mph) 20sec; 44.4kg/kW (33.1kg/bhp); 10.5L/100km (27mpg) at steady 64kph (40mph), average 10.9L/100km (26mpg).
PRODUCTION 20,026 DY, DX.
PRICE £205 standard saloon, £225 de luxe. Stratford sports tourer £250; Suffolk saloon £280; Tickford foursome coupe £285; Duple 2-seater £235; Duple tourer £240; Airline convertible 2-4-seater £257.10s.

Right: **Early Light Six in Wales with popular British "sunshine roof".**
Top right: **1936 DY 12HP Wingham cabriolet by Martin Walter.**

IMPRACTICABLE
FOR MOTORS
SAFETY FIRST

AMM 583

1937-1938 Light Six DX Fourteen

Although most of the changes to the 12HP DY and 14HPDX range for 1937 were cosmetic, they were nonetheless important. The cars were lengthened and widened, and as a change from the flat grille there was a chrome cascade and graceful teardrop headlamps. Wire wheels gave way to perforated steel disc wheels and, in a significant innovation, a new model was added to the 14HP alone. This was the Touring Saloon, 33cm (13in) longer than the ordinary 6-light saloon, with a stylish lidded trunk at the back. The spare wheel was affixed behind and the effect was similar to the big Continental touring saloons of Horch and Hispano-Suiza.

Mechanically the changes were mainly in details such as a larger sump, better lubrication for the valve-gear, and white-metal bearings for the camshaft. The new range was slightly cheaper than the one it replaced. The simplified Dubonnet front suspension was now suitable for production in Chevrolet, Pontiac, and Opel as well as Vauxhall. It incorporated a torsion bar as the principal springing medium with three coil springs inside the accompanying cylinder that also housed two tiny hydraulic shock absorbers. Annual tax was £10.10 (£10.50) against the 12hp's £9.00 following reductions in 1935.

BODY 6-light saloon; fixed head coupe, drophead, cabriolet, coachbuilt specials; 4 doors; saloon weight 1156kg (2548lb).
ENGINE 6 cylinders, in-line, front, 61.5mm x 100mm; 1782cc; compr: 6.25:1; 31.3kW (42bhp) @ 3500rpm; 17.6kW/L (23.6bhp/L).
ENGINE STRUCTURE pushrod overhead valves; side camshaft; cast iron cylinder head; chromidium iron cylinder block; 4-bearing crankshaft; Zenith downdraught carburettor; Lucas coil ignition, timing by combined vacuum and governor; water-cooled.
TRANSMISSION rear wheel drive; cable-operated single-plate clutch; 4-speed gearbox; synchromesh top and 3rd; spiral bevel final drive; ratio 4.7:1; semi-floating rear axle.
CHASSIS DETAILS steel X-braced box-section chassis; independent front suspension with coil springs torsion bars and hydraulic dampers; semi-elliptic leaf springs at rear; hydraulic Lovejoy dampers; rear anti-roll bar; semi-servo mechanical drum brakes; Burman Douglas worm and nut steering; 40.9L (9 Imp gal, 10.8 US gal) fuel tank; AC fuel pump 5.50in tyres, 16in rims.
DIMENSIONS wheelbase 256.5cm (101in); track 127cm (50in); ground clearance 19.7cm (7.75in); turning circle 10.7m (35ft); length 411.5cm (162in) (saloon), 444.5cm (175in) (touring saloon); width 162.5cm (64in); height 167.5cm (66in).
PERFORMANCE maximum speed 109.4kph (68mph); 25.5kph (16mph) @ 1000rpm; acceleration to 80kph (50mph) 20sec; 36.9kg/kW (27.5kg/bhp); fuel consumption 10.9-15.7L/100km (18-26mpg).
PRODUCTION 20,026 DY, DX.
PRICE £195 standard saloon, £215 de luxe. Coupe £235; Tickford foursome coupe £285; Wingham Cabriolet £310; de luxe Touring Saloon £220.

1937-1938 Light Six DY Twelve

Among the coachbuilders approved by Vauxhall to construct a wide range of special bodies were Martin Walter, Salmons, Howard Godfrey and Connaught, and the Grosvenor Carriage Company. Salmon's Tickford Foursome Coupe at £365 was a 2-door car available on DY or DX, with a hood raised and lowered by a detachable handle in the rear panel. Working through a train of hand-cut gears it was firm and taut when erect, and the lined hood was insulated and weatherproof. The Wingham Cabriolet by Martin Walter was a similarly substantial affair with four doors, selling for £400. The doors hung on a central pillar webbed to the frame and the head was spring-loaded to ease handling. It could be erected or taken down with, it was claimed, no more than a gentle push in contrast to the normal run of convertibles which needed much tugging and heaving. The rounded Wingham hood gave the appearance of a saloon, and folded flush with the rear of the body. Grosvenor's and Connaught's touring saloons had fashionable swept tails along the lines of MG or Jaguar, providing useful luggage space. Wheels were new-style perforated steel so-called "easiclene" instead of bolt-on wire-spoked.

BODY 4-door, 6-light saloon, fixed head coupe, drophead, 4-door cabriolet, coachbuilt specials; saloon weight 1172kg (2548lb).
ENGINE 6 cylinders, in-line, front, 57mm x 100mm; 1530cc; compr: 5.5:1; 26.9kW (36bhp) @ 4000rpm; 17.5kW/L (23.5bhp/L).
ENGINE STRUCTURE pushrod overhead valves; side camshaft; cast iron cylinder head; chromidium iron cylinder block; 4-bearing crankshaft; Zenith downdraught carburettor; Lucas coil ignition, timing by combined vacuum and governor; water-cooled.
TRANSMISSION rear wheel drive; cable-operated single-plate clutch; 4-speed gearbox; synchromesh top and 3rd; spiral bevel final drive; ratio 4.7:1; semi-floating rear axle.
CHASSIS DETAILS steel X-braced box-section chassis; independent front suspension with coil springs torsion bars and hydraulic dampers; semi-elliptic leaf springs at rear; hydraulic Lovejoy dampers; rear anti-roll bar; semi-servo mechanical drum

brakes; Burman Douglas worm and nut steering; 40.9L (9 Imp gal, 10.8 US gal) fuel tank; AC fuel pump 5.50in tyres, 16in rims.
DIMENSIONS wheelbase 256.5cm (101in); track 127cm (50in); ground clearance 19.7cm (7.75in); turning circle 10.7m (35ft); length 411.5cm (162in); width 162.5cm (64in); height 167.6cm (66in).
PERFORMANCE maximum speed 106.2kph (66mph); 25.7kph (16mph) @ 1000rpm; acceleration to 80kph (50mph) 23sec; 43.6kg/kW (32.6kg/bhp); fuel consumption 10.5-10.9L/100km (26-27mpg).
PRODUCTION 39,537 DY, DX.
PRICE £205 standard saloon, £225 de luxe. Stratford sports tourer £250; Suffolk saloon £280; Tickford foursome coupe £285; Duple 2-seater £235; Duple tourer £240; Arline convertible 2-4-seater £257.10s.

SALOON

TO

TOURER

—at a touch!

1937-1940 H-type Ten-Four

A notable milestone in automotive engineering, the first British unitary construction car the Vauxhall Ten-Four had hydraulic brakes, torsion bar independent front suspension and sold 10,000 inside five months. It was light, strong, lively, roomy, stylish and, astonishingly for a full 4-seater that would cruise happily close to 96kph (60mph), it could return under 7.1L/100km (over 40mpg). A number of tests showed its outstanding economy even when fuel was only 1/6d (7.5p) a gallon (4d [1.6p]/litre). "No exaggeration … the new Vauxhall Ten is one of the most brilliant pieces of design that has been seen in Britain for ten years," said *The Motor*, "… full of features of the highest technical interest but cleverly designed so that it could be made at an exceptionally low price."

It was true. There was not much to touch it at the price and a good deal not as good at any price. Vauxhall Tens kept Britain on its wheels throughout the following ten years or more. The 1940 model-year cars were stretched and the spare wheel carried outside on the bootlid. The umbrella-handle handbrake may have been retrograde but the rest of the car was a winner. Advertisements claiming "Placed 2nd" in the 1938 Monte Carlo Rally were a little wide of the mark. It was 2nd British finisher, yet a long way from what might be called a podium place.

BODY saloon, 4 doors; coupe, 2 doors; weight 915kg (2016lb).
ENGINE 4 cylinders, in-line, front, 63.5mm x 95mm; 1203cc; compr: 6.5:1; 25.7kW (34.5bhp) @ 3800rpm; 21.4kW/L (28.7bhp/L). Treasury rating 10hp.
ENGINE STRUCTURE pushrod overhead valves; chain-driven side camshaft; chromidium iron cylinder head and block; 3-bearing crankshaft; Zenith "Six Mixture" downdraught carburettor; coil ignition; water-cooled by fan, pump and thermostat; 6-volt electrics.
TRANSMISSION rear wheel drive; Borg & Beck single-plate clutch; 3-speed gearbox; synchromesh 2nd and top; spiral bevel final drive; ratio 5.14:1.
CHASSIS DETAILS integral body structure; independent front suspension with coil springs torsion bars and hydraulic dampers; semi-elliptic leaf springs at rear; single acting hydraulic dampers; Lockheed hydraulic drum brakes; Burman-Douglas worm and nut steering; 30.7L (6.75 Imp gal, 8.1 US gal) fuel tank; 5.00 x 16 tyres.
DIMENSIONS wheelbase 239cm (94in); front track 118cm (46.5in); 119.4cm (47in) rear; ground clearance 18.4cm (7.25in); turning circle 10.7m (35ft); length 396cm (156in); width 150cm (59in); height 157cm (62in).
PERFORMANCE maximum speed 96kph (60mph); 23kph (14.3mph) @ 1000rpm; acceleration 0-80kph (50mph) 18sec; 35.6kg/kW (26.5kg/bhp); fuel consumption 6.7-7.8L/100km (36-42mpg).
PRODUCTION 42,245.
PRICE de luxe saloon £182, standard saloon £159 to £168.

Right: the doors and middle hull of the Vauxhall Ten proved infinitely adaptable. It became the basis for Vauxhalls right up to the L-type Wyvern and Velox that remained in production until 1951, a 14 year lifespan.

Top Vauxhall. By the late 1930s any engine over 3.0-litre looked extravagant. Big cars that had been acceptable in the 1920s now seemed out of place and Vauxhall's new role was obstinately middle class. Yet every manufacturer needed an aspirational product and the 25hp replacement for the Big Six filled the bill. King Edward VIII had his Empire-made Buick, and a Vauxhall 25 with its curved grille, perforated disc wheels, and imposing appearance was just as agreeable without being showy. Coachbuilders could incorporate all the customary luxury fittings yet the outward appearance was still homely Vauxhall. The model was moreover popular with hire fleets, in particular the long wheelbase version which could accommodate fold-down seats in the rear. More spectacularly the Wingham Cabriolet had a mechanism, "release two clips and give the head a gentle push," to fold the roof down into the rear of the body.

The 25's engine was the familiar Chevrolet coupled to a four and later a three-speed gearbox with a long rather willowy lever. Integral body and chassis construction was now well established at Vauxhall and Opel, and the 25 was the last Vauxhall with a separate chassis. Many were converted during the 1940s emergency with ambulance bodywork.

BODY saloon, sports saloon, drophead coupe, 7-seat saloon, 4-door cabriolet, limousine; weight 1524kg (3360lb).
ENGINE 6 cylinders, in-line, front, 81.94mm x 101.6mm; 3215cc; 59.7kW (80bhp) @ 3400rpm; 18.6kW/L (24.9bhp/L). RAC fiscal rating 24.97hp.
ENGINE STRUCTURE pushrod ohv; chain-driven cam; chromidium iron cylinder head and cylinder block; 4-bearing crankshaft; downdraught Zenith carburettor; coil ignition; water-cooled, 12-volt electrics, Pedomatic starter.
TRANSMISSION rear wheel drive; single-plate clutch; 4 later 3-speed gearbox; synchromesh; spiral bevel final drive; ratio 4.44:1.
CHASSIS DETAILS steel x-braced chassis; ifs by torsion bars and coil spring damper units, half-elliptic rear suspension; hydraulic dampers; Lockheed hydraulic drum brakes; cam and roller steering; 55L (12 Imp gal, 14.4 US gal) fuel tank; 6.50x16tyres.
DIMENSIONS wheelbase 282cm (111in); track 146cm (57.5in); length 469cm (184.5in); width 181.5cm (71.5in).
PERFORMANCE maximum speed 124kph (77mph); 0-80kph (50mph) 16.6sec; 25.5kg/kW (19.1kg/bhp); consumption 15.7L/100km (18mpg).
PRODUCTION 6822 all models 25.
PRICE short chassis £210, 5-seat saloon £315.

1937-1940 25HP GL lwb

The exhaust overhead valves in the 25 engine were inclined and the inlets seated at a lower level just above the piston. The GY/GL had what was known as TT (torsion tube) independent front suspension incorporating torsion bars and stiff coil springs. The TT's torsion bar twisted inside a short tube that also acted as a torsion member. The coil springs were enclosed in an oil-bath casing and the only maintenance needed was an occasional top-up that also served to refill the shock absorbers. TT springing also found its way into the Vauxhall Ten.

An unusual item of equipment, according to *The Motor's* review of the 1937 London Motor Show at the new Earl's Court exhibition hall, was to be found on the Vauxhall stand. "On the 25HP saloon an internal heater not only provides warmth for the occupants of the car but also prevents frosting and misting of the windscreen."

On the Grosvenor Carriage Company's stand the Limousine offered plenty of room for seven people, with its wide doors and deep windows. There was also a seven-seat saloon without a division but with every form of useful accessory including picnic tables in the backs of the front seats, with concealed ashtrays.

BODY saloon, sports saloon, drophead coupe, 7-seat saloon, 4-door cabriolet, limousine; weight 1576kg (3475lb).
ENGINE 6 cylinders, in-line, front, 81.94mm x 101.6mm; 3215cc; 59.7kW (80bhp) @ 3400rpm; 18.6kW/L (24.9bhp/L). RAC fiscal rating 24.97hp.
ENGINE STRUCTURE pushrod overhead valves; chain-driven camshaft; chromidium iron cylinder head and cylinder block; 4-bearing crankshaft; downdraught Zenith carburettor; coil ignition; water-cooled, 12-volt electrics, Pedomatic starter.
TRANSMISSION rear wheel drive; single-plate clutch; 4 later 3-speed gearbox; synchromesh; spiral bevel final drive; ratio 4.44:1.
CHASSIS DETAILS steel x-braced chassis; independent front suspension by torsion bars and coil spring damper units, half-elliptic rear suspension; hydraulic dampers; Lockheed hydraulic drum brakes; cam and roller steering; 55L (12 Imp gal, 14.4 US gal)

fuel tank; 6.50x16 tyres.
DIMENSIONS wheelbase 330cm (130in); track 146cm (57.5in); length 468.5cm (184.5in); width 181.6cm (71.5in).
PERFORMANCE maximum speed 124kph (77mph); acceleration 0-80kph (50mph) 16.6sec; 26.4kg/kW (19.7kg/bhp); fuel consumption 15.7L/100km (18mpg).
PRODUCTION 6822 all models 25.
PRICE long chassis £240 7-passenger limousine £595.

Seven years elapsed between the first and last Twelve-Four yet production lasted barely 18 months at either end. A six-light saloon, based on the 10 with an extra 18cm (7in) on the wheelbase and a divided radiator grille, identified 1940 models and rare post-war ones. An integral body-chassis (the I stood for Integral), like the Ten with a sub-frame at the front carrying the engine and independent front suspension, made the Vauxhall Twelve a family car par excellence. The strong body tended not to rattle or squeak as much as contemporaries squirming about on a chassis but the suspension, modified from the original Dubonnet by Maurice Olley, was not an unqualified success. The short torsion bars were prone to break until the metallurgy had been improved and it carried on into the 1950s.

Alternatives to the 4-door Twelve-Four saloon in 1937 included a smart 2-door coupe with sliding roof and "no-draught" ventilation at £235, the Stratford open 4-seater at £255, Tickford Coupe at £285 and Wingham cabriolet £310. Post-war in a market desperate for cars at almost any price there was only one version and, the last 6-volt Vauxhall, it did not survive long.

BODY 6-light saloon; 4 doors, 5 seats; weight 940kg (2072lb).
ENGINE 4 cylinders, in-line, front, 69.5mm x 95mm; 1442cc; compr: 6.8:1; 26.1kW (35bhp) @ 3600rpm; 18.1kW/L (24.3bhp/L); 91Nm (68lb ft) @ 2000rpm.
ENGINE STRUCTURE pushrod overhead valves; chain-driven side camshaft; cast iron cylinder head and block; 3-bearing crankshaft; Zenith downdraught carburettor; mechanical AC fuel pump; Lucas coil ignition; water-cooled by pump, fan, and thermostat; 6-volt electrics.
TRANSMISSION rear wheel drive; single plate clutch; 3-speed gearbox; synchromesh; spiral bevel final drive; ratio 4.71:1.
CHASSIS DETAILS integral steel structure; independent front suspension by torsion bar and tube with coil spring and lever, integral hydraulic damper; live back axle with semi-elliptic springs and hydraulic dampers; Lockheed hydraulic drum brakes with cable handbrake to rear; Burman Douglas nut and screw steering; 30.7L (6.75 Imp gal, 8.1 US gal) fuel tank; 5.25x16 tyres.
DIMENSIONS wheelbase 257.17cm (101.25in); track 124cm (49in); ground clearance 19cm (7.5in); turning circle 11.7m (38.5ft); length 412cm (162.25in); width 155cm (61in); height 165cm (65in).
PERFORMANCE maximum speed 108kph (67mph); 25.8kph (16.1mph) @ 1000rpm; acceleration 0-80kph (50mph) 19.6sec; 36kg/kW (26.9kg/bhp); fuel consumption 7.8-8.8L/100km (32-36mpg).
PRODUCTION 10,164.
PRICE 1938 standard £189, de luxe £215. 1947 £330, £422.8.4 incl PT.

Right: four-light and six-light saloons compared. There was no consensus on titling; twelve-four or, as here, 12 four was just as likely as Twelve 4 or 12/4. Corporate consistency would in due course extend to areas like correct use and colour of Vauxhall logo.

THE CHEAPEST *Real* MOTORING
THAT MONEY CAN BUY

VAUXHALL
10 *four*
£168
40 M·P·G

VAUXHALL
12 *four*
£189
35 M·P·G

The outstanding feature of each of these Vauxhalls is the unusual combination of roominess, performance, comfort and economy. The 10-four provides the cheaper motoring; the 12-four costs slightly more to run, but it is an appreciably bigger car. We do not suggest that you buy either, but we do ask you to try every other Ten (or Twelve) before making your choice.

● **PERFORMANCE**: 10 h.p., 0 to 50 m.p.h. in 22.5 seconds. Maximum 60-65. 12 h.p., 0 to 50 m.p.h. in 21.9 seconds. Maximum 65-68 ● **ECONOMY**: 40 m.p.g. and 35 m.p.g. respectively. **INDEPENDENT SPRINGING** gives stability, changes riding to gliding ● **ALL STEEL CONSTRUCTION** results in greater rigidity with less weight ● **CONTROLLED SYNCHROMESH**—you can't help making a good change ● **HYDRAULIC BRAKES**, smooth, powerful, easy to apply ● **BODY CONFORMITY SEATING** for comfort on the longest journey ● **SOUND INSULATION** built into the cars under the direction of an acoustics specialist ● **NO DRAUGHT VENTILATION** on de luxe saloons. Many other features.

VAUXHALL

Full particulars from your local Vauxhall dealer, or, write for catalogues to Vauxhall Motors Ltd., Luton.

1939-1948 Fourteen-Six J-type

The archetypal middle-class market embraced the Vauxhall Fourteen with a warmth that stemmed from its comfort, its practicality, its good value, and its sheer size. It was large for a 14 and it had that trace of raciness that came with vaguely transatlantic styling. The teardrop headlights alongside the grille, the "speedbird" bonnet motif, the useful luggage boot with its let-down lid, the big instrument layout, leather upholstery, and the smooth purr of a 6-cylinder engine gave the Vauxhall 14 a certain cachet. It was never going to be posh like a Wolseley or a Rover but it was not going to be cheap either like a Ford. Post-war 14s had pink instead of green-faced instruments and fancier bonnet louvres, but more importantly they had optional heater and built-in radio. What bliss for drivers in the chill climate of 1947.

The Vauxhall was lighter than the opposition such as the dreary 4-cylinder Hillman 14, and only Morris ran to hydraulic brakes. Performance was extremely lively and widely spaced ratios in the all-synchromesh gearbox gave 25mph, 53mph and over 70mph. Among the good detail features was a steering column adjustable for reach, and *Practical Motorist* thought the luggage boot sufficiently large for a fortnight's holiday.

BODY saloon; 4 doors, 5 seats; weight 1136kg (2505lb).
ENGINE 6 cylinders, in-line, front, 61.5mm x 100mm; 1781cc; compr: 6.75:1; 35.8kW (48bhp) @ 3600rpm; 20.1kW/L (27bhp/L); 107Nm (80lb/ft) @ 1400rpm; RAC rating 14.07hp.
ENGINE STRUCTURE pushrod overhead valves; chain-driven side camshaft; cast iron cylinder head and block; 4-bearing crankshaft; Zenith downdraught carburettor; mechanical AC fuel pump; Lucas coil ignition; water-cooled by pump, fan, and thermostat; 12-volt electrics.
TRANSMISSION rear wheel drive; single plate clutch; 3-speed gearbox; all synchromesh; spiral bevel final drive; ratio 4.71:1.
CHASSIS DETAILS integral steel structure; independent front suspension by torsion bar and tube with coil spring and lever, integral hydraulic damper; live back axle with semi-elliptic springs and hydraulic dampers; Lockheed hydraulic drum brakes with cable handbrake to rear; Burman Douglas nut and screw steering.
DIMENSIONS wheelbase 267cm (105in); front track 128.3cm (50.5in), 129.5cm (51in) rear; ground clearance 19cm (7.5in); turning circle 12.8m (42ft); length 427cm (168in); width 162.5cm (64in); height 162.5cm (64in).
PERFORMANCE maximum speed 116kph (72mph); acceleration 0-50mph 18.4sec; 31.7kg/kW (23.7kg/bhp); fuel consumption 8.8-9.4L/100km (30-32mpg).
PRODUCTION 30,511 post-war, 45,499 total.
PRICE 1939 £230.

Right: the old wide running-boards were on their way out, the tall chrome grille and the voluptuous mudguards had a hint of the Buicks to which 1930s aristocrats often aspired.
Top right: 5-year-old (2nd from right) with his Uncle Bob's new J-type is author.

119

1940-1944 Churchill Tank Marks I-III, Infantry Tank Mark IV

Four years' work was compressed into one in the design and development of Vauxhall's tank and, although the Churchill was not perhaps the most notable armoured fighting vehicle of the Second World War, it was there when it was needed most. It fought in North Africa and despite being under-gunned with a meek 6-pounder, it was Churchills of 48 Royal Tank Regiment in 1943 that captured the first of the formidable new German Tiger tanks with its 88mm gun intact. The Mark III Churchill of 1942 was the only British tank whose armour was capable of withstanding the tungsten carbide shot of the powerful German 88mm. Churchills up to Mark V had 102mm (4in) frontal armour, Marks VII and VIII 152mm (6in) thick.

Hasty production resulted in a number of mechanical defects until the Mark IV was introduced in 1943. The transmission, incorporating an ingenious regenerative system used up to the 1990s, suffered from teething troubles. Its turret was too small to mount anything larger than a 75mm gun, which made the tank obsolete by 1943, although it remained in service throughout the war. Churchill IVs were converted into AVREs (Armoured Vehicle Royal Engineers) for close-range assaults, and laying down bridges. They did service clearing minefields and could be equipped with flame-throwing apparatus.

BODY armoured, 5 seats, 6 doors, weight 39,624kg (39 tons, 87,355lb). ENGINE 12 cylinders, horizontally opposed, rear, 127mm x 137.7mm; 1 cylinder 1770cc, total 21237cc; compr: 5.5:1; 261kW (350bhp); 1287Nm (960lb/ft) @ 1000-1800rpm. ENGINE STRUCTURE side valves, 2 per cylinder; 2 side camshafts; molybdenum iron cylinder head; cast iron block; 7-bearing crankshaft; 4 x Solex carburettors; coil ignition; water-cooled. TRANSMISSION Merrit-Brown triple differential, rear sprocket drive, 18in clutch 4-speed non-synchromesh gearbox, epicyclic final drive; ratio 7.1:1. CHASSIS DETAILS rivetted steel integral structure; independent coil spring suspension, coil spring dampers; hydraulic internal expanding brakes, controlled differential steering, 4 x 682L (150 Imp gal, 180US gal) fuel tanks, flanged steel rollers. DIMENSIONS track on ground 381cm (150in); width between track centres 223.5cm (88in); ground clearance 50.8cm (20in); length 767cm (302in); width 325cm (128in); height 249cm (98in). PERFORMANCE maximum speed 24.9kph (15.5mph); 151.8kg/kW (113.2kg/bhp); fuel consumption 332L/100km (0.85mpg). PRODUCTION 5640, Mark IV 1885. AVERAGE PRICE £15,000.

Right: Winston Churchill came to Luton to inspect the tank named after him. *Far right:* a Churchill passes through ruined Normandy following the D-Day landing. Data was compiled with the help of David Fletcher of The Tank Museum, Bovingdon, Dorset whose response to an enquiry about acceleration figures was, "There is no point in talking about acceleration with a Churchill tank, it is either going or it isn't."

121

The crucial dimension in the first post-war 10HP was wheelbase. The ground-breaking pre-war 10HP H-type was 163cm (94in). The broadly similar 12HP was 257cm (101.25in), the important difference in the body being an extra window in the rear quarter. When the 10HP was reintroduced in 1945 it fell in between at 249cm (98in) with four "lights" or windows on each side. Its spare wheel was carried under a cover on the outside of the bootlid, otherwise it was almost indistinguishable from its 1939 counterpart. There was not much incentive to change. Its monocoque hull was as innovative in 1946 as it had been in 1938. There was still almost nothing like it. The outrigger subframe carrying the engine and front suspension was much the same as before, the sturdy 1203cc engine as economical as ever although slightly less powerful in deference to the poor-quality fuel (now nearly 2/- [10p] a gallon) available. The supple suspension was comfortable and in a seller's market it scarcely mattered that the price had gone up to £422.

The rakish 2-door Coupe had no place in the austere post-war world but output got under way quickly with 53,586 cars of all models made in 1946, not far short of the 1938 total.

BODY saloon; 4 doors, 4 seats; weight 915kg (2016lb).

ENGINE 4 cylinders, in-line, front, 63.5mm x 95mm; 1203cc; compr: 6.5:1; 23kW (31bhp) @ 3600rpm; 75Nm (56lb/ft) @ 2200rpm.

ENGINE STRUCTURE pushrod overhead valves; chain-driven side camshaft; chromidium iron cylinder head and block; 3-bearing crankshaft; Zenith downdraught carburettor; coil ignition; water-cooled by fan, pump and thermostat, 6-volt electrics.

TRANSMISSION rear wheel drive; Borg & Beck single-plate clutch; 3-speed gearbox; synchromesh 2nd and top; spiral bevel final drive; ratio 5.14:1.

CHASSIS DETAILS integral body structure; independent front suspension with coil springs torsion bars and hydraulic dampers; semi-elliptic leaf springs at rear; single acting hydraulic dampers; Lockheed hydraulic drum brakes; Burman-Douglas worm and nut steering; 30.7L (6.75 Imp gal, 8.1 US gal) fuel tank; 5.00 x 16 tyres.

DIMENSIONS wheelbase 249cm (98in); front track 118cm (46.5in), 119.4cm (47in) rear; ground clearance 18.4cm (7.25in); turning circle 10.7m (35ft); length 402.6cm (158in); width 154.9cm (61in); height 157cm (62in).

PERFORMANCE maximum speed 96kph (60mph); acceleration 0-80kph (50mph) 18sec; 35.6kg/kW (26.5kg/bhp); fuel consumption 6.7-7.8L/100km (36-42mpg).

PRODUCTION 44,047 including 12-4.

PRICE 1946 £330, £422.8.4 (£422.41) incl PT.

123

The motor industry's frustration over the taxation system caused the rules to be changed in the 1947 Budget. The ascetic president of the Board of Trade, later Chancellor of the Exchequer, Sir Stafford Cripps, may have disapproved of luxury cars but he recognised that overseas markets did not like the high piston speeds of long-stroke British engines. In 1946 the RAC horsepower rating, based on cylinder bore but not stroke in an effort to relate taxation to piston area and thus power, was abandoned. A tax of £1.5s (£1.25) per 100cc was instituted in 1947 but it did not last long and a flat rate came in for engines of any capacity. Buyers were no longer discouraged by higher annual Road Tax from buying a 12HP instead of a 10HP and Vauxhall accordingly stopped making a Ten and brought out the HIX. This was the 98in Ten with the 1442cc engine from the Twelve.

The radiator grille bars were changed from the pre-war waterfall to horizontal bars which was as close as Vauxhall came to re-styling. A cloth-upholstered bench seat replaced the traditional buckets in what was not only the lowest-priced Twelve in Britain but also one of the half-dozen cheapest of any size.

BODY saloon, 4 seats, 4 doors, weight 953kg (2100lb).

ENGINE 4 cylinders, in-line, front, 69.5mm x 95mm; 1442cc; compr: 6.8:1; 26kW (35bhp) @ 3600rpm; 18kW/L (24.3bhp/L); 91Nm (68lb/ft) @ 2000rpm.

ENGINE STRUCTURE pushrod overhead valves; chain-driven side camshaft; chromidium iron cylinder head and block; 3-bearing crankshaft; Zenith downdraught carburettor; coil ignition; water-cooled by fan, pump and thermostat, 6-volt electrics.

TRANSMISSION rear wheel drive; Borg & Beck single-plate clutch; 3-speed gearbox; synchromesh 2nd and top; spiral bevel final drive; ratio 4.625:1.

CHASSIS DETAILS integral body structure; independent front suspension with coil springs torsion bars and hydraulic dampers; semi-elliptic leaf springs at rear; single acting hydraulic dampers; Lockheed hydraulic drum brakes; Burman-Douglas worm and nut steering; 30.7L (6.75 Imp gal, 8.1 US gal) fuel tank; 5.00 x 16 tyres.

DIMENSIONS wheelbase 249cm (98in); front track 122.5cm (48.25in), 125.9cm (49.6in) rear; ground clearance 18.4cm (7.25in); turning circle 11.58m (38ft); length 402.6cm (158in); width 154.9cm (61in); height 165cm (65in).

PERFORMANCE maximum speed 104kph (65mph); acceleration 0-80kph (50mph) 19.6sec; 36.6kg/kW (27.2kg/bhp); fuel consumption 7.1-8.1L/100km (35-40mpg).

PRODUCTION 44,047 including the 10-4.

PRICE 1946 £330, £422.8.4 (£422.41) incl PT.

12 H.P. SALOON
£330 plus £92.9.4 purchase tax

VAUXHALL

14 H.P. SALOON
£435 plus £121.11.8 purchase tax

An Invitation. A special exhibition "The story of Vauxhall" is being staged in the Vauxhall showrooms in Luton I. It is now open to the public daily (except Saturdays and Sundays) between 10.00 a.m. and 5.00 p.m. Admission Free.

Vauxhall Motors Ltd. Luton

1948-1951 Velox LIP

The first proper post-war design was essentially the doors and centre-section of the old HIY and HIX with a new boot and new front. The effect was vaguely transatlantic with a full-width horizontal grille and headlights sunk into voluptuous rounded wings. The entire range was reduced to two models; the Velox 6-cylinder and Wyvern 4-cylinder, sharing a common body shell with alligator bonnet-opening and similar mechanicals. Vauxhall was paying lip-service to the one-model policy encouraged by the Motor Industry Advisory Council, which allowed it enough steel to make 55,000 cars in 1947 instead of the 80,000 it wanted to. It was a time of government restriction and direction. The council suborned Standard into making the Vanguard, and British motorists' petrol ration allowed them about 270 miles a month. Two or three-year waits for new cars reflected an industry-wide obligation to export half of its output.

Changes in 1949 included larger headlamps with separate parking lamps and the introduction of Metallichrome paint, which shimmered in different colours when struck by sunlight. A 12-volt electrical system was standardised along with the steering column gearshift and bench front seat, without which the industry imagined export sales would be impossible.

BODY saloon; 4 doors; weight 1084kg (2390lb).
ENGINE 6 cylinders, in-line, front, 69.5mm x 100mm; 2275cc; compr: 6.75:1; 41kW (55bhp) @ 3300rpm; 18kW/L (24bhp/L); 142Nm (106lb/ft) @ 1100rpm.
ENGINE STRUCTURE pushrod overhead valves; chain-driven camshaft; cast iron cylinder head and block; 4-bearing crankshaft; Zenith 30VIG-5 carburettor; AC mechanical fuel pump; Lucas 12 volt coil ignition; water-cooled, pump, fan, thermostat.
TRANSMISSION rear wheel drive; 8in Borg & Beck sdp clutch; 3-speed gearbox; synchromesh 2nd and top, steering column change; spiral bevel final drive; ratio 4.125:1.
CHASSIS DETAILS integral structure; independent front suspension with coil springs torsion bars and hydraulic dampers; semi-elliptic leaf springs at rear; double acting hydraulic dampers; Lockheed hydraulic drum brakes; Burman-Douglas worm and nut steering, from 1950 Burman worm and peg; 45.5L (10 Imp gal, 12 US gal) fuel tank; 5.25 x 16in tyres, 5-stud disc wheels, from 1950 5.90 x 15.
DIMENSIONS wheelbase 97.75in; front track 50.6in, 52in rear; ground clearance 17.8cm (7in); turning circle 12.1m (39.85ft) right, 11.71m (38.45ft) left; length 418cm (164.5in); width 157.5cm (62in); height 165.3cm (65.1in).
PERFORMANCE maximum speed 119kph (74mph); 18.3mph @ 1000rpm; acceleration 0-60mph 22.7sec; 27.3kg/kW (20.3kg/bhp); fuel consumption 12.8-10.9L/100km (22-26mpg).
PRODUCTION 76,919.
PRICE at launch £430, £550.3s.11d incl PT, heater £8, radio £23.

Right: a 1949 car with larger headlights. Cream wheels and modest Vauxhall Six badges distinguished Velox from Wyvern.

127

1948-1951 Wyvern LIX

The 4-cylinder companion to the Velox had body-coloured not cream wheels, cloth upholstery and no rear seat arm-rest, but was otherwise almost indistinguishable. It had the same body with the same precious Vauxhall bonnet flutes, the same camshaft-driven wipers, same rather bleak metallic interior, and the same supple ride. It was the fourth lowest-priced car in Britain and certainly the roomiest and liveliest in its class. Its unitary construction, still a key to light weight and economy, gave it a fraction more than 1cc per lb of running weight.

Ride and handling were an improvement on the old Twelve from which it was derived. It was more stable, less floaty than its predecessor thanks to better damping and different spring-rates, although a curiosity of the new suspension set-up was a tendency of the nose of the car to rise under braking. Perhaps it was a reaction to the curtsey that had been the rule with Vauxhalls since the introduction of the Dubonnet independent front suspension. The steering was improved with less kick-back through the wheel. Most main road hills could be climbed in second gear although there was not much vigour left in it above 35mph. Top speed in 2nd was no more than 71kph (44mph).

BODY saloon; 4 doors; weight 994kg (2190lb).
ENGINE 4 cylinders, in-line, front, 69.5mm x 95mm; 1442cc; compr: 6.4:1; 26kW (35bhp) @ 3600rpm; 18kW/L (24.3bhp/L)l; 91Nm (68lb/ft) @ 2000rpm.
ENGINE STRUCTURE pushrod ohv; chain-driven camshaft; cast iron cyl head and block; 3-bearing crank; Zenith 30VIG-5 carb; AC mechanical fuel pump; Lucas 12 volt coil ignition; water-cooled, pump, fan, thermostat.
TRANSMISSION rear wheel drive; 8in Borg & Beck sdp clutch; 3-speed; synch 2nd and top, steering column change; spiral bevel final drive; ratio 4.625:1.
CHASSIS DETAILS integral structure; ifs with coil springs torsion bars and hydraulic dampers; semi-elliptic leaf springs at rear; double acting hydraulic dampers; Lockheed hydraulic drum brakes; Burman-Douglas worm and nut steering; 45.5L (10 Imp gal, 12 US gal) fuel tank; 5.00 x 16in tyres, 5-stud disc wheels.
DIMENSIONS wheelbase 248cm (97.75in); front track 124.7cm (49in), rear 126cm (49.6in); ground clearance 17.8cm (7in); turning circle 11.27m (37ft) right, 10.73m (35.2ft) left; length 418cm (164.5in); width 157.5cm (62in); height 165.1cm (65in).
PERFORMANCE maximum speed 96.3kph (60mph); 26.2kph (16.3mph) @ 1000rpm; 0-80kph (50mph) 27.8sec; 38.2kg/kW (28.4kg/bhp); 9.2L/100km (30.6mpg).
PRODUCTION 55,409.
PRICE at launch £350, £447.19.5 incl PT.

Right: 1950 L-type Wyvern manoeuvres during Thames Estuary Automobile Club Rally in 1956.

A 1949 Chevrolet was the basis of the 1951 Wyvern and Velox with full-width styling, still with flutes and a wide-mouthed grille, and lots of chrome. They followed their LIP and LIX predecessors in a common platform for 4-cylinders and 6-cylinders, ringing the changes with trim, paintwork, equipment and embellishment. Mechanical innovations for wider and longer cars included coil spring independent front suspension and a hypoid back axle. More room inside was important for the introduction at the Earls Court Motor Show in October 1951, with 9.5cm (3.75in) extra rear legroom, and no less than 45cm (17.75in) more width in the rear seat. The additional elbow-room made it a full 6-seater and the extra length increased the size of the luggage boot from the previous model's rather makeshift affair added-on to the pre-war monocoque.

In 1952-1953 E-types (EIPV) underwent a number of detail changes externally including stone-shields to protect the paintwork on the rear wing. More tangible alterations were shorter-stroke engines exploiting the taxation regime with a concomitant reduction in piston speeds to improve reliability and gain power. Recirculating ball steering reduced kick-back and annual facelifts provided buyers with incentives in the shape of new grilles, chrome flashes, and larger rear windows.

BODY saloon; 4 doors; weight 1126kg (2483lb).
ENGINE 6 cylinders, in-line, front, 69.5mm x 100mm; 2275cc; compr: 6.75:1, later 6.4:1; 41kW (55bhp) @ 3300rpm; 18kW/L (24.2bhp/L); 142Nm (106 lb/ft) @ 1100rpm (EIPV 2262cc 65bhp). From 1952: 79.4mm x 76.2mm, 2262cc, 47.7kW (64bhp) @ 4000rpm.
From 1954: 7.6:1 compression, 50.3kW (67.5bhp) @ 4000rpm.
ENGINE STRUCTURE pushrod overhead valves; chain-driven camshaft; cast iron cylinder head and cylinder block; 4-bearing crankshaft; Zenith downdraught carburettor; coil ignition; water-cooled.
TRANSMISSION rear wheel drive; Borg & Beck 8in sdp clutch; 3-speed gearbox; synchromesh; hypoid final drive, ratio 4.125:1.
CHASSIS DETAILS integral steel structure; ifs by coil springs and wishbones; live axle and semi-elliptic springs at rear; telescopic dampers; drum brakes; Burman worm and nut steering; (EIPV recirculating ball);

50L (11 Imp gal, 13.2 US gal) fuel tank; 5.90 -15tyres.
DIMENSIONS wheelbase 262cm (103in); front track 135cm (53in), rear 138cm (54.5in) rear; ground clearance 17.8cm (7in); turning circle 10.7m (35ft); length 438cm (172.5in); width 170cm (67.1in); height 161cm (63.5in).
PERFORMANCE maximum speed 129kph (80mph); 18.4mph @ 1000rpm; acceleration 0-96kph (60mph) 20.9sec; 27.5kg/kW (20.5kg/bhp); 10.1-11.8L/100km (24-28mpg). High compr, short-stroke 1954: 132kph (82mph), 20.4sec, 22.4kg/kW (16.7kg/bhp), 11.3L/100km (25mpg).
PRODUCTION 105,275 EIP; 13,777 EIPV.
PRICE at launch £515, £802.12.3 incl PT; 1954 £535, £759.0.10 incl PT.

Top: Novelty on E-type cars was side-opening bonnet.
Right: Coronation Safari Rally competitor of 1959 shows second-thoughts grille.

The 4-cylinder rendering of the E-type underwent similar changes to the Velox in 1953, with a short-stroke engine and later high-compression heads, to take advantage of the changeover from Pool to better quality petrol. Bore went up from 2.75 inches to 3.125 inches and stroke was reduced from 3.75 inches to 3 inches, which would have increased the defunct and anomalous RAC horsepower from 12 to 15.6. Cylinder volume went up from 1442cc to 1507cc, and power from 27kW (35bhp) @ 3600rpm to 30kW (40bhp) @ 4000rpm, a 14 per cent increase from 30 per cent more piston area. The change scarcely transformed the performance of the Wyvern, but top speed went up from 99.5kph (62mph) to 115kph (71.6mph), and usefully improved torque brought swifter hill-climbing and acceleration. Economy was in the region of 56.5-94L/100km (3-5mpg) better. A plastic-covered facia replaced the all-metal one and the damper settings were changed to improve the ride.

The E-type's side-opening though heavy bonnet was retained; it could be opened from either side or lifted off completely to give access to newly introduced items, such as the ducting for the interior heater and demister, and the windscreen washer bottle. The screen wipers were however still driven off the engine.

BODY saloon, 4 doors; weight 1003kg (2212lb).
ENGINE 4 cylinders, in-line, front, 69.5mm x 95mm; 1442cc; compr: 6.4:1; 27kW (35bhp) @ 3600rpm; 18kW/L (24.3bhp/L); 91Nm (68lb/ft) @ 2000rpm.
From 1952: 79.4mm x 76.2mm; 1507cc; 29.8kW (40bhp) @ 4000rpm.
ENGINE STRUCTURE pushrod overhead valves; chain-driven camshaft; cast iron cylinder head and cylinder block; 4-bearing crankshaft; Zenith downdraught carburettor; coil ignition; water-cooled.
TRANSMISSION rear wheel drive; Borg & Beck 7.5in sdp clutch; 3-speed gearbox; synchromesh; hypoid final drive; ratio 4.625:1.
CHASSIS DETAILS integral steel structure; independent front suspension by coil spring ad wishbone; live axle and half-elliptic springs at rear; telescopic dampers; drum brakes; Burman worm and peg steering; 50L (11 Imp gal, 13.2 US gal) fuel tank; 5.60-15 tyres.
DIMENSIONS wheelbase 262cm (103in); front track 135cm (53in), rear 138cm (54.5in); ground clearance 17.8cm (7in); turning circle 10.7m (35ft); length 438cm (172.5in); width 170cm (67in); height 161cm (63.25in).
PERFORMANCE (1952 short-stroke engine) maximum 115kph (71.6mph); 25.8kph (16.1mph) @ 1000rpm; acceleration 0-96kph (60mph) 37.2sec; 33.7kg/kW (25.1kg/bhp); fuel consumption 9.3L/100km (30.4mpg).
PRODUCTION 5315.
PRICE £495 £771.10.0 incl PT 1952.

Right: E-type Wyvern giveaway was still body-coloured wheels. By the time production ended there were 22,000 on the Vauxhall payroll, turnover was £76m, and the new plant at Dunstable was in full production.
Far right: interesting Vauxhall system of front suspension, incorporating torsion bar and spring.

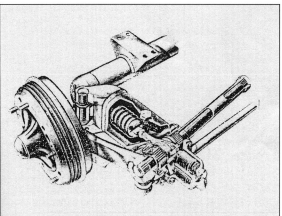

133

1953-1956 Grosvenor E-type estate

By December in the year of its introduction the first of three officially sanctioned estate car conversions, two by Grosvenor, one the Dormobile by Martin Walter, became available. Rustic-looking wooden estate car or "shooting brake" bodies became fashionable after the war when they were classified as commercial vehicles for a time and escaped purchase tax. The vogue continued with varnished timber panelling and traditional framing even when this no longer served any structural purpose. "Woody" bodies dated back to the 1920s when they were popular for taking shooting parties to the grouse moor. They were constructed to be spacious with gun-lockers and roof-racks for bringing home game, and the timber-framed bodies were designed to be flexible on chassis that were expected to buckle and twist when crossing rough terrain. Yet the Grosvenor was steel, part of the unitary structure, with appliqué polished oak-faced plywood and a horizontally split tailgate.

The Swansong name adopted in 1956 turned out to be appropriate. A supplier of Vauxhall bodywork since the 1920s the Grosvenor Carriage Co Ltd failed to develop the model and left the field to Friary. Grosvenor ceased trading under its own name by the 1960s.

BODY estate; 5 doors; weight 1157kg (2550lb).

ENGINE 6 cylinders, in-line, front, 69.5mm x 100mm; 2275cc; compr: 6.75:1, later 6.4:1; 41kW (55bhp) @ 3300rpm; 18kW/L (24.2bhp/L); 142Nm (106 lb/ft) @ 1100rpm (EIPV 2262cc 65bhp). From 1952: 79.4mm x 76.2mm, 2262cc, 48kW (64bhp) @ 4000rpm. From 1954: compr 7.6:1, 50.3kW (67.5bhp) @ 4000rpm.

ENGINE STRUCTURE pushrod overhead valves; chain-driven camshaft; cast iron cylinder head and cylinder block; 4-bearing crankshaft; Zenith downdraught carburettor; coil ignition; water-cooled.

TRANSMISSION rear wheel drive; Borg & Beck 8in sdp clutch; 3-speed gearbox; synchromesh; hypoid final drive, ratio 4.125:1.

CHASSIS DETAILS integral steel structure; independent front suspension by coil springs and wishbones; live axle and semi-elliptic springs at rear; telescopic dampers; drum brakes; Burman worm and nut steering; (EIPV recirculating ball);

50L (11 Imp gal, 13.2 US gal) fuel tank; 5.90 -15tyres.

DIMENSIONS wheelbase 262cm (103in); front track 135cm (53in), rear 138cm (54.5in); ground clearance 17.8cm (7in); turning circle 10.7m (35ft); length 438cm (172.5in); width 170cm (67in); height 161cm (63.25in).

PERFORMANCE maximum speed 129kph (80mph); 18.4mph @ 1000rpm; acceleration 0-96kph (60mph) 21sec; 28.2kg/kW (21kg/bhp); consumption 10.1-11.8L/100km (24-28mpg). High compr, short-stroke 1954: 132kph (82mph), 20.4sec, 23kg/kW (17.1kg/bhp), 11.3L/100km (25mpg).

PRICE Grosvenor Swansong £750, £1126.7.0 incl PT.

Three-phase two-tone was the term used to describe increasingly bizarre colour schemes employed to meet competition from the Ford Zodiac. This meant two colours in three layers, a rainbow sandwich effect which, together with chrome strips and mouldings, swept the Cresta along in the height of fashion. It was one of the smoothest, most effortless luxury cars under £1000. The wide bench seats were furnished with Nylon fabrics or leather (Nylon, still something of a novelty, was also used for the kingpin thrust washers) and in 1956 the combined hub and brake drum of the earlier Velox/Cresta was replaced with separate components. Mounting the cross-member of the independent front suspension on rubber cushions reduced road noise. Later models had slimmer A and C-post posts. The main instruments were contained in a single circular panel in front of the driver, a clock on the passenger's side allowing the same presswork to be used for left and right hand drive. Road testers were relieved that on this first Vauxhall without a starting handle, cold-weather starting was exemplary, and performance improved with a late 1956 7.7:1 compression engine. Another innovation, flashing direction indicators, controlled through a stalk on the right of the steering column pushed upwards for left turns, downward for right, were judged "very accessible" by *The Motor*.

BODY saloon; 4 doors; weight 1156kg (2549lb).
ENGINE 6 cylinders, in-line, front, 79.37mm x 76.2mm; 2262cc; compr: 7.3:1 (6.5 option, later 7.7 for premium fuel); 50.3kW (67.5bhp) @ 4000rpm; 22.3kW/L (29.8bhp/L); 138Nm (103lb/ft) @ 1100rpm.
ENGINE STRUCTURE pushrod overhead valves; chain-driven camshaft; cast iron cylinder head and block; 4-bearing crankshaft; Zenith VIGII downdraught carburettor; 12-volt coil ignition; water-cooled.
TRANSMISSION rear wheel drive; Borg & Beck 8in sdp clutch; 3-speed gearbox; synchromesh 2nd and 3rd; hypoid bevel final drive; ratio 4.125:1.
CHASSIS DETAILS integral steel structure; coil spring and wishbone independent front suspension; semi-elliptic leaf spring and live axle rear; double-acting telescopic dampers; anti-roll torsion bar; Lockheed-Vauxhall hydraulic drum brakes; Burman recirculating ball steering; 50L (11 Imp gal, 13.2 US gal) fuel tank; 5.90-15 tubeless tyres.

DIMENSIONS wheelbase 262cm (103in); track 135cm (53.3in) front, 139cm (54.8in) rear; ground clearance 17.8cm (7in); turning circle 10.4m (34ft); length 284.5cm (112in); width 169cm (66.5in); height 156cm (61.5in).
PERFORMANCE maximum speed 133kph (83mph), 136.5kph (85mph 7.7:1 compr); 29.5kph (18.4mph) @ 1000rpm; 0-96kph (60mph) 20.2sec; 23kg/kW (17.1kg/bhp); 12L/100km (23.5mpg), 11L/100km (26mpg) on premium fuel.
PRODUCTION 220,019.
PRICE £620 + £311.7.0, £931.7.0 (1956).

Right & far right: more toothsome grille for 1956 accompanied cosmetic changes and an increase in weight by 135lb on account of Cresta extras such as leather and Lurex upholstery. Extra colour now applied to side-stripe.
Right: Pet's Corner, Woburn Park.

1957-1960 Cresta PA

Longer, lower, and wider than its predecessor, the PA Vauxhall appeared at the 1956 motor show with radical thoroughly transatlantic full-width styling culminating in the classic 1950s feature, tail fins. The three-piece rear window was discarded after 1958, when the front air intake was enlarged, but the wrap-round windscreen with its dogleg pillar remained throughout the five years of the PA and its successor PASX series. Smooth-riding, with wide seats and a voluptuous appearance, the Cresta was a bold fashion statement. There were some sacrifices. Headroom was not generous. There was barely enough in the back for tall people, and no hat-room to speak of. Rear-seat legroom was restricted but the boot was vast. Yet the car soaked up bumps in a way that had hitherto been experienced only on large American sedans, and although there was a certain amount of body-roll on corners the customers proved more than willing to trade precise handling for comfort. It brought new standards of roadworthiness to large 5/6-seat saloons. More controversial perhaps were colour schemes that brought new pinks and greens to a market accustomed to sombre shades. Older motorists were surprised that there was no grease-gun in the toolkit even though chassis maintenance still expected one to be applied to 17 points every 1000 miles.

BODY saloon; 4 doors; 5/6 seats; weight 1194kg (2632lb).
ENGINE 6 cylinders, in-line, front, 79.4mm x 76.2mm; 2262cc; compr: 7.8:1 (6.8 opt); 61kW (82bhp) gross @ 4400rpm; 27kW/L (36.3bhp/L).
ENGINE STRUCTURE pushrod ohv; chain-driven cam; cast iron cyl head and block; 4-bearing crank; Zenith 34VNT downdraught carb; centrifugal and vacuum coil ignition; water-cooled.
TRANSMISSION rwd; Borg & Beck 8in sdp clutch; 3-speed, all sync; hypoid bevel final drive; ratio 4.11:1.
CHASSIS DETAILS integral steel structure; ifs by coil springs and wishbones; anti-roll bar, live rear axle with semi-elliptic leaf springs; Vauxhall telescopic dampers; Lockheed hydraulic drum brakes 2LS

at front; Burman recirculating ball steering; 49L (10.8 Imp gal, 13 US gal) fuel tank; 6.40-13 tubeless 4-ply tyres.
DIMENSIONS wheelbase 267cm (105in); track 136.5cm (53.75in) front, 137cm (54in) rear; ground clearance 17cm (6.75in); turning circle 10.4m (34ft); length 452cm (178in); width 174cm (68.5in); height 150cm (59in).
PERFORMANCE maximum speed 145kph (90mph); 27.8kph (17.3mph) @ 1000rpm; 0-96kph (60mph) 16.8sec; 19.6kg/kW (14.6kg/bhp); 12.3L/100km (23mpg).
PRODUCTION 81,841 all Velox/Cresta PA 1957-1960.
PRICE £715 + PT £358.17.0 £1073.17.0 1958.

Right: **no rally car, the Cresta's best affiliation with snow came through the association of its name with the famous bobsleigh run. This one took part in the 1960 Monte Carlo Rally, in which a similar car was 2nd in its class.**

Since the abandonment of the Wyvern and the introduction of the Victor, the Velox became the cheaper of the 6-cylinder pair. Only the Cresta came in two colours with white sidewall tyres. The Velox had painted mouldings instead of steel or chrome, and the wheels plain nave plates instead of full-size shiny discs. The poor Velox had no bonnet mascot but a circular piece of plastic with a crest instead, with down-market upholstery and trim, although until 1959 it did have the last token Vauxhall flutes. In an effort to retain a Vauxhall tradition dating back to Edwardian times, when the flutes became a feature of Vauxhall bonnets and radiators, concave chrome side-stripes graced PAs until 1959. The facia was black-topped, the instruments grouped in two circular dials ahead of the driver. A bench front seat and steering column gear lever were still standard equipment, road testers generally disliking both although conceding the shift was a good example of its type. Years of experience managed to eliminate most of the slack from the long linkage to the gearbox. There was some criticism of a shortage of rear seat legroom, counterbalanced by approval for the generous luggage boot. An optional Laycock de Normanville overdrive on second and top introduced in 1960 gave a 3.20:1 top gear and was operated by a right-hand tumbler switcher on the facia.

BODY saloon; 4 doors; weight 1194kg (2632lb).
ENGINE 6 cylinders, in-line, front, 79.4mm x 76.2mm; 2262cc; compr: 7.8:1 (6.8 optional); 61kW (82bhp) gross @ 4400rpm; 27kW/L (36.3bhp/L); 166Nm (124lb/ft) @ 1800rpm.
ENGINE STRUCTURE pushrod overhead valves; chain-driven camshaft; cast iron cylinder head and block; 4-bearing crankshaft; Zenith 34VNT downdraught carburettor; centrifugal and vacuum coil ignition; water-cooled.
TRANSMISSION rear wheel drive; Borg & Beck 8in sdp clutch; 3-speed gearbox; all synchromesh; hypoid bevel final drive; ratio 4.11:1.
CHASSIS DETAILS integral steel structure; independent front suspension by coil springs and wishbones; anti-roll bar, live rear axle with semi-elliptic leaf springs; Vauxhall telescopic dampers; Lockheed hydraulic drum brakes 2LS at front; Burman recirculating ball steering; 49L (10.8 Imp gal, 13 US gal)

fuel tank; 6.40-13 tubeless 4-ply tyres.
DIMENSIONS wheelbase 267cm (105.25in); track 136.5cm (53.75in) front, 137cm (54in) rear; ground clearance 17cm (6.75in); turning circle 10.4m (34ft); length 452cm (178in); width 174cm (68.5in); height 150cm (59in).
PERFORMANCE maximum speed 144.5kph (90mph); 27.8kph (17.3mph) @ 1000rpm; acceleration 0-96kph (60mph) 16.8sec; 19.6kg/kW (14.6kg/bhp); fuel consumption 12.3L/100km (23mpg).
PRODUCTION 81,841 all Velox/Cresta PA 1957-1960.
PRICE £655, £983.17.0 incl PT.

Right: **This 1958 PA, one of the oldest survivors, had the early model's 3-piece rear window.**

The Victor laid the foundations of a model range taking Vauxhall through to the second half of the 1970s. Its lively turn of speed, roomy body and useful boot was something of a departure for the 1.5-litre class that had suffered a surfeit of dreary Austin Cambridges, Hillman Minxes, Standard 10s, and Morris Oxfords. Here was a rival for the Ford Consul with overhead valves and styling that, whatever its demerits, was certainly eye-catching. It broke with Vauxhall tradition, relegating the famous flutes to the body sides, but it had a hydraulic clutch and synchromesh on first gear. There was an estate car, and in 1958 the option of the short-lived Newton two-pedal transmission.

The proportions of the Series I Victor (below) scarcely suited a narrow car with 13in wheels. There was a lot of rear overhang, the pillars of the wrap-around windscreen had a bruising dogleg, and the exhaust emerging from a bulbous bumper quickly discoloured the chrome. There was a logic in translating features popular in America, such as the oblique crease in the rear door and the jet-style nacelles, but within two years a hurried face-lift and the Series 2 tidied it up.

BODY saloon, 4 seats, 4 doors, weight 1016kg (2240lb); estate 1066kg (2352lb).
ENGINE 4 cylinders, in-line, front, 79.37mm x 76.2mm; 1508cc; compr: 7.8:1; 41kW (55bhp) gross @ 4200rpm, 28kW/L (36.5bhp/L); 113 Nm (84lb/ft) @ 2400rpm.
ENGINE STRUCTURE ohv; chain-driven camshaft; cast iron cylinder head and block; 4-bearing crank; Zenith VN434 carb; centrifugal and vacuum coil ignition; water-cooled.
TRANSMISSION rear wheel drive; Borg & Beck 7.25in sdp clutch; 3-speed all synchromesh; hypoid bevel final drive; 4.125:1 saloon, 4.625 estate; optional Newton clutch 1958 engaged at 800rpm.
CHASSIS DETAILS integral steel structure; front susp indep coil spring and wishbone; anti-roll bar; live axle half-elliptic springs rear (estate 25% stiffer); telescopic hydraulic dampers; hydraulic composite steel & cast iron drum brakes; Burman recirculating ball; 36.4L (8 Imp gal, 9.6US gal) fuel tank; 5.60-13 (5.90 estate) tyres.

DIMENSIONS wheelbase 249cm (98in); track 127cm (50in); ground clearance 16.5cm (6.5in); turning circle 10.5m (34.5ft); length 424cm (167in); width 158cm (62.25in); height 148cm (58.25in); estate permissible load 386kg (850lb), 1275L (45cu ft).
PERFORMANCE maximum speed 120kph (75mph); 26.5kph (16.5mph) @ 1000rpm (23.6kph, 14.7mph estate); 25kg/kW (18.5kg/bhp); 0-96kph (60mph) 28.1sec (30.9sec estate); 9.1L/100km (31mpg).
PRODUCTION 390,747 all F-type. PRICE £505 + PT £253 17s 0d, £758 17s 0d 1957 Super saloon; £637 + PT £319 17s 0d, £956.17s.0d 1958 estate car with Newton 2-pedal control, £931 7s 0d with manual transmission. £565 + PT £283 17s 0d, £848 17s 0d 1959 series II Super saloon.

Top right: **low loading floor for the estate was only 61cm (2ft) from the ground. Loads 152cm (5ft) long and 91cm (3ft) wide could be accommodated.**

A joint production of Vauxhall Motors and Friary Motors of Basingstoke, an estate conversion of the 2.3-litre Velox and Cresta was marketed as a fully approved Vauxhall model. It used the standard doors and body sides including the tailfin mouldings with the roofline extended rearwards to an upwards-opening tailgate. The rear seat folded forward to provide a large flat floor 180cm (71in) long (with a further 23cm [9in] of space to the folded seat) by 105cm (41.5in) wide, a generous 850L (30cu ft) with the seat up and 1473L (52cu ft) with it down. Loading height was only 66cm (26in) from the ground. The rear wheel arches were boxed-in and dual fuel tanks with a total capacity of 64L (14 Imp gal) could be fitted on either side of the spare wheel under the rear floor. The car's overall length was the same as the saloon. The effect of the conversion on performance was negligible, the increase in weight was only 50.8kg (112lb) adding about 1sec to the 0-60mph time and increasing the fuel consumption by about 1mpg. Heavy-duty rear springs, included to cope with the effects of weighty items in the back, had the effect of making the unladen ride firmer. Laden, the Friary coped quite well by the standards of the time. The Motor found it a "roomy and imposing dual-purpose car with a restful but lively performance."

BODY estate, 4 door, 5 seats, 1257kg (2771lb).
ENGINE 6 cylinders, in-line, front, 79.37mm x 76.2mm; 2262cc; compr: 7.8:1 (6.8 optional); 57kW (76bhp) net @ 4400rpm, 25kW/L (33.6bhp/L); 168Nm (125lb/ft) @ 1200rpm.
ENGINE STRUCTURE pushrod overhead valves; chain-driven camshaft; cast iron cylinder head and block; 4-bearing crankshaft; Zenith 34VNT downdraught carburettor; coil ignition; water-cooled.
TRANSMISSION rear wheel drive; Borg & Beck 8in sdp clutch; 3-speed gearbox; all synchromesh; Hardy Spicer open propellor shaft, hypoid bevel final drive; ratio 4.111:1.
CHASSIS DETAILS integral steel structure; independent front suspension by coil springs, wishbones and anti-roll bar; live axle and semi-elliptic heavy-duty springs at rear; telescopic hydraulic dampers; Lockheed hydraulic brakes, 2LS at front; Burman recirculating ball steering; 64L (14 Imp gal, 16.8 US gal) fuel tank; 6.40-13 6-ply tubeless tyres.

DIMENSIONS wheelbase 267cm (105in); front track 136.5cm (53.75in), 137cm (54in) rear; ground clearance 17cm (6.75in); turning circle 10.4m (34ft); length 452cm (178in); width 174cm (68.5in); height 150cm (59in).
PERFORMANCE maximum speed 145kph (90mph); 28kph (17.3mph) @ 1000rpm; acceleration 17.6sec; 22.1kg/kW (16.5kg/bhp); fuel consumption 12L/100km (21.8mpg). PRICE £862 + PT £360 5s 10d, £1222 5s 10d.

Right: Friary Estate retained the Vauxhall doors and even the familiar tail fins. Larger fronted grille identified later-series Cresta and Velox model in characteristic 1960s publicity shot.

A new 2.6-litre "square" (identical bore and stroke) engine, giving an extra 22.4kW (30bhp) with wedge-shaped combustion chambers for the Velox and Cresta, was accompanied by a restyling which enlarged both the air intake at the front and the tailfins. The steering was lower-geared which made wheel-twirling necessary in the event of skid correction. Crestas were luxury versions of Veloxes with anodised wheel trims, whitewall tyres and optional three-phase dual tone paintwork. Laycock de Normanville overdrive became optional on top and second gears. There was no change in rear axle ratio when overdrive was specified, yet the five ratios that became available were well-spaced.

The shortcoming of the extra power was what *The Motor* called "a certain degree of liveliness at the rear .. the driver is aware of the back axle's existence on rough surfaces .. sudden acceleration in sharp turns produces wheelspin." Road testers urged caution in opening the throttle in low gears to avoid rear-end breakaway. The new strip-type speedometer changed from green to amber at 48kph (30mph), then to red at about 88kph (55mph), yet the now familiar virtues of big Vauxhalls remained, quietness, refinement, smooth effortless performance, and above all a sense of style to which few rivals came close.

BODY saloon, 4 doors, 5/6 seats, weight 1219kg (2687lb).
ENGINE 6 cylinders, in-line, front, 82.55mm x 82.55mm; 2651cc; compr: 8.1:1; 84.3kW (113bhp) gross @ 4800rpm; 31.8kW/L (42.6bhp/L); 200Nm (149lb/ft) @ 2400rpm.
ENGINE STRUCTURE pushrod overhead valves; chain-driven camshaft; cast-iron cylinder head and block; ...-bearing crankshaft; Zenith 42VNT carburettor; coil ignition; water-cooled.
TRANSMISSION rear wheel drive; 9in sdp clutch; 3-speed gearbox; all-synchromesh; overdrive optional; hypoid bevel final drive; ratio 3.9:1, 3.03 overdrive.
CHASSIS DETAILS integral steel structure; independent front suspension by coil springs, wishbones and anti-roll bar; live axle and semi-elliptic springs at rear; hydraulic telescopic dampers; Lockheed hydraulic drum brakes 2LS at front; Burman recirculating ball steering; 49L (10.8 Imp gal, 13 US gal) fuel tank; 5.90-14 tubeless tyres.

DIMENSIONS wheelbase 267cm (105in); track 137cm (54in) front and rear; ground clearance 19cm (7.5in); turning circle 11.3m (37ft); length 457cm (180in); width 174cm (68.5in); height 98cm (58.5in).
PERFORMANCE maximum speed 153kph (96mph); 30kph (18.7mph) @ 1000rpm in top, 38kph (24mph) in overdrive top; acceleration 15.2sec; 14.5kg/kW (10.8kg/bhp); fuel consumption 14.9L/100km (19mpg).
PRODUCTION 91,923.
PRICE 1960 Cresta £760 + PT £317 15s 19d, £1077 15s 10d, without overdrive £1014 0s 10d.

Right: **upright plastic bonnet badge was abandoned as the one-piece back window improved the airiness of the interior. Venetian-blind rear window shade was popular accessory for keeping sun off rear passengers' necks.**

Second thoughts on the Victor exorcised the dogleg A-pillar, and inaugurated the well-proportioned FB series of 4-door saloons and 5-door estates. Also finally banished were the trademark flutes which, ever since they had become decorative strips, were anachronisms. The shape was a success. Crisp and well-proportioned rather than beautiful, it put the Victor more firmly than ever into the well-loved family category. Wheelbase, track, length and width were all increased over the F-series Victor. Only the height was reduced, by 3.8cm (1.5in). The spare wheel was mounted upright to increase luggage room, and Vauxhall's increasing knowledge of how to make unitary-structure bodies enabled it to reduce the weight by nearly 77kg (170lb).

A 3-speed gearbox was standard but most customers chose the optional 4-speed all-synchromesh box, criticised at first for being noisy, and having a spongy long-travel remote control gearshift. It was soon fixed. In any case it was so much more precise than the steering column change linkages that preceded it that the change was widely welcomed.

Bench seats were standard as well but most discerning customers specified the comfortable bucket seats. The Victor's steering swivels were re-designed so that grease gun applications now came at intervals of 12,000 miles.

BODY saloon, 4 doors; estate, 5 doors, 5 seats; weight 953kg (2100lb). ENGINE 4 cylinders, in-line, front, 79.4mm x 76.2mm; 1508cc; cr 8.1:1; 41kW (55bhp) @ 4600rpm, 27.2kW/L (36.5bhp/L); 107Nm (80lb/ft) @ 2000rpm. 1594cc, 44kW (59bhp) @ 4600rpm, 27.6kW/L (37bhp/L); 113Nm (84lb/ft) @ 2400rpm. ENGINE STRUCTURE pushrod ohv; chain-driven cam; cast iron cyl head and block; 4-bearing crank; Zenith 34VN downdraught carb; coil ignition; pressurised water-cooling. TRANSMISSION rear wheel drive; Borg & Beck 7.25in sdp clutch; 4-speed opt (3-speed standard), all sync; hypoid bevel final drive; ratio 3.9:1.

CHASSIS DETAILS integral steel structure; ifs by coil springs and wishbones; live axle and half-elliptic leaf springs at rear; telescopic dampers; front anti roll bar; Lockheed drum brakes; Burman recirculating ball steering; 45.5L (10 Imp gal, 12 US gal) fuel tank; 5.60-13 4-ply tyres. DIMENSIONS wheelbase 255cm (100.5in); track 129.5cm (51in); ground clearance 18cm (7in); turning circle 9.5m (31.25ft); length 439cm (173in); width 163cm (64in); height 147cm (58in). PERFORMANCE maximum speed 122kph (76mph); 27.8kph (17.3mph) @ 1000rpm; 0-96kph (60mph) 22.6sec; 23.2kg/kW (17.3kg/bhp); 8.8-10.9L/100km (26-32mpg). PRODUCTION 328,640 including VX4/90. PRICE with 4-speed gearbox £547, £781 8s 11d.

Left: **1961 Super model in Derwent valley.**
Right: **1964 FB estate.**
Far right: **1961 De Luxe.**

The VX 4/90 brought Vauxhall back to a sporting realm from which it had been absent since the 1920s. *The Motor* could scarcely believe it. "Twin carburettors are associated … with sports car characteristics whereas this is essentially a fast touring model." It was going to take more than a Victor with an extra 19kph (12mph) to convince the Establishment that the VX 4/90 was more than window-dressing. High gearing, an aluminium cylinder head, two downdraught Zenith carburettors, vacuum servo for disc and drum brakes, and big round instruments apparently were not enough to transform a family saloon into a sports car particularly if the interior was "finished entirely in modern synthetic materials," with painted metal panels of "nicely grained mock woodwork."

The VX4/90 however earned the respect of enthusiasts who saw Ford enter the same market in 1963 with the Cortina GT. It came into a world growing accustomed to high gearing for the new motorways yet still expecting good behaviour in top gear. The VX would pull away from 24kph (15mph) without hesitation or transmission snatch, the 4-cylinder pulling lustily although "individual power impulses … are felt until the speed rises above 25mph."

BODY saloon, 4 seats, 4 doors, weight 990kg (2184lb).
ENGINE 4 cylinders, in-line, front, 79.37mm x 76.2mm; 1508cc; compr: 9.3:1; 53kW (71bhp) net, 60.4kW (81bhp) gross, @ 5200rpm; 35kW/L (47bhp/L); 124Nm (92lb/ft) @ 2800rpm.
ENGINE STRUCTURE pushrod ohv; chain-driven cam; cast iron cyl head and block; 4-bearing crank; 2 Zenith 36WIP carbs; coil ignition; pressurised water-cooling.
TRANSMISSION rear wheel drive; Borg & Beck 8in sdp clutch; 4-speed; all synchromesh; hypoid bevel final drive; ratio 3.9:1.

CHASSIS DETAILS integral steel structure; ifs by coil springs, wishbones and anti-roll bar; live axle and half-elliptic springs at rear; Vauxhall telescopic dampers; Lockheed hydraulic brakes, 10.5in disc front, 8in drum rear, vacuum servo; Burman recirculating ball steering; 45.5L (10 Imp gal, 12 US gal) fuel tank; 5.60-14 tubeless 4-ply tyres.
DIMENSIONS wheelbase 254cm (100in); track 131cm (51.5in) front and rear; ground clearance 17.8cm (7in); turning circle 9.6 (31.5ft); length 439cm (172.8in); width 163cm (64in); height 145cm (57.25in).
PERFORMANCE maximum speed 145kph (90mph); 28.6kph (17.8mph) @ 1000rpm; 0-60mph 16.4sec; 18.7kg/kW (13.9kg/bhp); 7.2-11.3L/100km (25-39mpg).
PRODUCTION 328,640 all FB.
PRICE £674 + PT £253 15s 3d, £927 15s 3d (1962).

Right: instrument cluster including 100mph speedometer.

151

The resemblance of the 6-cylinder flagship Vauxhalls to the workaday Victor FB was no coincidence. Doors were costly to tool up for. A car that could be made with another car's doors saved an immense amount of money in development costs. Vauxhall had done it with the H Ten-Four of 1937 through to the LIX/LIP Wyvern/Velox of 1951. The doors were all the same. The British Motor Corporation did it. The doors of the Austin Maxi served the Austin 1800, and all its Wolseley and Morris counterparts for years. So it was with the PB. Victor FB doors, together with a front and back stretch (more shades of the LIX/LIP), made it with 12.7cm (5in) extra width and 45cm (17.75in) on the wheelbase. It was perfectly legitimate. Gone were the tailfins and wrap-round windows of the old P-type. A steering column gearshift and bench front seat were hangovers from an era that was passing unlamented. Light weight and clean lines made the Velox or Cresta's 145kph (90mph) less frenzied than the VX4/90's.

It was a quiet, almost lazy performer, and even if the handling was not exactly sporting (there was some body roll, and to a generation growing accustomed to better responses it felt mushy) it was safe and undemanding. The 3-speed gearbox retained the old car's steering column gearshift.

BODY saloon, 4 doors, 6 seats, weight 1220kg (2690lb).
ENGINE 6 cylinders, in-line front, 82.55mm x 82.55mm; 2651cc; compr 8.5:1, 70.8kW (95bhp) @ 4600rpm; 26.7kW/L (35.8bhp/L); 200Nm (149lb/ft) @ 2400rpm.
ENGINE STRUCTURE pushrod overhead valves; chain-driven camshaft; cast iron cylinder head and block; 7-bearing crankshaft; Zenith 42VNT downdraught carburettor; coil ignition.
TRANSMISSION rear wheel drive; sdp clutch; 3-speed all-synchromesh gearbox, optional Laycock de Normanville overdrive on top and 2nd; hypoid bevel final drive; ratio 3.9:1, 3.7:1 without overdrive.
CHASSIS DETAILS integral steel structure; ifs by coil springs and wishbones; live axle and half-elliptic springs at rear; telescopic dampers; anti roll bar at front; Lockheed disc front drum rear brakes; Burman recirculating ball steering; 49L (10.75 Imp gal, 12.9 US gal) fuel tank; 5.90-14 tubeless 4-ply tyres.

DIMENSIONS wheelbase 274cm (107.75in); track 141cm (55.5in) front, 143.5cm (56.5in rear); ground clearance 18cm (7in); turning circle 10.7m (35ft) left, 10.5m (34.5ft) right; length 462cm (182in); width 175cm (69in); height 149cm (59in).
PERFORMANCE maximum speed 149kph (92.7mph); 29.5kph (18.35mph) @ 1000rpm, 38kph (23.6mph) with overdrive; 0-96kph (60mph) 19.5sec; 17.2kg/kW (12.8kg/bhp); 11.8-14.5L/100km (19.5-24mpg).
PRODUCTION 87,047.
PRICE 1963 Cresta including overdrive £805, £973 5s 5d.

Right: 1965 Cresta. **Velox kept traditional distinguishing marks, body-colour wheels, less chrome, leather upholstery.** *Top:* Cresta/Velox interiors **had "safety-padded dash and steering-wheel centre, rich carpeting and walnut dash facing".**

1963 PB Estate by Martin Walter

Catalogued by Vauxhall, the PB estate car conversion carried out by Martin Walter of Folkstone was available as a Velox for £1203 or Cresta at £1305. The roof was removed from completed saloons and a new steel frame clad in glass reinforced plastic substituted, together with a folding rear seat and counterbalanced tailgate. The rear passenger doors were taken straight from a Victor estate.

The result was a luxury estate car; it might have been more workmanlike had the loading floor not been covered in splendid pile carpet with metal rubbing strips. As it was the platform was 127cm (50in) long with the rear seat in place, 185cm (73in) with it folded, although the fuel filler pipe and wheel arches reduced the usable width. The tailgate hinged upwards providing a useful shelter when loading. Stiff rear springs made the ride firmer than the saloon and the structure with the roof removed was less taut than the saloon, with the result that PB estates tended to shake and rattle after a large mileage. It was also less quiet than the saloon. GM's optional Hydramatic transmission had three epicyclic gears and a fluid coupling which multiplied the engine torque for swift getaways.

BODY estate, 5 doors, 5/6 seats, 1288kg (2839lb).
ENGINE 6 cylinders, in-line, front, 82.55mm x 82.55mm; 2651cc; compr: 8.5:1; 84.3kW (113bhp) gross @ 4800rpm, 70.5kW (94.6bhp) net @ 4600rpm; 26.6kW/L (35.7bhp/L); 197Nm (147lb ft) gross @ 2400rpm.
ENGINE STRUCTURE pushrod overhead valves; chain-driven camshaft; cast iron cylinder head and block; …-bearing crankshaft; Zenith 42VNT downdraught carburettor; coil ignition; water-cooled.
TRANSMISSION rear wheel drive; Borg & Beck 8.5in diaphragm spring sdp clutch; 3-speed gearbox; all synchromesh; automatic optional; overdrive optional; hypoid bevel final drive; ratio 3.9:1.
CHASSIS DETAILS integral steel structure with grp and steel-framed conversion; independent front suspension by coil springs and wishbone, anti-roll bar; live axle and semi-elliptic springs at rear; Vauxhall telescopic hydraulic dampers; Lockheed servo-assisted disc front drum rear brakes; Burman recirculating ball steering; 49L (10.8 Imp gal, 13 US gal) fuel tank; 5.90-14 6-ply tyres.
DIMENSIONS wheelbase 274cm (108in); front track 141cm (55.5in), 143.5cm (56.5in) rear; ground clearance 17.8cm (7in); turning circle 10.7m (35ft); length 462cm (182in); width 178cm (70.25in); height 149cm (58.5in).
PERFORMANCE maximum speed 151kph (94mph); 29.4kph (18.3mph) @ 1000rpm; acceleration 0-60mph 14.7sec; 18.3kg/kW (13.6kg/bhp); fuel consumption 12.3-14.9L/100km (19-23mpg).
PRICE £1080 +PT £225 11s 3d, £1305 11s 3d.

Right: **Cresta features included extra lights, large grille and chrome side-stripe, anodized wheel trims and white-wall tyres.**

Alliteration proved too tempting for the name of a small Vauxhall based on an Opel Kadett. It was well dubbed. It was lively and enjoyed a life span the best part of 20 years. Vauxhall had never made anything so small. The closest to a 1057cc engine it had come was the 1203cc Ten-Four of 1937, abandoned as soon as it decently could, when the tax regime changed after the war. The recipe for the new small car was hardly radical in an era when transverse engines, front wheel drive, all round independent suspension, and novel structures were becoming commonplace. An in-line water-cooled engine at the front driving the rear wheels in a frankly slab-sided 2-door steel monocoque did not seem exciting.

Yet there was a strong cadre of buyers to whom it was exactly right. It was simple to behold and just what they craved. It was cheap to make, cheap to run, reliable, and strong. It did break some new ground. The front transverse leaf spring deflected in a way that made it a roll stabiliser, and with fine attention to detail the wedge-shaped combustion chambers were not rough-cast but carefully machined in the cylinder head.

The additional HA90 high-compression 60bhp model had front disc brakes, optional on Vivas after 1965. 11,794 were made between 1965 and 1966.

BODY saloon, 2 doors, 4 seats, weight 724kg (1564lb).
ENGINE 4 cylinders, in-line front, 74.6mm x 60.96mm; 1057cc; compr 8.5:1, 7.3:1 option; 32.8kW (44bhp) @ 5200rpm high CR, 29.8kW (40bhp) @ 5200rpm low CR; 31kW/L (41.6bhp/L) high CR, 28kW/L (37.8bhp/L) low CR); 75Nm (56lb/ft) @ 3000rpm high CR, 71Nm (53lb/ft) @ 2900rpm low CR.
ENGINE STRUCTURE pushrod ohv; chain-driven camshaft; cast iron cylinder head and block; Solex downdraught B30PSE carburettor, mechanical fuel pump; 3-bearing crankshaft; pressurised water cooling.
TRANSMISSION rear wheel drive; 6.5in sdp cable operated diaphragm spring clutch; 4-speed gearbox, all synchromesh; hypoid final drive with two-pinion differential; ratio 4.13:1.
CHASSIS DETAILS integral steel structure; independent front suspension, double wishbone transverse leaf spring with anti-roll clamping; live axle with torque tube and half-elliptic springs at rear; telescopic dampers; Girling drum brakes with optional servo; rack and pinion steering; 32L (7 Imp gal, 8.4 US gal) fuel tank; 5.50-12 4-ply tubeless tyres, 3.50in rims.
DIMENSIONS wheelbase 232cm (91.5in); track 120cm (47.5in) front, 132cm (52.25in) rear; ground clearance 13cm (5in); turning circle 8.2m (27ft); length 394cm (155in); width 151cm (59.5in); height 136cm (53.3in).
PERFORMANCE maximum speed 125kph (78mph); 24kph (15mph) @ 1000rpm; 0-96kph (60mph) 19.6sec; 22kg/kW (16.5kg/bhp) high CR, 24.3kg/kW (18kg/bhp) low CR; 7-8.8L/100km (32-40mpg).
PRODUCTION 309,538.
PRICE £478, £578 2s 11d incl PT.

Right: 1966 HA Viva.
Top right: cosmetic changes for 1966 SL model included contrasting colour band, wheel trims, and optional fog and spot lamps and wing mirrors.

1964-1967 Victor 101 FC

Using much the same platform as the FB with a stiffer but slightly heavier body shell, the FC Victor 101 was 3.8cm (1.5in) longer, and just over 1.3cm (0.5in) wider. The body sides were curved, eliminating the strong waistline moulding on the window-sills, and giving 10cm (4in) extra shoulder room. The distinctive rear window was slightly concave and the boot was one of the biggest in the class somewhat at the expense of rear-seat legroom. The A-posts and C-posts were thinner and mechanical improvements included the option of disc brakes (£15) with vacuum servo assistance.

The engine carried over from the FB had the obligatory increase in power and was to be the last pushrod Victor. Powerglide automatic transmission or a 4-speed manual gearbox (£14 10s) was an option to the standard 3-speed. Hydraulic clutch operation fell out of favour at Luton, first on the Viva then with the Victor, and the 101 had a mechanical linkage between the pedal and the diaphragm-spring clutch. By contrast to the older FB models, the first 101 was relatively low-geared and at its top speed the engine could be over-revved by 500rpm. The extra weight affected fuel consumption more than anything and the Victor dropped behind rivals such as the Ford Corsair, Morris 1100, and Morris Oxford.

BODY saloon, estate, 4 seats, 4/5 doors, weight 1016kg (2240lb), estate weight 1086kg (2395lb).
ENGINE 4 cylinders, in-line, front, 81.64mm x 76.2mm; 1594cc; compr 9.0:1; 44.8kW (60bhp) net @ 4600rpm; 28kW/L (37bhp/L); 115Nm (86lb/ft) @ 2800rpm. 49kW (66bhp) @ 4800rpm, 30.9kW/L (41bhp/L), 127Nm (95lb/ft) @ 2600rpm.
ENGINE STRUCTURE pushrod ohv; chain-driven cam; cast iron cyl head and block; 3-bearing crank; Zenith 34IV carb; water-cooled.
TRANSMISSION rear wheel drive; Borg & Beck 8in sdp clutch; 3 or 4-speed, all synch; automatic optional;

spiral bevel final drive; ratio 4.125:1.
CHASSIS DETAILS integral steel structure; ifs by unequal length wishbones, coil springs, anti-roll bar; live axle and semi-elliptic springs at rear; Vauxhall telescopic dampers; Girling hydraulic brakes, duo servo drums at rear, discs front optional; recirculating ball steering; 46L (10 Imp gal, 12 US gal) fuel tank; 5.60-13 tyres, 4in rims, estate 5.90-13.
DIMENSIONS wheelbase 254cm (100in); front track 129.5cm (51in), rear 134cm (52.75in); ground clearance 17cm (6.75in); turning circle 9.1m (30ft); length 444cm (174.75in); width 165cm (64.75in); height 145cm (57.25in).
PERFORMANCE maximum speed 137kph (85mph); 26.2kph (16.3mph) @ 1000rpm, estate 27.1kph (16.9mph); 0-96kph (60mph) 17.1sec; 60bhp, 22.7kg/kW (16.9kg/bhp); 9.7-11.8L/100km (24-29mpg).
PRODUCTION 219,814 all FC.
PRICE with 4 gears and disc brakes 1965 £655 + PT £137 18s 4d, £792 18s 4d. Estate £725, £878 incl PT.

A real wood facia and 86 more cc enabled the FC VX4/90 to keep up with the competition from the more expensive Sunbeam Rapier and Fiat 1500, and the cheaper Cortina GT and Triumph Vitesse. Vauxhalls capable of 144.5kph (90mph) were becoming almost commonplace.

The new VX shared the Victor 101's better aerodynamics but now also used 13in instead of 14in wheels, the lower overall gearing making the car sound less relaxed. Overdrive was no longer an option and the resolute affiliation to a 3-bearing engine not much help. By way of compensation a Borg-Warner limited-slip differential was offered, which helped the car make a clean getaway on slippery surfaces. It also rid the VX back axle of a tendency to hop, but the emphasis was still on a supple ride rather than sporting handling with body roll remaining something of a bugbear. The front anti-roll bar was stiffened by 50 per cent but this improved the steering rather than reduced body-roll.

Better sound damping made the VX quieter than the Victor and even the Cresta, except at high speed when the engine revs reached 5,500. Avon radial-ply tyres were on offer which being slightly smaller in effective diameter further lowered the overall gearing.

BODY: saloon, 4 seats, 4 doors, weight 1020kg (2249lb).

ENGINE 4 cylinders, in-line, front, 81.64mm x 76.2mm; 1594cc; compr: 9.3:1; gross output 64kW (86bhp) @ 5200rpm; 40kW/L (54bhp/L); 115Nm (86lb/ft) @ 5200rpm. net output 55kW (74bhp) @ 5200rpm, 122.5Nm (91lb/ft) @ 2800rpm

ENGINE STRUCTURE pushrod overhead valves; chain-driven camshaft; aluminium cylinder head; cast iron block; 3-bearing crankshaft; 2 Zenith 34IV downdraught carburettors; AC mechanical fuel pump.

TRANSMISSION rear wheel drive; Borg & Beck 8in sdp clutch; 4-speed gearbox; all synchromesh; hypoid final drive; ratio 3.9:1.

CHASSIS DETAILS integral steel structure; independent front suspension by coil springs and wishbones; live rear axle with half-elliptic springs; telescopic dampers; front anti-roll bar; Girling disc front drum rear brakes, vacuum servo; recirculating ball steering; 45L (10 Imp gal, 12 US gal) fuel tank; 155-13 Avon radial-ply tubeless tyres, 4in rims.

DIMENSIONS wheelbase 254cm (100in); front track 129.5cm (51in), rear 134cm (52.75in); ground clearance 15.2cm (6.00in); turning circle 9.1m (30ft); length 444cm (174.75in); width 165cm (64.75in); height 145cm (57.25in).

PERFORMANCE: maximum speed 149kph (93mph); 27.8kph (17.3mph) @ 1000rpm; acceleration 0-96kph (60mph) 14.0sec; 18.5kg/kW (13.8kg/bhp); fuel consumption 10.5-12.8L/100km (22-27mpg).

PRODUCTION 13,449.

PRICE 1966 £730, £884 incl PT.

Right: **VX interior designers seemed undecided whether to go for a new sort of luxury car or emphasise a sporting role. In the end it came somewhere in between and proved a well-liked compromise.**

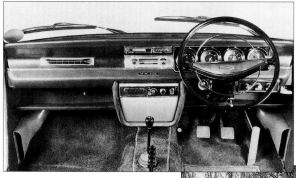

161

In a market disputed by the Ford Zodiac, Austin A110, and the Rover and Triumph 2000s, the big Vauxhall could not make much headway in top speed or economy, but it was swifter in acceleration and comfortably the cheapest. The Austin at £998 against the Cresta's £977 was a clumsy affair and the only serious foreign competition was the sleek Fiat 2300 which cost £1331, £38 more even that the redoubtable Rover.

In October 1964 the Cresta's engine capacity was increased by 25%, from 2651cc to 3293cc, producing 26% more torque and 21% more power. Its 0-80kph (50mph) acceleration time of 7.5sec was faster than a 1600SC Porsche, Ford Lotus-Cortina, Rolls-Royce Silver Cloud, or 1275S Mini Cooper. It nearly made 60mph under the 10sec barrier but could not quite muster 100mph because of low gearing, although its quickness off the mark made it a striking performer for a substantial family saloon. Not only that, it was also quiet and refined, just like the large American cars on which it was perhaps a little self-consciously modelled down to the wheel-twirling low geared steering with no fewer than five turns from lock to lock.

A bench front seat was standard, individual seats could be specified for £10, or an extravagant £30 with adjustable backs.

BODY saloon, 5/6 seats, 4 doors, weight 1179kg (2598lb).
ENGINE 6 cylinders, in-line, front, 96.13mm x 82.55mm; 3294cc; compr: 8.5:1; 91.7kW (123bhp) gross @ 4600rpm, 85.6kW (114.8bhp) @ 4200rpm; 26kW/L (35bhp/L); 235Nm (175lb/ft) @ 2200rpm.
ENGINE STRUCTURE pushrod ohv; chain-driven camshaft; cast iron cylinder head and block; 4-bearing crank; Zenith 42VNT downdraught carburettor; water-cooled.
TRANSMISSION rear wheel drive; 8.5in sdp diaphragm spring clutch; 4-speed, all synch; overdrive, auto optional; hypoid bevel final drive; ratio 3.7:1.
CHASSIS DETAILS integral steel structure; ifs by coil springs, wishbones, and anti-roll bar; live axle and semi-elliptic leaf springs at rear; telescopic hydraulic dampers; disc brakes front, drum rear; recirculating ball steering; 49L (10.75 Imp gal, 12.9 US gal) fuel tank; 5.90–14 tubeless tyres.
DIMENSIONS wheelbase 274cm (107.75in); front track 141cm (55.5ins), 143.5cm (56.5in) rear; ground clearance 18cm (7in); turning circle 10.7m (35ft); length 462.3cm (182in); width 270cm (106.25in); height 147.3cm (58in).
PERFORMANCE maximum speed 157kph (97.5mph); 31kph (19.3mph) @ 1000rpm; 0-60mph 10.6sec; 13.8kg/kW (10.3kg/bhp); 14.1-16.6L/100km (17-20mpg).
PRODUCTION 53,912.
PRICE £807 + PT £169 13s 9d, £976 13s 9d with 4-speed gearbox 1965.

With the Velox name in abeyance there were only Cresta *(right)* and Cresta de luxe *(far right)* to delineate premium-priced models from the rest. Two instead of four headlights, and the absence of wheel trim and cosmetic chrome, set the class distinctions.
***Top:* 2-spoke steering wheel on de luxe, with Powerglide automatic transmission.**

Concept cars: 1966 XVR; 1970 SRV

On show at the 36th Geneva Salon in March 1966, the XVR was largely the creation of David Jones, Vauxhall's charismatic head of design throughout the 1960s. Based on a backbone chassis with a VX4/90 engine and transmission, all independent wishbone suspension and outboard disc brakes, it was intended to show that Luton was sturdily autonomous in design generally and styling in particular. Its low-drag body, aggressive stance, shovel nose, and wrap-round windscreen found an echo in 1968 in the Opel GT whose pop-up headlamps and pointed tail made it something of a collector's item even though no great performer with a 67kW (90bhp) Rekord engine. The XVR had a distinctive interior with recessed dials and switchgear, which Jones was using to test reaction to ideas he had for the later Firenza.

The XVR was shown in Geneva with 10in tyres, a prophetic fashion initiative taken from the latest Formula 1 racing cars. In 1966 the grand prix formula changed, bringing in 3-litre engines, which needed to put more rubber on the road to cope with their enormous power. Goodyear, Dunlop, and Firestone were experimenting with ever-wider and lower-profile tyres to achieve it, and Jones with great prescience incorporated their appearance into XVR.

BODY coupe, 2 seats, 2 doors.
ENGINE 4 cylinders, in-line, front, 81.6mm x 76.2mm; 1595cc; compr: 9.3:1; 55kW (74bhp) net @ 5200rpm; 34.6kW/L (46.4bhp/L); 133Nm (99lb/ft) gross @ 3200rpm.
ENGINE STRUCTURE pushrod overhead valves; chain-driven camshaft; aluminium cylinder head; cast-iron block; 3-bearing crankshaft; two Zenith 34IV downdraught carburettors.
TRANSMISSION rear wheel drive; Borg & Beck 8in sdp clutch; 4-speed gearbox; all synchromesh; hypoid bevel limited slip final drive; ratio 3.9:1.
CHASSIS DETAILS steel backbone chassis; all independent suspension by coil springs and wishbones; telescopic dampers; outboard disc brakes; rack and pinion steering; 10in low profile cross-ply tyres, 13in dia rims.
PRODUCTION 1.

Animated perhaps by the exploits of the Ford GT40, Vauxhall determined to show that it could do something just as exciting "in house" and not be obliged to sub-contract elsewhere. The SRV was largely the work of David Jones's Luton design department, and was first shown at the 1970 Earls Court Motor Show. Sleek, low-built and imposing, the SRV's front doors hinged on the A-post, the rears upwards on the rear quarter roof rails or the nearest the car had to a C-post. With a shrewd prescience (aerodynamic aids were only just making their appearance in grand prix racing in 1970) it included an aerofoil to improve road grip, and electric self-levelling rear suspension. An instrument panel (right) in the driver's door included a manometer to measure air pressure on the car's hull as a means of gauging aerodynamic efficiency. Three turbo gauges measured boost, rpm, and exhaust temperature.

It was alas open season for wedge-shaped concept cars. The SRV was regarded as largely derivative, following Mercedes-Benz's C111 and similarly dramatic designs from Toyota (the EX-7) Pininfarina (Ferrari 512/S, Fiat-Abarth 2000 and others), Michelotti (Matra Laser), and Bertone (Stratos). More soon followed from an ex-Bertone stylist, Giorgetto Giugiaro, who left to form his own studio.

BODY: racing coupe 4 seats, 4 doors.
CHASSIS DETAILS: reinforced glass fibre and carbon fibre body.
DIMENSIONS: length 508cm (200in); width 194cm (76.5in); height 105cm (41.5in).

If the first HA Viva looked like a tentative effort at re-entry to the old Vauxhall Ten market, the HB looked more serious. Here was a fresh approach to styling, the exquisitely proportioned Coke-bottle look a generation ahead of any competitor. The style suited the new Viva's compact size perfectly and the stage was set for a model in many guises that would sell well over half a million inside four years. The pushrod engine was enlarged, there was more room inside, well-located coil spring rear suspension, tuned engines, and it was no longer a poor relation of an Opel. Indeed as the Kadett grew staid the Viva became something of a fashion icon. Customers could ring the changes to suit themselves and personalise their Viva with a choice of engines, transmissions, and trim packages on a single platform within a relatively narrow range of body styles, namely 2-door and, from June 1967, a neat estate. It was something of a market pioneer in this respect a full three years ahead of the Ford Capri. Automatic transmission was available from 1967. A collapsible steering column illustrated Vauxhall's growing commitment to safety in 1970, a 4-door saloon its loyalty to the family market. The Viva's 8% weight increase was balanced by 10% increase in engine capacity and 6.5% more power, so performance was little changed from the HA.

BODY saloon, 2 doors, 4 seats, weight 777kg (1714lb).
ENGINE 4 cylinders, in-line, front, 77.77mm x 61mm; 1159cc; compr: 8.5:1; 35kW (47bhp) @ 5200rpm; 30.2kW/L (40.6bhp/L); 83Nm (62lb/ft) @ 2800rpm.
ENGINE STRUCTURE pushrod overhead valves; chain-driven camshaft; cast iron cylinder head and block; 3-bearing crankshaft; Solex PSEI-7 carburettor.
TRANSMISSION rear wheel drive; Borg & Beck 6.25in clutch with mechanical linkage; 4-speed gearbox; all synchromesh; automatic optional; hypoid bevel final drive; ratio 3.9:1.
CHASSIS DETAILS integral steel structure; independent front suspension by coil springs and wishbones, no anti-roll bar; live rear axle located by lower trailing and diagonal upper arms, coil springs at rear; Vauxhall telescopic dampers; Girling disc front drum rear brakes; Burman or Cam Gears rack and pinion steering; 36L (8 Imp gal, 9.6 US gal) fuel tank; 5.50–12 tubeless tyres, 3.5J rims.
DIMENSIONS wheelbase 243cm (95.75in); track 139.5cm (51in) front and rear; ground clearance 13.3cm (5.25in); turning circle 8.5m (28ft) left, 9.1m (30ft) right; length 410cm (161.5in); width 159cm (62.75in); height 139cm (54.75in).
PERFORMANCE maximum speed 128kph (80mph); 25.7kph (16mph) @ 1000rpm; acceleration 0-96kph (60mph) 19.7sec; 22.2kg/kW (16.5kg/bhp); fuel consumption 7.6-9.7L/100km (29-37mpg).
PRODUCTION 566,391.
PRICE 1966 £508 + PT £118 2s 9d, £626 2s 9d disc brakes £12 10s extra.

Near right: **coil spring front and rear suspension.**
Far right: **Panda car of Bedfordshire and Luton constabulary contrasts with earlier traditional police transport.**

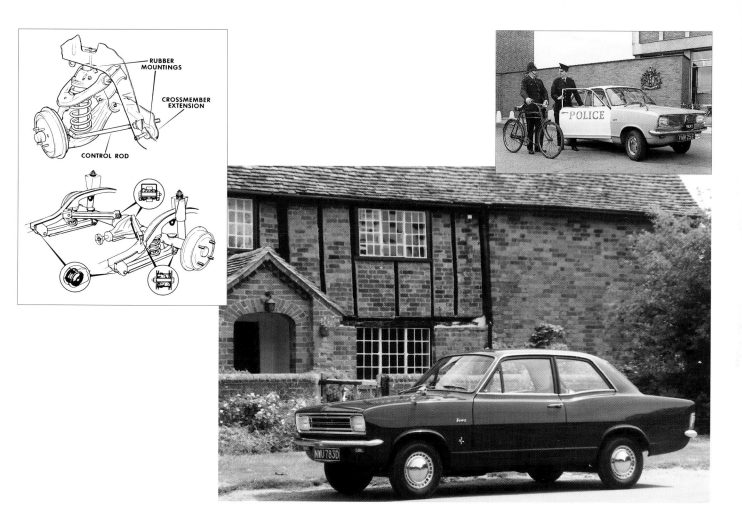

RUBBER
MOUNTINGS

CROSSMEMBER
EXTENSION

CONTROL ROD

POLICE

1967-1970 Viva HB Estate

Before the family hatchback more or less supplanted it, the small estate car exemplified by the Viva was close to the ideal family holdall. At the time of its introduction in 1967 it was available with a choice of three versions of the 1159cc pushrod engine, plus a 1600 overhead cam, and a tuned variant of the 2.0-litre. There were manual and automatic versions of all except the Viva GT which was manual only.

The Vauxhall ohc engine, introduced for the Victor, used the increasingly familiar toothed belt camshaft drive pioneered by Glas, Pontiac, and Cosworth. Its advantages over chain or gear drives included quietness, long mileages without appreciable wear, little need for lubrication or maintenance, easy assembly, and no tensioning device. Yet in 1967 it was a bold move. The cast iron camshaft ran in a detachable die-cast aluminium housing, its five bearings machined directly in the aluminium. A good number of practical engineering problems had to be solved before Europe's first volume production cambelt ohc engine reached production. Its only real demerit in the Viva was a sacrifice of the little car's light, crisp gearshift, and the fuel consumption showed no improvement over the small engine.

BODY estate, 4 seats, 3 doors, weight 870kg (1918lb).
ENGINE 4 cylinders, in-line, front, 77.77mm x 61mm; 1159cc; compr: 8.5:1; 44.7kW (60bhp) @ 5600rpm; 38.6kW/L (51.8bhp/L); 85.8Nm (64lb/ft) @ 3600rpm. 51.5kW (69bhp) @ 5800rpm, 44.4kW/L (59.5bhp/L); 88.5Nm (66lb/ft) @ 4200rpm. 85.73mm x 69.24mm, 1599cc, ohc, 62kW (83bhp) gross, 54kW (72bhp) net @ 5800rpm or 5600rpm;33.6kW/L (45bhp/L); 121Nm (90lb/ft) gross, 111Nm (83lb/ft) net @ 3200rpm or 2200rpm.
ENGINE STRUCTURE pushrod overhead valves 1159cc, 3-bearing crankshaft; overhead camshaft 1599cc; thin-wall cast iron cylinder head and block; 5-bearing crankshaft; Zenith 36IV carburettor.
TRANSMISSION rear wheel drive; 7.5in sdp Borg & Beck diaphragm spring mechanically operated clutch; 4-speed, all synch; automatic optional; hypoid bevel final drive; ratio 4.125:1.
CHASSIS DETAILS integral steel structure; ifs by coil springs and wishbones, no anti-roll bar; live rear axle located by lower trailing and diagonal upper arms, coil springs at rear; Vauxhall telescopic dampers; Girling disc front drum rear brakes; Burman or Cam Gears rack and pinion steering; 36L (8 Imp gal, 9.6 US gal) fuel tank; 5.50 – 12 tubeless tyres, 3.5J rims.
DIMENSIONS wheelbase 243cm (95.75in); track 129.5cm (51in) front and rear; ground clearance 13.3cm (5.25in); turning circle 8.5m (28ft) left, 9.1m (30ft) right; length 410cm (161.5in); width 159cm (62.75in); height 139cm (54.75in).
PERFORMANCE max 141kph (88mph); 23.8kph (14.8mph) @ 1000rpm; 0-96kph (60mph) 15.3sec; 19.5kg/kW (14.5kg/bhp) for 60bhp; 12.3-14.5L/100km (19.5-23mpg).
PRODUCTION 78,296.
PRICE £680 + PT £190 19s 6d, £870 19s 6d.

Right: facia of Viva de luxe with full-width parcel shelf and padded covers.

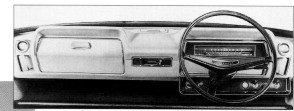

1967-1968 Viva HB90, Brabham Viva

Jack Brabham's connections with General Motors were by no means tenuous. The Formula 1 cars which brought him the world constructors' championships in 1966 and 1967 were powered by the Australian-developed Repco whose origins lay in an American Buick V-8. They also won him and Denny Hulme the 1966 and 1967 drivers' titles.

Yet the little Vivas with cosmetic bonnet stripes and up-rated 1159cc engines were no sports cars even though they were homologated with the FIA for Group 2 racing. There were two uprated models, the 90 and the SL90 with optional Brabham fittings. Engine modifications included a high-lift camshaft and a long curved aluminium manifold linking a side-draught carburettor to the vertical inlet ports. The compression ratio was raised, the final drive ratio lowered from 3.89 to 4.125:1, the same as the HA Viva. Peak torque was achieved 800rpm further up the rev band and there was a free-flow exhaust with three silencers and polished end-trim all at a price only £37 10s (plus £10-£12 for fitting) over the standard SL90. The changes raised its top speed by 4mph. An SL90 was already about 7mph faster than the standard Viva. The most marked improvement was in acceleration above 3000rpm and the engine could be taken to 7000rpm without undue stress.

BODY saloon, 4 seats, 2 doors, weight 777kg (1714lb).
ENGINE 4 cylinders, in-line, front, 77.77mm x 61mm; 1159cc; compr: 9.0:1; 50.7kW (68bhp) @ 5800rpm; 43.7kW/L (58.7bhp/L); 88.5Nm (66lb/ft) @ 3800rpm.
ENGINE STRUCTURE pushrod overhead valves; chain-driven camshaft; cast iron cylinder head and block; 3-bearing crankshaft; 2 Stromberg 150CD variable choke carburettors; coil ignition; water-cooled.
TRANSMISSION rear wheel drive; Borg & Beck 6.25in clutch with mechanical linkage; 4-speed gearbox; all synchromesh; hypoid bevel final drive; ratio 4.125:1.
CHASSIS DETAILS integral steel structure; independent front suspension by coil springs and wishbones; live rear axle located by lower trailing and diagonal upper arms, coil springs at rear; Vauxhall telescopic dampers; Girling disc front drum rear brakes; Burman or Cam Gears rack and pinion steering; 36L (8 Imp gal, 9.6 US gal) fuel tank; low profile wide-rim tubeless tyres.
DIMENSIONS wheelbase 243cm (95.75in); track 129.5cm (51in) front and rear; ground clearance 13.3cm (5.25in); turning circle 8.5m (28ft) left, 9m (30ft) right; length 410cm (161.5in); width 159cm (62.75in); height 139cm (54.75in).
PERFORMANCE maximum speed 144.5kph (90mph); 23.8kph (14.85mph) @ 1000rpm; acceleration 0-96kph (60mph) 14.4sec; 15.3kg/kW (11.4kg/bhp); fuel consumption 8.8-10.9L/100km (26-32mpg).
PRODUCTION 78,293 all HB90.
PRICE 1968 basic Viva £606, de luxe £653, Viva 90 £690, SL £699, SL90 £736, prices include Purchase Tax.

Right: Jack Brabham with Braham Viva de luxe 90.

1966-1972 Viscount

Once the Velox had been discarded and Cresta made sole 6-cylinder, the new prestige model was the Viscount. It was given a fabric-covered roof, walnut veneer and leather interior, reclining seats, electric windows, picnic tables, reading lights, four headlights, little coronets on the door trim, Powerglide 2-speed automatic as standard, all the stuff of the luxury car trade at a premium price. A 4-speed manual gearbox was available with an £86 reduction on the price. Sound damping was improved, there were bigger wheels and wider tyres, and heated rear window for one of the last essentially transatlantic 6-cylinder Vauxhalls. The extra cost over the standard Cresta was a formidable £400, so although the cheaper version outsold it by nearly eight to one, the Viscount had the appointments of a top grade executive car. The extra equipment accounted for an additional 100kg (220lb) weight.

In October 1970 a GM 3-speed automatic replaced the 2-speed Powerglide with a floor control lever. The 2-speed was never quite up to the mark. It was satisfactory on large V-8s with an abundance of power and torque, but overtaking was either sluggish or noisy if the low ratio was held. The extra weight affected acceleration against the Cresta and the fuel consumption.

BODY saloon, 5 seats, 4 doors, weight 1397kg (3080lb).
ENGINE 6 cylinders, in-line, front, 92.08mm x 82.55mm; 3294cc; compr: 8.5:1 (7.0 optional); 89.5kW (120bhp) @ 4700rpm; 236Nm (176lb/ft) @ 2400rpm.
ENGINE STRUCTURE pushrod overhead valves; chain-driven camshaft; cast iron cylinder head and block; 4-bearing crankshaft; Zenith 42Wiat carburettor.
TRANSMISSION rear wheel drive; optional 4-speed gearbox; all synchromesh; 2-speed automatic standard; final drive ratio 3.46:1.
CHASSIS DETAILS integral steel structure; independent front suspension by wishbones, coil springs, and anti-roll bar; live axle, inclined tie-rod, and semi-elliptic leaf springs at rear; Vauxhall telescopic dampers; disc front drum rear brakes with vacuum servo and inertia valve for rear brakes; Burman recirculating ball PAS; 68L (15 Imp gal, 18 US gal) fuel tank; 7.00-14 tyres, 5J rims.
DIMENSIONS wheelbase 274cm (107.75in); front track 140cm (55.25in), 143cm (56.25in) rear; ground clearance 15cm (6in); turning circle 10.4m (34ft); length 478cm (188.25in); width 178cm (70in); height 145cm (57in).
PERFORMANCE maximum speed 157cm (98mph); 34.4kph (21.4mph) @ 1000rpm; acceleration 0-96kph (60mph) 15.5sec; 15.6kg/kW (11.6kg/bhp); fuel consumption 12.8-17.7L/100km (16-22mpg).
PRODUCTION 7025.
PRICE 1966 £1205 + PT £277 17s 4d, £1482 17s 4d, radio £22 7s 3d. Retractable aerial £2 27s 3d, fog lamps £3 10s each.

Right: 1971 PC Viscount
Far right: **front compartment of Viscount had luxurious individual reclining seats upholstered in soft, rich hide, with deep-pile carpet and burr walnut veneer.**

173

1967-1972 Victor FD 1600, 2000

A hemi-head overhead camshaft engine gave Vauxhall a technical advantage in one of the most stylish cars of its time. Following the Coke-bottle silhouette of the Viva that had been such a success, the Victor also adopted rack and pinion steering, and even in its most basic form could reach 145kph (90mph). An estate car version appeared in May 1968 and the GM Strasbourg automatic was added in 1970 when the model name became Victor Super. Inclined at 45 degrees, the engine featured a short shaft for the distributor drive, and a rigid short-throw crankshaft, safe according to John Alden chief engineer to 9000rpm. Thinwall casting techniques newly developed in the United States (which had rendered the famous aluminium Buick V-8 obsolete) were incorporated.

Some suspension features were shared with the Viva such as the rubber-mounted sub-frame for the front suspension. At the back instead of the Viva's four inclined links there were five in the form of parallel trailing arms plus a Panhard rod. Roll height was raised by about 6.4in (2.5in), cutting body lean by 20%. Front track was 7.6cm (3in) wider than the 101's, wheelbase and length were both 5cm (2in) longer, and rear overhang reduced to move the passenger compartment rearwards following styling trends.

BODY saloon, 5 seats, 4 doors, 1600: 1053kg (2321lb), 2000: 1066kg (2350lb).
ENGINE 4 cylinders, in-line, front, 85.73mm x 69.24mm; 1599cc; compr: 8.5:1; 62kW (83bhp) gross @ 5800rpm, 54kW (72bhp) net @ 5600rpm; 33.6kW/L (45bhp/L); 121Nm (90lb/ft) @ 3200rpm. 95.25mm x 69.24mm; 1975cc; 77.6kW (104bhp) gross @ 5800rpm, 65.7kW (88bhp) net @ 5500rpm; 33.3kW/L (44.6bhp/L); 158Nm (118lb/ft) @ 3200rpm.
ENGINE STRUCTURE overhead valves; overhead camshaft; cast chromidium iron cylinder head and block; 5-bearing crankshaft; Zenith 36IV carburettor.
TRANSMISSION rear wheel drive; sdp diaphragm spring clutch; 3 or 4-speed; all synchromesh; overdrive opt; automatic opt Borg Warner Model 35 later GM; hypoid bevel final drive; 1600 4.125:1, 2000 3.9:1.
CHASSIS DETAILS integral steel structure; ifs by wishbones, coil springs and anti-roll bar; live axle coil, springs, parallel trailing arms and Panhard rod at rear; telescopic dampers; drum front and rear 1600, disc and drum 2000, vacuum servo; rack and pinion; 54.5L (12 Imp gal, 14.4 US gal); 5.60-13 low profile cross-ply tyres 1600, 6.2-13 2000 4.5J rims.
DIMENSIONS wheelbase 305cm (102in); track 137cm (54in), front track 2000 138cm (54.6in); ground clearance 16.5cm (6.5in); turning circle 10.2m (33ft 4in); length 449cm (176.7in) 449cm; width 170cm (66.9in); height 1600 133cm (52.4in), 2000 131cm (51.7in).
PERFORMANCE maximum speed 2000 152.5kph (95mph); 26.2kph (16.3mph) @ 1000rpm 1600, 26.3kph (16.4mph) 2000; acceleration 2000 0-60mph 14.0sec; 17kg/kW (12.7kg/bhp) 1600, 16.2kg/kW (12.1kg/bhp) 2000; fuel consumption 10.5-12.8L/100km (22-27mpg).
PRODUCTION 198,085 including Ventora.
PRICE 1600 £819, 2000 £739 + PT £171 6s 0d, £910 6s 0d. 4-speed gearbox £14 10s 0d extra.

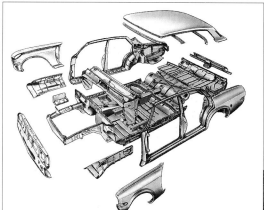

Top: integral body
construction giving
strength and rigidity with
durability and lightness.
Right: 3 generations
of Victor. 1968 2000 *(front)*,
with 1964 de luxe *(back left)*
and 1967 101 de luxe
(back right).

1968-1970 Viva HB 1600, 2000GT

The GT label was a mixed blessing. Matt black bonnet, air scoops that scooped air to nothing in particular, bright wheel trims, and four exhaust pipe stubs did little for the car's credibility never mind the owner's. Yet the 2.0-litre Viva GT had nothing to apologise for. Despite strong understeer it handled well, it was well proportioned, and it nearly managed 96kph (60mph) in the 10sec that traditionally distinguished the lively from the lazy. Although 160kph (100mph) may not sound fast to generations accustomed to its attainment by the humblest hatchback, it was quite quick in 1968.

The equivalent Ford Escort was a good deal faster, but it was essentially a detuned competition car, whereas the Viva was a speeded-up road car with the new Victor's inclined-four ohc five main bearing two-carburettor engine. The ride was a shade wallowy for a sports car and the price quite high, within £100 of the large luxurious new Ventora 3.3-litre six. Among the first Vauxhalls to leave the factory with radial-ply tyres as standard, it took the firm a little closer to the sporting driver than any time since the 1920s. The GT label was short-lived, and the model reappeared as the 1600SL without its distinctive black bonnet in the HC series.

BODY saloon, 4 seats, 4 doors 1600, 2 doors GT, 925kg (2038lb).
ENGINE 4 cylinders, in-line, front, 85.73mm x 69.24mm; 1599cc; compr: 8.5:1; 62kW (83bhp) gross @ 5800rpm, 54kW (72bhp) net @ 5600rpm; 33.4kW/L (45bhp/L); 121Nm (90lbft) gross @ 3200rpm, 111Nm (83lbft net) @ 2200rpm. 95.25mm x 69.24mm; 1975cc; 83.5kW (112bhp) gross @ 5400rpm, 78kW (104bhp) net @ 5600rpm; 39.5kW/L (52.7bhp/L); 170Nm (127lb/ft) gross @ 3400rpm, 157Nm (117lb/ft) net @ 3400rpm.
ENGINE STRUCTURE belt-driven overhead cam; cast iron cyl head and block; 5-bearing crankshaft; Zenith 36IV downdraught carburettor 1600; two Zenith 175 CD-25 GT.
TRANSMISSION rear wheel drive; 7.5in sdp Borg & Beck diaphragm spring clutch 1600; 8in Laycock GT; 4-speed gearbox; all synchromesh; Borg Warner automatic 1600 option; hypoid bevel final drive; ratio 3.9:1.
CHASSIS DETAILS integral steel structure; ifs by coil springs, wishbone, and anti-roll bar; live rear axle located by parallel links, coil springs, Panhard rod GT; telescopic dampers; servo-assisted Girling disc and drum brakes; rack and pinion; 36.4L (8.0 Imp gal, 9.6 US gal); 6.2-12 tyres, 4in rims 1600, 155SR–12 radial-ply Avon tyres GT, 4.5in rims.
DIMENSIONS wheelbase 243cm (95.75in); track 130cm (51in) front and rear; ground clearance 13.3cm (5.25in); turning circle 8.5m (28ft) left 9.1m (30ft) right; length 410cm (161.5in); width 159.4cm (62.75in); height 139cm (54.75in).
PERFORMANCE Maximum speed 148kph (92mph) 1600, 160.5kph (100mph) GT; 25.7kph (16.0mph) @ 1000rpm 1600, 27.3kph (17.0mph) @ 1000rpm GT; acceleration 0-60mph 14.4sec 1600, 10.7sec GT; 17.1kg/kW (12.8kg/bhp) 1600; fuel consumption 11.7-12.8L/100km (22-24mpg) 1600, 10.9-13.5L/100km (21-26mpg) GT.
PRODUCTION 18,123.
PRICE £657 + PT 203 0s 10d, £860 0s 10d. 1600 £830 + PT £232 12s 10d, £1062 12s 10d.

Right: Shaw and Kilburn
Viva Special, developed
for racing in collaboration
with WB Blydenstein,
testing at Snetterton.

1968-1975 Ventora, Victor 3300

The temptation to squeeze a 3.3-litre Cresta engine under the FD Victor's shapely bonnet proved too much. The pushrod 6-cylinder was something of an antique (it was designed in the 1950s although well over-square) compared with the FD's usual 5-bearing overhead cam 4-cylinder, but it was smooth and quiet even though it never got much above 160kph (100mph). The estate version was known as Victor 3300, and from 1970 to 1972 Ventora with the FE's long wheelbase was suffixed "II".

With 92kW (123bhp) against the Victor 2000's 66kW (88bhp) and only 92kg (203lb) extra, a rather livelier turn of speed might have been expected, but using the Cresta's 3.45:1 axle instead of the Victor's 3.9:1 the gearing was high. Coil springs and dampers were beefed-up, there was a larger diameter front anti-roll bar, and the brakes were equipped with Cresta calipers. The extra cylinders stretched forward into the engine bay where the extra weight affected the handling and the steering was not so responsive as on the Victor. The Ventora II had rosewood facia and console, decorative door casings, and deeper pile carpets. The seat facings were brushed nylon and at the back of the car were a satin-finish trim panel and chrome exhaust pipe finisher.

BODY saloon, estate, 4 seats, 4 doors; 1158kg (2553lb), estate 1124kg (2478lb).
ENGINE 6 cylinders, in-line, front, 92.08mm x 82.55mm; 3294cc; compr: 8.5:1; 92kW (123bhp) net @ 4600rpm; 27.9kW/L (37.3bhp/L); 236Nm (176lb/ft) net @ 2400rpm.
ENGINE STRUCTURE pushrod ohv; chain-driven camshaft; cast iron cylinder head and block; 4-bearing crank; Zenith 42WIAT downdraught carb.
TRANSMISSION rear wheel drive; Borg & Beck 8.5in diaphragm spring clutch; 4-speed gearbox; all synchromesh; Laycock overdrive, 2-speed Powerglide automatic optional; hypoid bevel final drive; ratio 3.45:1.
CHASSIS DETAILS integral steel structure; ifs by wishbones and coil springs, anti-roll bar, live axle, coil springs, radius arms and Panhard rod at rear; telescopic dampers; servo-assisted disc front drum rear Girling brakes; Burman or Cam Gears rack and pinion steering; 55L (12 Imp gal, 14.4 US gal) fuel tank; 165-13 radial-ply tubeless tyres, 4.5in rims.
DIMENSIONS wheelbase 259cm (103in); front track 139cm (54.6in); 137cm (54in) rear; ground clearance 15.5cm (6.1in); turning circle 10.2m (33ft 4in); length 449cm (176.7in); width 170cm (65.9in); height 133cm (52.5in).
PERFORMANCE maximum speed 164kph (102mph); 31.3kph (19.5mph) @ 1000rpm, overdrive top 40.1kph (25.0mph); acceleration 0-60mph 10.5sec; saloon 12.6kg/kW (9.4kg/bhp), estate 12.2kg/kW (9.1kg/bhp);12.3-14.1L/100km (20-23mpg).
PRODUCTION 25,185.
PRICE £895 + PT £206 16s 6d, £1101 16s 6d. Vinyl roof £9 10s 6d, radio £27 16s 0d, fog and spot lights £11 2s 6d, reverse lights £3 14s 6d, wing mirrors £3 19s 0d, cigar lighter £1 12s 0d extra.

The revival of the VX4/90 title, which had been in abeyance for two years, neatly avoided using GT as a label for the speediest Victor. Grand Touring was devalued through over-use and attracted unwelcome attention from insurers. Vauxhall nevertheless produced a car that deserved the title more than most. The VX's Rostyle wheels furnished it with a racy identity at a time when wheel trim tended to be shiny chrome and turbo-decoration, and well before alloys became fashionable.

Inside the car the trend was towards black leather, imposing dials preferably sunk in tunnels in the facia and a central console that finally cast out that 1940s aberration, the bench seat. A generation of drivers who had lolled and swayed on benches sank thankfully into bucket seats from which they could enjoy the newly discovered superior handling of their VX4/90.

Still no racer, it lacked the crisp handling and competitive edge of its competitors. It could still only just manage 160kph (100mph) and even with Vauxhall's now well-established affection for rack and pinion steering and five-link rear axles, the emphasis was more on ride than handling. The VX4/90 exemplified speed with style and as little discomfort as possible.

BODY saloon, 4 seats, 4 doors, 1102kg (2430lb).
ENGINE 4 cylinders, in-line, front, 96.25mm x 69.24mm; 1975cc; compr: 8.5:1; 83.5kW (112bhp) gross @ 5400rpm, 77.6kW (104bhp) net @ 5600rpm; 39.3kW/L (52.7bhp/L); 170Nm (127lbft) gross, 157Nm (117lb/ft) net @ 3400rpm.
ENGINE STRUCTURE belt-driven ohc; cast iron cylinder head and block; 5-bearing crankshaft; 2 Zenith 175 CD-25 variable choke carburettors.
TRANSMISSION rear wheel drive; Borg & Beck 8in sdp diaphragm spring clutch; 4-speed, all synchro; Laycock de Normanville overdrive optional; hypoid bevel final drive; ratio 3.9:1.

CHASSIS DETAILS integral steel structure; ifs by wishbones, coil springs, and anti-roll bar, live axle located by 4 trailing links and Panhard rod, coil springs; telescopic dampers; Girling 10.3in disc front, 9in drum rear brakes with vacuum servo; Burman or Cam Gears rack and pinion steering; 55L (12 Imp gal, 14.4 US gal) fuel tank; 6.9–13 Goodyear Grand Prix tyres, 5J rims, 175/70 radial-ply tyres optional.
DIMENSIONS wheelbase 262cm (103in); track 138cm (54.25in); ground clearance 16.5cm (6.5in); turning circle 9.1m (30ft); length 448cm (176.25in); width 170cm (67in); height 140cm (55.25in).
PERFORMANCE maximum speed 162kph (101mph); 27.3kph (17.0mph) @ 1000rpm, 35kph (21.8mph) overdrive; acceleration 12.4sec; 14.2kg/kW (10.6kg/bhp); fuel consumption 10-13.5L/100km (21-28mpg).
PRODUCTION 14,277.
PRICE £970 +PT £283 8s 1d, £1203 8s 1d (1970).

Vauxhall VX4/90.

The HC Viva dropped the curvy Coke-bottle line and appeared with two distinct engine specifications, pushrod and overhead cam. The mechanical platform was hardly altered, some body panels were carried over, and the opportunity was taken to make detail engineering changes such as a shorter nose on the differential housing. This had been long to make the propellor shaft short and vibrationless, but stiffening the pinion shaft inside the diff casing produced better results. The widely copied four-link rear suspension was retained. The basic HC was 1159cc with 36.5kW (49bhp), or the 90 with 44.7kW (60bhp). There were three trim options De Luxe and SL for saloons and estates and Standard for the 2-door. All had alternators (dynamos were long gone), seat belts, and one car a week was subjected to a test programme at the new 700-acre proving ground Vauxhall had inaugurated at Lidlington later known as Millbrook.

An inch extra in wheelbase, length and width made the Viva more grown-up, increasing body-in-white weight by some 14kg (30lb), extra equipment such as dual-circuit brakes and additional sound-damping accounting for a further 25 making about 25kg (55lb). Power to restore the performance was supplied by bigger valves and 13in wheels instead of 12in raised overall gearing.

BODY: saloon, 4 seats, 2/4 doors, weight 1800lb (817kg); estate, 3 doors.
ENGINE: 4 cylinders, in-line, front, 77.8mm x 61.0mm; 1159cc; compr: 8.5:1; 36.5kW (49bhp) @ 5300rpm, 31.5kW/L (42.3bhp/L); 85Nm (63lb/ft) @ 2900rpm. 3800rpm. 45kW (60bhp DIN) @ 5600rpm, 38.8kW/L (52bhp/L); 87Nm (64lb/ft) @ 3600rpm. From 1972 81mm x 61mm; 1256cc; 40.3kW (54bhp) @ 5200rpm, 32kW/L (43bhp/L); 88Nm (65lb/ft DIN) @ 2600rpm.
ENGINE STRUCTURE: pushrod ohv; chain-driven camshaft; cast iron cylinder head and block; 3-bearing crank; Zenith 301Z or 150CDS carb.
TRANSMISSION: rear wheel drive; Borg & Beck 6.5in diaphragm spring clutch; 4-speed gearbox; all synchromesh; 3-speed GM automatic optional; hypoid bevel final drive; ratio 4.125:1.
CHASSIS DETAILS: unitary steel structure; ifs by coil springs and wishbones, no anti-roll bar; live rear axle located by lower trailing and diagonal upper arms, coil springs at rear; Vauxhall telescopic dampers; Girling disc front drum rear brakes; Burman or Cam Gears rack and pinion steering; 36L (8 Imp gal, 9.6 US gal) fuel tank; 5.50–13 cross-ply tubeless tyres, 4in rims.
DIMENSIONS: wheelbase 246cm (97in); track 131cm (51.4in); ground clearance 12.6cm (4.9in); turning circle 10m (31ft); length 411cm (162in); width 164cm (64.7in); height 135cm (53.1in).
PERFORMANCE: max 126kph (78.3mph); 25.4kph (15.8mph) @ 1000rpm; 18-22.4kg/kW (13.6-16.7kg/bhp); 0-96kph (60mph) 20.6sec; 7.6-9.4L/100km (30-37mpg).
PRODUCTION: 640,863 all HC.
PRICE: at introduction including PT £783, De Luxe £851, 4-door £884, estate £949, 90 engine + £40. SL £963, SL 4-door £996, SL estate £1055.

Right: 2-door Viva.
Far right: De Luxe interior.

183

The power of the overhead camshaft Vivas more than made up for the small increase in weight that came with the somewhat bland new style with its straight and level waistline and increased room inside. Wind and road noise were suppressed, the ride improved, and the facia arranged more sensibly.

The 1.6 engine grew to 1.8-litre and carried forward well to the slightly bigger body, the GT label was discarded and by 1972 there was a 2300cc engine as well. The estate's fastback styling had no aerodynamic advantage, although in an era of Lancia, Reliant, and Volvo high speed estates it looked racy enough. The lighter saloons showed a small advantage in acceleration as well. Driving had a large influence on fuel consumption of the 2300. Making full use of its extremely lively turn of speed brought it to 13L/100km (21.5mpg).

On 20 July 1971 the millionth Viva was produced at Luton and chassis no 1,000.001 was produced at Vauxhall's Ellesmere Port plant. By 1973 the overhead camshaft Vivas were being tested at the new 700 acre Millbrook facility with its huge 2-mile motorway-standard speed saucer and 1.5 miles of country roads. Vivas were exported to Canada with left hand drive and Pontiac Firenza badges.

BODY saloon, 4 seats, 2 doors, weight 948kg (2090lb); 4 doors, 965kg (2127lb); estate, 3 doors, 990kg (2183lb); 2300 saloon 960kg (2116lb); estate 975kg (2150lb).
ENGINE 4 cylinders, in-line, front, inclined 45deg, 85.72mm x 76.2mm; 1759cc; compr: 8.5:1; 57kW (77bhp) @ 5200rpm, 32.6kW/L (44bhp/L); 131.4Nm (97lb/ft) @ 3000rpm. 65.6kW (88bhp) @ 5800rpm, 133Nm (99lb/ft) @ 3500rpm. 97.54 x 76.2; 2279cc; 82kW (110bhp) @ 5200rpm, 36kW/L (48bhp/L); 187.8Nm (140lb/ft) @ 3200rpm.
ENGINE STRUCTURE ohv; ohc; ci cyl head, block; 5-bg crank; Zenith 36NE. 2300 2 Zenith 175 CD-2S.
TRANSMISSION rwd; Borg & Beck 6.5in diaphragm spring clutch; 4-speed all synchromesh; 3-speed GM auto optional; hypoid bevel final drive; 3.7:1, 3.45:1 auto 2300, 3.34:1.
CHASSIS DETAILS unitary steel structure; ifs by coil springs and wishbones, no anti-roll bar; live rear axle located by lower trailing and diag upper arms, coil springs rear; Vauxhall telesc dampers; 2300 rear anti-roll bar; Girling disc front drum rear brakes; Burman or Cam Gears rack and pinion; 36L (8 Imp gal, 9.6 US gal) tank; 155–13 radial-ply tubeless tyres, 4J rims. 2300 175/70 HR 13.
DIMENSIONS wheelbase 246cm (97in); track 131cm (51.4in); ground clearance 12.6cm (4.9in); turning circle 10m (31ft); length 411cm (162in); width 164cm (64.7in); height 135cm (53.1in).
PERFORMANCE maximum speed 161kph (100.3mph); 28.4kph (17.7mph) @ 1000rpm; 0-100kph 13.6sec; 26-36kg/kW (19.5-27kg/bhp); 10.8 L/100km (26.2mpg). 2300 max 168kph (104.7mph); 30.9kph (19.2mph) @ 1000rpm, 0-100 11.4sec; 12.1L/100km (23.3mpg).
PRODUCTION 640,863 Viva HC.
PRICE 1972 2300SL £1219 incl PT.

Right: **1000 special edition 1972 Viva X14 had automatic transmission and 1800ohc of the newly-announced Victor.**

1971-1973 Firenza

A year behind the HC Viva saloon, the stylish Firenza had the HB's 246cm (97in) wheelbase and was intended to compete with its arch-rival the Ford Capri. The first short-lived version launched in May 1971 had a range of engines starting with the original and somewhat feeble 1159cc pushrod with 46kW (62bhp). Despite the lightweight look it was 29.5kg (65lb) heavier than its saloon equivalent, so the 1600 engine was offered as an option with a single downdraught Zenith 36 1V carburettor providing 52kW (70bhp) DIN @ 5100rpm and 121Nm (90lb/ft) torque at 2500rpm. For the 1972 model year the pushrod engine was quickly bored out to 1256cc but the car's reputation was already sullied.

With hindsight it was probably badly treated. The press always saw it as slightly effete, which it scarcely deserved. The Firenza was well proportioned, crisply designed, and well furnished with individual seats upholstered in Ambla. Its misfortune was that the ohc cars were too noisy and the quiet, smooth, smaller engined ones too slow. It was a splendid touring car with a huge boot and although the rear seats were a tight fit for two adults they accommodated children easily. De luxe Firenzas had square headlights, GTs four round ones.

BODY coupe, 4 seats, 2 doors, weight 846kg (1865lb), de luxe 856kg (1888lb) SL.
ENGINE 4 cylinders, in-line, front, 77.77mm x 60.96mm; 1159cc; compr: 8.5:1; 46kW (62bhp) @ 5500rpm; 40kW/L (53.5bhp/L); 87Nm (65lb/ft) @ 3800rpm. 1256cc, 39.5kW (53bhp) @ 5200rpm, 87Nm (65lb/ft) @ 2600rpm.
ENGINE STRUCTURE pushrod overhead valves; chain-driven camshaft; cast iron cylinder head and block; 3-bearing crankshaft; Zenith 150-CD carburettor.
TRANSMISSION rear wheel drive; rear wheel drive; Borg & Beck 6.5in diaphragm spring clutch; 4-speed gearbox; all synchromesh; 3-speed GM automatic optional; hypoid bevel final drive; ratio 4.125:1.
CHASSIS DETAILS unitary steel structure; independent front suspension by coil springs and wishbones, anti-roll bar; live rear axle located by lower trailing and diagonal upper arms, coil springs; Vauxhall telescopic dampers; Girling disc front drum rear brakes with vacuum servo; Burman or Cam Gears rack and pinion steering; 55L (12 Imp gal, 14.4 US gal) fuel tank; 6.20–13 cross-ply tubeless tyres, 4J rims. 6.50-13 optional low-profile cross-ply or 155-13 radial-ply.
DIMENSIONS wheelbase 246cm (97in); front track 135cm (53in), 131cm (52in) rear; ground clearance 13.5cm (5.3in); turning circle 9.6m (31.5ft); length 414cm (163in); width 164cm (65in); height 133cm (52in).
PERFORMANCE maximum speed 135kph (84mph); 25kph (15.5mph) @ 1000rpm; acceleration 0-100kph (62mph) 22sec; 18.4kg/kW (13.6kg/bhp); fuel consumption 8-11 L/100km (25.6-35.3mpg).
PRODUCTION 18,352 all Firenza.
PRICE £1017 incl PT, SL £1099.

Far right: demonstration of step-in access to **Firenza**.

1971-1973 Firenza ohc

The Viva GT developed into a satisfactory if short-lived model. Its heirs were the overhead camshaft versions of the Firenza, of which the fastest at launch in May 1971 was the 2000SL with two Stromberg carburettors. Its high axle ratio provided easy top-gear cruising on the motorways proliferating throughout Europe, so that 160kph (100mph) represented 5184rpm, well within the engine's capacity. The 2000's acceleration and top speed still fell short of its principal rival although fuel consumption was better. The Firenza's ride was now more absorbent and body roll reduced. Contemporary testers were unstinting in their praise of the five-link rear axle which in many respects was ahead of its time, and lent support to the contention that a well-located live axle was still superior to an indifferent independent set-up.

The 2279cc Firenza was a vigorous performer and its seven-dial instrument was in tune with Vauxhall policy of appealing to younger buyers. Dealer Team Vauxhall, near enough a works team, assuaged General Motors' scepticism about motor racing. By 1975 mainstream Firenzas were being phased out, and the rump of bodyshells was sold off as the Viva E (for Economy) with the standard 1256cc engine, at £1399 undercutting the new Chevette and the basic Viva saloon.

BODY coupe, 4 seats, 2 doors, weight 964kg (2126lb).
ENGINE 4 cyls, in-line, incl 45deg, front, 85.72mm x 76.2mm; 1759cc; cr 8.5:1; 58kW (78bhp) @ 5200rpm; 33kW/L (44bhp/L); 131Nm (98lb/ft) @ 3000rpm. 95.25mm x 69.24mm, 1975cc, 78kW (104bhp) @ 5600rpm, 39.5kW/L (52.7bhp/L), 157Nm (117lb/ft) @ 3400rpm. 97.54mm x 76.2mm, 2279cc, 82kW (110bhp) @ 5200rpm, 36kW/L (48bhp/L); 189Nm (141lb/ft) @ 3000rpm.
ENGINE STRUCTURE ohv; belt-driven ohc; cast iron cyl head and block; 5-bearing crank; 1759cc Zenith 36NE, 1975cc 2 Stromberg 175CD-2S carbs, 2279cc 2 Zenith 175CD-2S.
TRANSMISSION rear wheel drive; Laycock diaphragm spring clutch; 4-speed, all synch; auto opt; hypoid bevel final drive; ration 3.7:1, 3.45:1 automatic. 1975cc and 2279cc 3.45:1.
CHASSIS DETAILS unitary steel structure; ifs by coil springs and wishbones, anti-roll bars front and rear; live rear axle located by lower trailing and diagonal upper arms, coil springs; Vauxhall telescopic dampers; Girling disc front, drum rear with vacuum servo brakes; Burman or Cam Gears rack and pinion; 55L (12 Imp gal, 14.4 US gal); 1975cc 165HR-13 radial ply tubeless tyres.
DIMENSIONS wheelbase 246cm (97in); front track 135cm (53in), 131cm (51.5in) rear; ground clearance 13.5cm (5.3in); turning circle 9.6m (31.5ft); length 414cm (163in); width 164cm (65in); height 133cm (52in).
PERFORMANCE 1975cc maximum speed 160.5kph (100mph); 31kph (19.3mph) @ 1000rpm; 0-96kph (60mph) 10.6sec; 12.4kg/kW (9.3kg/bhp); 10.5-13.5L/100km (21-27mpg).
PRODUCTION 18,352 all Firenza.
PRICE 2000SL 1971 £1282 incl PT, auto £104, radial-ply tyres and Rostyle wheels £33.

Right: Gerry Marshall in Dealer Team Firenza 2000SL. *Far right:* double coachline on 2000SL, with Vinyl roof an extra-cost SL option.

Vauxhall's fifth Victor was the biggest yet. An increase in wheelbase from the FD's 259cm (102in) to 267cm (105in) brought the simultaneous introduction in February 1972 of the Victor, Victor SL, Victor Estate, VX4/90, and Ventora. It was a classic example of building an entire range of cars on a single platform, in this case the Opel Rekord's, long before such a thing became industry jargon.

Although it was in many respects a development of the FD, with enlarged versions of the 45 degree sloper 4-cylinder engines, it needed more power to cope with the increased weight and keep up with the competition. In both cases the stroke was increased to 7.6cm (3in), making the 1599cc unit 1759cc, with the same cylinder bore of 8.57cm (3.375in). The larger engine's stroke was similarly increased, which meant both shared the same 5-bearing crankshaft, and the block was bored out from 95.2 to 97.5mm giving a capacity of 2279cc.

There were three versions of the engine in the Victor range, the smallest 1759cc for the Victor de luxe, 2279cc Victor SL (and an option for the de luxe) with a twin-carburettor

BODY saloon, 4 seats, 4 doors; weight Victor 1109kg (2445lb), SL 1116kg (2460lb), VX4/90 1178kg (2595lb), Ventora 1254kg (2765lb); estate, 5 doors.
ENGINE 4 cylinders in-line, inclined 45deg, front, 85.7mm x 76.2mm; 1759cc; compr: 8.5:1; 57kW (77bhp) @ 5200rpm; 32.6kW/L (43.8bhp/L); 130Nm (97lb/ft) @ 3000rpm. SL and VX 97.5 x 76.2, 2279cc, SL 74.6kW (100bhp) @ 5200rpm, 32.7kW/L (43.9bhp/L), VX 82kW (110bhp) @ 5200rpm, SL 186Nm (138lb/ft) @ 3000rpm, VX 188Nm (140lb/ft) @ 3000rpm. ENGINE STRUCTURE 45deg inclined, belt-driven ohc; cast iron cyl head & block; 5-bearing crank; Zenith-Stromberg 175CD-2 carb.

TRANSMISSION rear wheel drive; diaphragm spring 8.5in sdp clutch; 4-speed, all synchromesh; automatic, overdrive optional until 1973; hypoid bevel final drive; ratio Victor 3.9:1, estate 4.1:1, SL 3.73:1, VX 3.73:1, Ventora 3.09:1.
CHASSIS DETAILS unitary steel structure; ifs by double wishbones, coil springs, anti-roll bar; live axle, parallel trailing links with Panhard rod and coil springs at rear; AC-Delco telesc dampers; Lockheed disc and drum brakes, vacuum servo; rack and pinion steering; 65L (14.25 Imp gal, 17 US gal) tank; tyres 6.40-13 Victor, estate, SL; 185/70-14 VX and Ventora.
DIMENSIONS wheelbase 267cm (105in); front track 143cm (56.2in), 141cm (55.4in) rear; ground clearance 20cm (8in); turning circle 11.3m (37ft) left, 11m (36ft) right; length 455cm (179in); width 170cm (67in); height 137cm (54in).

Right: 1975 Victor.
Left: 2279cc engine.

version for the VX4/90. The Ventora represented the final fling of the venerable Bedford/Chevrolet 6-cylinder used since 1963, which while being a touch smoother than the VX4/90 was no faster, and after 1976 it was no more.

Suspension was much the same as before but the body was larger. It was longer and the same width (the track was 2.5cm, an inch, wider at the rear, and 5cm, 2in at the front) and slightly taller. It was also heavier but not by much. Rear legroom and overall shoulder room was increased. Ride was improved with anti-dive suspension geometry and compliant springing with 8.6cm (3.4in) on bump and 10cm (4in) on rebound. There were 23cm (9in) of suspension movement at the back. Front roll centre was 7.6cm (3in) high, rear 25cm (10in), making a downward-sloping roll axis, promoting safe-driving understeer. After 1973 the overdrive option was withdrawn.

The David Jones styling was distinctively Vauxhall with upright radiator grilles, big glass area, and moulded seats with Ambla upholstery, with rosewood in the Ventora. The 267cm (105in) wheelbase made the Victor appreciably larger than the 257cm (101in) Cortina, 20cm (8in) bigger than the Viva and only 5cm (2in) shorter than the seven year old PC Cresta. A great deal of thought was going into Vauxhall model policy.

PERFORMANCE maximum speed Victor 2300SL 156kph (97mph), Victor 1800 148kph (91.7mph), VX 162kph (101mph); 29.2kph (18.2mph) @ 1000rpm Victor, 27.5kph (17.1mph) estate, 30.3kph (18.9mph) SL, 30.2kph (18.8mph) VX, 36.4kph (22.7mph) Ventora; acceleration 0-96kph (60mph) Victor 1800 15.9sec, 2300SL 12.4sec, VX 12sec; Victor 19.5kg/kW (14.4kg/bhp); fuel consumption 2300SL 11.3-13.1L/100km (21.6-25mpg).
PRODUCTION 44,078.
PRICE £1299 incl PT 2300SL 1972, overdrive £66, automatic £99, reclining front seats £13, heated rear window £14, radial-ply tyres £12, metallic paint £7.

Top left: 6-cylinder 3-litre **Ventora.**
Centre left: Victor **2300 SL.**
Bottom left: twin-carb **VX4/90.**
Right: safety features of **Victor VX4/90 and Ventora shown on Victor 2300SL.**

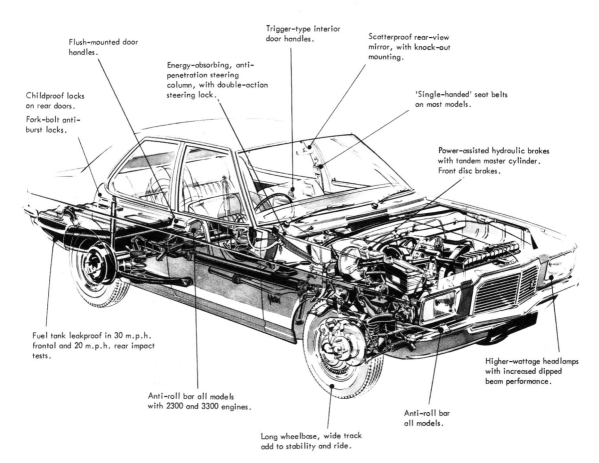

Trigger-type interior door handles.

Scatterproof rear-view mirror, with knock-out mounting.

Flush-mounted door handles.

Energy-absorbing, anti-penetration steering column, with double-action steering lock.

'Single-handed' seat belts on most models.

Childproof locks on rear doors.

Fork-bolt anti-burst locks.

Power-assisted hydraulic brakes with tandem master cylinder. Front disc brakes.

Fuel tank leakproof in 30 m.p.h. frontal and 20 m.p.h. rear impact tests.

Anti-roll bar all models with 2300 and 3300 engines.

Long wheelbase, wide track add to stability and ride.

Anti-roll bar all models.

Higher-wattage headlamps with increased dipped beam performance.

1973-1975 Firenza Droopsnoot

In 1973 Firenza models were reduced to two. The larger Vivas became Magnums, and the Firenza 2300 the Magnum Coupe, little different from the 2300SL. The Firenza HP (for High Performance) was based on the Magnum Coupe with Silver Starfire metallic paintwork and aerodynamic appendages at the front, giving rise to its nickname droopsnoot. It was the most exciting Vauxhall for a generation, and the cornerstone of the return to sport. Making it was not without its difficulties. The reinforced glass fibre nosecone manufactured by Specialised Mouldings had to be hand-fitted. The engine's combustion chambers, inlet tracts, and valve throats were hand-finished but with 15.7kW (21bhp) more than the Magnum the performance was rewarding, even though the ride was harsh and the model's bugbear body resonance persisted. It was the first Vauxhall with five gears (made by ZF) and first to break the 10sec barrier to 96kph (60mph).

Hopes for a long production run were dashed when the Yom Kippur War, petrol shortages, and industrial unrest imposed a three-day working week on Britain. Fast cars looked like a luxury and plans for 1000 Firenza HPs a year were soon abandoned. The survivors of the 204 made became prized (and expensive) collectors' items.

BODY coupe, seats, 2 doors, 4 seats; weight 1015kg (2238lb).
ENGINE 4 cylinders, in-line, inclined 45deg, front, 97.4mm x 76.2mm; 2279cc; compr: 9.2:1; 98kW (131bhp) @ 5500rpm; 42.9kW/L (57.5bhp/L); 195Nm (145.5lb/ft) @ 3500rpm.
ENGINE STRUCTURE single overhead camshaft; aluminium cylinder head; cast iron block; 5-bearing crankshaft; two Stromberg 175CD-2SE carburettors; AC Delco mechanical ignition.
TRANSMISSION rear wheel drive; Borg & Beck sdp diaphragm spring cable-actuated clutch; ZF 5-speed gearbox; all synchromesh; hypoid bevel final drive; ratio 3.7:1.
CHASSIS DETAILS unitary steel structure with grp; independent front suspension by short upper wishbone, long lower single arm, anti-roll bar, coil springs; live axle, four-link location at rear, coil springs; telescopic dampers; disc front drum rear brakes, dual circuit, vacuum servo; rack and pinion steering; 54.5L (12 Imp gal, 14.4 US gal) fuel tank; Michelin XVS radial ply tubeless tyres 185–70 HR13, cast alloy 4-stud wheels 6J rims.
DIMENSIONS wheelbase 246cm (97in); front track 138cm (54.3in); 136cm (53.5in) rear; ground clearance 12cm (4.8in); turning circle 11m (36ft); length 480cm (189in); width 164cm (64.6in); height 131.5cm (334in).
PERFORMANCE maximum speed 193kph (120mph); 33.9kph (21.1mph) @ 1000rpm; acceleration 0-96kph (60mph) 9.4sec; 10.4kg/kW (7.7kg/bhp); fuel consumption 12.8L/100km (22mpg).
PRODUCTION 204.
PRICE £2625 incl car tax and VAT seat belts standard.

195

A key figure in Vauxhall's modern competitions history, Bill Blydenstein, made his reputation with an unlikely and surprisingly fast Borgward Isabella. He next prepared and drove a VX4/90 in touring car races in Britain and on the Continent which encouraged London dealers Shaw & Kilburn to entrust him with preparing for racing a Viva HB. Gerry Marshall was the driver but the car had insufficient power to score well until the inclined 2.0-litre 4 cylinder engine became available. It then became almost unbeatable in British club racing, until in 1971 with money from 600 Vauxhall Dealers a new racing organisation was formed. It was official GM policy not to support racing from the factory, so Dealer Team Vauxhall was something of a way round the internal rules following similar examples in other GM territories notably Australia.

The engine developed in co-operation with Lotus was the 4-valve LV220 giving 164kW (220bhp) which, installed in a suitably modified Magnum, produced another consistent race winner. It also produced a highly competitive rally car in Groups 1 and 2, and in 1974 Will Sparrow won the RAC Group 1 British championship. The rally team was operated from Coburn Improvements, and later Magard.

Vauxhall's own LV220 head with cranked cam carriers was introduced alongside Lotus's until the oil crisis of the early 1970s stalled a number of production programmes including those for Jensen-Healey. The 2300HS programme was under some pressure until new chairman Bob Price, irked by Ford's success in rallying, asked DTV for its response. The resulting car won Pentti Airikkala the Welsh, Manx, and Castrol rallies, losing the RAC British rally championship only by a narrow margin. Only the highly specialised works Lancia Stratos was faster.

In racing Gerry Marshall won his class in the 1976 Tricentrol British saloon car championship in the Group 1 Magnum and finished a fine second overall in the 1977 Spa 24 Hours with co-driver Peter Brock. Marshall won 96 British national special saloon car races, and five championships, with DTV-built 5.0-litre V8 engined specials, the Ventora-based Big Bertha and later Magnum-based Baby Bertha.

Right: 1971 ex-works Firenza 'The Old Nail' owned and raced by Gerry Marshall. *Far right:* 1977 DTV Chevette 2300 driven by Pentti Airikkala.

1973-1977 Magnum 1800, 2300

While the 1256cc HC remained a Viva, the 1759cc and 2279cc saloons, estate cars and coupes were renamed Magnum. Rubber-faced bumpers, a side strip and four headlights reflecting qualitative improvements in the new range. Automatic transmission was available on SLs with the 1759cc engine. Power unit improvements included higher compression ratios, changes to the combustion chamber design, firmer engine mountings and a stiffer cylinder block. Power of 1800 was increased in 1975 mutation. A rear anti-roll bar improved the saloons' handling although it made the ride quite hard, wheel rims were made wider, radial-ply tyres standardised, and a divided propellor shaft reduced vibration without quite eliminating the model's customary resonance. Skittish behaviour especially over mid-corner bumps was a criticism of contemporary road testers, together with the estate car's inability to accommodate large square loads owing to the fastback styling. The ride was much better when the car was heavily laden. The same suspension was used for the newly introduced Jensen-Healey sports car, which not surprisingly exhibited some of the same characteristics. Magnums gained reclining seats with brushed nylon facings, seven-dial instrument panels in the 2300, and prices in line with the inflationary pressures of the 1970s.

BODY saloon, 4 seats, 2 doors, weight 970kg (2139lb); 4 drs, 985kg (2172lb). Estate, 3 drs, 1020kg (2249lb). Coupe, 2 drs, 970kg (2139lb).
ENGINE 4 cylinders, in-line, inclined 45deg, front, 85.73mm x 76.2mm; 1759cc; compr: 8.5:1; 57kW (77bhp) @ 5200rpm; 32.6kW/L (43.8bhp/L); 130Nm (97lb/ft) @ 3000rpm. 65.6kW (88bhp) @ 5800rpm, 37.3kW/L (50bhp/L), 133Nm (99lb/ft) @ 3500rpm. 2279cc, 82kW (110bhp) @ 5000rpm, 36kW/L (48.3bhp/L), 188Nm (140lb/ft) @ 3000rpm. 1976 power increase 1759cc 65.5kW (88bhp) @ 5800rpm.
ENGINE STRUCTURE belt-driven ohc; cast iron cyl head and block; 5-bearing crankshaft; Zenith Stromberg 175CD carburettor, two on 2279cc.
TRANSMISSION rear wheel drive; sdp diaphragm spring clutch; 4-speed gearbox; all synchromesh; auto optional 1759cc; hypoid bevel final drive; 3.727:1. 3.455:1 on 2279cc.
CHASSIS DETAILS unitary steel structure; ifs by upper wishbones lower transverse links, reaction arms

coil springs and anti roll bar; live axle, coil springs, four locating links at rear, anti roll bar on saloons; telescopic dampers; disc front drum rear brakes with vacuum servo; rack and pinion; 54.5L (12 Imp gal, 14.4 US gal) fuel tank; Michelin ZX 175-70SR13 tyres, 5J rims. HR13 on 2279cc.
DIMENSIONS wheelbase 246cm (97in); front track 130.6cm (51.4in), 131cm (51.6in) rear; ground clearance 12.7cm (5in); turning circle 9.8m (32.2ft); length 413.5cm (163in); width 164.3cm (64.7in); height 135cm (53in).
PERFORMANCE maximum speed 159.5kph (99.1mph); 28.4kph (17.7mph) @ 1000rpm, 30.3kph (18.9mph) 2279cc; 0-96kph (60mph) 11.7sec, 11.2sec 2279cc car; 17kg/kW (12.6kg/bhp)l 10.1-11.8L/100km (23.9-28.1mpg), 11.0-11.9L/100km (23.7-25.6mpg) 2279cc.
PRODUCTION 20,300.
PRICE 1974 1800 2dr £1304; 4dr £1346. 2300 2dr £1409; 4dr £1450. 1800 estate £1424; 2300 estate £1528. 1800 coupe £1359, 2300 coupe £1464. automatic transmission £113.

199

The most important and one of the most successful Vauxhalls ever was launched almost secretly, certainly apologetically, and even a little acrimoniously. The Opel Ascona was already being sold in the UK, but as *Autocar* pointed out in August 1975, not in large numbers. There was, it seemed, "no logical reason … to explain the poor sales performance of Opel in this country." Only 1148 Asconas and 1738 Manta coupes were bought in the UK during 1974. By September there were rumours that Asconas made in GM's Antwerp plant rebadged as Vauxhall Cavaliers would be brought in instead. The stories were neither confirmed nor denied, but by October they were on view as Vauxhalls with 1.3, 1.6 or 1.9-litre engines and 2-door saloons and coupes, 3-door "sportshatch" or 4-door saloon bodies, their Opel antecedents slightly abridged by a different front. GM was distinctly edgy in case they were seen as alien.

They were not. They were cars of rich quality. They may have failed as Opels, but were a resounding success as Vauxhalls, filling the gap between the 246cm (97in) wheelbase Viva and the 267cm (105in) Victor. Opel immediately matched the Vauxhall's price but it was too late. The Cavalier was already on its way to becoming one of the best-selling and best-loved cars in Britain.

BODY saloon, 5 seats, 2 doors, 950kg (2094lb); 4 doors 970kg (2139lb); GL 980kg (2489lb).
ENGINE 4 cyl, in-line, front, 81mm x 61mm; 1256cc; cr 8.7:1; 43kW (58bhp) @ 5400rpm; 34.4kW/L (46.1bhp/L); 88.5Nm (66lb/ft) @ 2600rpm.79mm x 61mm; 1584cc; cr 8.8:1; 51.5kW (69bhp) @ 5000rpm; 32.5kW/L (43.6bhp/L); 111Nm (82.7lb/ft) @ 3600rpm. 93mm x 69.8mm, 1897cc, 66kW (88.5bhp) @ 4800rpm, 34.8kW/L (46.7bhp/L), 147Nm (109.8lb/ft) @ 3800rpm. 1897cc, 74.6kW (100bhp) @ 5400rpm, 37.7kW/L (50.5bhp/L), 151.5Nm (113lb/ft) @ 3800rpm.
ENGINE STRUCTURE pushrod ohv; chain-driven cam in head; cast iron cyl head and block; 5-bg crank; Solex 32DIDTA-4 downdraught carb. 1897cc Zenith 35/40 downdraught twin choke.
TRANSMISSION rwd; clutch sdp diaphragm spring cable-operated; 4-spd, all synch; 3.67:1. 1.3 no auto.
CHASSIS DETAILS unitary steel; ifs wishbones, coils, anti roll bar; live axle, trailing arms, torque tube, Panhard rod, coils, rear anti roll bar; telescopic dampers; disc front rear drum brakes, vacuum servo dual circuit; rack & pinion; 50L (11 Imp gal, 13.2 US gal) fuel tank; 165SR13 tyres, 5J rims.
DIMENSIONS wb 252cm (92in); track 137.5cm (54in); g c 13cm (5in); turning circle 10.1m (33ft); length 444cm (175in); width 165cm (66in); height 132cm (52in).
PERFORMANCE max 156kph (96.3mph); 29.5kph (18.4mph) @ 1000rpm; 0-96kph (60mph) 13.3sec; 18.4kg/kW (13.8kg/bhp); 9.0-10.8L/100km (26.1-31.3mpg).
PRODUCTION 238,980 all types.
PRICE 1976 £2124 incl tax.

There were five Opel Mantas, the smallest with a Kadett 1200 engine, two 1584cc versions, a 1897cc and the GT/E with Bosch L-Jetronic fuel injection. The Cavalier Coupe had a 3.67:1 final drive for acceleration rather than speed. The Manta's optional 3.18:1 axle, which would have given 33.4kph (20.7mph) instead of a fussy (and not very economical) 29.6kph (18.5mph) per 1000rpm in top gear, was not on offer. Still the Cavalier was in many ways a revelation, with a strong driver appeal, and the Coupe had a well-balanced raciness that eluded even the Firenza. Middle-weight rack and pinion steering, a well-located back axle, commendably low angles of roll, a smooth gearshift, supple ride, and true straight-line running even in crosswinds that autobahn-developed cars tended to have, were by no means the rule in the 1970s.

Yet some of the Cavalier's best features were not immediately apparent. It was better made than many British cars. It had an 11-stage anti-corrosion process, a Bitumen undersealant, wax injection into sills and some of its most vulnerable panels were zinc coated. Opels had a good reputation for keeping rust at bay and the Cavalier quickly set an example that the rest of the industry had to follow.

BODY coupe, 2 doors, 5 seats, weight 960kg (2116lb).
ENGINE 4 cyl, in-line, front, 81mm x 61mm; 1256cc; cr 8.7:1; 43kW (58bhp) @ 5400rpm; 34.4kW/L (46.1bhp/L); 88.5Nm (66lb/ft) @ 2600rpm.79mm x 61mm; 1584cc; cr 8.8:1; 51.5kW (69bhp) @ 5000rpm; 32.5kW/L (43.6bhp/L); 111Nm (82.7lb/ft) @ 3600rpm. 93mm x 69.8mm, 1897cc, 66kW (88.5bhp) @ 4800rpm, 34.8kW/L (46.7bhp/L), 147Nm (109.8lb/ft) @ 3800rpm. 1897cc, 74.6kW (100bhp) @ 5400rpm, 37.7kW/L (50.5bhp/L), 151.5Nm (113lb/ft) @ 3800rpm.
ENGINE STRUCTURE pushrod ohv; chain-driven camshaft in head; cast iron cylinder head and block; 5-bearing crankshaft; Solex 32DIDTA-4 downdraught carb. 1897cc Zenith 35/40 downdraught twin choke.
TRANSMISSION rear wheel drive; sdp diaphragm spring cable-operated clutch; 4-spd, all synch; 3.67:1. 1.3 no auto.
CHASSIS DETAILS unitary steel; ifs wishbones, coils, anti roll bar; live axle, trailing arms, torque tube, Panhard rod, coils, rear anti roll bar; telescopic dampers; disc front rear drum brakes, vacuum servo dual circuit; rack & pinion; 50L (11 Imp gal, 13.2 US gal) fuel tank; 165SR13 tyres, 5J rims.
DIMENSIONS wheelbase 252cm (99in); track 137.5cm (54in); g c clearance 13cm (5in); turning circle 10.1m (33.1ft; length 449.5cm (177in); width 165cm (65in); ht 127cm (50in).
PERFORMANCE 1897cc max 171kph (106mph); 29.7kph (18.5mph) @ 1000rpm; 0-96kph (60mph) 11.2sec; 18.6kg/kW (13.9kg/bhp); 11.9-13.1L/100km (21.6-23.7mpg).
PRODUCTION 238,980 all Cavalier.
PRICE 1976 £2843 incl tax, seat belts standard, radio £40.

1975-1984 Chevette

The internationalisation of GM was the T-car programme. Later so-called world cars had more shared features, but the T-car was an important step towards them. It appeared in Brazil, then in Germany as the Opel Kadett, in Japan as the Isuzu 1600 and in Britain as the Chevette. Although the intention had been to build a common design they all looked different. Subsequent T-cars were different again, yet although the world car programme was judged on the whole a success it did not result in one universal car. That awaited the platform concept of flexible design with common or adaptable components.

Introduced as one model 3-door hatchback, Chevette buyers at first had little choice except colour. A 4-door and estate followed in 1976 sharing the fore-part of the floorpan with the Opel Kadett as well as windscreen, suspension, and brakes. The engine and transmission were pure Viva 1300. A shorter car than the Kadett, it was at the economy end of the market, the Viva having grown-up to become the Magnum. The Chevette's aim was 50mpg at 50mph and its success made a useful contribution to Vauxhall's 1976 return from a £14M loss back towards profitability.

BODY hatchback, 3 doors, E 850 kg (1874lb), L 860kg (1896lb), GL 870kg (1918lb). Saloon, 2 doors, 835kg (1840lb); 4 doors 875kg (1929lb). Estate 895kg (1973lb).
ENGINE 4 cylinders, in-line, front, 81mm x 61mm; 1256cc; compr: 9.2:1; 43.5kW (59bhp) @ 5600rpm; 34.6kW/L (47bhp/L); 92.2Nm (68.8lb/ft) @ 2600rpm.
ENGINE STRUCTURE pushrod ohv; chain-driven camshaft; cast iron cylinder head and block; 3-bearing crankshaft; Zenith Stromberg 150CDS (E)V carburettor.
TRANSMISSION rear wheel drive; sdp 7.25in diaphragm spring cable operated clutch; 4-speed, all synchromesh; final drive; 4.111:1.

CHASSIS DETAILS unitary steel structure; independent front suspension by wishbone, lower transverse arms, brake reaction rods, coil springs, anti roll bar; live axle, trailing arms, Panhard rod, torque tube, coil springs, anti roll bar at rear; telescopic dampers; disc and drum brakes with vacuum servo; rack and pinion steering; 43L (9.9 Imp gal, 11.9 US gal) fuel tank, 3 door hatch 38L (8.4 Imp gal, 10 US gal); 155SR-13 tyres, 5J rims.
DIMENSIONS wheelbase 239cm (94in); track 130cm (51.2in); ground clearance 13cm (5in); turning circle 9.2m (30.2ft); length 394cm (155in); width 158cm (62.2in); height 131cm (51.6in).
PERFORMANCE maximum speed 141kph (87.7mph); 25.7kph (16mph) @ 1000rpm; acceleration 0-96kph (60mph) 16.7sec; 19.5kg/kW (14.4kg/bhp); fuel consumption 9.1L/100km (31mpg).
PRODUCTION 415,608.
PRICE 1976 3-door L £1829, 1975 4-door L £1894 incl tax.

205

By 1976 the Victor was no more. It had its ups and downs over 20 years before being replaced by an amended FE with 1.8 and 2.3-litre engines, known simply as VX. The old running gear was retained, servo disc brakes and inertia reel seat belts were included, automatic was optional, but overdrive was discontinued and the body stayed much the same. Larger than a Ford Cortina, smaller than a Granada, with in-between-sized engines when the Cavalier came in to compete more directly in the Morris Marina and Cortina market, the VX could afford to move up-market. Unfortunately its decor failed to live up to its price. Decoration on the standard VX 1800 (the 2300 looked almost identical) was reduced, with plain rectangular headlights (using the new wonder halogen bulbs) and an uncompromising square eggbox-pattern grille. It did have woody-look cappings and ribbed velour inside, chrome window surrounds and a coachline, but somehow it failed to capture the public imagination. There was a fastback estate with hard-wearing Ambla upholstery until the customers demanded the ribbed velour. Like the saloons it had plenty of room for people, but its carrying capacity was diminished by the sloping rear. Ride was good, handling fair, and progressive development made it commendably quiet.

BODY saloon, 4 seats, 4 doors; weight 1156kg (2549lb). Estate, 5 door, 1205kg (2657lb).
ENGINE 4 cylinders, in-line, inclined 45deg, front, 85.72mm x 76.2mm; 1759cc; compr: 8.5:1; 65.5kW (88bhp) @ 5800rpm; 37.2kW/L (50bhp/L); 135.5Nm (101lb/ft) @ 3500rpm.
 ENGINE STRUCTURE overhead camshaft; cast iron cylinder head and cylinder block; 5-bearing crankshaft; Stromberg CD carburettor.
TRANSMISSION rear wheel drive, sdp clutch, 4-speed gearbox; all synchromesh; automatic option; hypoid bevel final drive; ratio 3.727:1.
CHASSIS DETAILS unitary steel structure; independent front suspension by wishbone, bottom link coil springs, anti-roll bar; live axle, 4 trailing arms, Panhard rod at rear; hydraulic dampers; disc and drum brakes with vacuum servo; rack and pinion steering; 65L (14.25 Imp gal, 17 US gal) fuel tank; 175SR-13 tyres, 5J rims.
DIMENSIONS wheelbase 266.5cm (105in); front track 142.5cm (56in), rear 140.5cm (55.3in); ground clearance 12.5cm (4.9in); turning circle 11.5m (37.7ft); length 454cm (178.7in); width 170cm (66.9in); height 137cm (53.9in).
PERFORMANCE maximum speed 160kph (100mph); 29.6kph (18.4mph) @ 1000rpm; acceleration 0-100kph (62mph) 14.9sec; saloon 17.6kg/kW (13.1kg/bhp); fuel consumption 10.7-11.9L/100km (23.7-26.4mpg).
PRODUCTION 25, 185, 1800 and 2300.
PRICE 1976 saloon £2592 incl tax, estate £2803.

Right: **1977 VX 4/90 had sports-type road wheels, black-painted centre pillars and side-window surrounds, and distinctive grille (see copy). Halogen foglamps incorporated the turn-indicators.**

1976-1978 VX 2300 FE

The 6-cylinder Ventora was discontinued, so the new 4-cylinder had to do duty not only at the luxury and performance end of the old Victor spectrum, but also in what was becoming known as the executive sector. Special editions abounded, starting in 1974 with the 2300S in metallic blue or green and with not one but two coachlines. Its Vinyl roof was a dignified black matched by black wheels and chrome wheel arch trims, and the interior was in trendy colour-keyed brushed nylon. The radio mono cassette player was standard equipment. This car evolved into the 1976 flagship 2300GLS in new colours with a different grille, chrome-covered door sills and Vinyl roof. Power steering, tachometer, and a deep spoiler, giving the front an imposing aspect, added to the effect.

At nearly 2.3-litres the old sloper engine was among the biggest 4-cylinder power units in regular production. The proliferation of the V6 lay a long way in the future; balancer shafts to damp out the vibrations of a big four had been invented at the turn of the century by Dr Fred Lanchester, but were still the stuff of production engineers' pipe dreams.

BODY saloon, 4 seats, 4 doors; weight 1180kg (2601lb). Estate, 5 doors, 1220kg (2690lb).
ENGINE 4 cylinders, in-line, inclined 45deg, front, 97.54mm x 76.2mm; 2279cc; compr. 8.5:1; 81kW (109bhp) @ 5000rpm; 35.5kW/L (48bhp/L); 187.5Nm (140lb/ft) @ 3000rpm.
ENGINE STRUCTURE overhead camshaft; cast iron cylinder head and cylinder block; 5-bearing crankshaft; Stromberg CD carburettor.
TRANSMISSION rear wheel drive, sdp clutch, 4-speed or Getrag 5-speed gearbox; all synchromesh; automatic option; hypoid bevel final drive; ratio 3.455:1.
CHASSIS DETAILS unitary steel structure; independent front suspension by wishbone, bottom link coil springs, anti-roll bar; live axle, 4 trailing arms, Panhard rod at rear; hydraulic dampers; disc and drum brakes with vacuum servo; rack and pinion steering; 65L (14.25 Imp gal, 17 US gal) fuel tank; 175SR-13 tyres, 5J rims.

DIMENSIONS wheelbase 266.5cm (105in); front track 142.5cm (56in), rear 140.5cm (55in); ground clearance 12.5cm (4.9in); turning circle 11.5m (37.7ft); length 454cm (179in); width 170cm (66.9in); height 137cm (54in).
PERFORMANCE maximum speed 166.5kph (103.5mph); 29.6kph (18.4mph) @ 1000rpm; acceleration 0-96kph (60mph) 11.3sec; saloon 14.6kg/kW (10.8kg/bhp); fuel consumption 9.7-11.2L/100km (25.2-29.2mpg).
PRODUCTION 25, 185, 1800 and 2300.
PRICE 1976 saloon £2709 incl tax, £2920 estate.

Right: VX 2300 GLS.

1976-1980 Chevette 2300HS

Conceived as a small economy hatchback with better handling than ride, the Chevette was developed for competition as part of an initiative to make Vauxhall a younger buyer's car. This meant challenging Ford in motor sport. GM's traditional reluctance to support a works team meant one was created with the backing of Vauxhall dealers instead. Only the car could be from the factory, so Luton found the resources to create a model to fit the regulations. The catalogued HS Chevette had a Vauxhall-designed 16-valve twin-cam cylinder head and Getrag gearbox to satisfy the rules. The Chevettes that took part in rallies had Lotus-designed heads and ZF gearboxes giving rise to problems with the 400 laid down to satisfy the homologation certification. The structure was as near production Chevette as made no matter, reinforced where necessary to take the turret mountings for the huge gas-filled suspension dampers. Likewise the Viva driveline was beefed-up with the torque tube drive from the Opel Kadet GT/E and the brakes were Cavalier-size.

Too noisy to have much appeal as a road car, it certainly brought new life to Vauxhall. It also brought Pentti Airikkala three major wins in its first season and second place in the British rally championship.

BODY hatchback, 2 seats, 3 doors; weight 970kg (2138lb).
ENGINE 4 cylinders, in-line, inclined 45deg, front, 97.5mm x 76.2mm; 2279cc; compr: 8.2:1; 100.7kW (135bhp) @ 5500rpm; 44kW/L (59bhp/L); 180Nm (134lb/ft) @ 4500rpm.
ENGINE STRUCTURE overhead valves; 2 belt-driven overhead camshafts; 16-valve aluminium cylinder head; cast iron cylinder block; 5-bearing crankshaft; two 175CD Stromberg carburettors.
TRANSMISSION rear wheel drive; sdp clutch; 5-speed gearbox; all synchromesh; no automatic option; final drive ratio 3.44:1.
CHASSIS DETAILS unitary steel structure with airdams and spoilers reducing drag coefficient from 0.475 to 0.407; double wishbone and coil spring independent front suspension, anti-roll bar, gas-filled dampers; live rear axle with trailing arms, Panhard rod, torque tube, anti-roll bar; telescopic dampers; disc brakes 9.6in front 9.0in drums rear, dual circuit, vacuum servo; rack and pinion steering 3.5 turns lock to lock; 32L (8.5 Imp gal, 10.2 US gal) fuel tank; Dunlop 205-60HR tyres, 6J alloy wheels.
DIMENSIONS wheelbase 239cm (94in); track 130cm (51in); ground clearance 10cm (3.9in); turning circle 9.2m (30.2ft); length 394cm (155in); width 158cm (62.2in); height 131cm (51.6in).
PERFORMANCE maximum speed 188kph (117mph); 30.6kph (19mph) @ 1000rpm; acceleration 0-96kph (60mph) 8.8sec; 9.6kg/kW (7.2kg/bhp); fuel consumption 11.1-15.4L/100km (18.3mpg-25.5mpg).
PRODUCTION 450.
PRICE £5107 incl tax.

Top and bottom right: **wind-tunnel testing resulted in front air dam and rear spoiler on tailgate of 2300HS.**

1978 Equus concept car

Vauxhall had not made an open car since the 1930s. There were some special-bodied conversions, notably Bob Jankel's Panther Westwinds and Lima open 2-seater. As part of the 1970s programme of revitalising Vauxhall design, director Wayne Cherry used the Lima as the basis for an in-house motor show project.

The components were a cut-down Magnum floor-pan and a glass reinforced plastic body with angular lines and crisp profile, and the prototype was built by Panther. Cherry wanted to demonstrate that Vauxhall could design a sports car in the modern idiom. It had an Austin-Healey Sprite Mark 1-style luggage compartment with no lid and luggage loaded through an aperture behind the seats. The armadillo-style louvres on the sides were designed to break up the long body side panel and the grey paint was shaded at the windscreen roots to try and integrate the upright screen into the low-built body. There were optimistic hints that Vauxhall would like to enter into competition with the MGB, even then under threat, with an affordable sports car but they came to naught. In the event the Equus was the last all-British Vauxhall. In 1980 the design department was closed down and Vauxhall development was concentrated largely in Germany by the talented Wayne Cherry.

BODY open, 2 seats, 2 doors; weight approx 885kg (1951lb).
ENGINE 4 cylinders, in-line, inclined 45deg, front, 97.54mm x 76.2mm; 2279cc; compr: 8.5:1; 81kW (109bhp) @ 5000rpm; 35.5kW/L (47.7bhp/L); 187.5 Nm (140lb/ft) @ 3000rpm.
ENGINE STRUCTURE overhead valves; belt-driven overhead camshaft; cast iron cylinder head and block; 5-bearing crankshaft; Zenith Stromberg carburettor; water-cooled.
TRANSMISSION rear wheel drive; sdp clutch; 5-speed ZF gearbox; all synchromesh; hypoid bevel final drive; ratio 3.7:1.
CHASSIS DETAILS braced steel floor pan with tubular reinforcement and grp body; independent front suspension by upper wishbones lower transverse links, reaction arms coil springs and anti roll bar; live axle, coil springs, four locating links at rear, anti roll bar on saloons; telescopic dampers; disc front drum rear brakes with vacuum servo; rack and pinion steering; 54.5L (12 Imp gal, 14.4 US gal) fuel tank; Michelin ZX 175-70SR13 tyres, 5J rims.
DIMENSIONS wheelbase 246cm (97in); front track 133cm (52.4in), 132cm (52in) rear; ground clearance 11.5cm (4.5in); turning circle 9.8m (32.2ft); length 361cm (142in); width 161cm (63.4in); height 122cm (48in).
PERFORMANCE maximum speed 177kph (110mph); 28.4kph (17.7mph) @ 1000rpm, 30.4kph (18.9mph); acceleration 0-96kph (60mph) 7-8sec; 10.9kg/kW (8.1kg/bhp)l fuel consumption 9-14L/100km (20.1-31.4mpg).
PRODUCTION 1.

1978-1982 Royale saloon and coupe

The first 6-cylinder Vauxhall since the Ventora, the Royale was based on the Opel Senator and Monza of 1977. Some of the body structure was common to the Carlton announced at the same time in October 1978, and with the whole of Europe in the grip of an inflationary spiral, it was the first Vauxhall to retail for over £8000. This was eight times what Alexander Wilson was pleading for to save the company in 1889.

Vauxhall's answer to the Rover 3500 and the slightly cheaper Ford Granada Ghia did not have the top Opel's fuel injection 3.0-litre 134kW (180bhp) engine but an optional single carburettor 2.7-litre 104kW (140bhp) affair which sold for a good deal less in saloon form, £7956 against the big Opel's £9548. It was also the first production Vauxhall with independent suspension to all four wheels, the first 6-cylinder overhead camshaft, and the first with optional air conditioning at a price twice that of an entire pre-war Ten horsepower car. What the Royale did however was raise Vauxhall's sights from the popular-priced Vivas, Chevettes, and Cavaliers to something like the 25 of the 1930s. The Royale was a cut above the Veloxes, Crestas and even the Viscounts of the 1950s and 1960s.

BODY saloon, 5 seats, 4 doors, weight 1370kg (3020lb); Coupe, 2 doors, weight 1375kg (3031lb).
ENGINE 6 cylinders, in-line, front, 92.0mm x 69.8mm; 2784cc; compr: 9.0:1; 104kW (140bhp) @ 5200rpm; 37.5kW/L (50.3bhp/L); 216Nm (161lb/ft) @ 3400rpm.
ENGINE STRUCTURE overhead valves; chain-driven cam-in-head, short pushrods; hydraulic tappets; cast-iron cylinder head and block; 7-bearing crankshaft; Zenith twin choke carburettor; water-cooled, viscous-coupled fan.
TRANSMISSION rear wheel drive; sdp clutch; 4-speed gearbox; all synchromesh; GM Strasbourg automatic optional; hypoid bevel final drive; ratio 3.45:1.
CHASSIS DETAILS unitary steel structure; ifs by Macpherson struts; irs by trailing arms and coil springs; telescopic dampers; anti-roll bars front and rear; brakes 10.6in ventilated discs, front 10.9in rear with vacuum servo; dual circuit; recirculating ball PAS; 75L (16.3 Imp gal, 19.6 US gal) fuel tank, Coupe 70L (15.4 Imp gal, 18.5 US gal); 195-70HR 14 tyres, 6J rims.
DIMENSIONS wheelbase 268.5cm (105.7in); front track 144.5cm (56.9in), rear 147cm (57.9in); ground clearance 14cm (5.5in); turning circle 10.8m (35.4ft); length 481cm (189.3in), Coupe 469cm (185in); width 173cm (68in); height 141.5cm (56in), Coupe 138cm (54.3in).
PERFORMANCE maximum speed 190kph (118mph); 20.9mph @ 1000rpm; acceleration 0-96kph (60mph) 11.4sec; 13.2kg/kW (9.8kg/bhp); 12.8-15.7L/100km (18-22mpg).
PRODUCTION 7119.
PRICE saloon £7956 incl tax, Coupe £8248 manual or automatic.

Centre right: Royale all-independent suspension.

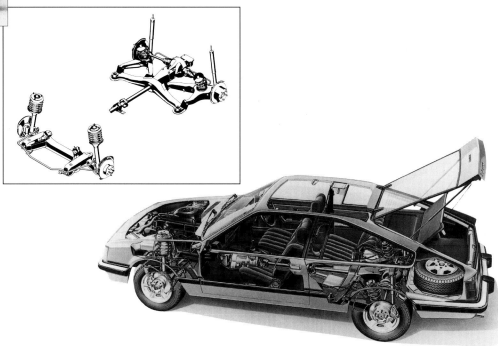

1978-1986 Carlton

It seemed for a while that Vauxhall and Opel might contest the British market together. In the case of the Carlton, a clone of the Opel Rekord, a strategy emerged which made the Opel a £4762 special-equipment version of the Vauxhall-badged £4600 Carlton. Yet Wayne Cherry in charge of styling at GM Europe contrived to maintain a Vauxhall identity, replacing the old VX 4/90 and keeping a trace of droopsnoot Firenza, so that the British public quite forgot its alter ego. It was well-made, handled like a sports car, and its comfort (with superb air-blending heating and ventilation) was exemplary.

Essentially a 4-cylinder version of the Royale and 15cm (6in) shorter, its accommodation was about the same. The estate car version had a platform 194cm (76.5in) long and 143.5cm (56.5in) wide and a practical roofline. The engine was typically Opel with the camshaft high in the cylinder head operating the valves through short pushrods, hydraulic tappets, and rockers. In some respects it was scarcely a match for the old sloper overhead cam Vauxhall, notably low-speed pulling and indifferent economy, but like the rest of the car it was beautifully made and thoroughly reliable. A 1983 facelift introduced fuel injection and an optional seven function trip computer.

BODY saloon, 4 doors; estate, 5 doors; 5 seats; weight saloon 1120kg (2469lb), estate 1145kg (2524lb).
ENGINE 4 cylinders, in-line, front, 95mm x 69.8mm; 1979cc; compr: 9.0:1; 74.6kW (100bhp) @ 5200rpm, 37.7kW/L (50.5bhp/L); 157Nm (117lb/ft) @ 3600rpm. 82kW (110bhp) @ 5400rpm, 41kW/L (55.6bhp/L); 160Nm (119lb/ft) @ 3400rpm. 2197cc, 86kW (115bhp) @ 4800rpm, 39kW/L (52.3bhp/L); 180Nm (134lb/ft) @ 2800rpm. 2260cc diesel, 48.5kW (65bhp) @ 4200rpm, 21.4kW/L (28.8bhp/L); 126Nm (94lb/ft) @ 2500rpm.
ENGINE STRUCTURE overhead valves; chain-driven cam-in-head, short pushrods; hydraulic tappets; cast-iron cylinder head and block; 5-bearing crankshaft; Zenith downdraught carburettor. From 1983 Bosch LE-Jetronic fuel injection
TRANSMISSION rear wheel drive; 20.3cm 8.0in sdp diaphragm spring clutch; 4-speed; synchromesh; 1983 5-speed; automatic option; hypoid bevel final drive; ratio 3.67:1.

CHASSIS DETAILS integral steel structure; independent front suspension by Macpherson struts; live axle, trailing arms, Panhard rod, and coil springs at rear; anti-roll bars front and rear; telescopic dampers, adjustable at rear; disc front drum rear brakes with vacuum servo; dual circuit; recirculating ball steering, optional PAS (std from 1983); 65L (14.3 Imp gal, 17.2 US gal) fuel tank; Pirelli P3 175SR14 tyres, 5.5J rims.
DIMENSIONS (saloon) wheelbase 267cm (105in); front track 140cm (55in), 142cm (56in) rear; ground clearance 14cm (5.5in); turning circle 10.8m (35.4ft); length 459.5cm (181in); width 172.5cm (68in); height 142cm (56in).
PERFORMANCE maximum speed 170kph (106mph) 1983 186.7kph (116mph); 31.4kph (19.53mph) @ 1000rpm; 0-96kph (60mph) 11.4sec; 15kg/kW (11.2kg/bhp) 100bhp saloon; fuel consumption 10.1-12.8L/ 100km (22-28mpg).
PRODUCTION 80,000 estimate.
PRICE £4600.

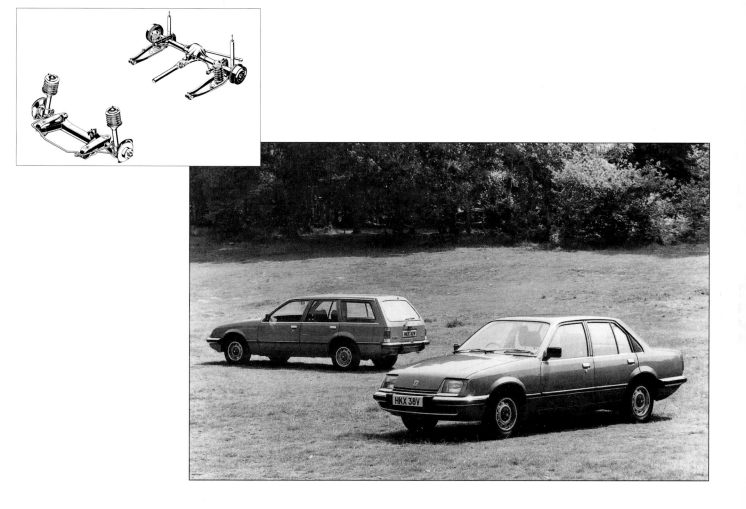

1980-1982 Viceroy

In October 1980 GM relaunched the Opel Commodore and brought out the Vauxhall Viceroy. This was a 6-cylinder car based on the Rekord/Carlton body shell, and fitted between them and the Senator/Royale saloons. A curious amalgam of Carlton from the windscreen back and Royale front it had a fetching white cross motif on the grille. The Commodore came out at Frankfurt in 1977, production starting in earnest about a year later, but its in-between status made it less of a success than its fine dynamic qualities deserved.

A sort of luxury Carlton/Commodore, there was only one model of Viceroy and it came with central locking, radio stereo cassette player, and electric boot release as standard equipment. There was a six-dial instrument pack and the CD Commodore had electric window lifts, a manual steel sunroof and alloy wheels; an impressive array of equipment in 1980. It was short-lived. A facelift in time for the 1981 motor show blacked the window surrounds and introduced stripy seats, trendy features that did not last long, and brought in an Opel-style facia without the tasteful wood veneer.

BODY saloon, 4 doors, 5 seats; weight 1220kg (2646lb).
ENGINE 6 cylinders, in-line, front, 87mm x 69.8mm; 2490cc; compr: 9.2:1; 85kW (114bhp) @ 5200rpm; 34kW/L (45.8bhp/L); 177Nm (132lb/ft) @ 3800rpm.
ENGINE STRUCTURE overhead valves; chain-driven cam-in-head, short pushrods; hydraulic tappets; cast-iron cylinder head and block; 7-bearing crankshaft; Zenith twin choke carburettor; water-cooled, viscous-coupled fan.
TRANSMISSION rear wheel drive; 20.3cm 8.0in sdp diaphragm spring clutch; 4-speed; synchromesh; GM 3-speed automatic optional; hypoid bevel final drive; ratio 3.7:1, automatic 3.45:1. overdrive optional; final drive ratio 3.7:1.
CHASSIS DETAILS integral steel structure; independent front suspension by Macpherson struts; live axle, trailing arms, Panhard rod, and coil springs at rear; anti-roll bars front and rear; telescopic dampers; disc front drum rear brakes with vacuum servo; dual circuit; recirculating ball PAS; 65L (14.3 Imp gal, 17.2 US gal) fuel tank; 175/70HR14 tyres, 6J rims.
DIMENSIONS wheelbase 267cm (105in); front track 144.5cm (57in), 142.5cm (56in) rear; ground clearance 14cm (5.5in); turning circle 11.5m (37.7ft); length 470.5cm (185in); width 172cm (67.7in); height 141cm (55.5in).
PERFORMANCE maximum speed 180kph (112mph), 175kph (109mph) automatic; 31.1kph (19.4mph) @ 1000rpm (manual); acceleration 0-96kph (60mph) 11.5sec, automatic 13sec; 14.4kg/kW (10.7kg/bhp); fuel consumption 10.9L/100km (26mpg), automatic 11.9L/100km (23.7mpg).
PRODUCTION 2295.
PRICE £7864 (Opel Commodore 2.5S Berline £7714, CD £8702).

Style for the 1980s.
Top right: **The Viceroy had a distinguished crisp line.**
Bottom right: **Button pads on steering wheel operated horn.**

1980-1984 Astra 1.2, 1.3

Vauxhall's transition from in-line to transverse engines, and rear wheel to front wheel drive, was accomplished by the Astra. It came between the top Chevette and lowest-priced Cavalier and inherited three Opel Kadett engine families, pushrod, ohc and diesel, only the latter pair available in Britain at launch. The cylinder dimensions of the new 1.3 overhead cam engine were nearly "square", 73mm x 73.4mm, and it was notably powerful with 55kW (74bhp) at a time when its contemporaries were producing between 45kW and 52kW (60 and 70bhp). The 3-bearing 1196cc pushrod engine was reserved for the entry-level Astra known as the 1.2S.

It was not a notable period for automotive haute couture. The new Vauxhalls were flat-panelled and plain, rather like the first Viva. Bodies included 3 and 5-door hatchbacks, 3 and 5-door estates, and a 4-door saloon. Only the 5-door saloons and estates were brought to Britain at first, and since there was no international British motor show in 1979 and no Motorfair at Earls Court, the Astra made its debut at the Scottish Motor Show at Kelvin Hall. Opel put its new and almost identical Kadett on sale to coincide with it, so Vauxhall responded by displaying two Astras even though the model was not available until the following April.

BODY saloon, 4 seats; 2 doors, weight 815kg (1797lb), 5 doors 835kg (1841lb); estate, 5 doors, 895kg (1973lb).
ENGINE: 4 cylinders, in-line, transverse, front; 79mm x 61mm, 1196cc, 7.8:1, 39kW (52bhp); 32.6kW/L (43.5bhp/L); 82Nm (61lb/ft) @ 3600rpm. 75mm x 73.4mm, 1297cc, compr 9.2:1; 55kW (74bhp) @ 5800rpm, 42.4kW/L (56.9bhp/L), 101Nm (75lb/ft) @ 3800rpm.
ENGINE STRUCTURE (ohc) belt-driven overhead camshaft; hydraulic tappets, aluminium cylinder head; cast iron cylinder block; 5-bearing crankshaft; GMF Varijet twin-choke downdraught carburettor. 1196cc Solex 35PDSI.
TRANSMISSION front wheel drive; sdp clutch; 4-speed gearbox; synchromesh; automatic optional; final drive 1196cc 4.20:1, 1297cc 4.18:1.
CHASSIS DETAILS integral steel structure; independent front suspension by Macpherson struts, coil springs, anti-roll bar; rear suspension trailing arms with torsional cross-beam, coil springs, anti-roll bar; 9.2in disc front 7.8in drum rear servo brakes, diagonally-split; rack and pinion steering; 42L (9.2 Imp gal, 11.1 US gal) fuel tank, estate 50L (11 Imp gal, 13.2 US gal); 145 or 155SR13 tyres, 5J rims.
DIMENSIONS wheelbase 251.4cm (99in); front track 140cm (55in), 140.5cm (55.3in) rear; ground clearance 13.5cm (5.3in); turning circle 10.6m (34.8ft); length 400cm (157.5in); width 163.5cm (64.4in); height 138cm (54.3in). Estate length 420.5cm (165.5in), height 140cm (55in).
PERFORMANCE maximum speed 157kph (98mph); 26kph (16.2mph) @ 1000rpm; 0-96kph (60mph) 12.6sec; 20.9kg/kW (15.7kg/bhp); 7.8-9.4L/100km (30-36mpg). 1196cc, 140kph (87mph), 0-96kph (60mph) 16sec, 14.8kg/kW (11kg/bhp).
PRODUCTION 1,117,662 all Astra including Mk II.
PRICE 1982 1.2S 3-door £4233; 1.3 G: 5-door £5371.

1980-1984 Astra 1.6, 1.8

The clever overhead camshaft unit that GM conceived for its new transverse-engined front wheel drive cars was known as Family I when it was a 1.3-litre, and Family II when it was a 1.6-litre. The 1.3 went into Astras as soon as they were announced, the 1.6 followed when the engine was developed for GM's J-car, the autumn 1981 Ascona/Cavalier, one of the series of "world" cars inspired by the accountants of mega-manufacturers but rarely endorsed by "world" customers. Not that the new overhead cam engine was not clever. It was. It remained successful throughout the decade and its descendants prospered long after. It differed from the 16-year-old cam-in-head design by dispensing with the rockers; this was a real overhead camshaft engine working the valves by cantilever followers. Unlike some transverse engines, it was a crossflow with diagonal oval combustion chambers in the face of the two-piece aluminium cylinder head, the upper part of which was a pressure die-casting. At 119kg (263lb) without oil or clutch it weighed 25kg (55lb) less than its predecessor. It was a compact engine with the distributor driven off the overhead camshaft and transistorised ignition. The 1983 Astra GTE was a strong contender in the so-called hot hatchback market.

BODY saloon, 2/3 doors, 4 seats, 825kg (1819lb); saloon 4/5 doors, 845kg (1863lb); estate, 3/5 doors 885kg (1951lb); 1.6 +70kg (154lb).
ENGINE 4 cylinders, in-line, transverse, front, 80.0mm x 79.5mm, 1598cc, cr: 9.2:1; 66kW (88.5bhp) @ 5800rpm; 41.3kW/L (55.4bhp/L); 126Nm (94lb/ft) @ 4000rpm. GTE 84.8mm x 79.5mm, 1796cc, compr: 9.5:1, 84kW (113bhp) @ 5800rpm; 46.8kW/L (62.7bhp/L); 149Nm (111lb/ft) @ 4800rpm.
ENGINE STRUCTURE belt-driven ohc; aluminium cyl head, cast iron block; 5-bearing crankshaft; GMF Varijet downdraught carburettor; GTE 1796cc Bosch LE-Jetronic fuel injection transistorised ignition.
TRANSMISSION front wheel drive; sdp clutch; 4 and 5-speed gearboxes; synchromesh; automatic optional; final drive ratios 3.94:1 4-speed, 3.74 5 speed, 4.18 estate 3.74 automatic, 3.33 1598cc auto, 3.94, 1796cc.
CHASSIS DETAILS integral steel structure; ifs by Macpherson struts, coil springs, anti-roll bar; rear suspension trailing arms with torsional cross-beam, coil springs, anti-roll bar; 9.2in disc front 7.8in drum rear servo brakes, diagonally-split; rack and pinion steering; 42L (9.2 Imp gal, 11.1 US gal) fuel tank, estate 50L (11 Imp gal, 13.2 US gal); 145 or 155SR13 or 175/70SR13 or +67kW 195/60HR tyres, 5J 5.5J rims.
DIMENSIONS wheelbase 251.4cm (99in); front track 140cm (55in), 140.5cm (55.3in) rear; ground clearance 13.5cm (5.3in); turning circle 10.6m (34.8ft); length 400cm (157.5in); width 163.5cm (64.4in); height 138cm (54.3in). Estate length 420.5cm (165.5in), ht 140cm (55in).
PERFORMANCE 1796cc 84kW: 186kph (115mph); 38.6kph (24mph) @ 1000rpm; 0-62kph (99mph) 9.5sec; 9.8kg/kW (7.3kg/bhp); 6-9.7L/ 100km (29-47mpg).
PRODUCTION 1,117,662 all Astra including Mk II.
PRICE 1.6S 5-door estate £5951, 1.6S SR 3-door £5867.

Right: **1.6-litre ohc engine.**

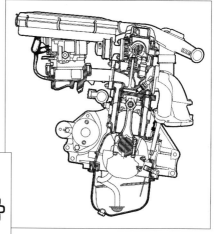
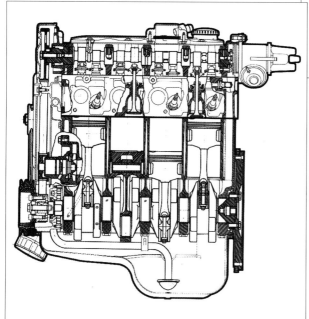

1981-1988 Cavalier II 1.3, 1.6

GM's encouragement of competition between its brand names in some parts of the world had led to Opels and Vauxhalls competing in Britain. This began to change with the introduction of the J-car, one of GM's repeated attempts at what it liked to call a world car and in some respects an enhancement of the successful Astra platform. The economics were always persuasive and some economies of scale were achieved, but the cars generally ended up differently made for different markets. Not so with the Opel and Vauxhall Astras, nor the Cavalier/Ascona, although after production of the Cavalier began in earnest at Luton things changed.

Cavaliers had been assembled from kits supplied from Germany and Belgium. The car that Ferdie Beickler, Vauxhall chairman and managing director, drove off the line on 17 August 1981 was the first with a large amount of domestic content, but with body panels pressed in Germany and Belgium, engines from as far away as Australia, and transmissions from Germany and Japan.

Opel and Vauxhall dealerships were combined, only the Manta Coupe remaining an Opel, since there was meantime no Vauxhall equivalent. There were two Cavalier bodies, five trim and equipment variations, and until 1983 no estate car.

BODY saloon, 4 doors, 4/5 seats, weight 940kg (2072lb); 5 doors, 970kg (2139lb). CD +25kg (55lb), automatic +30kg (66lb), 1.6 + 50kg (110lb). Estate 1040kg (2293lb).
ENGINE 4 cylinders, in-line, transverse front, 75mm x 73.4mm; 1297cc; compr: 9.2:1; 56kW (75bhp) @ 5800rpm; 43kW/L (57.8bhp/L); 99Nm (74lb/ft) @ 4000rpm. 80mm x 79.5mm, 1598cc, compr: 8.2:1; 67kW (90bhp) @ 5800rpm; 42kW/L (56.3bhp/L); 125Nm (93lb/ft) @ 4000rpm.
ENGINE STRUCTURE belt-driven overhead camshaft; hydraulic tappets aluminium cylinder head; cast iron block; 5-bearing crankshaft; Solex carburettor 56kW engine, Varajet carburettor 67kW engine.
TRANSMISSION front wheel drive; sdp clutch; 4-speed gearbox; synchromesh; automatic optional; helical spur final drive ratio 3.74:1, 3.33:1 automatic. 5-speed option on 67kW 3.94:1.
CHASSIS DETAILS integral steel structure; independent front suspension by Macpherson struts, anti-roll bar; rear suspension trailing arms, torsion beam, coil springs, anti-roll bar; disc front drum rear brakes; rack and pinion steering 3.5 turns lock-lock; 61L (13.4 Imp gal, 16.1 US gal) fuel tank; 165SR13 tyres 185/70HR 13 CD.
DIMENSIONS wheelbase 257.5cm (101.4in); front track 140cm (55in), 140.5cm (55.3in) rear; ground clearance 14cm (5.5in); turning circle 11m (36.1ft); length 436.5cm (172in); width 167cm (65.7in); height 139.5cm (55in). Fastback length 426.5cm (168in), height 138.5cm (54.5in).
PERFORMANCE 1598cc: max speed 170kph (106mph); 29.2kph (18.2mph) @ 1000rpm; acceleration 0-96kph (62mph) 12.5sec; 14kg/kW (12.5kg/bhp); fuel consumption 7.4-9.7L/100km (29-38mpg).
PRODUCTION 806,359 all Cavalier II.
PRICE 1982 1.3S 4-door £4820 manual, £5267 automatic; 1.6S GLS 5-door £6932 manual, £7389 automatic.

1982-1988 Cavalier II 1.8, 2.0

By 1982 there was a 1.8 Cavalier with fuel injection, which in due course evolved into the sporty 1.8Sri with optional two-tone paintwork like Crestas of old. In January Vauxhall said it expected to sell 50,000 Cavaliers a year, but by September the calculations were well wrong. It was sixth best selling car in Britain and with three months to go 70,000 had been sold. A 5-speed gearbox was introduced on the GLS and SRi, then the 1.6-litre.

Alongside the 1.8SRi the luxury CD had velour seats and electric windows and basked in the refinement of the 5-speed gearbox. The Cavalier was if anything under-geared and fidgety at motorway speeds. Instead of third gear being 1.37 in the old 4-speed gearbox it was now 1.28. The overall ratio was unchanged but 4th in the 5-speed was 0.89:1, giving 31.8kph (19.8mph) per 1000rpm, instead of 30kph (18.7mph) on the 0.97:1 top of the 4-speed. The new 5th, with a ratio of 0.71:1, gave 40.9kph (25.5mph) per 1000rpm, so with the engine doing under 4000rpm at 100mph, high-speed cruising was leisurely.

In the autumn of 1987 the 2.0 litre completed a range that now encompassed everything from basic economy to chief executive.

BODY saloon, 4 doors, 5 seats, weight 1010kg (2227lb); 5 doors 1060kg (2337lb); CD + 25kg (55lb), SRi + 90kg (198lb), automatic + 30kg (66lb). 2.0 5-door 1075kg (2370lb). Estate 1040kg (2293lb).
ENGINE 4 cylinders, in-line, transverse front, 84.8mm x 79.5mm; 1796cc, compr 9.2:1; 85kW (113bhp) @ 5800rpm; 47.1kW/L (63bhp/L); 150Nm (112lb/ft) @ 4800rpm. 86.0mm x 86mm, 1998cc, compr 9.2:1; 84.5kW (113bhp) @ 5600rpm; 42.3kW/L (56.6bhp/L); 175Nm (130.5lb/ft) @ 3000rpm.
ENGINE STRUCTURE belt-driven overhead camshaft; hydraulic tappets aluminium cylinder head; cast iron block; 5-bearing crankshaft; Bosch LE Jetronic fuel injection, 2.0 Motronic.
TRANSMISSION front wheel drive; sdp clutch; 5-speed gearbox; synchromesh; automatic optional; helical spur final drive ratio 3.94:1, 3.33:1 automatic, 2.0 3.55.
CHASSIS DETAILS integral steel structure; independent front suspension by Macpherson struts, anti-roll bar; rear suspension trailing arms, torsion beam, coil springs, anti-roll bar; disc front drum rear brakes; rack and pinion steering 3.5 turns lock-lock; 61L (13.4 Imp gal, 16.1 US gal) fuel tank; 165SR13 tyres 185/70HR 13 CD.
DIMENSIONS wheelbase 257.5cm (101.4in); front track 140cm (55in), 140.5cm (55.3in) rear; ground clearance 14cm (5.5in); turning circle 11m (36.1ft); length 441cm (173.6in); width 168.5cm (66.3in); height 139.5cm (55in). Fastback length 426.5cm (168in), height 138.5cm (54.5in).
PERFORMANCE Sri: maximum speed 185kph (115mph); 41.1kph (25.6mph) @ 1000rpm; acceleration 0-96kph (60mph) 9.4sec; 13kg/kW (9.7kg/bhp); fuel consumption 9.1-10.1L/100km (28-31mpg).
PRODUCTION 806,359 all Cavalier II.
PRICE 1982 1.8SRi 5-door £1759, £6775 automatic; 1.8cd 4-door £7598, £7941 automatic.

227

1982-1984 Astra diesel

The diesel that went into Astra and Cavalier from 1982 was a Family II overhead camshaft 4-cylinder, which had a good deal in common with the petrol engine, the main differences lying in the aluminium cylinder head and reinforced cast-iron connecting rods. A Ricardo Comet V combustion chamber gave around 95 per cent of the maximum torque between 1400rpm and 3800rpm. GM Europe revealed the new engine at the Brussels motor show in January to meet growing demand for diesel cars in Continental Europe. In 1981 diesel car sales reached nearly a million, with 15,000 expected in the United Kingdom in 1982.

When the Astra went on sale in the summer it was available only as a 3-door hatchback or 5-door estate. Expected to sell principally to the fleet market, or high-mileage working drivers who would offset the 20-30 per cent economy advantage against the higher first cost of the car, it was available only in L trim. This was the lowest-spec available, with tweed upholstery and fairly basic equipment, although it did run to a push-button radio. The Astra and Cavalier diesels had identical gearing, the difference in kph (mph) per 1000rpm accounted for by different size tyres.

BODY saloon, 2/3 doors, 4 seats, 925kg (2039lb); 4/5 doors, 960kg (2116lb); estate, 3/5 doors, 985kg (2172lb).

ENGINE 4 cylinders, in-line, transverse, front, 80.0mm x 79.5mm; 1598cc compr 23:1; 39.5kW (54bhp) @ 4600rpm; 24.8kW/L (33.5bhp/L); 95Nm (71lb/ft) @ 2400rpm.

ENGINE STRUCTURE: belt-driven overhead camshaft; aluminium cylinder head; cast iron cylinder block; 5-bearing crankshaft; Bosch VER82 fuel injection.

TRANSMISSION: front wheel drive; 7.5in cable-operated clutch; 4/5-speed gearbox; synchromesh; automatic optional; final drive ratio automatic and 4- speed 3.74:1.

CHASSIS DETAILS: integral steel structure; independent front suspension by Macpherson struts, coil springs, anti-roll bar; rear suspension trailing arms with torsional cross-beam, coil springs, anti-roll bar; 9.2in disc front 7.8in drum rear servo brakes, diagonally-split; rack and pinion steering; 42L (9.2 Imp gal, 11.1 US gal) fuel tank, estate 50L (11 Imp gal, 13.2 US gal); 155R 13 tyres, 5J rims.

DIMENSIONS wheelbase 251.4cm (99in); front track 140cm (55in), 140.5cm (55.3in) rear; ground clearance 13.5cm (5.3in); turning circle 10.6m (34.8ft); length 400cm (157.5in); width 163.5cm (64.4in); height 138cm (54.3in). Estate length 420.5cm (165.5in), height 140cm (55in).

PERFORMANCE: maximum speed 143kph (89mph); 37.7kph (23.5mph) @ 1000rpm; acceleration 0-96kph (60mph) 19.1sec; 23.4kg/kW (17.1kg/bhp); fuel consumption 7.1-8.1L/100km (35-40mpg).

PRODUCTION 1,117,662 all Astra including Mk II.

PRICE 1982 1.6LD 3-door £5203; 5-door estate £5758.

229

Two years after its introduction Vauxhall brought out an estate Cavalier. It had always maintained that the Astra and Carlton catered for estate car customers but demand persisted and assent was finally given in 1983. It was not entirely home-grown. It was based on the Cavalier's 256.5cm (101in) wheelbase but was 5cm (2in) longer, a development carried out by General Motors Holden in Australia and designed by attached engineer Peter Hannenberger. It became available in Britain with the 1.6-litre 67kW (90bhp) petrol engine and 40kW (54bhp) diesel and 40,856 were sold by the time the Cavalier II production ended in 1988. In 1986 it helped the model to its best UK year when one new car in ten was a Cavalier. There never was an Opel equivalent.

The petrol estate automatic managed 165kph (103mph) and accelerated to 96kph (60mph) in 13.5sec, but the diesel Cavalier introduced together with the Astra diesel in 1982 was scarcely sprightly. It barely kept abreast of traffic on the motorway and the automatic was even more leisurely. It did have new high-energy pre-heater plugs to make starting quicker however and automatic cold-start enrichment amounting to 180 per cent of the full-load fuel supply.

BODY saloon, 4 doors, 5 seats; weight 1015kg (2238lb); estate, 5 doors, 1040kg (2293lb).

ENGINE 4 cylinders, in-line, transverse front, 80.0mm x 79.5mm; 1598cc compr 23:1; 40kW (54bhp) @ 4600rpm; 24.8kW/L (33.5bhp/L); 95Nm (71lb/ft) @ 2400rpm.

ENGINE STRUCTURE belt-driven overhead camshaft; aluminium cylinder head; cast iron cylinder block; 5-bearing crankshaft; Bosch VER82 fuel injection.

TRANSMISSION front wheel drive; sdp clutch; 4 or 5-speed gearbox; synchromesh; automatic optional; final drive ratio 3.94:1, 3.43:1 automatic.

CHASSIS DETAILS integral steel structure; independent front suspension by Macpherson struts, anti-roll bar; rear suspension trailing arms, torsion beam, coil springs with dampers inclined at 45deg, anti-roll bar; disc front drum rear brakes; rack and pinion steering 3.5 turns lock-lock; 61L (13.4 Imp gal, 16.1 US gal) fuel tank; 165SR13 or 185/70 SR13 tyres, 5 or 5.5J rims.

DIMENSIONS wheelbase 257.5cm (101.4in); front track 140cm (55in), 140.5cm (55.3in) rear; ground clearance 14cm (5.5in); turning circle 11m (36.1ft); length 436.5cm (172in); width 167cm (65.7in); height 139.5cm (55in).

PERFORMANCE maximum speed 143kph (89mph); 36kph (24.4mph) @ 1000rpm; 0-100kph (63mph) 21sec, 26sec automatic; 25.4kg/kW (18.8kg/bhp); fuel consumption 5.1-6.8 L/100km (41.5-55mpg).

PRODUCTION 806,359 all Cavalier II.

PRICE 1983 diesel saloon LD 4-door £5913, 5-door £6040. 1986 estate 1.6GL £8847, diesel estate £8194.

1982-1987 Senator and Monza Coupe

Rationalising what was still a joint Vauxhall-Opel range, Viceroy, Commodore, and Royale were replaced by Senator, an upgraded Royale with every extra in the Vauxhall armoury including alloy wheels. Velour carpets, steering wheel height adjustment, tinted glass, and a headlamp wash-wipe were included in the price. Both Senator and Monza remained Opels until October 1984 when the Senator was rebadged Vauxhall. There was a Senator 2.5E saloon in C trim, Senator 3.0E in C and CD trim, and Monza 3.0E C Coupe. External changes reduced drag, the Senator being credited with a coefficient of 0.39 and the Monza 0.35. These stemmed from a more sloping bonnet and frontal treatment similar to the Carlton while the rear deckline of the Senator was raised with a sharper trailing edge giving a useful increase in luggage capacity.

Air conditioning was standard on the Senator CD which also introduced the short-lived vogue for digital instruments. The Monza's limited-slip differential was also available on the Senator and fuel injection was standardised. An impact sensor automatically unlocked the doors in an accident. The 5-speed gearbox with overdrive top was standard on the 2.5E Senator and 3.0E Monza and a no-cost option on the 3.0E C Senator.

BODY saloon, 4 doors, 5 seats Senator; Coupe Monza, 3 doors, 5 seats; weight 1335kg (2943lb).
ENGINE 6 cylinders, in-line, front, 87.0mm x 69.8mm; 2490cc; compr: 9.2:1; 100kW (134bhp) @ 5200rpm; 40.2kW/L (53.8bhp/L); 186Nm (138lb/ft) @ 4600rpm. 95mm x 69.8mm, 2969cc, compr: 9.4:1, 132kW (177bhp) @ 5800rpm, 44.5kW/L (59.6bhp/L), 248Nm (185lb/ft) @ 4400rpm. 2969cc, 152kW (204bhp) @ 6000rpm, 51.2kW/L (68.7bhp/L), 267Nm (199ft/lb) @ 3600rpm.
ENGINE STRUCTURE overhead valves; chain-driven overhead camshaft; hydraulic tappets; cast iron cylinder head and block; 7-bearing crankshaft; Bosch LE Jetronic fuel injection; electronic ignition; water-cooled, viscous fan.
TRANSMISSION rear wheel drive; 9.0in dia clutch (Monza 9.5in); 5-speed gearbox, overdrive top; synchromesh; 3 speed later 4 speed automatic optional; hypoid bevel final drive; ratio 3.45:1.

CHASSIS DETAILS integral steel structure; ifs by MacPherson struts; irs by semi-trailing arms coil springs, telescopic dampers; anti-roll bars front and rear; disc brakes all round; vacuum servo; split system front-rear; recirculating ball PAS; 75L (16.5 Imp gal, 19.8 US gal) fuel tank, Monza 70L (15.4 Imp gal, 18.5 US gal); 195/70R 206/60VR15 tyres, 6.0in rims.
DIMENSIONS wheelbase 268.5cm (105.7in); front track 144.5cm (57in), 147cm (58in) rear; ground clearance 14cm (5.5in); turning circle 10.2m (33.5ft); length 484cm (190.6in); width 172cm (67.7in); height 141.5cm (55.7in).
PERFORMANCE Senator 2.5E maximum speed 195kph (122mph); 33.7kph (21mph) @ 1000rpm; acceleration 0-96kph (60mph) 11.5sec, automatic 12.5sec; 13.4kg/kW (10kg/bhp); fuel consumption 11.8-14.1L/100km (20–24mpg).
PRODUCTION 33,125 Senator I and II.
PRICE 1984 Senator 2.5E £10,923, Monza 3.0E GSE £13,801.

Vauxhall was riding the crest of a wave with 11.5 per cent of the UK market, so it was with some dismay that it found itself forced to cope with an industrial dispute over the import of the new Nova from the Spanish factory where it was made. The problem was solved in due course and the car, which had gone through its design phase in 1976, went into production at Zaragoza as GM's S-car with plans to make 270,000 a year.

This rival to the Ford Fiesta, VW Polo, Fiat 127, and Renault 5 had its steering and suspension made in Cadiz, soft trim at Rioja, and overhead camshaft "Family 1"engine and F10 transmission made at Aspern near Vienna. Hatchback, 5-door, and 33cm (13in) longer but mechanically identical notchback 4-door versions came out at the same time.

There were three engine options at first, 1.0, 1.2, and 1.3-litre petrol, and the transverse power pack was unusual in having the gearbox alongside so that the driveshafts were of unequal length. Designer Herbert Oberhaus added a flywheel on the longer shaft to damp out vibration, claiming elimination of torque-steer by installing the engine a degree or two offset from true "east-west".

BODY saloon, 3/4/5 doors, 5 seats; 3-dr 745kg (1642lb), 5-dr 805kg (1775lb).
ENGINE 4 cyls, in-line, transverse front, 72mm x 61mm; 993cc; compr: 9.2:1; 33.5kW (45bhp) @ 5400rpm; 33.8kW/L (45.3bhp/L); 67Nm (50lb/ft) @ 2600rpm. 77.8mm x 62.9mm, 1196cc, 41kW (55bhp) @ 5600rpm; 34.3kW/L (46bhp/L), 88.5Nm (66lb/ft) @ 2200rpm. 75mm x 73.4mm, 1297cc, 52kW (70bhp) @ 5800rpm, 40.1kW/L (54bhp/L), 99Nm (74lb/ft) @ 3800rpm. From 1987 79mm x 81.5mm, 1598cc, 75kW (101bhp) @ 5600rpm; 47kW/L (63bhp/L); 134Nm (100lb/ft) @ 3400rpm.
ENGINE STRUCTURE pushrod ohv (993cc), belt-driven ohc (others); cast iron (993cc) aluminium (others) cyl head; cast iron block; 3-bearing crank; Weber carb 993cc, Pierburg 1.2, 1.3 Varajet 1.6; 1.2, 1.3, 1.6 electronic ignition.
TRANSMISSION front wheel drive; diaphragm spring clutch; 4- & 5-spd; synchro; 3.74, 3.94:1; electric fan.
CHASSIS DETAILS integral steel structure; ifs by MacPherson strut, anti-roll bar; irs by compound crank system, coil springs, hydraulic dampers, optional anti-roll bar 1.3; disc front, drum rear, vacuum servo, diagonal split circuit; rack and pinion; 42L (9.2 Imp gal, 11 US gal) fuel tank; 135SR13, 145SR13 tyres 4.5 rims.
DIMENSIONS wheelbase 234.5cm (92in); front track 132cm (52in), 130.5cm (51in) rear; ground clearance 14cm (5.5in); turning circle 10m (32.8ft); length 362cm (142.5in); width 153cm (60in); height 136.5cm (54in).
PERFORMANCE 1.0 max 140kph (87mph); 28.6kph (17.8mph) @ 1000rpm; 0-96kph (60mph) 19.5sec; 22.2kg/kW (16.6kg/bhp); 7.1-7.8L/100km (36-40mpg). 1.3 max 161kph (100mph); 37kph (59.4mph) @ 1000rpm; 0-96kph (60mph) 13.5sec; 14.3kg/kW (10.6kg/bhp); 6.4-8.8L/100km (32-44mpg).
PRODUCTION 446,462.
PRICE 1983 1.0 hatchback £3635, radio + £75. 1.2 hatchback £4273, 5-speed + £128, alloy wheels + £176. 1988 1.3SR £6999, 1.6GTE £8512.

1984-1991 Astra II 1.2, 1.3

Aerodynamics were much in vogue when the second series of Astra came out. A low coefficient of drag (Cd) was almost as keenly sought as a high ratio of power to weight. But some new cars of the period, like the Ford Sierra, had not been well received despite their favourable aerodynamics. The customers did not like the shape so it was a bold initiative on the part of the normally conservative General Motors to sanction a new Vauxhall with a Cd of 0.30 or less. This was a figure achieved two years earlier by Audi which carefully streamlined underneath its costly new 100. Yet here was a mainstream volume production car matching it by eliminating drag-inducing features such as rain-guttering, fitting flush windows, a polypropylene nose blended with a wrap-round bumper, and reducing the size of the air intake to what was necessary rather than too large. The underfloor fuel tank was faired-in, wheel arch lips were removed, and gaps between the bonnet and headlamps filled.

Code-named T-85, the Astra II was a success from the start. It carried over much of its predecessor's platform and five engines with many useful improvements.

BODY saloon, estate, convertible, 5 seats; weight 3 doors, 850kg (1874lb), 5 doors 870kg (1918lb), estate 3 doors 895kg (1973lb), 5 doors 915kg (2017lb). 1297cc + 15kg (33lb), automatic + 35kg (77lb).
ENGINE 4 cyls, in-line, transverse, front, 79mm x 61mm; 1196cc; compr: 9.0:1; 41kW (55bhp) @ 5600rpm; 34.2kW/L (46bhp/L); 83Nm (62lb/ft) @ 3600rpm. 75mm x 73.4mm, 1297cc; compr 9.2:1; 56kW (75bhp) @ 5800rpm; 43.2kW/L (57.8bhp/L); 101Nm (75lb/ft) @ 3800rpm.
ENGINE STRUCTURE pushrod overhead valves 1196cc; overhead camshaft 1297cc; cast iron cylinder head and block 1196cc, aluminium head 1297cc; 3-bearing crankshaft (5 for 1297cc); 1196cc Weber 32TL single choke carburettor, 1297cc Pierburg 2E twin choke.
TRANSMISSION front wheel drive; sdp clutch; 4 or 5-speed gearbox; synchromesh; automatic option 1297cc; 3.94:1 final drive, 4.18 estate and 5-speed.
CHASSIS DETAILS integral steel structure; ifs by Macpherson struts, coil springs, anti-roll bar; rear suspension trailing arms with torsional cross-beam, coil springs, anti-roll bar; 9.2in disc front 7.8in drum rear servo brakes, diagonally-split; rack and pinion, PAS optional; 52L (11.4 Imp gal, 13.7 US gal) fuel tank, estate 50L (11 Imp gal, 13.2 US gal); 145SR 13 tyres, 155SR 13 or 175/70SR 13, 4.5, 5.0, or 5.5J rims.
DIMENSIONS wheelbase 252cm (99in); front track 140cm (55in), 140.5cm (55.3in) rear; ground clearance 13.5cm (5.3in); turning circle 10.5m (34.5ft); length 400cm (157.5in); width 166.5cm (65.5in); height 140cm (55in). Estate length 423cm (166.5in), height 143cm (56.3in).
PERFORMANCE 1196cc maximum speed 155kph (96.5mph); 34.9kph (21.7mph) @ 1000rpm; 0-96kph (60mph) 17sec; 20.7kg/kW (15.5kg/bhp); 5.1-8.4L/100km (34-56mpg).
PRODUCTION 1,117,662.
PRICE 1985 1.2S 3 door £4494; 1.3S L 5 door £5678.

237

1984-1991 Astra II 1.6, 1.8, 2.0

The "Family II" engines of the Astra or T-car range were 1.6 and 1.8-litres on introduction, followed in 1986 by a 2.0-litre. Variations were introduced throughout the Astra II's seven-year run under names such as Merit, Antibes, Shadow, Jubilee (marking 25 years' production at Ellesmere Port), Diamond, Swing, Tiffany, Celebrity, Starlight and Starmist, many denoting special Limited Editions which proved popular with dealers and customers alike.

In 1987 the pretty Convertible provided competition for VW and Ford. Vauxhall sent partly finished body shells to Bertone in Turin but the conversion was not wholly successful. A good deal of rear seat space was lost in providing stowage for the hood and even with a full safety roll bar the structure was not sufficiently stiff to prevent scuttle shake. Erecting the hood manually was not easy.

The Convertible GTE was offered initially with the 86kW (115bhp) engine. The most potent Astra was the 16v GTE with four valves per cylinder and 110kW (148bhp). Production was concentrated at Ellesmere Port from August 1984 and in 1985 the model was elected Car of the Year. Quick Silver was a special edition made for the Birmingham Motor Show of 1987.

BODY saloon, estate, convertible, 5 seats; 3 doors 915kg (2017lb), 5 doors 935kg (2061lb), estate 3 doors 975kg (2150lb), 5 doors 995kg (2194lb). Automatic + 25kg (55lb). 1796cc 3 doors 950kg (2094lb), 5 doors 970kg (2139lb). Convertible 1015kg (2238lb). ENGINE 4 cyls, in line, transverse front, 71.0mm x 89.5mm; 1598cc; compr: 10.0:1; 60kW (80.5bhp) @ 5400rpm; 37.7kW/L (50.4bhp/L); 130Nm (97lb/ft) @ 2600rpm. 84.8mm x 79.5mm, 1796cc, 82kW (110bhp) @ 5600rpm, 45.7kW/L (61.2bhp/L), 158Nm (118lb/ft) @ 3000rpm. 86mm x 86mm, 1998cc, 95kW (127bhp) @ 5600rpm; 547.5kW/L (63.8bhp/L); 180Nm (150lb/ft) @ 4800rpm. 1998cc 16v compr: 10.5:1, 110kW (148bhp) @ 6000rpm; 55.1kW/L (73.8bhp/L); 196Nm (146lb/ft) @ 4800rpm. ENGINE STRUCTURE belt-driven ohc; 1998cc 110kW 16v chain-driven 2 ohc; al cyl head; ci block; 5-bg crank; Varajet II carb 1598cc, Bosch LE-Jetronic inj 1796cc; Motronic 1998cc. TRANSMISSION fwd; 4 or 5 spd;

synchro; auto optional; 3.74:1 4-spd, 3.94:1 5-spd, 3.43 auto 3.55 2.0-litre. CHASSIS DETAILS integral steel structure; ifs by Macpherson struts, coil springs, anti-roll bar; rear susp trailing arms with torsional cross-beam, coil springs, anti-roll bar; 9.2in disc front, 7.8in drum rear servo, diagonally-split; rack and pinion, PAS optional; 52L (11.4 Imp gal, 13.7 US gal), estate 50L (11 Imp gal, 13.2 US gal); 155SR 13 tyres 1598cc, 175/70HR 13 and 185/60HR 14 others. DIMENSIONS wheelbase 252cm (99in); front track 140cm (55in), 140.5cm (55.3in) rear; ground clearance 13.5cm (5.3in); turning circle 10.5m (34.5ft); length 400cm (157.5in); width 166.5cm (65.5in); height 140cm (55in). Estate length 423cm (166.5in), ht 143cm (56.3in). PERFORMANCE 1987 1998cc 95kW max 206kph (128mph); 34.5kph (21.5mph) @ 1000rpm; 0-96kph (60mph) 8.5sec; 9.6kg/kW (7.2kg/bhp); 5.7-10.1L/100km (28-49.5mpg). PRICE 1985 GTE £7344 PAS £299; GTE Convertible 1987 £11600.

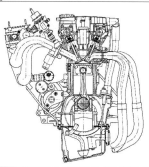

1984-1991 Astra II Diesel

Vauxhall abstained from direct injection, turbochargers and intercoolers for the Astra diesel, preferring to emphasise economy and practicality at a price only £330 above the 1.6-litre petrol-engined car. The 1.7-litre diesel engine introduced in 1987 was a development of the older 1.6, and the aluminium cylinder head was based on the Family II with indirect injection, the increase in capacity obtained by widening the cylinder bore from 80mm 82.5mm. Noise reduction was accomplished by lighter pistons and a redesign of the inlet manifold that also provided 6 per cent more power than the 1598cc.

Spring and damper settings of the 1.3 and 1.6-litre petrol engined cars remained unchanged, and the 1989 cosmetic alterations included minor alterations to the suspension mountings derived from the Cavalier. In view of the additional weight of the diesel engine, the optional power steering with 3.4 turns lock to lock was necessary to avoid the manual's four whole turns which could make parking tiresome.

Equipment was plain with cloth upholstery, no tachometer or steering rake adjustment, but a radio-cassette player with four speakers and a tilt-slide glass sunroof were standard.

BODY saloon, 5 seats; weight 3 doors 940kg (2072lb), 5 doors 960kg (2116lb); estate, 5 seats, weight 3 doors 990kg (2183lb), 5 doors 1010kg (2227lb). Automatic + 25kg (55lb).
ENGINE 4 cylinders, in-line, front transverse; 80mm x 79.5mm, 1598cc; compr: 23:1; 41kW (55bhp) @ 4600rpm; 25.7kW/L (34.4bhp/L); 95Nm (71lb/ft) @ 2400rpm. 82.5mm x 79.5mm 1699cc, 42.5kW (57bhp) @ 4600rpm; 25.5kW/L (34.2bhp/L); 103Nm (77lb/ft) @ 2400rpm.
ENGINE STRUCTURE belt-driven overhead camshaft; aluminium cylinder head; cast iron block; 5-bearing crankshaft; Bosch 5L fuel injection.
TRANSMISSION: front wheel drive; 7.5in cable-operated clutch; 4/5-speed gearbox; synchromesh; automatic optional; final drive ratio automatic and 4- speed 3.74:1, 5-speed 3.94:1.
 CHASSIS DETAILS: integral steel structure; independent front suspension by Macpherson struts, coil springs, anti-roll bar; rear suspension trailing arms with torsional cross-beam, coil springs, anti-roll bar; 9.2in disc front 7.8in drum rear servo brakes, diagonally-split; rack and pinion steering PAS optional; 52L (11.4 Imp gal, 13.7 US gal) fuel tank, estate 50L (11 Imp gal, 13.2 US gal); 155SR 13 or 175/70 SR13 tyres.
DIMENSIONS wheelbase 252cm (99in); front track 140cm (55in), 140.5cm (55.3in) rear; ground clearance 13.5cm (5.3in); turning circle 10.5m (34.5ft); length 400cm (157.5in); width 166.5cm (65.5in); height 140cm (55in). Estate length 423cm (166.5in), height 143cm (56.3in).
PERFORMANCE 1699cc maximum speed 146kph (91mph); 37.7kph (23.5mph) @ 1000rpm; acceleration 0-96kph (60mph) 15.1sec; 22.1kg/kW (16.5kg/bhp); fuel consumption 6L/100km (47mpg).
PRODUCTION 1,117,662 all Astra. PRICE 1987 1.7DL £8569, PAS £410.

Launched at Frankfurt in 1985 to meet a demand for classic non-hatchback three-box saloons, the Belmont shared the Astra's 252cm (99.2in) wheelbase and mechanical platform with an additional 22cm (8.7in) overall length to accommodate a roomy rear luggage boot. The 19.4cu ft space could be increased to 43.4cu ft by folding the 60/40 split rear seat backs flat giving the Belmont class-leading carrying capacity. The boot lid opened down to bumper height enabling bulky loads to be handled with ease. The extra length impaired the carefully-contrived aerodynamics very little, the Cd rising only a fraction from the Astra's 0.30 to 0.32.

GLSi specification included fashionable accessories such as alloy wheels, reclining seats, remote control door mirrors, tinted glass, and central locking in the price. The demand for economy and relaxed cruising was met by ever-higher gearing, and the overdrive top gear (0.71:1) of the 1.8 Belmont gave almost 40kph (25mph) per 1000rpm, making changes down to 4th necessary for motorway hills.

The Belmont was also available with the Astra's wide range of engines including the diesel but not the 16 valve 2.0-litre. There was a variety of trims including the luxury CD and even an estate.

BODY saloon, 4 doors, 5 seats, weight 885kg (1951lb).
ENGINE 4 cyls, in-line, transverse, front, 79mm x 61mm; 1196cc; compr: 9.0:1; 41kW (55bhp) @ 5600rpm; 34.3kW/L (46bhp/L); 83Nm (62lb/ft) @ 3600rpm. 75mm x 73.4mm, 1297cc; compr 9.2:1; 56kW (75bhp) @ 5800rpm; 43.1kW/L (57.8bhp/L); 101Nm (75lb/ft) @ 3800rpm. 71.0mm x 89.5mm; 1598cc; compr: 10.0:1; 60kW (80.5bhp) @ 5400rpm; 37.5kW/L (50.4bhp/L); 130Nm (97lb/ft) @ 2600rpm. 84.8mm x 79.5mm, 1796cc, 82kW (110bhp) @ 5600rpm, 45.7kW/L (61.2bhp/L), 158Nm (118lb/ft) @ 3000rpm. 86mm x 86mm, 1998cc, 95kW (128bhp) @ 5600rpm; 47.5kW/L (63.8bhp/L); 180Nm (150lb/ft) @ 4800rpm. Diesel: 80mm x 79.5mm, 1598cc; compr: 23:1; 41kW (55bhp) @ 4600rpm; 25.7kW/L (34.4bhp/L); 95Nm (71lb/ft) @ 2400rpm. 82.5mm x 79.5mm 1699cc, 42.5kW (57bhp) @ 4600rpm; 25.5kW/L (34.2bhp/L); 103Nm (77lb/ft) @ 2400rpm.
ENGINE STRUCTURE belt-driven ohc; aluminium cylinder head; 1998cc 116kW 16 valve; cast iron block; 5-bearing crank; Pierburg 2E 1297cc, Varajet II carburettor 1598cc, Bosch LE-Jetronic fuel injection 1796cc; Motronic 1998cc; electric fan, water-cooled.
TRANSMISSION front wheel drive; 4 or 5-speed gearbox; synchromesh; automatic optional; final drive ratios 3.74:1 4-speed, 3.94:1 5-speed, 3.43 auto, 3.55 2.0-litre.
CHASSIS DETAILS integral steel structure; ifs by Macpherson struts, coil springs, anti-roll bar; rear susp trailing arms with torsional cross-beam, coil springs, anti-roll bar; 9.2in disc brakes front, 7.8in drum rear servo, diagonally-split; rack and pinion, PAS optional; 52L (11.4 Imp gal,13.7 US gal); estate 50L (11 Imp gal, 13.2 US gal); 155SR 13 tyres 1598cc, 175/70HR 13 and 185/60HR 14 others.
DIMENSIONS wheelbase 252cm (99in); front track 140cm (55in), 140.5cm (55.3in) rear; ground clearance 13.5cm (5.3in); turning

circle 10.5m (34.5ft); length 422cm
(166in); width 166cm (65.3in); height
140cm (55in).
PERFORMANCE 1986 1.8GLS
maximum speed 174kph (108mph);
39.9kph (24.9mph) @ 1000rpm; 0-
96kph (60mph) 9.2sec; 10.8kg/kW
(8kg/bhp); average fuel consumption
8.8L/100km (32mpg).
UK SALES 40,150.
PRICE 1986 1.8GLS £8095,
automatic £573, PAS £323, electric
windows £338.

Below: 1.8 Astra and
Belmont engine.
Centre right: LXi estate.

1986-1993 Carlton II 1.8, 1.8i, 2.0i, 2.3D

Replacing the Carlton of 1978, the Mark II gained 6cm (2.4in) in wheelbase, 3.6cm (1.4in) in length, 4.8cm (1.9in) in width and height, and although the frontal area was also up, improved aerodynamics kept the Cd to 0.28. In the mid 1980s anything under 0.30 was extremely creditable, and its predecessor had been 0.36.

It was a merit of the long slim envelope as well as carefully curved contours and fine detailing that the Carlton was not only an efficient shape but looked well proportioned. Its flush-glass treatment was a success and in plan form it had a noticeable taper towards the rear. Refinement was enhanced in a number of ways. Pistons and connecting rods were lightened by 1.2kg (2.6lb) and the rods were lengthened by 7mm (0.275in) by positioning the gudgeon pin higher up the piston. This reduced the unbalanced secondary forces by about 25 per cent, and a 30 per cent heavier flywheel produced one of the smoothest-running 4-cylinder engines of the time. The engine had pioneering long curved inlet tracts that contributed to a useful wide spread of pulling power, and mapped electronic ignition which could be reset by the driver for 91 or 95RON lead-free fuel.

BODY saloon, 5 seats, 4 doors; weight 1.8 1178kg (2598lb), 1.8i 1212kg (2673lb), 2.3D 1296kg (2857lb); estate, 5 doors, 1255kg (2766lb).
ENGINE 4 cylinders, in-line, front, 84.8mm x 79.5mm; 1796cc; compr: 10:1; 1.8/1.8i: 67/86kW (90/115bhp) @ 5200/5600rpm; 37.3/47.9kW/L (50.1/64bhp/L); 146/149Nm (109/111lb/ft) @ 3400/4600rpm. 86mm x 86mm 1998cc, 91kW (122bhp) @ 5400rpm; 45.5kW/L (61.1bhp/L); 173Nm (129lb/ft) @ 2600rpm. 92.0mm x 85.0mm, 2260cc diesel; compr 22:1; 54kW (73bhp) @ 4400rpm; 24.1kW/L (32.3bhp/L); 137Nm (102lb/ft) @ 2400rpm. Turbodiesel compr 23:1, 66kW (88.5bhp) @ 4200rpm, 29.2kW/L (39.2bhp/L), 119Nm (160lb/ft) @ 2200rpm.
ENGINE STRUCTURE belt-driven ohc (diesel chain); al cyl head, ci block; 5-bg crank; Pierburg 2E carb 1.8, Bosch LE Jetronic fuel inj 1.8i/2.0i; diesel Bosch mechanical inj; petrol electronic ign; turbodiesel KKK K24.

TRANSMISSION rwd; diaphragm spring clutch; GM 3-rail 5-speed; synchro; auto optional; final drive ratio 3.7, 3.9:1, 5-speed 3.45:1.
CHASSIS DETAILS integral steel structure; ifs MacPherson struts, anti-roll bar; irs semi-trailing arms, coils, telescopic dampers, anti-roll bar; dual circuit split front-rear vacuum servo disc brakes, ABS opt; recirculating ball PAS; 75L (16.5 Imp gal, 19.8 US gal) tank; Estate 70L (15.4 Imp gal, 18.5 US gal); 185/70TR-14 tyres, 5.5 rims.
DIMENSIONS wheelbase 273cm (107.5in); front track 145cm (57in), rear 147cm (58in); ground clearance 14cm (5.5in); turning circle 10.8m (35.4ft); length 469cm (184.6in); width 177cm (70in); height 144.5cm (57in). Estate front track 145cm (57in), rear 146cm (57.5in), length 473cm (186in), height 148cm (58in).
PERFORMANCE 1.8i max 194kph (121mph); 0-96kph (60mph) 12sec; 14.1kg/kW (10.5kg/bhp); 8.3-10.9L/100km (26-34mpg).
PRODUCTION 241,051.
PRICE 1986 2.0i CD£12340.

1987-1993 Carlton 2.4i, GSi 3000

The beautifully-detailed 6-cylinder Carlton had separate power outputs quoted with or without catalytic converters. The 3.0i went on sale in the spring of 1987 with or without emission control equipment in different markets; non-cat cars had 9.4:1 compression ratio, 3.7:1 axle, and developed 43.9kW/L. Catalyser cars had a compression ratio of 8.5:1 and developed 114.5kW (153.5bhp) or 38.7kW/L and 230Nm @ 3800rpm on lead-free petrol. The difference gave cat cars a top speed of 213kph (133mph), 9kph (5.6mph) slower. The cat added a full second to the 0-60mph time and increased fuel consumption by 3-4 per cent. The Carlton acquired a reputation for sporting performance. The newly smoothed engine revved to 6000 for its top speed of 221.5kph (138mph). Drivers found that 100mph came up quickly and easily, and the car still felt relaxed at 120mph, but the expected broad torque band did not materialise and the engine was rather inflexible.

Handling and roadholding benefited from the trendy wide tyres, and even though the ride was on the firm side, they were not yet sufficiently low-profile to make it harsh. A 4-cylinder 2.4i engine was introduced in 1988 and 24v GSi 3000 in 1989.

BODY saloon, 5 seats, 4 doors; weight 1250kg (2756lb), 2.4i 1330kg (2932lb); estate 1.8 1255kg (2766lb).
ENGINE 6 cyls, in-line, front, 95.0mm x 69.8mm; 2969cc; compr: 9.4:1; 132kW (177bhp) @ 5600rpm; 44.5kW/L (59.6bhp/L); 245Nm (183lb/ft) @ 4800rpm. 152kW (204bhp) @ 6000rpm; 51.2kW/L (68.7bhp/L); 267Nm (199lb/ft) @ 3600rpm.
4 cyls, 95mm x 85mm, 2410cc, compr 9.2:1, 92kW (124bhp) @ 4800rpm 38.2kW/L (bhp/L); 195Nm (145lb/ft) @ 2400rpm. 24v 152kW (204bhp) @ 6000rpm; 63.1kW/L (84.6bhp/L); 270Nm (199lb/ft) @ 3600rpm.
ENGINE STRUCTURE chain-driven ohc (2 cams 24v); cast iron cyl head and block; 4cyl 5-bearing crank, 7-bearing 6 cyl; Bosch LE-Jetronic fuel injection, Motronic 6 cyl, twin closed-loop catalytic converters.
TRANSMISSION rear wheel drive; diaphragm spring clutch; GM 3-rail 5-speed; synchromesh; 4 speed GM automatic no-cost option; final drive ratio 3.45:1, 3.70; 24v limited slip diff.

CHASSIS DETAILS integral steel structure; ifs by MacPherson struts, anti-roll bar; irs by semi-trailing arms, coil springs, telescopic dampers, anti-roll bar; dual circuit split front-rear vacuum servo disc brakes, ABS standard on 24v; recirculating ball PAS; 75L (16.5 Imp gal, 19.8 US gal) tank; 195/65VR-14 tyres, 7in rims.
DIMENSIONS wheelbase 273cm (107.5in); front track 145cm (57in), rear 147cm (58in); ground clearance 14cm (5.5in); turning circle 10.8m (35.4ft); length 469cm (184.6in); width 177cm (70in); height 144.5cm (57in). Estate front track 145cm (57in), rear 146cm (57.5in), length 473cm (186in), height 148cm (58in).
PERFORMANCE (3000GSi) maximum speed 221.5kph (138mph), 239kph (149mph) 24v; 37.4kph (23.3mph) @ 1000rpm; 9.5kg/kW (7.1kg/bhp); fuel consumption 10.8-14.1L/100km (20-26mpg).
PRICE 1987 GSi 3000 £16999; 1989 GSi 3000 £21,690.
PRODUCTION 1463.

247

There were two Novas introduced at the 1987 Frankfurt Motor Show with a diesel engine 4EC1 designed by GM's Japanese partner Isuzu. These were a 37kW non-turbo and a 50kW turbocharged version. The turbo was an outstanding performer accelerating to 96kph (60mph) in 12.2sec and reaching 162kph (101mph) while returning over 6.5L/100km (43mpg). It had a substantial advantage on almost all its rivals, even though it cost £860 on top of the non-turbo Nova diesel's 1992 price of £8600, or the best part of £2500 over the cheapest petrol Nova, the 1.2 Trip 3-door. The turbo was surprisingly economical, *Autocar's* testers obtaining 46.7mpg against the turbo's extremely praiseworthy 43.8mpg. The 1.5TD turbo furthermore had a catalytic converter unavailable on the 1.5D.

Autocar was also relieved over not having to make much use of the Nova's gearbox, which it described as notchy. It found the driveline taut and the clutch deftly cushioned. By the 1990s however, some of the Nova's rivals had caught up, notably the supple-riding Peugeot. Non-power steering made it feel cumbersome against nimbler superminis and many owners endorsed the testers' view that only dedicated economy motorists would be likely to prefer it against the turbo.

BODY hatchback, saloon, 5 seats, 2/3/4/5 doors, weight 850kg (1874lb).
ENGINE 4 cylinders, in-line, transverse, front, 76mm x 82mm; 1488cc; compr 23:1, turbo 22.5:1; 37/50kW (50/67bhp) @ 4600/4800rpm; 25/33.6kW/L (33.6/45bhp/L); 88.5/130Nm (66/97lb/ft) @ 2600/3000rpm.
ENGINE STRUCTURE single belt-driven overhead camshaft; aluminium cylinder head; cast iron block; 5 bearing crankshaft; Bosch VE fuel injection.
TRANSMISSION front wheel drive; sdp clutch; 5-speed gearbox; synchromesh; final drive ratio 3.74:1.
CHASSIS DETAILS integral steel structure; independent front suspension by MacPherson strut, anti-roll bar; independent rear suspension by compound crank system, coil springs, hydraulic dampers, optional anti-roll bar 1.3; disc front drum rear brakes, vacuum servo, diagonal split circuit; rack and pinion steering; 42L (9.2 Imp gal, 11 US gal) fuel tank; 145SR13 tyres 4.5 J rims.

DIMENSIONS wheelbase 234.5cm (92.3in); front track 132cm (52in), 130.5cm (51.4in) rear; ground clearance 14cm (5.5in); turning circle 10m (32.8ft); length 362cm (142.5in); width 153cm (60.2in); height 136.5cm (53.7in).
PERFORMANCE non-turbo maximum speed 142kph (88mph); 38.9kph (24.24mph) @ 1000rpm; acceleration 0-96kph (60mph) 15.4sec; 17/23kg/kW (12.7/17kg/bhp); fuel consumption 5.7-6.3L/100km (44.8-50mpg).
PRODUCTION 446,462.
PRICE 1.5 D Merit 3 door £7957, 5-door £8600, 1.5 TD Merit 5-door £9111.

249

1987-1993 Senator

The second rendering of the Senator in the autumn of 1987 was one of the best Vauxhalls of the time. It bore a passing resemblance to the Carlton but subtle differences made it look quite different. They included the egg-crate grille reminiscent of old Formula 1 Ferraris, and a window in the C-pillar that lightened the entire aspect of the car.

Active Chassis Technology was a switchable system setting the dampers to Hard Soft and Intermediate and standard on the CD. The ZF Servotronic steering was light for parking and heavier at speed yet it never had the sensitive nature keen drivers might prefer. The ACT was also speed-perceptive, switching itself to Hard when doing over 112kph (70mph), reverting to its previous setting when it was going slower.

The Senator was an effortless car with a smooth ride, quiet engine, and lots of lounging room. The interior was carefully detailed and the CD air conditioned a cold box in the facia. The 24-valve engine was entirely new, sharing only cylinder spacings and dimensions in a thin-wall cast block. The twin-cam aluminium head had direct acting hydraulic bucket tappets. Bosch Motronic engine management controlled sequential fuel injection and Dual Ram tuned intake system.

BODY saloon, 5 seats, 4 doors, weight 1435kg (3163lb).
ENGINE 6 cylinders, in line, front, 87.1mm x 69.6mm; 2490cc; compr: 9.2:1; 103kW (138bhp) @ 5200rpm; 39.9kW/L (53.5bhp/L); 205Nm (153lb/ft) @ 4200rpm. 95mm x 69.8mm, 2969cc, compr 10:1; 130kW (175bhp) @ 5800rpm; 43.8kW/L (59bhp/L); 240Nm (179lb/ft) @ 4800rpm. 24v 150kW (201bhp) @ 6000rpm, 50.5kW/L (67.8bhp/L), 270 Nm (201lb/ft) @ 3600rpm.
ENGINE STRUCTURE chain-driven ohc (2 cam 24v); cast iron cyl head (aluminium on 24v) and block; 7-bearing crank; Bosch Motronic fuel injection with digital management; twin closed-loop catalytic converters.
TRANSMISSION rear wheel drive; diaphragm spring clutch; GM 3-rail 5-speed; synchromesh; 4-speed GM automatic no-cost option; final drive ratio 3.70; 24v limited slip diff.
CHASSIS DETAILS integral steel structure; ifs MacPherson struts, anti-roll bar; irs semi-trailing arms, coil springs, telescopic dampers, anti-roll bar; dual circuit split front-rear vacuum servo disc brakes, ABS standard on 24v; recirculating ball PAS; 75L (16.5 Imp gal, 19.8 US gal) fuel tank; 205/65 ZR15 tyres.
DIMENSIONS wheelbase 272cm (111in); front track 145cm (57in), 147cm (58in) rear; ground clearance 14cm (5.5in); turning circle 10.8m (35.4ft); length 484.5cm (191in); width 176.5cm (69.5in); height 145cm (57in).
PERFORMANCE 24v maximum speed 240kph (150mph); 39.3kph (63.1mph) @ 1000rpm; 0-96kph (60mph) 7.8sec; 9.6kg/kW (7.1kg/bhp); fuel consumption 11.8-14.7L/100km (19-24mpg).
UK SALES 22,325.
PRICE1989 3.0i CD £22308; 1990 24v £24879.

The idea of a "platform" as the basis of a car was gaining ground. A platform was not the same as a "chassis" with firm dimensions and fixed mechanical units on which coachbuilders could mount bespoke bodywork. Nor was it a common bodyshell to which different cosmetics and badges could be grafted to distinguish entry-level from de luxe. A platform was becoming a concept around which many common components could cluster to provide a range of models and even different makes of car.

Thus when the third rendition of the Cavalier came out it was on a stretched evolutionary platform that provided 22 model variants from the beginning, with more to come. The wheelbase was extended by 2.5cm (1in) and a 6.4cm (2.5in) longer front overhang helped secure a sleek Cd of 0.29. It was an adaptable platform accommodating six engines from 1.4 to 2.0 litres, with 75bhp to 168bhp introduced throughout the model's seven year lifespan, and made provision for four wheel drive, hatchback, saloon, and in due course coupe and estate car bodywork. The GM mid-range platform would even form the basis for the development of a new range of Saab models.

BODY saloon, 4 seats, 4 doors, weight 1005kg (2216lb); hatchback, 5 doors, weight 1035kg (2282lb), 1.4 990/1020kg (2183/2249lb), 1.8 1040/1070kg (2293/2359lb).

ENGINE 4 cylinders, in-line, front transverse; 77.8mm x 73.4mm, 1396cc; compr: 9.4:1; 56kW (75bhp) @ 5600rpm; 40.1kW/L (53.7bhp/L); 107Nm (80lb/ft) @ 3000rpm. 79mm x 81.5mm, 1598cc, 61kW (82bhp) @ 5200rpm; 38.3kW/L (51.3bhp/L); 126Nm (94lb/ft) @ 2600rpm. 84.8mm x 79.5mm, 1796cc, 67kW (90bhp) @ 5400rpm; 37.4kW/L (50.1bhp/L); 144Nm (107lb/ft) @ 3000rpm.

ENGINE STRUCTURE belt-driven overhead camshaft; aluminium cylinder head; cast iron block; 5-bearing crankshaft; 1.4 2-choke Pierburg carburettor, 1.6 Rochester fuel injection, 1.8 Bosch/Pierburg electronic, later Multec fuel injection.

TRANSMISSION front wheel drive; diaphragm spring clutch; 5-speed gearbox; synchromesh; Aisin-Warner automatic optional; final drive ratios 1.6 4.18 or 3.94:1, automatic 2.8:1; 1.4 4.29:1; 1.8 3.72 auto 2.8:1.

CHASSIS DETAILS integral steel structure; ifs by MacPherson struts; anti-roll bar; irs by semi-trailing arms, coil springs, telescopic dampers, anti-roll bar (not on 1.4); dual circuit split front-rear vacuum servo disc brakes Teves ABS; rack and pinion PAS; 61L (13.4 Imp gal, 16.1 US gal) fuel tank; 195/60 HR14 tyres, 5.5J rims.

DIMENSIONS wheelbase 260cm (102.4in); front track 142cm (55.9in), 142.5cm (56.1in) rear; ground clearance 14cm (5.5in); turning circle 11m (36.1ft); length 443cm (174.4in); width 170cm (66.9in); height 140cm (55in). Fastback length 435cm (171.25in).

PERFORMANCE 1.6 max speed 176kph (110mph); 35.8kph (22.3mph) @ 1000rpm; 0-96kph (60mph) 14.0sec; 16.7kg/kW (12.4kg/bhp); 9.4-11.3L/100km (25-30mpg).

UK SALES 862,000 all Cav III.

PRICE 1990 1.4 £9615, 1.6L £10420, 1.8GL £11860, 4/5 door prices identical.

When the third, and as it turned out the last, Cavalier came out it had almost a full complement of engines with three sorts of 2.0-litre (85kW 114bhp, 95kW 127bhp and 16v 110kW 147bhp). They were followed in 1993 by the first Vauxhall engine with the cylinders not in line. This was the 2.5 V6 with twin overhead camshafts per bank known as Ecotec and destined for a wide range of Vauxhalls, Opels and Saabs. One bank of cylinders was designed for all Family II engines providing a range of multi-valve 4 cylinder units between 1.6 and 2.0 litres. Built at the Ellesmere Port factory, refurbished at a cost of £190 million, the engine was also the basis of a 3.0 litre V6. The 54 deg angle between the cylinders made it compact enough to fit sideways into a small front-drive engine bay, yet big enough to accommodate twin-cam heads that inclined the exhaust valves at a greater angle than the inlets.

The V6 took the Cavalier into new territory, meeting the need of an emerging market for customers down-sizing, as sales jargon had it, into leisurely middle-class cars with the feel and pace of bigger cars forsaken for economic and social reasons.

BODY saloon, 4 seats, 4 doors, weight 1085kg (2392lb); hatchback, 5 doors, 1115kg (2458lb), V6 1245kg (2745lb), 5 doors 1265kg (2789lb).
ENGINE 4 cylinders, in-line, front transverse, 86.0mm x 86.0mm; 1998cc; compr 9.2:1; 85kW (114bhp) @ 5200rpm; 42.5kW/L (57.1bhp/L); 170 Nm (127lb/ft) @ 2600rpm. 95kW (127bhp), compr 10:1, 47.5kW/L (63.4bhp/L), 180Nm (134lb/ft) @ .....rpm. 16v 110kW (147bhp) @ 6000rpm; 55.1kW/L (73.6bhp/L); 196Nm (146lb/ft) @ 4800rpm. 81.6 x 79.6, 2498cc V6, compr: 10.5:1, 125kW (168bhp) @ 6000rpm, 50.1kW/L (67.3bhp/L); 227Nm (169lb/ft) @ 4000rpm.
ENGINE STRUCTURE belt-driven ohc (16v: 2 chain-driven); aluminium cyl head; cast iron block; 5-bearing crank; Bosch Motronic ML 4.1 fuel inj. V6 54deg; 4 valves per cyl; 2x2 chain-driven ohc; aluminium heads; 4-bearing crank, Bosch Motronic 2.8.
TRANSMISSION front wheel drive; diaphragm spring clutch; 5-speed gearbox; synchromesh; automatic optional; final drive ratios 3.55:1, 2.4:1 automatic. V6 3.38:1 2.86:1 automatic.
CHASSIS DETAILS integral steel structure; ifs by MacPherson struts; anti-roll bar; irs by semi-trailing arms, coil springs, telescopic dampers, anti-roll bar (not on 1.4); dual circuit split front-rear vacuum servo disc brakes (V6 ventilated discs) Teves ABS; rack and pinion PAS; 61L (13.4 Imp gal, 16.1 US gal) fuel tank; 195/60 HR14 tyres, V6 ZR16, 6J rims.
DIMENSIONS wheelbase 260cm (102in); front track 142cm (55.9in), 142.5cm (56.1in) rear; ground clearance 14cm (5.5in); turning circle 11m (36.1ft); length 443cm (174in) (fastback 435cm (171.25in); width 170cm (67in); height 140cm (55in).
PERFORMANCE 2.0 16v maximum 198kph (123mph); 42.8kph (26.7mph) @ 1000rpm; 0-96kph (60mph) 10.5sec; 9.9kg/kW (7.4kg/bhp); 11.3-12.8L/100km (22-25mpg).
UK SALES 862,000 all Cav III.
PRICE 1994 2.0i LS 5-door £12650; 2.0 SRi 16v 5-door £15125; 2.5 V6 4-door CDX £18350.

1988-1995 Cavalier III 4x4, diesel & turbodiesel

Vauxhall probably joined in the vogue for four wheel drive out of necessity more than enthusiasm. There was always a place for four wheel drive saloons and estates for country vets and engineers, but it never looked like a large market and the keen sporty driver wanting to emulate rally stars was going to demand extremes of power in any case.

The Cavalier 4x4 used a viscous coupling to take the drive from the front-mounted transmission to the rear axle. Torque distribution to front and rear wheels was adjusted automatically and there was a separate clutch to disengage 4wd and accommodate ABS. The rear suspension on the 4x4 was fully independent with semi-trailing arms replacing the torsion beam. This raised the boot floor to make room for the rear differential and meant losing some luggage room. Among the other side-effects were an indifferent ride, but the 16v would accelerate to 100kph (62mph) in 8.5sec and reach 205kph (128mph). Fuel consumption was 9.4-11.8L/100km (24-30mpg).

The diesel Cavalier tended to be unglamorous until the introduction in 1992 of a turbocharged version with indirect injection. This was not the old 1699cc engine but a quieter, more powerful, and more refined Isuzu 1686cc.

BODY saloon, 5 seats, 4 doors, weight 1245kg (2745lb); diesel 1080kg (2381lb), 5 doors 1095 kg (2414lb).
ENGINE 4 cylinders, in-line, front transverse, 86.0mm x 86.0mm; 1998cc; compr 9.2:1; 86kW (115bhp) @ 5200rpm; 43kW/L (57.7bhp/L); 170Nm (127lb/ft) @ 2600rpm. 16v 1998cc, 110kW (147.5bhp) @ 6000rpm, 55.1kW/L (73.8bhp/L); 196Nm (146lb/ft) @ 4800rpm. Turbodiesel: 79mm x 86mm 1686cc, compr 22:1; 60kW (80.5bhp) @ 4400rpm; 35.6kW/L (47.7bhp/L); 168Nm (125lb/ft) @ 2400rpm.
ENGINE STRUCTURE belt-driven overhead camshaft; chain-driven 2 ohc 16v; aluminium cylinder head, cast iron block; 5-bearing crankshaft; diesel injection; turbocharger and intercooler; Bosch Motronic petrol injection.
TRANSMISSION front wheel drive, 4x4; sdp clutch; 5-speed gearbox; 6-speed 204bhp engine; synchromesh; automatic optional not diesel; final drive ratio 3.72:1 4x4, 3.55:1 4x4 16v, 3.94:1 diesel.

CHASSIS DETAILS integral steel structure; ifs by MacPherson struts; anti-roll bar; irs by semi-trailing arms, coil springs, telescopic dampers, anti-roll bar; dual circuit split front-rear vacuum servo disc brakes (front ventilated discs 16v) Teves ABS; rack and pinion PAS; 61L (13.4 Imp gal, 16.1 US gal) fuel tank; 205/55 VR 15 tyres 16v.
DIMENSIONS wheelbase 260cm (102.4in); front track 142cm (55.9in), 142.5cm (56.1in) rear; ground clearance 14cm (5.5in); turning circle 11m (36.1ft); length 443cm (174.4in); width 170cm (66.9in); height 140cm (55in). Fastback length 435cm (171.25in).
PERFORMANCE turbodiesel maximum 178kph (111mph); 41.4kph (25.8mph) @ 1000rpm; 0-96kph (60mph) 12.8sec; 18kg/kW (13.4kg/bhp); fuel consumption 7.6-8.8L/100km (32-37mpg).
UK SALES 862,000 all Cav III.
PRICE 1989 2000 16v 4x4 £17567; 1990 1.7DL £10805; 2.0GSi 4x4 £18370.

257

The shades of Laurence Pomeroy and Percy Kidner must have shuddered over the controversy surrounding the launch of the Lotus Carlton. They were showered with praise for their efforts to reach 100mph, while their successor Paul Tosch was thrown on the defensive concerning the promotion of a technical *tour de force* of which Pomeroy and Kidner would have been proud.

They would certainly have been astonished at the speed and precision resulting from the twin-turbocharged straight-six with which Vauxhall made-do after finding that the 281kW (377bhp) Chevrolet Corvette ZR-1 quad-cam 32 valve V8 Lotus had developed would not fit. In the event it did not much matter, the home-grown and Garrett-turbocharged unit developed almost as much anyway and managed it with remarkable poise and water-cooled intercoolers.

Lotus Engineering developed the Carlton's MacPherson strut front and multi-link rear suspension lowering it, stiffening it, and increasing wheel travel in turn. The result was one of the fastest and most confident big luxury saloons in the world. The balance of the handling was superb with a benign progressive oversteer and quick, sharp steering responses enabling its enormous power to be used, if not with abandon, certainly with equanimity.

BODY saloon, 5 seats, 4 doors, weight 1690kg (3726lb).
ENGINE 6 cylinders, in-line, front, 95mm x 85mm; 3615cc; compr: 8.2:1; 281kW (377bhp) @ 5500rpm; 77.7kW/L (104.3bhp/L); 562Nm (419lb/ft) @ 4200rpm.
ENGINE STRUCTURE two chain-driven overhead camshafts, 24 valves; aluminium cylinder head; cast iron block with siamesed liners; 7-bearing counterbalanced forged crankshaft; Rochester fuel inj; 2 Garrett T25 turbochargers with charge-coolers; distributorless ignition, 3 coils.
TRANSMISSION rear wheel drive; sdp clutch; ZF 6-speed gearbox; synchromesh; no automatic option; limited slip diff; final drive 3.34:1.

CHASSIS DETAILS integral steel structure; independent front suspension by MacPherson struts, anti-roll bar; independent rear suspension by semi-trailing arms, coil springs, telescopic dampers, anti-roll bar; dual circuit split front-rear vacuum servo 13in ventilated disc brakes with AP 4-pot calipers at front, 2-pot rear, GM-Bosch ABS; recirculating ball PAS; 75L (16.5 Imp gal, 19.8 US gal) fuel tank; 235/45 ZR 17 front tyres, 265/40 ZR 17 rear; 8/9J rims.
DIMENSIONS wheelbase 273cm (107.5in); front track 149cm (58.7in), rear 153.5cm (60.4in); turning circle 11.2cm (36.7ft); length 477cm (188in); width 181cm (71.25in); height 143.5cm (56.5in).
PERFORMANCE maximum speed 282kph (176mph); 68.3kph (42.5mph) mph @ 1000rpm; acceleration 0-100kph (62mph) 5.4sec; 6kg/kW (4.5kg/bhp); fuel consumption 8.1-16.1L/100km (17.5-35mpg).
PRODUCTION 440.
PRICE £48000.

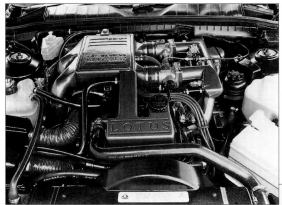

1990-1996 Calibra

The Cavalier had established such a fine reputation that rumours of a coupe version were enough to get cheque-books rustling. Prior to its launch at the Frankfurt motor show, pictures of the Calibra became widely available with the manufacturers' tacit accord if not their actual connivance, since it was replacing the old Opel Manta.

The sleek appearance that was the Calibra's hallmark reflected a commendable Cd of 0.26, and while it shared the Cavalier's platform it was tempting to regard it as a sports car albeit an adequately roomy four-seater. It looked as though four wheel drive might be the answer but no sooner was this offered in 1991 than the testers were asking for more power.

Like the Cavalier, the rear differential and the splaying of the rear suspension reduced the depth of the luggage boot but it was all necessary to keep abreast of the competition which included 4x4 Ford Sierra, Audi 80, Renault 21, and Peugeot 405. The call for more power was not long in coming and the turbocharged version lifted it into contention against Sierra Cosworth, Toyota Celica, and Lancia Integrale. The Calibra, made throughout its production run by Valmet in Finland, was in distinguished company.

BODY coupe, 4 seats, 2 doors, weight 2.0 1215kg (2679lb); 2.0 16v 1250kg (2756lb), 2.5 V6 1325kg (2921lb); 4x4 2.0 1310kg (2888lb), turbo 1375kg (3031lb).
ENGINE 4 cylinders, in-line, front transverse; 86mm x 86mm, 1998cc; cr 9.2:1; 86kW (115bhp) @ 5200rpm; 43kW/L (57.6bhp/L); 168Nm (125lb/ft) @ 2600rpm. 1998cc 16v, 110kW (147.5bhp) @ 6000; 55.1kW/L (73.8bhp/L); 196Nm (146lb/ft) @ 4600rpm. 81.6mm x 79.6mm, 2498cc V6, cr 10.8:1; 125kW (168bhp) @ 6000rpm; 50kW/L (67bhp/L); 227Nm (169lb/ft) @ 4200rpm. 4x4 1998cc turbo, 150kW (201bhp) @ 5600rpm; 75.1kW/L (100.6bhp/L); 280Nm (209lb/ft) @ 2400rpm.
ENGINE STRUCTURE belt-driven ohc, 16v twin chain; al cyl head, ci block; 5-bg crank; Bosch Motronic M1.5 fuel inj (M2.5 16v). KKK 16 turbocharger and intercooler.
TRANSMISSION front wheel drive, 4x4; sdp clutch; 5-spd; synchromesh; auto optional not 4x4; 6-spd 4x4; final drive 3.55:1, 3.72:1 auto, 4x4 3.72:1.

CHASSIS DETAILS integral steel structure; ifs by MacPherson struts; anti-roll bar; irs by semi-trailing arms, coil springs, telescopic dampers, anti-roll bar; dual circuit split front-rear vacuum servo disc brakes (front vent discs 16v) Teves ABS; rack and pinion PAS; 63L (13.9 Imp gal, 16.6 US gal) tank; 195/60VR 14 tyres, 5.5J rims, 202/55 VR 15, 6J rims 150bhp 4x4.
DIMENSIONS wheelbase 260cm (102in); front track 142.5cm (56in), rear 144.5cm (57in) rear; ground clearance 14cm (5.5in); turning circle 11.5m (37.7ft); length 449cm (177in); width 169cm (66.5in); height 132cm (52in).
PERFORMANCE 86kW 115bhp maximum 205kph (128mph); 34.3kph (21.4mph) @ 1000rpm; 0-96kph (60mph) 10.0sec; 14.1kg/kW (10.6kg/bhp); 9.4-11.8L/100km (24-30mpg).
UK SALES 40,460.
PRICE 1990 2.0i £14750; 2.0i 16v 4x4 £18890. 1992 turbo 4x4 £20950.

Right: Calibra V6, with engine, airbags and facia.

261

1991-1998 Frontera 2.0i, 2.2 16v, 2.4i, 2.3 turbodiesel

Ringing the changes with three engines and two wheelbases, Vauxhall's entry into the all-terrain market brought a swift response. The Frontera moved almost at once into second place in the sales charts behind a leader that had dominated the category for the best part of 40 years. It was decided to use an established Japanese design and make the vehicles in a new production facility at Luton. This was IBC, a joint venture between General Motors and Isuzu to make a vehicle already popular with American engines such as the Amigo and Rodeo, and the Isuzu Mu in Japan.

Big, chunky, with a robust box-section ladder chassis, the Frontera was a serious off-roader even though four wheel drive was selectable and ground clearance seemingly modest. There were no high-tech viscous couplings or centre differentials like some rivals, but the Frontera was much cheaper than the Mitsubishi Shogun or Land Rover Discovery and it was bigger than rivals from Daihatsu and Suzuki.

Engines were derived from the Vauxhall range, the Cavalier's 2.0-litre 4-cylinder that gave a useful advantage over 1.6-litre rivals, and the 2.4-litre petrol/ 2.3 diesel derived from the all-iron six in the Carlton/Senator. After 1995 6,825 were sold with the 2.0 16v engine.

BODY sport utility, 5 seats, 3 doors, weight 1635kg (3605lb). 5 doors, 1800kg (3968lb). Turbodiesel 5 doors 1860kg (4101lb).
ENGINE 4 cylinders, in-line, front, 86mm x 86mm; 1998cc; compr: 9.2:1; 86kW (115bhp) @ 5200rpm; 43kW/L (57.6bhp/L); 168Nm (125lb/ft) @ 2600rpm. 95mm x 85mm, 2410cc; compr 9.2:1; 93kW (125bhp) @ 4800rpm; 38.7kW/L (51.9bhp/L); 193Nm (144lb/ft) @ 2600rpm. 92mm x 85mm, 2260cc diesel; compr 23:1; 75kW (100bhp) @ 4200rpm; 33.2kW/L (44.2bhp/L); 212Nm (158lb/ft) @ 2200rpm.
ENGINE STRUCTURE belt-driven ohc 2.0 (chain-driven others); aluminium cyl head, cast iron block 2.0 (all iron others); 5-bearing crank; Bosch Motronic fuel injection; diesel Bosch fuel injection and KKK K24 turbocharger with intercooler.
TRANSMISSION rear wheel drive, selectable 4x4; 5-speed; synchromesh; no automatic option; low ratio 1.87; final drive ratio 4.88:1 2.4 4.56:1, diesel 4.30:1; both low ratio 2.28.

CHASSIS DETAILS box-section chassis, separate steel body; ifs by double wishbones, torsion bars, anti-roll bar; rear suspension live axle, leaf springs (1995 coils with links), oblique telescopic dampers; brakes discs all round, ventilated at front, servo; recirculating ball PAS; 80L (17.6 Imp gal, 21.2 US gal) fuel tank; 225/75 R15 tyres, 6J rims.
DIMENSIONS wheelbase 233cm (91.7in); front track 149.5cm (58.9in), 149.5cm (58.9in) rear; ground clearance 23.5cm (9.25in); turning circle 11.4m (37.4ft); length 404cm (159in); width 171cm (67.3in); height 170cm (66.9in).
PERFORMANCE 1991 2.3TD 5-door max 133kph (83mph); 35kph (21.8mph) @ 1000rpm; 0-96kph (60mph) 18.1sec; 17.6kg/kW (13.1kg/bhp); 11.8-14.1L/100km (20-24mpg). UK SALES 51,925.
PRICE 1991 2.0 Sport 3-door £12250; 2.4 5-door Estate £15740; 2.3 TD Estate £16830.

Right: **Frontera Sport.**

1992-1998 Astra III 1.4, 1.6

The Astra II was an outstanding success with 631,000 European sales in 1989, of which 1176,000 were in the UK offering the most formidable challenge ever to the Ford Escort. Astra III was the first joint Vauxhall GM model to carry the same name. After 55 years Opel dropped Kadett, Belmont was allowed to atrophy, and the new mid-range T-car was known as the Astra wherever it was made and sold. It was scarcely radical technically. It continued with the same platform and restyled 3-door and 5-door hatchbacks and estates, and a 4-door saloon. A longer wheelbase gave more room inside, and a taller roofline more headroom in the back. Engine options in the Wayne Cherry restyled body (34 per cent torsionally stiffer than the old one) were much the same and catalytic converters became standard equipment in the UK. This meant the final abandonment of carburettors even in the 1.4 and the 1.2 was dropped. Power steering was available throughout. The new shape received a warm welcome at the Frankfurt Motor Show in September 1991. Flush glass contributed to the light appearance of a car produced at five plants across Europe; Ellesmere Port, Antwerp, Bochum, Saragossa, and Azambula in Portugal with extra capacity planned at Eisenach in the former East Germany and Szengot-thard in Hungary.

BODY saloon, 3/5 doors, 5 seats; 930/950kg (2050/2094lb); estate, 5 doors, 995kg (2194lb). Automatic 35kg (77lb) extra.
ENGINE 4 cylinders, in-line, front, transverse, 77.6mm x 73.4mm; 1389cc; compr 9.4:1; 44kW (59bhp) @ 5200rpm; 31.7kW/L (42.5bhp/L); 103Nm (76lb/ft) @ 2800rpm. Opel version without catalytic converter 55kW (74bhp) @ 5800rpm; 39.6kW/L (53.1bhp/L); 110Nm (82lb/ft) @ 3000rpm. Vauxhall multi-point 61kW (82bhp) @ 4400rpm; 111Nm (83lb/ft) @ 3400rpm. 79mm x 81.5mm, 1598cc, compr 9.2:1; 55kW (74bhp) @ 5200rpm, 34.4kW/L (46.3bhp/L); 125Nm (93lb/ft) @ 2800rpm. Vauxhall multi-point, compr 10:1; 74kW (99bhp) @ 5600rpm, 46.3 kW/L (62.1bhp/L); 132Nm (98lb/ft) @3400rpm.
ENGINE STRUCTURE ohc, belt-driven with automatic tensioner; hydraulic tappets; aluminium cylinder head, cast iron block; 5-bearing crank; Rochester single-point fuel injection or Multec multi-point; electronic ign.

TRANSMISSION front wheel drive; sdp clutch; 5-speed gearbox; synchromesh; automatic optional 1598cc; final drive ratio 4.18 1389cc, 3.94 1598cc 3.94, 2.81:1 automatic.
CHASSIS DETAILS integral steel structure; ifs by Macpherson struts, coil springs, anti-roll bar; rear suspension trailing arms with torsional cross-beam, coil springs, anti-roll bar; 9.2in disc front 7.8in drum rear servo brakes, diagonally-split; rack and pinion PAS optional; 52L (11.4Imp gal, 13.7US gal) fuel tank; 175/70TR tyres, 5.5J rims.
DIMENSIONS wheelbase 251.5cm (99in); track 142.5cm (56in); ground clearance 13.5cm (5.3in); turning circle 10.5m (34.5ft); length 405cm (159.5in); width 169cm (66.5in); height 141cm (55.5in).
PERFORMANCE 1.4 max 160kph (99.7mph); 35.9kph (22.4mph) @ 1000rpm; 0-96kph (60mph) 16sec; 21.1kg/kW (16.1kg/bhp); 6.7L/100km (42.2mpg).
UK SALES 606,350 all Astra III.
PRICE 1.4L 5-door £8749.

Top: CD. *Centre:* Club /
California interior.
Far right: GSi 16v.

Big reductions in noise vibration and harshness (NVH in motor industry jargon) and ride were claimed for the Astra following the adoption of a separate Cavalier-style sub-frame carrying the front suspension. Although bolted directly to the body, it was effectively insulated with rubber mountings, in particular at the top of the Macpherson struts where road noise tended to reverberate through the body structure. The subframe was reinforced to improve crash resistance, spreading impact loads to a crossbeam in the toe-board. Negative camber was increased front and rear to improve handling and the back suspension kept the compound torsion beam axle introduced with the first front wheel drive T-car in 1979. With a lot of power being transmitted through the front wheels, wheelspin in the lower gears could be problematical. Electronic Traction Control (ETC), developed in conjunction with Hella, sensed when a front wheel lost traction and brought in the brake anti-lock mechanism to communicate with the management system, progressively reducing engine power. Vauxhall brought electronic surveillance into popular cars much as it transformed the 1930s family car with synchromesh. New techniques reduced the parts needed to make the car by 30 per cent, while safety reinforcements increased weight by 15kg (33lb).

BODY saloon, 3/5 doors, 5 seats; weight 1015/1035kg (2238/2282lb). 4 door and estate weight 1080kg (2381lb). 2.0 3/5 doors, 1050kg (2315lb). 2.0 dohc 1100kg (2425lb).
ENGINE 4 cylinders, in-line, front, transverse, 84.8mm x 79.5mm; 1796cc; cr 9.2:1; 66kW (89bhp) @ 5400rpm; 36.8kW/L (49.3bhp/L);145Nm (108lb/ft) @ 3000rpm. 86mm x86mm, 1998cc, cr 9.2:1; 85kW (114bhp) @ 5400rpm; 42.5kW/L (57bhp/L); 170Nm (127lb/ft) @ 2600rpm. dohc 110kW (148bhp) @ 6000rpm; 55.1kW/L (74bhp/L); 196 Nm (146lb/ft) @ 4800rpm.
ENGINE STRUCTURE belt-driven ohc, automatic tensioner; hydraulic tappets; aluminium cyl head, ci block; 5-bg crank; Multec fuel inj; electronic ign. 2.0 Bosch Motronic fuel inj; dohc 2 belt-driven cams 16 valves at 46 deg, Bosch Motrinic M2.5.
TRANSMISSION front wheel drive; sdp clutch; 5-speed, synchro; auto opt; final drive ratio 3.72, automatic 2.81:1. 2.0 3.35:1; Electronic Traction Control; dohc 3.42:1.

CHASSIS DETAILS integral steel struct; ifs by Macpherson struts, coil springs, anti-roll bar; rear susp trailing arms with torsional cross-beam, coil springs, anti-roll bar; 9.2in disc front 7.8in drum rear servo brakes, diag-split; 2.0 vent front discs; GSi discs all round, ABS; rack & pinion PAS; 52L (11.4 Imp gal, 13.7 US gal); 175/75 TR14, 2.0 195/60HR15 opt 205/50HR15 tyres, 5.5/6J rims.
DIMENSIONS wheelbase 251.5cm (99in); track 142.5 (56in); ground clearance 13.5cm (5.3in); turning circle 10.5m (34.5ft); length 405cm (159in); width 169cm (66.5in); height 141cm (55.5in).
PERFORMANCE GSi maximum speed 195kph (121.5mph); 42.6kph (26.5mph) @ 1000rpm; 0-96kph (60mph) 9.5sec; 12.3kg/kW (9.2kg/bhp); 7.8L/100km (36mpg).
UK SALES 606,350 all Astra III.
PRICE 1.8 GSi £12995; 2.0 £15320.

Top right: **Sport 2.0 16v.**
Right: **GTE 2.0i 16v engine.**
Far right: **GSi 16v.**

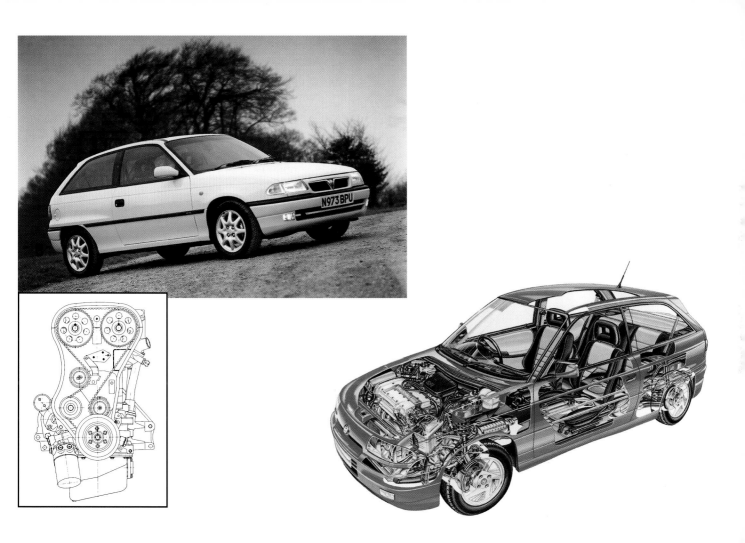

1992-1998 Astra III 1.7TD, petrol Convertible

The launch diesel for the Astra III was an Opel non-turbo of 42.5kW (57bhp) with an uncontrolled oxidising catalyst exceeding the current European diesel emission standards by a comfortable margin. The later Isuzu-built 60kW (80.5bhp) 1.7-litre turbo, developed from the catalysed 1.5 with which the Nova was already equipped, only cost £775 more than the somewhat feeble non-turbo. The price included power steering bringing the effective difference to around £400. The Astra was priced aggressively and scored heavily on economy. Keen rivals from Citroën, Peugeot, Volkswagen, and Renault were not within £750 of it although the engine was never quite in the same class for refinement.

The Bertone plant at Grugliasco built the Astra Convertible based on the platform of the 4-door saloon, the door sills strengthend by 3mm sheet steel, a cross member under the rear seat, braced wheel arches, and reinforcement round the door pillars and the well containing the furled hood. The hood space took up quite a lot of the rear seat space and there was a weight penalty of an extra 70kg (154.3lb). Although theoretically almost as stiff as the saloon the pretty Convertible was never completely free from scuttle shake. Most buyers chose the option of electric operation of the hood.

BODY (turbodiesel data) saloon, 3/5 doors, 5 seats; weight 1065/1085kg (2348/2392lb). 4 doors, 1095kg (2414lb); estate 1130kg (2491lb).
ENGINE 4 cylinders, in-line, front, transverse, 79mm x 86mm; 1686cc; cr 22:1; 60kW (80.5bhp) @ 4400rpm; 35.6kW/L (47.7bhp/L); 168Nm (125lb/ft) @ 2400rpm. Non-turbo 82.5mm x 79.5mm, 1700cc; compr 23.1:1; 42kW (56bhp) @ 4600rpm; 24.7kW/L (33.1bhp/L); 105Nm (78lb/ft) @ 2400rpm; alternative version 42kW (56bhp) @ 3900rpm.
ENGINE STRUCTURE belt-driven ohc; aluminium cylinder head, cast iron block; hydraulic tappets; 5-bearing crankshaft; turbocharger and intercooler; fuel injection.

TRANSMISSION front wheel drive; sdp clutch; 5-speed gearbox; synchromesh; final drive ratio 3.74:1.
CHASSIS DETAILS integral steel structure; ifs by Macpherson struts, coil springs, anti-roll bar; rear suspension trailing arms with torsional cross-beam, coil springs, anti-roll bar; 9.2in disc front 7.8in drum rear servo brakes, diagonally-split; rack and pinion PAS optional; 52L (11.4 Imp gal, 13.7US gal) tank; 175/75 TR14, 2.0 195/60HR15 opt 205/50HR15 tyres, 5.5/6J rims.
DIMENSIONS wheelbase 251.5cm (99in); track 142.5 (56in); ground clearance 13.5cm (5.3in); turning circle 10.5m (34.5ft); length 405cm (159in); width 169cm (66.5in); height 141cm (55.5in).
PERFORMANCE maximum speed 173kph (108 mph); 40.3kph (25.1mph) @ 1000rpm; acceleration to 60mph 13.5sec; 17.8kg/kW (13.2kg/bhp); fuel consumption 5.7-6.1L/100km (46-50mpg).
UK SALES 606,350 all Astra III.
PRICE £9995. Convertible £15,800.

By April 1993 the small car sector was ready for further development as Corsa replaced Nova with a strongly made safety cage car. A range of seven 4-cylinder engines was available at launch, including an economy 1.2-litre that promised fuel consumption of over 4.7L/100km (60mpg), with a speedy eighth due in the autumn. The 3-door and 5-door body shells had styles of their own and an automatic transmission was imminent.

The Corsa had more room than the Nova and among its luxuries were power steering, air conditioning, anti-lock brakes, and a car alarm. The range of trim and equipment was wide with seatbelt pre-tensioners, anti-submarining seats, door beams, height-adjustable belt mountings, and an airbag. Water-based paints caught the mood of the moment along with CFC-free air conditioning, coded plastic components and a pledge to 90 per cent recyclability.

The Corsa was as much a car of the 1990s as the Ten-Four was of the 1930s, with its innovatory one-piece steel bodies and independent front suspension. Corsa was made at Zaragoza, Spain, and Eisenach in the former East Germany. Among 1999 changes was the introduction of the SXi with 1.2 16v engine, close ratio gearbox, sports suspension, and alloy wheels at £9480.

BODY hatchback, 5 seats, 3/5 doors, weight 835/870kg (1841/1918lb); 1.4 850/920kg (1874/2028lb); 1.6 945/975kg (2083/2150lb); diesel 880/930kg (1940/2050lb).
ENGINE 4 cylinders, in-line, front transverse; 72.0mm x 73.4mm, 1195cc; cr 10:1; 32.8kW (44bhp) @ 5000rpm; 27.4kW/L (36.8bhp/L); 87Nm (65lb/ft) @ 2800rpm. 77.6mm x 73.4mm, 1389cc; cr 9.4:1; 44kW (59bhp) @ 5200rpm; 31.7kW/L (42.5bhp/L); 102Nm (76lb/ft) @ 2800rpm. 77.6mm x 73.4mm, 1389cc, 60kW (80.5bhp) @ 5800rpm; 43.2kW/L (59-7.9bhp/L); 114Nm (85lb/ft) @ 3400rpm. 79mm x 81.5mm, 1598cc, 2ohc; cr 10.5:1; 78kW (105bhp) @ 6000rpm; 48.8kW/L (65.5bhp/L); 149Nm (111lb/ft) @ 4000rpm. 76mm x 82mm, 1488cc diesel, compr 23:1; 36.5kW (49bhp) @ 4800rpm; 24.5kW/L (32.9bhp/L); 88.5Nm (66lb/ft) @ 2400rpm; turbodiesel cr 22:1; 49kW (65.7ch) @ 4600rpm; 32.9kW/L (44.2ch/L), 132 Nm (98lb/ft) @ 2600rpm.
ENGINE STRUCTURE belt-driven ohc (2 ohc 16v); aluminium cyl head, cast iron block; 5-bearing crank; Multec fuel injection; Bosch diesel.
TRANSMISSION front wheel drive; 5-spd; synchro; auto opt not 1195cc, 1389cc 82/89bhp, 2ohc, or diesel;3.74, 3.94, 4.18:1.

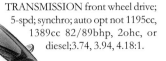

CHASSIS DETAILS integral steel structure; ifs by MacPherson struts; rear susp torsion beam axle, coil springs, dampers, anti roll bar; discs (some ventilated) front, drum rear brakes; rack and pinion PAS; 46L (10.1 Imp gal, 12.1US gal) fuel tank; 145/R13, 165/70 185/50 tyres.
DIMENSIONS wheelbase 244.5cm (96.3in); front track 138.5cm (54.5in), rear 139cm (54.7in); ground clearance 14cm (5.5in); turning circle 10.4m (34.1ft); length 373cm (147in); width 161cm (63.4in); ht 143.5cm (56.5in).
PERFORMANCE SRi 1993 max speed169kph (105mph); 29.7kph (18.5mph) @ 1000rpm; 0-96kph (60mph) 11.5sec; 15.3kg/kW (11.4kg/bhp); 7.4-8.3L/100km (34-38mpg).
PRICE 1993 1.2i Merit 3-door £6495; 1.6i GSi 3-door 5-speed; 1.2i 5-door £6900; 1.5TD GLS £9360. 1999 Club 16v £9295 on the road, CDX £10595.

Right: Corsa CDX.
Far right: demonstration of Corsa's fuel consumption.

Ever since the demise of the traditional flutes, Vauxhall had been seeking a graphic identifying feature. With the arrival of the Omega it found one that embodied something of the old convention, a V in the air intake, which provided the brand identity that rival makes were achieving with chrome replicas of their old grilles. Yet Omega was much more than that. It replaced Carlton and the much-admired Senator with a body shell stiffer and slightly larger than its predecessor. The saloon was 4.9cm (1.9in) longer, 2.6cm (1in) wider and the estate was 5.1cm (2in) longer; torsional stiffness was 26 per cent better giving better handling and reducing resonance. Modern big Vauxhalls aimed to be a match for BMW and Mercedes-Benz with zinc-coated steel over 65 per cent of its surface area.

The venerable straight six was no more and Omega engines were 16v 2.0, 2.5 and 3.0 quad-cam V6s. The turbo-diesel was a BMW-sourced 2.5 6-cylinder, and the level of electronic control of engine management, traction control, four-channel ABS braking, and even air conditioning increased hugely. Crashworthiness improved too, with airbags, a stiff roll cage, and "shear-off" front wheels to dissipate collision energy. Remote-control deadlocks prevented the doors being opened even if a window was smashed.

BODY saloon, estate, 5 seats, 4/5 doors; 1400/1460kg (3086/3219lb); 16v 1426/1495kg (3144/3296lb); V6 1595/1625kg (3516/3583lb); diesel 1525/1575kg (3362/3472lb).
ENGINE 6 cylinders, in-line, front, 86mm x 86mm; 1998cc; compr: 10:1; 86kW (115bhp) @ 5400rpm; 43kW/L (57.6bhp/L); 176Nm (131lb/ft) @ 2800rpm. 1998cc 2ohc; compr 10.8:1; 99kW (133bhp) @ 5600rpm; 49.6kW/L (66.6bhp/L); 182Nm (136lb/ft) @ 4000rpm. 81.6 x 79.6, 2498cc V6, 125kW (168bhp) @ 6000rpm; 50kW/L (67.3bhp/L); 224Nm (167lb/ft) @ 3200rpm. 86 x 85, 2962cc V6 156.5kW (210bhp) @ 6200rpm; 52.9kW/L (70.9bhp/L); 267Nm (199ft/lb) @ 3600rpm. 80 x 82.8, 2498cc 6 cylinder diesel; compr 22:1; 95.5kW (128bhp) @ 4500rpm; 38.2kW/L (51.2bhp/L); 247Nm (184lb/ft) @ 2200rpm
ENGINE STRUCTURE ohv; ohc 1998cc and 2498cc diesel, 2ohc 1998cc 133bhp engine; V6 2 ohc per bank; aluminium cyl head, cast iron block; 5-bearing crank (4-bearing V6, 7-bearing diesel); Bosch Motronic inj; diesel digital inj, turbo and intercooler.
TRANSMISSION rear wheel drive; 5-speed; synchromesh; auto optional; final drive 3.9:1, 3.7:1, 3.45 diesel; switchable traction control on V6.
CHASSIS DETAILS integral steel structure; ifs by MacPherson struts; semi-trailing arm multi-link irs, coil springs; disc brakes ABS; ZF Servotronic PAS; 75L (16.5 Imp gal, 19.8 US gal) fuel tank, estate 70L (15.4 Imp gal, 18.5 US gal);195/55 HR 15, 225/55 VR 16 6. tyres 6.5/7J rims.
DIMENSIONS wheelbase 273cm (107.5in); front track 145cm (57.1in), rear 147cm (57.8in); ground clearance 14cm (5.5in); turning circle 11m (36.1ft); length 474cm (186.6in); width

176cm (69.3in); height 144.5cm
(56.9in). Estate rear track 146.5cm
(57.7in), length 477cm (187.8in),
height 148cm (58.3in).
PERFORMANCE 1994 1998cc
2.0iGLS max 209kph (130mph);
35kph (21.8mph) @ 1000rpm; 0-
96kph (60mph) 9.3sec; 14.7kg/kW
(11kg/bhp); 10.1-12.3L/100km (23-
28mpg).
UK SALES 65,840.
PRICE 1994 Edition S 2.0i £15995;
CD 2.5TD £21350; Elite 3.0 V6 24v
£26950; Estate GLS 2.0 16v £18300;
CD 2.5 V6 24v £21650.

Above: Omega Elite.
Left: 2.5TD Omega engine.
Right: Omega safety.
Far right: GLS estate.

1994-1998 Monterey

GM's affinity with Isuzu bore a number of fruits including a 4x4 leisure off-roader up-market of the Frontera. Large, tough-looking, strong, six Montereys went on sale with identical prices for petrol or diesel. They were sold by 269 specialist 4x4 Vauxhall dealers against Land Rover's 127. Vauxhall expected Monterey to compete with luxury saloons not other 4x4s. It had a refined road performance and good furnishings, speed-sensitive power steering, supple suspension, and the four wheel drive only worked when asked for, so the extra pair of tyres and driveshafts did not waste fuel. Thanks to strong torque it was lively enough to keep up with the traffic, yet the emphasis on performing well on the road was perhaps a reflection of its abilities off-road.

For those whose need for four wheel drive was less than compelling, the superior ride and refinement made the Monterey tempting. So was the six-seat option on the long wheelbase LTD, and the fully galvanised steel bodywork which provided corrosion protection almost a match for aluminium-bodied rivals. The interior was roomy, the facia undistinguished, and it had curious asymmetrically split rear doors, the larger swinging on to the kerbside complete with the spare wheel in a genteel metal casing.

BODY sport utility, 5 seats, 3/5 doors, weight 1795/1880kg (3957/4145lb).
ENGINE V6 cylinders, front, 93.4mm x 77.0mm; 3165cc; compr: 9.3:1; 132kW (177bhp) @ 5200rpm; 258Nm (192lb/ft) @ 3750rpm. 4 cylinder turbodiesel 95.4mm x 107mm, 3059cc, 83.5kW (112bhp) @ 3600rpm; 27.3kW/L (36.6bhp/L); 258Nm (192lb/ft) @ 2000rpm.
ENGINE STRUCTURE ohv; 2 chain-driven ohc, 4 valves per cyl, diesel 1ohc, 2 valves; aluminium cyl head and block (cast iron diesel); 4-bearing crank V6, 5-bearing diesel; fuel injection, diesel 0.8bar turbo.
TRANSMISSION rear wheel drive, selectable four wheel drive; 5-speed; synchromesh; automatic optional; final drive ratio 4.3:1, diesel 4.56.
CHASSIS DETAILS Box-section chassis; independent front suspension by double wishbones and torsion bar; live axle, multi-link trailing arms, coil springs and Panhard rod at rear; ventilated disc brakes, ABS standard; recirculating Ball PAS; 85L (18.7 Imp gal, 22.4 US gal) fuel tank; 245/70 R16 107S tyres.
DIMENSIONS wheelbase 276cm (108.7in); front track 145.5cm (57.3in), 146cm (57.5in) rear; ground clearance 21cm (8.3in); turning circle 12.4m (40.7ft); length 470cm (185in); width 470cm (185in); height 184cm (72.4in). 3 door: wheelbase 233cm (91.7in); turning circle 10.8m (35.4ft), length 427cm (168in).
PERFORMANCE maximum speed (petrol) 170kph (106mph); 39.3kph (24.5mph) @ 1000rpm; acceleration 0-96kph (60mph) 11.5sec; 13.6kg/kW (10.1kg/bhp); fuel consumption 14.1-15.7L/100km (18-20mpg).
UK SALES 4,495.
PRICE 1994 3.2 V6 24v LTD £23510; 3.1 TD LTD £23510.

1994 Tigra

Introduced at the Frankfurt motor show, the Tigra was officially a concept car to gauge public reaction, yet it was too well finished and mature to look as though it would not reach production. Work on an open roadster was halted before the model was cleared for sale. A chipper three-door hatchback with small back seats and promoted as a concept car, it held its own against contemporary plastic and glass motor show mock-ups with the grace of a catwalk model, sleek, vogue-ish, and fresh as paint.

There were two versions, a 1.4i and a 1.6i based on the platform of the economical but plain Corsa. The Vauxhall-Opel design studio evolved distinctive sweeping curves for the Tigra. - a rare asset when so many cars looked alike. The 1.6 Tigra was noisy and the gearshift stiff and notchy, but it was well-equipped with pretty alloy wheels, twin airbags, anti-lock brakes, and deadlocks. The body was 81mm (3.2in) lower than a Corsa and it rode 13mm (0.5in) lower on its springs. Weight distribution was 61 per cent on the front wheels instead of 63 per cent, so although 100kg (220lb) or so heavier than a Corsa the handling was better with recalibrated springs, dampers, and anti-roll bars.

BODY coupe, 4 seats, 2 doors, weight 1010kg (2227b), 1.6 1030kg (2271lb). ENGINE 4 cylinders, in-line, front transverse, 77.6mm x 73.4mm; 1389cc; compr: 10.5:1; 66kW (89bhp) @ 6000rpm; 47.5kW/L (64.1bhp/L); 123Nm (92lb/ft) @ 4000rpm. 79mm x 81.5mm, 1598cc, 78kW (105bhp) @ 6000rpm; 49kW/L (65.7bhp/L); 109lb/ft @ 4000rpm
ENGINE STRUCTURE belt driven 2 overhead camshafts; 16 valve; aluminium cylinder head; cast iron block; 5-bearing crankshaft; Multec sequential fuel injection.
TRANSMISSION front wheel drive; 5-speed gearbox; synchromesh;

automatic optional; final drive ratio 4.12:1 1.4; 3.74:1 1.6. automatic 4.12:1.
CHASSIS DETAILS integral steel structure; independent front suspension by MacPherson struts; rear suspension torsion beam axle, coil springs, dampers, anti roll bar; servo ventilated disc front, drum rear brakes ABS option; rack and pinion PAS; 46L (10.1 Imp gal), 12.1 US gal) fuel tank; 175/65 HR 14, 185/55 HR15 tyres, 5.5/6J rims.
DIMENSIONS wheelbase 243cm (95.7in); front track 138.5 (54.5in), rear 139cm (54.7in); ground clearance 13.5cm (5.3in); turning circle 10.5m (34.5ft); length 392cm (154.3in); width 181cm (71.25in); height 134cm (52.75in).
PERFORMANCE 1.6 maximum speed 203kph (126mph); 32.1kph (20mph) @ 1000rpm; acceleration 0-96kph (60mph) 9.8sec; 13.2kg/kW (9.8kg/bhp); average fuel consumption 7.1-8.8L/100km (32-40mpg).
PRICE 1994 1.4i 16v £10995; 1.6i 16v £12995.

1995 Maxx

The Geneva Motor Show was traditionally an occasion for set-piece concept car displays. In 1995, responding to a survey of European motorists, the Vauxhall Maxx accompanied the springtime blossoms by Lake Geneva. Half of those surveyed wanted something to do double duty as a city car, a pick-up, a convertible, or even an off-roader when required. The notion of a multi-function vehicle inspired other designers for years.

The prescient Maxx was designed round an aluminium spaceframe, 75cm (29in) shorter than a Corsa, with the 3-cylinder Ecotec engine that went into production two years later. The framework of aluminium extrusions was part of a reinforced safety perimeter at the waistline and the body was made up of plastic or composite panels that could be removed or replaced according to what role the car was playing. A rocker switch beside the steering wheel controlled gearchanges on the sequential gearbox or the driver could resort to fully automatic on the lines of the Porsche Sportmatic. The modular design of the Maxx would have provided almost limitless scope for development. There was also a 4-door Opel equivalent with a built-in telephone, navigation system and fax, and a roadster version, the so-called Mad Max with turbocharger, was contemplated but not built.

BODY 2 doors, 4 seats; weight 550kg (1213lb).
ENGINE 3 cylinders, in-line, front transverse, 72.5mm x 78.6mm; 973cc; compr: 10.1:1; 40kW (54bhp) @ 5600rpm; 41.1kW/L (5.9ch/L); 82Nm (61lb/ft) @ 2800rpm.
ENGINE STRUCTURE 2 hollow chain-driven overhead camshafts; 12-valve; hydraulic tappets; aluminium cylinder head, cast iron; 4-bearing crankshaft; Bosch Motronic fuel injection, electronic ignition, separate coils to each plug; water-cooled.
TRANSMISSION front wheel drive; 5-speed sequential gearbox convertible to fully automatic; synchromesh; final drive ratio 3.74:1.
CHASSIS DETAILS extruded aluminium space frame with clip-on plastic or composite body panels; Macpherson strut independent front suspension; torsion beam rear suspension; telescopic dampers; disc brakes; rack and pinion PAS; 46L (10.1 Imp gal, 12.1US gal) fuel tank; 165/65 TR14 tyres, 5.5J rims.
DIMENSIONS wheelbase 244.5cm (96.25in); track 139cm (54.7in); length 297.5cm (117in); width 161cm (63.4in).
PERFORMANCE maximum speed 151kph (94mph); acceleration 0-96kph (60mph) 12.0sec; fuel consumption 3.9L/100km (72mpg) @ 90kph (56mph).
PRODUCTION limited to experimental models.
PRICE not sold.

The Maxx featured a bench front seat pivoted in the middle and swung round to give access to the back. Modules for communications, entertainment, navigation and heating systems were fixed to aluminium cross-member in facia.

Vauxhall had some long-running names such as Velox, Cresta, Victor and Viva, yet none was relinquished so reluctantly as Cavalier. There had been times when the survival of the Vauxhall brand was in doubt and the Cavalier saved the day with a dynasty of mid-range cars. It won its spurs in the civil war with Ford as slightly more flamboyant, slightly livelier, well made, unlikely to rust, and fun to drive. Cavalier was well named. The replacement Vectra at first seemed more Roundhead, looked less lavish, even a little severe. The interior of the entry-level 1.6-litre and the 1.8-litre had large areas of dark-coloured plastic, it was well upholstered, but the furnishings were sombre. The specification included new subframe-mounted suspension and an RDS clock of great accuracy.

Quality was superb, and the Vectra was one of a growing number of European cars able to match competitors from the Far East in reliability and low warranty costs, so there was little doubt of its success.

The cheapest 1.6 Envoy gave buyers the choice of 8-valve or 16-valve engines, and although early road tests were critical of the handling, praise for the ride and refinement was pretty well unanimous.

BODY saloon, 4 doors, 5 seats; weight 1170kg (2579lb). 5 doors 1185kg (2613lb).
ENGINE 4 cylinders, in-line, front transverse, 79.0mm x 81.5mm; 1598cc; compr: 9.6:1; 55kW (74bhp) @ 5200rpm; 34.4kW/L (46.3bhp/L); 126Nm (94lb/ft) @ 2800rpm. 16v; compr 10:5; 74kW (99bhp) @ 6200rpm, 46.2kW/L (62bhp/L), 148Nm (110lb/ft) @ 3200rpm. 1.8 16v 81.6mm x 86.0mm 1799cc compr 10.8:1; 85kW (113bhp) @ 5400rpm, 42.5kW/L (56.6bhp/L), 168Nm (125lb/ft) @ 3600rpm.
ENGINE STRUCTURE one belt-driven overhead camshaft, 2ohc 16v; aluminium cylinder head, cast iron block; 5-bearing crankshaft; Multec fuel injection; Siemens-Simtec 16v, electronic ignition.
TRANSMISSION front wheel drive; 5-speed gearbox; synchromesh; automatic optional; final drive ratios 3.94:1, 4.19:1 16v 4.12:1 automatic: 3.94:1 1.8, 2.81:1 automatic.
CHASSIS DETAILS integral steel structure; independent front

suspension by MacPherson struts; multi-link rear suspension; coil springs, telescopic dampers; anti-roll bar; vacuum servo disc brakes; rack and pinion PAS; 61L (13.4 Imp gal, 16.1 US gal) fuel tank, 2.0 4x4: 63L (13.9 Imp gal, 16.6 US gal); 175/70 R 14, 185/70 HR 14, 195/65 VR 15 tyres, 5.5, 6J rims.
DIMENSIONS wheelbase 260cm (102.4in); front track 140cm (55in), 142.5cm (56in) rear; ground clearance 14cm (5.5in); turning circle 11m (36.1ft); length 443cm (174.4in); width 170.5cm (67in); height 140cm (55in). Hatchback length 435cm (171in). 2.0 track 142.5cm (56in) front, 144.5cm (57in) rear.
PERFORMANCE 1.6 16v, maximum speed 183kph (114mph); 35.4kph (22.1mph) @ 1000rpm; acceleration 0-96kph (60mph) 12.5sec; 15.8kg/kW (11.8kg/bhp); fuel consumption 6.6-7.4L/100km (38-43mpg).
UK SALES 162,735.
PRICE 1995 1.6i Envoy £12235; 1997 1.8 Envoy £14700, 1.8 GLS £17105.

281

1995-1999 Vectra direct injection diesel and turbodiesel

The direct injection diesel announced in 1996 was designed by GM in Japan and was the world's first in production with a 16-valve cylinder head. The Ecotec TD arrived first with 60kW (81bhp) and was followed a year later by a version producing 75kW (101bhp). The engines' most unusual feature was the operation of all 16 valves from one chain driven overhead camshaft, each cam actuating two valves by means of a patented bridge piece on the tappets. Making-do with only one camshaft reduced internal friction by around one-third, and with the pressure pump for the fuel injection working at up to 1500bar giving an unusually fine spray, torque was generated evenly between 1800 and 2500rpm. This flat delivery of strong pulling power provided the car with great refinement made possible by high gearing. It had an impressive performance coupled with spectacular economy that could touch over 5.5L/100km (50mpg) with circumspect driving.

The rationale for a small price premium over rivals from Ford, Citroen, Renault, and Peugeot was good ride comfort, quietness, and a high equipment level including anti-lock brakes. Racy road testers were critical of the handling but workaday drivers buying Vectras found them highly competent.

BODY saloon, hatchback, estate, 5 seats, 4/5 doors; weight 1320kg (2910lb); estate 1360kg (2998lb).
ENGINE 4 cylinders, in-line, front, transverse, 84.0mm x 90.0mm; 1995cc; compr: 18.5:1; 60kW (81bhp) @ 4300rpm; 30.1kW/L (40.3bhp/L); 185Nm (138lb/ft) @ 1800rpm. 75kW (101bhp) @ 4300rpm; 37.6kW/L (50.4bhp/L); 205Nm (153lb/ft) @ 1600rpm.
ENGINE STRUCTURE chain-driven overhead camshaft; 16-valve; aluminium cylinder head; cast iron block; 5-bearing crankshaft; Garrett T15 turbocharger with intercooler, Bosch fuel injection.
TRANSMISSION front wheel drive;

5-speed gearbox; synchromesh; final drive ratios 3.74:1, 3.74:1.
CHASSIS DETAILS integral steel structure; independent front suspension by MacPherson struts; multi-link rear suspension; coil springs, telescopic dampers; anti-roll bar; vacuum servo disc brakes; rack and pinion PAS; 61L (13.4 Imp gal, 16.1 US gal) fuel tank; 185/70 R14 tyres.
DIMENSIONS wheelbase 260cm (102.4in); front track 140cm (55in), 142.5cm (56in) rear; ground clearance 14cm (5.5in); turning circle 11m (36.1ft); length 443cm (174.4in); width 170.5cm (67in); height 140cm (55in). Hatchback length 435cm (171in). 2.0 track 142.5cm (56in) front, 144.5cm (57in) rear.
PERFORMANCE 60kW maximum speed 176kph (110mph); 44.5kph (27.7mph) @ 1000rpm; acceleration 0-100kph (62mph) 15.5sec; 22kg/kW (16.3kg/bhp); fuel consumption 4.6/6.9L/100km (41-61mpg).
UK SALES 52,535.
PRICE 1996 TDS £14495.

1995-1999 Vectra 2.0, 2.5V6

The 2.0 Vectra had perfectly adequate performance but the expectations for the V6 were high. The suspension was 25 per cent firmer and the tyres beefed up to 205/55s or 60s, and with twin tailpipes and an aerofoil on the bootlid, it looked as though it was aimed at the sporty driver.

In the end the V6 was not just about speed. Six cylinders gave a smooth response, so it appealed to the CD trim buyer just as much as the enthusiast looking for sharp handling and a top speed well above UK motorway limits. In any case the V6 did not quite have the low-rev thrust to make it truly sporting, nor the swift turn-in to make it as racy as the £25000 Super Touring model, akin to the British Touring Car Championship (BTCC) car. This was a 149kW (200bhp) development of the 2.0-litre of which a production run of 500 was planned by the developer Ray Mallock. The engine developed 75kW/L (101bhp/L) by reconfiguring the fuel injection electronics, reworking the inlet and exhaust manifolds, and altering the camshafts. The Super Touring stripped for racing would do 152kph (150mph) and reach 100kph in about 7sec.

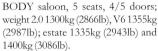

BODY saloon, 5 seats, 4/5 doors; weight 2.0 1300kg (2866lb), V6 1355kg (2987lb); estate 1335kg (2943lb) and 1400kg (3086lb).
ENGINE 4 cylinders, front transverse, 86mm x 86mm, 1998cc; compr 10.8:1; 100kW (134bhp) @ 5600rpm; 50kW/L (67.1bhp/L); 188Nm (140lb/ft) @ 3200rpm. V6 81.6mm x 79.6mm; 2498cc; compr: 10.8:1; 125kW (168bhp) @ 5800rpm; 50kW/L (67.3bhp/L); 230Nm (172lb/ft) @ 3200rpm.
ENGINE STRUCTURE 2 belt-driven overhead camshafts (V6, 2 per bank); aluminium cylinder head, cast iron block; 5-bearing crankshaft (V6 4); Siemens-Simtec fuel injection 2.0, Bosch Motronic V6; electronic ignition.
TRANSMISSION front wheel drive; 5-speed gearbox, auto 4 or 5-speed 2.0, 4-speed V6; synchromesh; automatic optional; final drive ratios 3.94:1 2.0 manual, 2.81:1 4-speed auto; V6 4.05:1 manual, 2.81 auto.
CHASSIS DETAILS integral steel structure; independent front suspension by MacPherson struts; multi-link rear suspension; coil springs, telescopic dampers; anti-roll bar; vacuum servo disc brakes; rack and pinion PAS; 61L (13.4 Imp gal, 16.1 US gal) fuel tank; 195/65 R 15, 205/55 R 16 tyres, 6J 7J rims.
DIMENSIONS wheelbase 260cm (102.4in); front track 140cm (55in), 142.5cm (56in) rear; ground clearance 14cm (5.5in); turning circle 11m (36.1ft); length 443cm (174.4in); width 170.5cm (67in); height 140cm (55in). Hatchback length 435cm (171in). 2.0 track 142.5cm (56in) front, 144.5cm (57in) rear.
PERFORMANCE maximum speed 233kph (145mph), auto 230kph (143mph); 38.3kph (23.9mph) @ 1000rpm; 0-100kph (62mph) 7.8sec, auto 8.8sec; 10.1kg/kW (7.8kg/bhp); 6.7-11.4L/100km (25-42mpg).
UK SALES 95,690.
PRICE 1996 2.5 V6 SRi £17695; 2.0i GLS £15900.

Left & right: **SRi.**
Far right: **CDX estate.**

1997 Corsa 1.0 12V 3-cylinder

The bold decision to replace an old 4-cylinder Family II engine, dating back to the 1980s, with a 3-cylinder was taken in 1990. It was based on the need for a new generation of power units to meet approaching exhaust emission laws and use less fuel than existing Ecotec models. Joachim Quarg, head of development at the new GM engine facility in Aspern, Austria, outlined the rationale for the modular layout of the first 3-cylinder European engine to have 4 valves per cylinder. Quarg's thesis was that small petrol engines were at their most efficient with cylinder displacements of between 300 and 500cc. At 107mm shorter, 51mm narrower, and 27mm lower than the 1.2 litre engine it replaced, it was built round a lightweight steel block and weighed 82.5kg (182lb), a saving of 12.5kg (27.6lb). Only 5.5mm separated each cylinder and their spacing was closed up by 6mm to 78mm. Hollow camshafts, tiny hydraulic valve lifters, and a magnesium cam cover contributed to the low weight while roller valve followers reduced internal friction by some 70 per cent. The facelifted model had new electric power steering that dispensed with the need for an engine-driven hydraulic pump, making further fuel savings of up to five per cent.

BODY hatchback, 5 seats, 3/5 doors; weight 855kg (1885lb).
ENGINE 3 cylinders, in-line, front transverse, 72.5mm x 78.6mm; 973cc; compr: 10.1:1; 40kW (54bhp) @ 5600rpm; 41.1kW/L (55.1bhp/L); 82Nm (61lb/ft) @ 2800rpm.
ENGINE STRUCTURE chain-driven ohc; aluminium cylinder head; iron/steel block; 4-bearing crankshaft; Bosch Motronic fuel injection.
TRANSMISSION front wheel drive; 5-speed; synchromesh; final drive ratio 3.74:1.

CHASSIS DETAILS integral steel structure; ifs by MacPherson struts; rear susp torsion beam axle, coil springs, dampers, anti roll bar; discs (some ventilated) front drum rear brakes; rack and pinion electric PAS; 46L (10.1 Imp gal, 12.1 US gal) fuel tank; 165/70 R13 tyres, 5J rims.
DIMENSIONS wheelbase 244cm (96.1in); track 139cm (54.8in); ground clearance 14cm (5.5in); turning 10.1m (33.1ft); length 373cm (147in); width 161cm (63.4in); height 142cm (55.9in).
PERFORMANCE max 150kph (93.4mph); 30.9kph (19.2mph) @ 1000rpm; acceleration 0-100kph (62mph) 18sec; 21.4kg/kW (15.8kg/bhp); 4.9-6.4L/100km (44-58mpg).
PRICE 1997 Sting £8540; 1999 Trip £6820; GLS £9495 with PAS on the road.

Colour-keyed bumper and new grille with corporate "V" was ultimately applied to all Corsas. Testers compared smooth-running engine to a V6.

287

1997 Omega

The evolution into an entire range of luxury saloons and estate cars meant that the Omega could spread itself across a wide spectrum of prices (roughly between £20,000 and £30,000) and engine sizes. There was a choice of five between 2.0 and 3.0-litres with two diesels leading to a variety of options, such as Traction Control Plus (TC-Plus) on both V6 petrol engines, but anti-lock brakes were standard throughout. TC-Plus monitored the speed of all four wheels, and when those at the rear went faster than those at the front it automatically shut off engine pull to prevent wheelspin. It was clever enough to detect wheelspin on just one wheel, and gently apply the brakes to it, transferring drive to the one opposite. It averted skids so subtly that most drivers were quite unaware they had been overruled.

PAS was standard throughout the range, the V6s having Servotronic, which was sensitive to speed, reducing the amount of assistance when the car was going fast to improve feel and increasing it when parking. The top Elite had the self-levelling rear suspension that was optional on other models, satellite navigation, and load-sensing automatic transmission that adapted its shift patterns to the driver's style.

Spec for 3.0iV6.
BODY saloon, 4 doors; estate, 5 doors; 5 seats; weight saloon 1590kg (3505lb), estate 1655kg (3649lb).
ENGINE V6 cylinder, front, 86.0mm x 85.0mm; 2962cc; compr: 10.8:1; 155kW (208bhp) @ 6200rpm; 52.3kW/L (70.2bhp/L); 270Nm (167.4lb/ft) @ 3600rpm.
ENGINE STRUCTURE 2 belt-driven overhead camshafts per bank; sodium-cooled valves; aluminium cylinder head; graphite iron block; 4-bearing crankshaft; Motronic sequential fuel injection.
TRANSMISSION rear wheel drive; asbestos-free sdp clutch; 5-speed gearbox; synchromesh; 4-speed automatic; final drive ratio 3.7:1, 3.9:1 automatic.
CHASSIS DETAILS integral steel structure; independent front suspension by MacPherson struts; independent multi-link rear suspension; twin-tube gas pressure dampers; anti roll bars front and rear; disc, diagonally split hydraulic dual circuit, tandem servo brakes, ABS; recirculating ball PAS; 75L (16.5 Imp gal, 19.8 US gal) fuel tank; 225 55 R16 tyres, 7J rims.
DIMENSIONS wheelbase 273cm (107.5in); front track 151cm (59.4in), 153cm (60.2in) rear; ground clearance 14cm (5.5in); turning circle 11m (36.1ft); length 479cm (188.6in); width 179cm (70.5in); height 146cm 57.5in). length 482cm (189.8in), height 151cm (59.4in).
PERFORMANCE manual saloon maximum speed 238kph (149mph); 39.5kph (24.6mph) @ 1000rpm; 0-06kph (60mph) 8.3sec; 10.3kg/kW (7.6kg/bhp); fuel consumption 11.1L/100km (25.4mpg).
PRICE 1997 Tdi 16v GLS estate £20400; 1999 V6 3.0 Elite £31650.

1997-1999 Sintra 2.2 16v, 3.0 V6 24v

The Sintra was designed to look less like the front of an Inter-City train than some MPVs. Its creators decided it would be better if it looked and behaved like a big estate car, with seats for up to eight, rather than feel like an adapted van. Accordingly it was based on a GM American platform with sliding doors and a driver's eyeline about the same height as it would be in a car. Similarly the facia was arranged so that the instruments were in the driver's normal line of sight, not below it.

Sintra was part of a world GM programme which expected to sell 300,000 a year, with Europe taking 50,000, not a large number by GM standards but in the event it proved unattainable. Heavy Europeanisation including firmer spring-damper rates, quicker-geared steering, and negative-camber front suspension giving better steering response and more feel. European specification included four wheel disc brakes, ABS as standard equipment, a completely different interior and controls to suit local tastes in trim and seating positions. A great deal of thought went into weight-saving with aluminium alloy hub carriers, tubular anti-roll bars and aluminium seat-rails and frames. Following the introduction of the Zafira multi-purpose vehicle, imports from the US were discontinued in 1999.

BODY MPV 5/8 seats, 5 doors; weight 2.2 1620kg (3572lb), V6 1710kg (3770lb), turbodiesel 1690kg (3726lb). ENGINE 54deg V6 cylinders, front, 86mm x 85mm; 2962cc; compr: 10.8:1; 148kW (199bhp) @ 6000rpm; 50kW/L (67.2bhp/L); 260Nm (194lb/ft) @ 3600rpm. 4 cylinders 86.00mm x 94.6mm; 2198cc; compr 10.5:1; 104kW (140bhp) @ 5400rpm; 47.3kW/L (63.4bhp/L); 202Nm (151lb/ft) @ 2600rpm. Diesel 84mm x 90mm; 1995cc; compr 18.5:1; 74kW (99bhp) @ 4300rpm; 37.1kW/L (49.7bhp/L); 205Nm (153lb/ft) @ 1600rpm.
ENGINE STRUCTURE 2 belt-driven overhead camshafts V6 2 per bank; 4 valves per cylinder; aluminium cylinder head, iron block; 4-bearing crankshaft V6, 5 2.2; electronic fuel injection; diesel chain-driven ohc 4 cylinder 16-valve Bosch VP55 injection and Garrett T15 turbo.

TRANSMISSION front wheel drive; 2.2 5-speed gearbox; V6 4-speed automatic; final drive ratios 3.09:1, 2.2 4.05:1.

CHASSIS DETAILS integral steel structure; independent front suspension by MacPherson struts; rear suspension torsion beam, coil springs; telescopic dampers; anti-roll bars front and rear; servo discs, ABS brakes; rack and pinion PAS; 70L (15.4 Imp gal, 18.5 US gal) fuel tank; 205/65 R15 tyres, 6J rims.

DIMENSIONS wheelbase 285cm (112in); front track 156cm (61.4in), 161cm (63.4in) rear; ground clearance 16cm (6.3in); turning circle 11.4m (37.4ft); length 467cm (184in); width 183cm (72in); height 176cm (69.3in).

PERFORMANCE maximum speed 201kph (125mph); 39.1kph (24.4mph) @ 1000rpm; acceleration 0-100kph (62mph) 10.8sec; 11.6kg/kW (8.6kg/bhp); fuel consumption 8-13.6L/100km (20.8-35.3mpg).

UK SALES 4000.

PRICE 2.2 CD £19450; 3.0 V6 CDX £25350.

1998 Astra 1.2 16v, 1.6 8v

Vauxhall's TV slogan was "Quality is a right not a privilege." Well-chosen words. The Astra had whole-body galvanising once found only on cars twice the price. Vauxhall's galvanising gave the Astra a 12-year warranty against rusting through, effectively banishing body-rot to the recollections of older motorists and classic car restorers.

There was a wide range of engines from 1.2 (not sold in the UK), 1.4, 1.6 and 1.8 petrol, and 1.7 and 2.0 diesel. All the petrol engines were 16-valve except the 1.6 55kW (74bhp) 8v entry-level. Vauxhall priced the Astra keenly against the radically-styled Escort replacement, not yet on the road. The appearance was relatively safe and conservative although the car was a profound improvement over worthy but scarcely dynamic predecessors. The three main trim levels were Envoy, Club, and CD, with the addition of LS (electric windows, manual sunroof, steering wheel tilt, tinted glass standard), CDX (ABS and traction control, passenger and side airbags, leather steering wheel as well as the CD's air conditioning and wood-trimmed console), and Sport (sports suspension, close ratio gears, white instrument dials). Demand for the Astra was so high that a third shift at Ellesmere Port, which produced its 3 millionth vehicle in 1999, was inaugurated to meet it.

BODY saloon, estate; 3/4/5 doors; 5 seats; weight 3-dr 990kg (2183lb), estate 5-dr 1060kg (2337lb), saloon 1110kg (2447lb), 1.6 saloon 1050kg (2315lb).
ENGINE 4 cylinders, in-line, front transverse, 72.5mm x 72.6mm; 1199cc; compr: 10:1; 48kW (64bhp) @ 5600rpm; 40kW/L (53.7bhp/L); 110Nm (82lb/ft) @ 4000rpm. 79mm x 81.5mm, 1598cc; compr 9.5:1; 55kW (74bhp) @ 5200rpm; 34.4kW/L (46.1bhp/L); 128Nm (95.5lb/ft) @ 2800rpm.
ENGINE STRUCTURE 2 chain-driven overhead camshafts; 16v; aluminium cylinder head; cast iron block; 5-bearing crankshaft; Multec S multi-point fuel injection. 1.6, belt-driven sohc; 8v; Multec single-point fuel injection.
TRANSMISSION front wheel drive; hydraulic asbestos-free sdp clutch; 5-speed gearbox; synchromesh; final drive ratio 3.94:1. 1.6 4.18:1 automatic 4.12:1.
CHASSIS DETAILS integral steel structure; independent front suspension by MacPherson struts, gas-pressure dampers and anti-roll bar, rear suspension torsion tube with compound links, double-conical springs; gas-pressure dampers; servo disc brakes ventilated at front, dual circuit diagonally split; rack and pinion PAS; 52L (11.4 Imp gal, 13.7 US gal) fuel tank; 175/70 R14 tyres, 5.5J rims. 1.6 195/60 R15.
DIMENSIONS wheelbase 261cm (102.75in); front track 148.5cm (58.5in), 146cm (57.5in) rear; ground clearance 13cm (5.1in); turning circle 10.8m (35.4ft); length 411cm (161.8in); width 171cm (67.3in); height 143cm (56.3in).
PERFORMANCE 1.2 maximum speed 165kph (103mph); 34.7kph (21.6mph) @ 1000rpm; acceleration 0-96kph (60mph) 16sec; 20kg/kW (14.7kg/bhp); fuel consumption 5-8L/100km (35-57mpg).
PRICE 1999 Astra Envoy 1.6i 8-valve 3-door £11,150; LS 5-door £12,470.

1998 Astra 1.4 16v, 1.6 16v Ecotec

Almost every aspect of the Astra was remarkable. Road noise was reduced to a distant hum, engine noise subdued, and ride and handling were exemplary after Lotus became involved in fine-tuning the suspension. Former grand prix racing driver John Miles worked with Lotus chassis engineer Steve Swift on the damper settings and bump stops that determine suspension travel and steering response. The rear anti-roll bar was deleted in favour of a well-trimmed torsion bar and the front suspension was mounted in a lightweight aluminium subframe. The only real criticism of the car concerned the gloomy interior. Body styles at launch were 3 and 5-door and an estate, followed by a 4-door saloon, and although there were some delays to the start of production, quality standards were high.

The aerodynamic coefficient of drag was 0.29 and the new car was larger and roomier than any of its predecessors. Since 1981 the Astra wheelbase had grown by more than 9cm (3.5in), length by over 11cm (4.3in), and height by 5cm (1.9in). The saloon's body shell was 80 per cent stiffer than before, the estate car an astonishing 100 per cent, explaining much of the new-found refinement that was a match for anything in its class.

BODY saloon, estate, 3/4/5 doors, 5 seats; weight 1085kg (2392lb), estate 1145kg (2524lb).

ENGINE 4 cylinders, in line, front, transverse, 77.6mm x 73.4mm; 1389cc; compr: 10.5:1; 66kW (88.5bhp) @ 6000rpm; 47.5kW/L (63.7bhp/L); 125Nm (93lb/ft) @ 4000rpm. 79mm x 81.5mm; 1598cc; 74kW (99bhp) @ 6200rpm; 46.3kW/L (62.1bhp/L); 159Nm (119lb/ft) @ 3200rpm.

ENGINE STRUCTURE 2 belt-driven overhead camshafts; 16v; aluminium cylinder head; hydraulic tappets; cast iron block; 5-bearing crankshaft; Multec S multi-point fuel injection; electronic mapped ignition, knock control.

TRANSMISSION front wheel drive; hydraulic asbestos-free sdp clutch; 5-speed gearbox; synchromesh; 4-speed automatic with electronic control of adaptive shifts optional 1.6i; 3.74, 3.94, 4.12 or 4.18:1 final drive ratio.

CHASSIS DETAILS integral steel structure; independent front suspension by MacPherson struts,

gas-pressure dampers and anti-roll bar, rear suspension torsion tube with compound links, double-conical springs; gas-pressure dampers; servo disc brakes ventilated at front, dual circuit diagonally split; rack and pinion PAS; 52L (11.4 Imp gal, 13.7 US gal) fuel tank; 185/65 R14 tyres, 5.5J rims.

DIMENSIONS wheelbase 261cm (102.75in); front track 148.5cm (58.5in), 146cm (57.5in) rear; ground clearance 13cm (5.1in; turning circle 10.8m (35.4ft); length 411cm (161.8in); width 171cm (67.3in); height 143cm (56.3in).

PERFORMANCE 1.4i maximum speed 180kph (112mph); 31.3kph (19.5mph) @ 1000rpm; acceleration 0-96kph (60mph) 11.5sec; 16.4kg/kW (12.3kg/bhp); fuel consumption 7.1L/100km (39.8mpg).

PRICE 1999 1.4i 16v Envoy 5 door £11800; 1.6I 16v LS Estate £13720.

Far right: the author samples Astra cornering on a special course at the press launch.

295

1998 Astra 1.8 16v, 2.0 16v

Most notable of the new Astra's engines engine was the smooth-running balancer-shaft 2.0-litre Ecotec as used in the Vectra. The suppression of tyre and wind noise made both hatchback and 4-door saloon Astras refined even in the face of opposition from Peugeot and Volkswagen. The steering rack was mounted on the lightweight hydroformed aluminium subframe, not the front bulkhead.

A feature of the automatic transmission, optional throughout the range except for the 1.2 and 1.7TD, was its shift into neutral when the car stopped with the brakes applied. Creep was eliminated and there was no drag when the engine was idling. Fuel consumption in traffic was reduced by 3 per cent and as soon as the brake was released Drive re-engaged of its own accord. Vauxhall's pioneering work with synchromesh was recalled with new rings and shift lever sleeves to make shifting easier and smoother on manual-transmission cars.

Like the 1.2, the 1.8 engine was new, with a lighter crankshaft to improve smooth-running and a variable intake manifold to give better pulling power throughout the speed range. Transmission refinements included on the 3-door 2.0SRi included traction control and there was a 15 per cent stiffening of spring rates.

BODY saloon, estate; 3/4/5 doors, 5 seats; weight 1095kg (2414lb), estate 1190kg (2624lb).
ENGINE 4 cylinders, in-line, front, transverse, 80.5mm x 88.2mm; 1796cc; compr: 10.5:1; 85kW (114bhp) @ 5400rpm; 47.3kW/l (63.5bhp/L); 170Nm (127lb/ft) @ 3400rpm. 86mm x 86mm; 1998cc; compr 10.8:1; 100kW (134bhp) @ 5600rpm; 50kW/L (67.1bhp/L); 188Nm (140lb/ft) @ 3200rpm.
ENGINE STRUCTURE 2 belt-driven ohc; aluminium cyl head; cast iron block; 5-bearing crank; Siemens-Simtec multi-point fuel injection; electronic mapped direct ignition.
TRANSMISSION front wheel drive; hydraulic asbestos-free sdp clutch; 5-speed; synchromesh; 4-speed auto optional; final drive ratio 3.74, 4.12:1

auto 1.6 3.74 or 3.94, 2.8:1 auto 2.0.
CHASSIS DETAILS integral steel structure; ifs by MacPherson struts, gas-pressure dampers and anti-roll bar, rear suspension torsion tube with compound links, double-conical springs; gas-pressure dampers; servo disc brakes ventilated at front, dual circuit diagonally split; rack and pinion PAS; 52L (11.4 Imp gal, 13.7 US gal) fuel tank; 195/60R15 tyres, 5.5J rims.
DIMENSIONS wheelbase 261cm (102.75in); front track 148.5cm (58.5in), 146cm (57.5in) rear; ground clearance 13cm (5.1in); turning circle 10.8m (35.4ft); length 411cm (161.8in); width 171cm (67.3in); height 143cm (56.1in).
PERFORMANCE 2.0i, maximum speed 208kph (129.5mph); 33.8kph (21.1mph) @ 1000rpm; 0-96kph (60mph) 8.5sec; 11kg/kW (8.2kg/bhp); 6.6-12L/100km (23.5-43mpg).
PRICE 1999 1.8i Sport 16v 5-door £14250; 2.0i SRi 16v 3-door with aircon £15300.

Left: SRi. *Right:* Sport.

Below: Introduced at the 1999 Earls Court motor show, the Bertone Astra Coupe for model year 2000 came with a 2.0-litre 185bhp turbo engine or a choice of aluminium 4-valve units giving 112bhp or 143bhp.

1998 Astra 1.7 TD, 2.0 Di

Astras were the best-selling estate cars in Britain throughout most of the 1990s, and the new version was provided with more loading bay space by keeping the ingenious torsion beam rear suspension and setting the rear dampers at an unusually steep angle. Estates were 18cm (7.1in) longer than the hatchback, mostly owing to extra rear overhang and a modest increase in wheelbase, and had a capacity of 1500 litres with the seatbacks folded down, or 480 litres with them in place. The rear seat split 60/40.

A favourite engine among estate buyers was the 1995cc turbodiesel, a direct injection four-valve unit whose cylinder head was something of a masterpiece of miniaturisation. There was not much room for four valves, all operated from one camshaft, in the small combustion space of a diesel. Performance was adequate rather than spectacular, and although the engine was clattery on start-up it quietened down at speed. Economy was outstanding and, driving prudently, it was possible to get 50mpg (5.7L/100km) even from the smooth-changing automatic. This gave a range on a 52 litre (11.4gal) tankful of some 917kms (570 miles). The 1.7TD was a modest performer and not so economical as the ECOTEC 16-valve 2.0.

BODY 3/4/5 door, 5 seats; weight 1115kg (2458lb), estate 1175kg (2590lb); 2.0 1225kg (2701lb) and 1280kg (2822lb).
ENGINE 4 cylinders, in-line, front, transverse, 82.5mm x 79.5mm; 1700cc; compr: 22:1; 50kW (67bhp) @ 4500rpm; 29.4kW/L (39.4bhp/L); 132Nm (98lb/ft) @ 2400rpm. 84mm x 90mm, compr 18.5:1, 1995cc, 60kW (80bhp) @ 4300rpm, 30.1kW/L (40.3bhp/L), 185Nm (138lb/ft) @ 1800rpm.
ENGINE STRUCTURE overhead camshaft (1.7 belt 2.0 chain, 16-valve); aluminium cylinder head; cast iron block; 5-bearing crank; turbocharger, intercooler, Bosch fuel injection. 2.0 Garrett T15 turbocharger.
TRANSMISSION front wheel drive; hydraulic asbestos-free sdp clutch; 5-speed gearbox; synchromesh; 2.0 automatic optional; final drive ratios 3.55, 3.74, 2.6:1 auto.
CHASSIS DETAILS integral steel structure; independent front suspension by MacPherson struts, gas-pressure dampers and anti-roll bar, rear suspension torsion tube with compound links, double-conical springs; gas-pressure dampers; servo disc brakes ventilated at front, dual circuit diagonally split; rack and pinion PAS; 52L (11.4 Imp gal, 13.7 US gal) fuel tank; 195/65 R15 tyres, 5.5J rims.
DIMENSIONS wheelbase 261cm (102.75in); front track 148.5cm (58.5in), 146cm (57.5in) rear; ground clearance 13cm (5.1in); turning circle 10.8m (35.4ft); length 411cm (161.8in); width 171cm (67.3in); height 143cm (56.1in).
PERFORMANCE 2.0 maximum speed 175kph (109mph); 43.5kph (27.1mph) @ 1000rpm; acceleration 0-96kph (60mph) 13.5sec; 20.4kg/kW (15.3kg/bhp); fuel consumption 4.7-7.5L/100km (38-60mpg).
PRICE 1999 Envoy 1.7TD 3-door £11700; CD 2.0Di 16v estate with aircon £15220.

1998 Frontera 2.2 and 3.2V6

Although it had similar chunky lines to the 1991 original, nearly all the Frontera of 1998 was completely new. The body was subtly reshaped, there were no panels carried over, and the interior was completely revised to meet criticisms of the facia switchgear and materials. The 2.2-litre 4-cylinder had balancer shafts added and the new 3.2-litre V6 gave a further option. Automatic transmission became available, it was claimed to be 50 per cent quieter inside, it was up to139kg (306lb) lighter and had 16.5 per cent better economy.

Four wheel drive was selectable on the move, the steering was changed to power assisted rack and pinion, and wider front and rear track enhanced the appearance and improved the handling. The V6 even had a cruise control. Both models had longer wheelbases than before but came closer in overall length with the 3-door 8cm (3.1in) longer and the 5-door 10cm (3.9in) shorter overall. Vauxhall retained the separate chassis so essential to a serious off-roader, and interior space was much increased. The sporty swb version was not available with the V6, but in lwb form it was an effective replacement for the Monterey, which was discontinued.

Spec for 2.2i Estate
BODY estate, 5 doors, 5 seats; weight 1730kg (3814lb). Sport, 3 doors (2.2 only) 1667kg (3675lb).
ENGINE 4 cylinders, in-line, front, 86.0mm x 94.6mm; 2198cc; compr: 9.6:1; 100kW (134bhp) @ 5200rpm; 45.5kW/L (61bhp/L); 148.9Nm (111lb/ft) @ 2500rpm. V6 3165cc; compr 9.4:1; 151kW (203bhp) @ 5400rpm; 47.7kW/L (64bhp/L); 290Nm (214lb/ft) @ 3000rpm.
ENGINE STRUCTURE 2 belt-driven overhead camshafts; 16 valves; aluminium cylinder head; cast iron block; 5-bearing crankshaft; balancer shafts; Motronic multi-point fuel injection; electronic ignition. V6 2ohc per bank, aluminium crankcase, sodium-filled exhaust valves.
TRANSMISSION rear wheel drive, selectable 4WD; 5-speed gearbox; automatic optional V6; final drive ratio 4.78:1. V6 4.3:1. auto 4.1:1.
CHASSIS DETAILS box-section chassis, separate steel body; independent front suspension by double wishbones, gas-pressure dampers, torsion bars, anti-roll bar; rear suspension live axle, four trailing links with Panhard rod, coil springs and twin-tube hydraulic gas pressure dampers; anti-roll bar; ventilated disc brakes, dual circuit, servo; ABS optional, V6 std; rack and pinion PAS; 75L (16.5 Imp gal, 19.9US gal) fuel tank (estate);245/70OR tyres, 7J rims.
DIMENSIONS wheelbase 270.2cm (106.4in); track 146cm (57.5in); ground clearance 23cm (9.1in); turning circle 11.48m (37.7ft); length 465.8cm (183.4in); width 203.6cm (80.2in); height 174cm (68.5in).
PERFORMANCE 2.2i maximum speed 165kph (103mph); 35.3kph (22mph) @ 1000rpm; 0-96kph (60mph) 12.5sec; 17.3kg/kW (12.9kg/bhp); fuel consumption 11.1L/100km (25.4mpg).
PRICE 1999 2.2 16v Sport 3-door £16095; 3.2i V6 24v 5-door Estate Limited £21770.

Far right: the author verifies the Frontera's cross-country credentials.

300

1998 Frontera 2.2 DTi

Independent front suspension was by no means general for off-road leisure 4x4s, but one aim of the Frontera was an improvement in on-road performance where the competition was forging ahead. Vauxhall's response to the good road manners of its Nissan and Land Rover adversaries was the installation of a diesel engine more sophisticated than either, with four valves per cylinder, balancer shafts as developed by the redoubtable Dr Lanchester, more power and more torque. Noisy on start-up, it quietened down on the road to become quieter in operation than its rivals as well as faster and swifter in acceleration.

Off-road the Frontera was a match for anything with 50cm (19.7in) wading depth, maximum departure, ramp, and approach angles of 29deg, 20deg, and 32deg (lwb 23, 19, and 32), and a safe maximum angle of tilt at 45.7deg. The long wheelbase Frontera could tilt to 46deg without falling over. Improvements to the new model in chassis stiffness and durability were achieved following experience of the TransGlobe Challenge, an 18,000 mile circumnavigation of the world over four continents and 16 countries in three weeks, a record for a production 4x4 standard except for satellite navigation and a larger fuel tank.

BODY estate, 5 door, 5 seats; weight 1813kg (3997lb). Sport, 3 doors, 1727kg (3807lb).
ENGINE 4 cylinders, in-line, front, 84mm x 98mm; 2171cc; 85kW (114bhp) @ 3800rpm; 39.2kW/L (52.5bhp/L); 260Nm (194lb/ft) @ 1900-2500rpm.
ENGINE STRUCTURE chain-driven overhead camshaft; balancer shafts; aluminium cylinder head; cast iron block; 5-bearing crankshaft; Bosch fuel injection; water-cooler turbocharger and intercooler.
TRANSMISSION rear wheel drive, selectable 4WD; 5-speed gearbox; synchromesh; final drive ratio 4.56:1.
CHASSIS DETAILS box-section chassis, separate steel body; independent front suspension by double wishbones, gas-pressure dampers, torsion bars, anti-roll bar; rear suspension live axle, four trailing links with Panhard rod, coil springs and twin-tube hydraulic gas pressure dampers; anti-roll bar; ventilated disc brakes; ABS optional; rack and pinion PAS; 75L (16.5 Imp gal, 19.8 US gal)

fuel tank (estate); 245/70ORtyres, 7J rims.
DIMENSIONS wheelbase 270.2cm (106.4in); track 146cm (57.5in); ground clearance 23cm (9.1in); turning circle 11.48m (37.7ft); length 465.8cm (183.4in); width 203.6cm (80.2in); height 174cm (68.5in).
PERFORMANCE maximum speed 154kph (96mph); 38kph (23.7mph) @ 1000rpm; acceleration 0-96kph (60mph) 13.7sec; 21.3kg/kW (15.9kg/bhp); fuel consumption 9.1L/100km (31mpg).
PRICE 1999 Sport RS 2.2DTi 3-door £18770; 2.2 DTi 16v 5-door estate £19570.

Far right: CARIN navigation system was option in Vectra and Omega.

303

1999 Zafira 1.6, 1.8

Vauxhall's 70-year tradition of family cars stretched into the 21st century with a compact Astra-based multi purpose vehicle (MPV). The Zafira entered a segment of the market almost unknown in western Europe before 1992. Then less than one car in a hundred could be described as an MPV, but by 1997 registrations of them had grown four-fold, and the vigorous growth was expected to continue.

Encouraged by the strong sales of Astra estate, always strong in the UK and top of its class in Europe, Zafira came in with accommodation for seven occupants or 1700 litres of load space. It had an ingenious foldaway seating system that provided room for seven, or converted it to a single seater in 15sec, without removing a seat. Instead of having to be taken out and carried off, the two individual third row seats folded easily into the floor. Only 9.3cm (3.7in) longer than an Astra, 3cm (1.2in) longer than an Astra estate, with the familiar Astra instruments and switchgear, the Zafira had plenty of door bins, map pockets, cup holders, and a drawer under the passenger seat to cater for families just as Vauxhall had been doing since just after the turn of the century. Even before the Zafira officially went on sale in May 1999, planned output at its European manufacturing plant was increased from 120,000 to 145,000 a year.

BODY MPV, 7 seats, 5 doors; weight 1300kg (2866lb).
ENGINE 4 cyls, in-line, front, t'verse, 79mm x 81.5mm; 1598cc; cr 10.5:1; 74kW (99bhp) @ 6200rpm; 46.3kW/L (62.1bhp/L); 159Nm (119lb/ft) @ 3200rpm. 80.5mm x 88.2mm; 1796cc; cr 10.5:1; 85kW (114bhp) @ 5400rpm; 170Nm (127lb/ft) @ 3400rpm.
ENGINE STRUCTURE 2 belt-driven ohc; 16v; aluminium cyl head; hydraulic tappets; ci block; 5-bg crank; Multec S multi-point fuel inj; electronic mapped ign, knock control.
TRANSMISSION fwd; sdp clutch; 5-spd, synch; auto opt; final drive 4.19:1.
CHASSIS DETAILS integral steel structure; ifs by MacPherson struts, gas-pressure dampers, anti-roll bar,

rear susp torsion tube, compound links, double-conical springs; gas dampers; servo electro-hydraulic disc brakes ventil front, dual circ diag split; r & p PAS; 52L (11.4 Imp gal, 13.7 US gal); 195/60R15 tyres, 5.5J rims.
DIMENSIONS wb 270cm (106in); track 147cm (58in), 149cm (59in) rear; g c 15cm (6in); turning circle 10.5m (34.5ft); length 432cm (170in); width 176cm (69in); height 164cm (64in).
PERFORMANCE 1.6: max 176kph (110mph); 31.1kph (19.4mph) @ 1000rpm; 0-96kph (60mph) 13.5sec; 17.6kg/kW (13.1kg/bhp); 6.8-10.9L/100km (25.9-41.5mpg).
PRICE: 1.6 16v £14,500; Comfort 1.6 16v £17,500; Comfort 1.8 16v £16,250; Elegance 1.8 16v £17,500.

1999 Zafira 2.0D

Like the petrol Ecotec-engined models that preceded it, the turbo-diesel Zafira came with a choice of trim. The entry-level petrol-engined 1.6 already had the energy-saving electro-hydraulic power steering, electric front windows, tinted glass, and fabric seat covering. Zafira Comfort trim added an adjustable steering wheel, air conditioning, and roof rails, and Zafira Elegance had a CDR 500CD sound system with eight speakers, cosmetic chrome, and 6-spoke alloy wheels. Cruise control and add-on accessories to the roof bars were among the optional extras when it came on the market to meet competition from the well-established Renault Scenic, Toyota Picnic, and the radical 6-seat Fiat Multipla.

The Zafira was received with almost as much enthusiasm as the Astra had been, with praise for the low level of road noise, crisp gearchange, and nicely-weighted high geared steering with only 3.1 turns from lock to lock. The handling remained good and firm although there was a little more body roll than the lower Astra. Like the Astra however the interior was regarded as unworthy of such an innovative Vauxhall and the larger body carried more engine and wind noise resonance than the praiseworthy Astra. Yet at around £1000 more than the Astra estate and offering astonishing versatility, it was excellent value.

BODY MPV, 7 seats, 5 doors; weight 1430kg (3153lb).
ENGINE 4 cylinders, in-line, front, transverse; 84mm x 90mm; 1995cc; compr: 18.5:1; 60kW (80bhp) @ 4300rpm; 30.1kW/l (40.3bhp/l) 185Nm (138lb/ft) @ 1800rpm.
ENGINE STRUCTURE one chain driven ohc; 16v; alumin cyl head, cast iron block; 5-bg crank; Bosch fuel injection; Garrett T15 turbocharger.
TRANSMISSION front wheel drive; sdp clutch; Getrag 5-speed gearbox; synchromesh; final drive ratio 4.17:1.
CHASSIS DETAILS integral steel structure; ifs, MacPherson struts, gas-pressure dampers and anti-roll bar, rear suspension torsion tube with compound links, double-conical springs; gas-pressure dampers; servo disc brakes ventilated at front, dual circuit diagonally split; rack and pinion electro-hydraulic PAS; 52L (11.4 Imp gal, 13.7 US gal) fuel tank; 195/60R15 tyres, 5.5J rims.
DIMENSIONS wheelbase 270cm (106.25in); front track 147cm (57.9in), 149cm (58.7in) rear; ground clearance 15cm (6in); turning circle 10.5m (34.5ft); length 432cm (170in); width 176cm (69in); height 164cm (64in).
PERFORMANCE maximum speed 160kph (100 mph); 0-100kph (62mph) 17sec; 39.3kph (24.5mph) @ 1000rpm; 23.8kg/kW (17.9kg/bhp); fuel consumption EU 5.5-8.4L/100km (34-51mpg).

1999 Vectra

The Vectra underwent a facelift in 1999. Styling revisions gave it a closer family resemblance to the thriving Astra, an upgraded interior to meet the demand for more style, and safety improvements developed by Vauxhall's Swedish GM counterpart Saab. These included headrests that pivoted to meet the driver's head in a rear impact, reducing the load on the neck by 40-50 per cent. There were also suspension enhancements. Vectra handling had gained detailed improvements soon after launch and now they were consolidated into road behaviour almost a match for the widely praised Astra. Chassis response and cornering were improved, body roll reduced, and bigger wheels and tyres made room for larger front brake discs. The balancer shaft 2.0-litre was included in the changes and the 1.8-litre was given the Astra's new 1.8 engine, providing more power and 10 per cent better economy.

Among the cosmetic changes were larger body-contoured bumpers, a chrome grille, and what was called "jewel-effect" one-piece headlamp and indicators giving 20 per cent more light. Xenon headlamps with dynamic beam levelling became an option from the autumn of 1999. Vauxhall stretched the valuable anti-perforation warranty from 6 to 10 years, and claimed that a total of over 2,500 changes in all had been made.

Spec for 1.8 16v:
BODY saloon, 4/5 doors, 5 seats; weight 1246kg (2747lb); estate 1310kg (2888lb).
ENGINE 4 cylinders, in-line, front, transverse, 81.6mm x 88.2mm; 1796cc; compr: 10.5:1; 85kW (114bhp) @ 5400rpm; 47.2kW/l (63.5bhp/l); 170Nm (127lb/ft) @ 3400rpm.
ENGINE STRUCTURE 2 overhead camshafts; 16valves; aluminium cylinder head; cast iron block; 5-bearing crankshaft; Siemens-Simtec electronic fuel injection.
TRANSMISSION front wheel drive; sdp clutch; 5-speed gearbox; synchromesh; 4-speed automatic optional; final drive ratio 3.74:1, 4.12:1 automatic; Traction Control Plus on 2.0 16v and 2.5V6.
CHASSIS DETAILS integral steel structure; independent front suspension by MacPherson struts; multi-link rear suspension; coil springs, telescopic dampers; anti-roll bar; vacuum servo disc brakes, ventilated at front; rack and pinion PAS; 60L (13.2 Imp gal, 15.8US gal)

fuel tank;185/70R14 tyres, 5.5J rims.
DIMENSIONS wheelbase 263.5cm (104in); front track 146.5cm (57.7in), 147cm (57.9in) rear; ground clearance 14cm (5.5in); turning circle 11.3m (37.1ft); length 449.5cm (177in); width 171cm (67in); height 142cm (56in).
PERFORMANCE maximum speed 199kph (124mph); 34.8kph (21.7mph) @ 1000rpm; acceleration 0-96kph (60mph) 11.0sec; 14.9kg/kW (10.9kg/bhp); fuel consumption EU 5.8-10.6 L/100km (27-50mpg).
PRICES on-the-road Envoy 1.6i £14,695; Arctic 1.8 16v £14,800; SRi 2.5i V6 £18.260 with side airbags, air conditioning, and 16in alloy wheels £20,575.

The new Vectra had three interior colour schemes, black, grey, and light neutral with a further option of two-colour black-and-beige.

1999 Vectra (2)

Engine	Max power	Max torque	Top speed*	0-96kph
1.6i	55kW (74bhp) @ 5200rpm	128Nm (96lb/ft) @ 2800rpm	175kph (109mph)	14.5sec
1.6i 16v	73.5kW (99bhp) @ 6000rpm	150Nm (112lb/ft) @ 3000rpm	183kph (114mph)	12.9sec
1.8i 16v	84kW (113bhp) @ 5400rpm	170Nm (127lb/ft) @ 3400rpm	199kph (124mph)	11.5sec
2.0i 16v	100kW (134bhp) @ 5600rpm	188Nm (140lb/ft) @ 3200rpm	210kph (131mph)	9.5sec
LPG mode	98.5kW (132bhp) @ 5600rpm	185Nm (138lb/ft) @ 3200rpm	n/a	n/a
2.0 Di 16v	60kW (81bhp) @ 4300rpm	185Nm (138lb/ft) @ 1800-2500rpm	177kph (110mph)	14.5sec
2.0 DTi 16v	73.5kW (99bhp) @ 4300rpm	205Nm (153lb/ft) @ 1600-2750rpm	194kph (121mph)	12.0sec
2.5i V6 24v	125kW (168bhp) @ 5800rpm	230Nm (172lb/ft) @ 3200rpm	230kph (143mph)	8.0sec
2.5i V6 GSi	143kW (192bhp) @6000rpm	250Nm (186lb/ft) @ 5000rpm	238kph (148mph)	7.6sec

* figures for hatch and saloon models.

2000 VX220

Shown as the Speedster Concept Car at the 1999 Geneva Motor Show, the VX220 was a high-performance aluminium 2-seater with a composite body, designed by the Opel/Vauxhall international technical centre at Rüsselsheim, together with Lotus Engineering at Hethel. Peter Hannenberger, management board member for engineering, said at its launch, "Lotus is acknowledged as a master of ride and handling and is expert in the art of making great sports cars." The mid-engined car, which reached production in 2000, had the aluminium 4-cylinder produced at Kaiserslautern in a range of sizes for several Vauxhalls and Opels. Lotus's experience with aluminium extrusions for the Elise proved invaluable for the prototype although the production version was more sophisticated. The stiff light chassis conferred exemplary handling and precise responsive steering to keep the driver well informed about the behaviour of the front wheels. The ride was unusually smooth for such a thoroughgoing sports car. The VX220 was also surprisingly refined with a reasonable 206litres (7.27cuft) of luggage space, although the aperture was small. Getting in and out of the small cockpit demanded some agility. The 16-valve engine was economical with a combined official figure of 8.5 l/100km (33.2mpg). The production car was £22,815. *What Car?* named it roadster of the year in 2002.

BODY open, 2 seats, 2 doors; weight 800kg (1764lb)
ENGINE 4 cylinders, in-line, mid; 2200cc; 110Kw (147bhp); 49.8kW/l (66.8bhp/l).
ENGINE STRUCTURE 2 ohc; aluminium cyl head and block; 5-bearing crank; direct fuel injection; water-cooled.
TRANSMISSION rear wheel drive; sdp clutch; 5 speed close ratio gearbox; synchromesh.
CHASSIS DETAILS fabricated aluminium extrusions; composite body; independent wishbone front and rear suspension; servo disc brakes.
PERFORMANCE maximum speed 220kph (137mph); 0-96kph (60mph) 5.9sec; 7.3kg/kW (5.4kg/bhp)

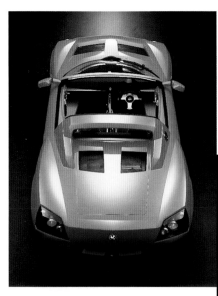

2000 Astra Coupe Bertone

Launched as a co-operative concept, with the Italian design house of Bertone at the Frankfurt Motor Show in 1999, production was planned at 30,000 cars a year and began in Turin the following spring. Vauxhall estimated the British coupe market was 73,000, around 3.3 per cent and as with Royale, Calibra and Cavaliers of the past was worth pursuing. Although wheelbase and width remained the same, the Coupe was 1.5cm (.5in) longer than an Astra saloon and 15.7cm (6.1in) more than the 3 and 5-door hatchbacks. The roofline was 3.4cm (1.3in) lower and the steeply raked windscreen gave a drag coefficient of Cd 0.28. Frameless doors and black C-pillars gave the impression of a single one-piece side window; door handles and side mouldings were body-coloured. The fully galvanised body had a 12-year warranty and by way of completing its sporting credentials the suspension was lowered by 2cm (.7in) and stiffened. The Astra Coupe provided a launch platform for a new 2.2 16v engine complying with Euro4 emissions standards, not due to come into force until 2005. A 2.0 turbo, based on the existing Astra and Vectra, with counter-rotating balancer shafts was added to the Coupe range in the autumn of 2000, and both engines were used throughout the Astra range in 2002.

INTRODUCTION Frankfurt 1999. Production February 2000, Convertible 2001.
Specification 2.2 Ecotec
BODY Coupe; 2-doors, 4-seats; weight 1200kg (2645.5lb); Convertible 1320kg (2910lb).
ENGINE 4-cylinders, in-line; front; transverse; 86mm x 94.6mm; 2198cc; compr 10:1; 108kW (144.8bhp) @ 5800rpm; 49.1kW (65.8bhp)/l; 203Nm (149.7lbft) @ 4000rpm.
ENGINE STRUCTURE Z22XE in hydroformed subframe; 16-valves; 2 chain-driven overhead camshafts; aluminium cylinder head, block; electronic Siemens-Simtec fuel injection, ignition; 5-bearing crank.
TRANSMISSION front wheel drive; hydraulic sdp clutch; 5-speed gearbox; optional 4-speed auto; final drive 3.95:1, 2.81:1 auto.
CHASSIS integral steel structure; MacPherson strut independent front suspension; anti roll bar; rear suspension torsion tube with compound links; anti roll bar;

telescopic dampers; hydraulic servo disc brakes, front 28cm (11in) dia ventilated, rear 26.4cm (10.3in) dia, ABS; electro-hydraulic PAS; 52l (11.4gal) fuel tank; 195/60 R15, 205/50 R16 tyres 6J rims.
DIMENSIONS wheelbase 260.5cm (102.5in); track front 146.5cm (57.6in) rear 145cm (57in); Convertible 147.5cm (58in), 148cm (58.2in); length 426.5cm (167.9in); width 171cm (67.3in); height 139cm (54.7in); ground clearance 13cm (5.1in); turning circle 10.9m (35.7ft).
EQUIPMENT Electronic Stability Programme (ESP) from 2002; Traction Control, Electronic brake force distribution.
PERFORMANCE maximum speed 218kph (135.7mph); 35.3kph (21.9mph) @ 1000rpm; 0-100kph (62mph) 8.8sec; fuel consumption 8.2l/100km (34.4mpg).
1.8: 1185kg (2612.4lb); 80.5mm x 88.2mm; 1796cc; 92kW (123.3bhp) @ 5600rpm; 51.2kW (68.6bhp)/l; 170Nm (125.4lbft) @ 3800rpm; Z18XE engine; final drive 3.74:1;

210kph (130.8mph); 33.9kph (21.1mph) @ 1000rpm; 9.5sec; 7.8l/100km (36.2mpg).

2.0 Turbo 1260kg (2777.7lb); 86mm x 86mm; 1998cc; compr 8.8:1; 140kW (187.7bhp) @ 5400rpm; 70kW (93.8bhp)/l; 250Nm (184.4lbft) @ 1950rpm; Z20LET engine; Motronic management; turbocharger, intercooler; Traction Control; final drive 3.63:1; 30.8cm (12.1in) dia brake discs; 245kph (152.6mph); 39.3kph (24.4mph) @ 1000rpm; 7.5sec; 8.9l/100km (31.7mpg)

PRICE 1.8 £14,970; 2.2 £16,470; Convertible £18,815; 2.0 Turbo £18,815.

315

2000 Omega: MY2000

Speculation about a flagship with a Chevrolet Corvette 5.7litre pushrod V8 as a spiritual successor to the Lotus-Carlton of 1989-1993 (qv), flourished at the Frankfurt Motor Show in 1999. Prototypes had been tried out in America with the Cadillac Catera, as the Omega was known, but the plan never materialised. Instead a new 2.2litre Ecotec engine with twin overhead camshafts and two balancer shafts led the changes to the European Omega. A £100million investment led to better handling with DSA (Dynamic Safety) chassis and enhanced safety, through front and side airbags. Restyling included a stronger V grille, and new headlamp clusters. The interior gained a restyled instrument panel, central console and anti-whiplash head restraints, yet it never quite matched luxury rivals from Jaguar or Germany. The inclusion of what was known as intelligent dual-zone electronic climate control as standard went some way to redressing the balance. However the Omega saloons and commodious estates remained good value; "a lot of car for the money" was road testers' conclusion. Following the chassis revisions, which included altering the front axle geometry, dampers, and power steering, it remained an outstanding long-distance touring car, whose high quality finish came with a ten-year anti-perforation warranty.

INTRODUCTION Frankfurt 1999. Specification 2.2 16v
BODY Saloon; 4-doors, 5-seats; weight 1530kg (3373lb); 1550kg (3417.1lb).
ENGINE 4-cylinders, in-line; front; 86mm x 94.6mm; 2198cc; compr 10.5:1; 106kW (142bhp) @ 5400rpm; 48.2kW (64.6bhp)/l; 205Nm (152.2lbft) @ 4000rpm.
ENGINE STRUCTURE 16v Y22XE; 2 belt-driven overhead camshafts; aluminium cylinder head; Siemens-Simtec electronic fuel injection; 5-bearing crankshaft. X30XE 24v; 2x2 belt-driven ohc; aluminium heads; Bosch Motronic; 4-bearing crank. X25TD 12v; 1 chain-driven ohc; digital fuel injection, turbocharger, intercooler; 7-bearing crank.
TRANSMISSION rear wheel drive; sdp clutch; 5-speed gearbox; 4-speed automatic option; final drive manual 3.9:1, automatic 4.22:1. 3.0 manual, 2.7:1; diesel 3.45:1.
CHASSIS integral steel structure; independent front suspension by MacPherson struts; independent multi-link rear suspension with coil springs, twin-tube gas pressure dampers; anti roll bars front and back; hydraulic dual circuit servo disc brakes front 28.6cm (11.2in), rear 29.6cm (11.6in); ABS; recirculating ball PAS; 75l (16.4gal) fuel tank; 195/65R15 tyres 6.5J rims. 3.0, 225/55R16, 7J. diesel, 205/65R15.
DIMENSIONS wheelbase 273cm (107.4in); track front 151.5cm (59.6in) rear 153cm (60.2in); length 490cm (192.9n); width 177.5cm (69.8in); height 145cm (57in); ground clearance 14cm (5.5in); turning circle 11m (36ft).
EQUIPMENT Combined audio and Siemens satellite navigation; load protector for estate cars; quick power brake booster; GLS, CD, CDX, and Elite trim.
PERFORMANCE maximum speed 210kph (130.8mph); 35kph (21.8mph), @ 1000rpm; 0-100kph (62mph) 10.5sec; fuel consumption 10l/100km (28.2mpg).
3.0 V6: 1590kg (3505.3lb); V6 54deg;

86mm x 85mm; 2962cc; 155kW
(207.8bhp) @6000rpm; 52.3kW
(70.1bhp)/l; 270Nm (199lbft) @
3400rpm; 243kph (151.3mph);
39.9kph (24.8mph) @ 1000rpm;
8.5sec; 11.3l/100km (25mpg).
2.5 turbodiesel: 6-cyl, in-line; 80mm
x 82.8mm; 2497cc; compr 22.5:1;
96kW (128.7bhp) @4500rpm;
38.4kW (51.4bhp)/l; 250Nm
(184lbft) @ 2200rpm; 200kph
(124.5mph) 45.2kph (28.1mph) @
1000rpm; 12 sec; 8.5l/100km
(33.2mpg).
PRICE 2.2 GLS £19,775, CDX
Estate £23,925; 3.0i £31,650; 2.5TD
Elite £27,750

317

2000 Agila 1.0, 1.2

The main difference from the Suzuki Wagon R was that Agila had no four wheel drive. However removing responsibility for driving the rear wheels through a central viscous coupling did not seem to save much weight, and Suzuki production versions of the 1.2litre gave only 65PS against the Vauxhall's 75PS. The 1.0 re-used the 3-cylinder engine introduced for the Corsa in 1997 (qv) but both versions felt fairly leisurely. Itself based on the smallest Suzuki, the Alto, the Wagon R appeared at Geneva in 1994 as an upright microvan with a transverse engine. The Agila was just as versatile, had useful space within a compact wheelbase, four door access and an agreeably composed ride. However the steering was heavy for such a little car, it was noisy, and failed to keep up with the latest standards of safety and security. It gained the 1.3 CDTi diesel in 2004, with which it could reach 4.4l/100km (64.2mpg) in urban driving. For 2005 ABS was included on the Expression models, so it was standard across the entire range, and the addition of Twinport technology to the 1.2 gave 79PS, a top speed over 160kph (100mph) and 0-60mph time of 12.2sec. The Twinport also improved fuel consumption to 5.9l/100km (47.1mpg). Prices remained the same as for the outgoing 1.2.

INTRODUCTION Summer 2000. Specification for 1.0
BODY Saloon; 5-doors, 4-seats; weight 940kg (2072.3lb).
ENGINE 3-cylinders, in-line; front; transverse; 72.5mm x 78.6mm; 973cc; compr 10.1:1; 43kW (57.6bhp) @ 5600rpm; 44.2kW (59.2bhp)/l; 85Nm (62.7lbft) @ 3800rpm.
ENGINE STRUCTURE Z10XE 12-valves; 2 chain-driven overhead camshafts; aluminium cylinder head, iron/steel block; Bosch Motronic fuel injection; 4-bearing crankshaft.
TRANSMISSION front wheel drive; hydraulic sdp clutch; 5-speed gearbox; final drive 4.39:1.
CHASSIS steel monocoque; MacPherson strut independent front suspension; rear suspension 3-link rigid axle; Panhard rod, anti roll bar; telescopic dampers; hydraulic servo brakes, front 24.7cm (9.7in) dia disc, rear drums, Nishimbo ABS; Mando electric PAS; 41l (9gal) fuel tank; 155/65 R14, 165/65 R14 tyres 4.5J rims.

DIMENSIONS wheelbase 236cm (92.9in); track front 142cm (55.9in) rear 139cm (54.7in); length 350cm (137.7in); width 162cm (63.7in); height 169.5cm (66.7in); turning circle 10.6m (34.7ft).
EQUIPMENT 3 seat belts in rear bench seat, airbags.
PERFORMANCE maximum speed 142kph (88.4mph); 28.6kph (17.8mph) @ 1000rpm; 0-100kph (62mph) 18sec; fuel consumption 6.4l/100km (44.1mpg)
1.2: 920kg (2028.2lb); Z12XE 4-cylinders; 72.5mm x 72.6mm; 1199cc; 55kW (73.7bhp) @ 5600rpm; 45.9Kw (61.5bhp)/l; 110Nm (81.1lbft) @ 4000rpm; Z12XE engine 5-bearing crank; final drive 4.11:1; 155kph (96.5mph); 30.3kph (18.8mph) @ 1000rpm; 13.5sec; 6.3l/100km (44.8mpg).
PRICE 1.0 £6850; 1.2 £7305, Enjoy £7,995, Design £8,450.

2001 Corsa 1.2 and 1.0 with Easytronic 5-speed, 1.4 and 1.7CDTi

Known since 1983 as the Vauxhall Nova (qv), improvements had been steadily introduced on the Spanish-built Corsa. In 1990 a new 1.4litre engine, in 1993 a complete re-style, in 1997 the 3-cylinder then another new version in 2000 with Easytronic 5-speed transmission. The improvements brought an 8 per cent increase in Corsa sales in the UK and for the 2002 model year prices were decreased by up to £765. Air conditioning was included as standard on Comfort models and even the entry-level Corsa Club gained electric windows and a sunroof. Although security equipment was satisfactory, the furnishings looked ungenerous, and Corsas no longer measured up to class standards of noise and refinement. Quality and reliability were good, ride and handling praiseworthy, and the swift 1.8 16-valve SRi satisfactory if not quite in the top drawer of so-called hot hatchbacks. The facelift for MY 2004 with the Vauxhall V grille brightened the car's prospects with new 1.0 and 1.4 Twinport petrol engines that not only provided greatly improved economy, but also achieved low emissions that took the Corsa into the lowest tax category for company car drivers. Two important safety features included as standard throughout the range, were ABS and EBA (Emergency Brake Assist), and the speed-dependent electro-hydraulic steering was sharpened up.

INTRODUCTION Spring 2001. Specification 1.7CDTi
BODY Saloon; 3/5-doors, 5-seats; weight 1050kg (2314.8lb).
ENGINE 4-cylinders, in-line; front; transverse; 79mm x 86mm; 1686cc; compr 18.4:1; 55kW (73.7bhp) @ 4400rpm; 32.8kW (43.9bhp)/l; 165Nm (121.7lbft) @ 1800rpm .
ENGINE STRUCTURE Y17DT: 2 belt-driven overhead camshafts; 4-valve; aluminium cylinder head; Bosch direct injection; turbocharger 0.9bar, intercooler; 5-bearing crankshaft.
TRANSMISSION front wheel drive; hydraulic sdp clutch; 5-speed gearbox; final drive 3.55:1. Easytronic on petrol 1.2, 5-speed automatic, final drive 3.94:1
CHASSIS integral steel structure, ifs by MacPherson struts; rear suspension torsion beam axle; coil springs, dampers, anti-roll bar; hydraulic servo disc brakes front ventilated 26cm (10.2in), rear drums; ABS; electric PAS; 44l (9.6gal) fuel tank; 175/65R14 tyres 5.5J rims.

DIMENSIONS wheelbase 249cm (98in); track front 143cm (56.2in) rear 142cm (55.9in); length 381.5cm (150.1in); width 164.5cm (64.7in); height 144cm (56.6in); ground clearance 14cm (5.5in); turning circle10.4m (34.1ft) .
EQUIPMENT rear seatbelts, Easytronic optional
PERFORMANCE maximum speed 170kph (105.8mph); 39.5kph (24.6mph) @ 1000rpm; 0-100kph (62mph) 13.5sec; fuel consumption 4.86l/100km (58.1mpg).
1.0 12v Twinport: 910kg (2006.1lb); 3-cylinders; 72.5mm x 78.6mm; 973cc; compr 10:1; 43kW (57.6bhp) @ 5600bhp; 44.2kW (59.2bhp)/l; 85Nm (62.7lbft) @ 3800rpm; Z10XE; 4-bearing crank; final drive 3.94:1; 155kph (96.5mph); 30kph (18.6mph) @ 1000rpm; 17sec; 5.8l/100km (48.4mpg).
1.4 16v Twinport: 1010kg (2226.6lb); 4-cylinders; 77.6mm x 73.4mm; 1389cc; compr 10.5:1; 66kW (88.5bhp) @ 6000rpm; 47.5kW (63.6bhp)/l; 125Nm (92.2lbft) @

4000rpm; Z14XE; 5-speed final
drive 3.94:1; 4-speed auto 4.12;
ventilated 26cm (10.2in) front disc
brakes; 180kph (112.1mph); 30.5kph
(18.9mph) @ 1000rpm; 11.5sec;
7.6l/100km (37.1mpg)
PRICE 1.0 12v £6995; 1.2i 16v
£8495; 1.7CDTi £8995

Above: **The facelift for 2004 with
prominent V grille strengthened
the Vauxhall identity on 3 and 5
door models.**

2002 Vectra 1.8, 2.2, 3.2 V6

Since the SRi accounted for one Vectra in five, both it and the GSi were developed for the third generation of Vauxhall's mainstream car. Their spoilers, alloy wheels, and chromed exhausts had proved popular and stiffer springing and revised gear ratios were retained for the new model. Both were available only as 5-door hatchbacks and SRi buyers had the option of 1.8, 2.2 and the Ellesmere Port-made 3.2 V6, the largest ever in a production Vectra. This 3175cc, 211PS unit managed 0-60mph in 7.5sec and gave a top speed of 248kph (154mph). The 2.0 turbo became available as a third option for the SRi in 2003. *What Car?* liked what it drove, finding the Vectra handled more tidily than its predecessor, although the power steering was faulted for not giving the feedback required for twisting roads. Refinement was the biggest gain: "If it's noisy you're speeding. The absence of significant noise is hugely impressive, making the cabin a hushed place until you are well above the UK speed limit. All the controls, with the exception of the gearlever, move with slick precision." Testers also noticed improvements in Vauxhall quality and reliability. Vectra's steering ratio was reduced from 16:1 to 15:1 to improve response, the body sat 2cm (.8in) lower and front wheel vertical travel was 1.5cm (.6in) less.

INTRODUCTION autumn 2001, in production, spring 2002.
Specification 1.8 122 PS
BODY Saloon; 4-doors, 5-seats; weight 1320kg (2910.1lb) 5-door 1390kg (3064.39lb).
ENGINE 4-cylinders, in-line; front; transverse; 80.5mm x 88.2mm; 1796cc; compr 10.5:1; 90kW (120.69bhp) @ 5600rpm; 50kW (67.05bhp)/l; 167Nm (123.2lbft) @ 3800rpm.
ENGINE STRUCTURE Z18XE 4-valves; 2 belt-driven ohc; aluminium cylinder head; fuel injection, electronic ignition; 5-bearing crank.
TRANSMISSION front wheel drive; hydraulic sdp clutch; 5-speed gearbox; final drive 3.94 or 3.74:1; optional CVT.
CHASSIS steel monocoque with sub-frames; MacPherson strut independent front suspension; anti roll bar; rear suspension torsion beam axle, transverse arms, coil springs; anti roll bar; telescopic dampers; hydraulic servo disc brakes, front 28.5cm (11.2in) dia

ventilated, rear 27.8cm (10.9in), V6 29.2cm (11.5in) dual circuit, ABS; EPAS; 60l (13.2gal) fuel tank; 195/65 R15 tyres, 5.6J rims.
DIMENSIONS wheelbase 270cm (106.3in); track front 153.5cm (60.4in), rear 152.5cm (60.1in); length 459.5cm (180.9in); width 179.8cm (70.8in); height 146cm (57.5in); ground clearance 14cm (5.5in); turning circle 11.4m (37.4ft)
EQUIPMENT air conditioning, Brake Assist, cruise control, electric front windows, 5-speed automatic optional on SRi and Gti 2.2, 3.2.
PERFORMANCE maximum speed 205kph (127.7mph); 38.8kph (24.2mph) @ 1000rpm; 0-100kph (62mph) 11.2sec; fuel consumption 8.38.3l/100km (34mpg).
2.2 147PS: 1380kg (3042.3lb); 86mm x 94.6mm; 2198cc; comp 10:1; 108kW (144.8bhp) @ 5800rpm; 49.1kW (65.8bhp)/l; 203Nm (149.7lbft) @ 4000rpm; Z22XE; GM Powertrain engine management; final drive 3.38:1 or 3.95:1; auto 2.:1; 215/55 R16 tyres, 7J rims;

200kph (124.6mph); 36.9kph (23mph) @ 1000rpm; 10.2sec; 9.1l/100km (31mpg).
2.0 Turbo 175PS: 1395kg (3075.4lb); 86mm x 86mm; 1988cc; compr 9.5:1; 129kW (173bhp)@ 5500rpm; 64.9kW (87bhp)/l; 265Nm (185.4lbft) @ 2500rpm; turbocharger 0.7 bar, intercooler; final drive 3.91:1; 230kph (143.3mph); 9.1sec; 9.4l/100km (30.1mpg).
PRICE 1.8 £14,645; 2.2 £15,145; 1.8SRi £16,545; 2.2SRi £17,045, GSi V6 £20,980

323

2002 Vectra 2.0 and 2.2 DTI

Hatchback production began following £200 million investment at Ellesmere Port, a month after saloon production was started at Rüsselsheim. Some £500million had been invested at the German plant for the new model, which had better aerodynamics and a Cd down to 0.28. The longer wheelbase Signum and Vectra Estate were promised for 2003, along with the 2.0 turbo petrol and V6 diesel to complete the engine range. One innovation was a flexible service indicator, providing information on when servicing was needed, depending on how the car was used. Petrol engines needed oil changes every 20,000 miles or two years, while diesels could go up to 30,000 miles. The 5-speed automatic available on the 2.2DTi worked adaptively, recognised the driving style, and shifted gears to suit it. The 74 per cent stiffer body structure used 15 sorts of high-strength steel, but despite more aluminium and magnesium components there was an increase in weight over the outgoing Vectra. More space inside (excepting headroom) and 6cm (2.3in) on the wheelbase was traded for a bit less speed and slightly heavier fuel consumption. Testers mostly welcomed the strong pull and good driveability of the diesels but found the weight gain exhausted the smaller petrol engines.

INTRODUCTION on sale May/June 2002.
Specification 2.0 101PS
BODY Saloon; 4-doors, 5-seats; weight 1430kg (3152.6lb).
ENGINE 4-cylinders, in-line; front; transverse; 84mm x 90mm; 1995cc; compr 18.5:1; 74kW (99.2bhp) @ 4300rpm; 37.1kW (49.8bhp)/l; 230Nm (169.6lbft) @ 1950rpm.
ENGINE STRUCTURE Y20DTH; 4-valve parallel; 1 chain-driven overhead camshaft; aluminium head; Bosch VP44 fuel injection; Garrett T15 turbocharger; 5-bearing crank.
TRANSMISSION front wheel drive; hydraulic sdp clutch; 5-speed gearbox; final drive 3.74:1.
CHASSIS steel monocoque with sub-frames; MacPherson strut independent front suspension; anti roll bar; rear suspension torsion beam axle, transverse arms, coil springs; anti roll bar; telescopic dampers; hydraulic servo disc brakes, front 28.5cm (11.2in) dia ventilated, rear 27.8cm (10.9in), V6 29.2cm (11.5in) dual circuit, ABS;

EPAS; 60l (13.2gal) fuel tank; 195/65 R15 tyres, 5.6J rims.
DIMENSIONS wheelbase 270cm (106.3in); track front 153.5cm (60.4in), rear 152.5cm (60.1in); length 459.5cm (180.9in); width 179.8cm (70.8in); height 146cm (57.5in); ground clearance 14cm (5.5in); turning circle 11.4m (37.4ft)
EQUIPMENT optional park assist, tyre pressure monitor, rain sensors. Standard flexible service indicator, 5-speed automatic option on 2.2DTi
PERFORMANCE maximum speed 192kph (119.6mph); 45kph (28mph) @ 1000rpm; 0-100kph (62mph) 13sec; fuel consumption 6.2l/100km (45.6mpg).
2.2 125PS: 84mm x 98mm; 2171cc; 92kW (123.4bhp) @ 4000rpm; 42.4kW (56.9bhp)/l; 280Nm (206.5lbft) @ 1500rpm; Y22DTR; final drive 3.61:1; automatic 2.4:1; 206kph (128.3mph); 46.6kph (29mph) @ 1000rpm; 10.8sec; 6.8l/100km (41.5mpg).
3.0 176PS (on Opel Vectras, Vauxhalls from 2005): 1530kg

(3373lb); 66deg V6 87.6mm x 82mm; 2962cc; compr 18:1; 129kW (173bhp) @ 4000rpm; 43.6kW (58.5bhp)/l; 350Nm (258.2lbft) @ 1800rpm; Garrett common rail injection, turbocharger, intercooler; 2x2 belt-driven overhead camshafts; aluminium block and heads; 4-bearing crankshaft; 6-speed gearbox; 3.91:1 final drive; Aisin-Warner 5-speed automatic; 2.44:1 final drive; 226kph (140.8mph); 9.1sec; 7.5l/100km (37.7mpg). PRICE 2.0DTi £15,545, 2.2DTi £16,095, 2.2DTi SRi £17,995.

2002 Astra Convertible. 2.2, 2.0 turbo, 1.8, 1.7 CDTi Euro IV, 2.0 DTi

In 2001 a Convertible joined the Coupe at Bertone. It had an electrically operated lined and insulated hood, which stowed flush with a belt line rising towards the rear. Also in 2002 the engines for the entire Astra range were reorganised. There were soon ten - seven petrol and three diesel. The 1.6 versions gained Twinport technology, there was a new 1.7 common rail diesel meeting Euro IV regulations, and an extension of the aluminium 2.2 16v units. Three of the engines had a dual fuel option. A 3-year/60,000 mile warranty was introduced, and in September Vauxhall confirmed that following a successful defence of its British Touring Car Championship manufacturer's and team's titles, it would again enter two Astra Coupes with its race partner Triple Eight Race Engineering. This was Vauxhall's fifteenth consecutive season of competing in the series and it was duly rewarded, in its centenary year, with its third championship in a row. The new diesel used second generation Bosch common rail direct fuel injection to provide emissions of only 118gm/km without expensive additional complex gas emission treatment. It was introduced at a modest 80PS in Euro IV configuration and its power was increased progressively to 100PS. For 2004 the Convertible Exclusiv sold for £16,995 with a claimed £950's worth of extra equipment.

INTRODUCTION Production February 2000, Convertible 2001. Specification 2.2 Ecotec, 1.8, 2.0 turbo.

BODY Convertible; 2-doors, 4-seats; weight 1320kg (2910lb).

ENGINE 4-cylinders, in-line; front; transverse; 86mm x 94.6mm; 2198cc; compr 10:1; 108kW (144.8bhp) @ 5800rpm; 49.1kW (65.8bhp)/l; 203Nm (149.7lbft) @ 4000rpm.

ENGINE STRUCTURE Z22XE in hydroformed subframe; 16-valves; 2 chain-driven overhead camshafts; aluminium cylinder head, block; electronic Siemens-Simtec fuel injection, ignition; 5-bearing crank.

TRANSMISSION front wheel drive; hydraulic sdp clutch; 5-speed gearbox; optional 4-speed auto; final drive 3.95:1, 2.81:1 auto.

CHASSIS integral steel; MacPherson strut ifs; anti roll bar; rear suspension torsion tube, compound links; anti roll bar; tele dampers; hydraulic servo disc brakes, front 28cm (11in) dia ventilated, rear 26.4cm (10.3in) dia, ABS; electro-hydraulic PAS; 52l (11.4gal) fuel tank; 195/60 R15, 205/50 R16 tyres 6J rims.

DIMENSIONS wheelbase 260.5cm (102.5in); track front 146.5cm (57.6in) rear 145cm (57in); Convertible 147.5cm (58in), 148cm (58.2in) length 426.5cm (167.9in); width 171cm (67.3in); height 139cm (54.7in); ground clearance 13cm (5.1in); turning circle 10.9m (35.7ft).

EQUIPMENT Electronic Stability Programme (ESP) from 2002; Traction Control, Electronic brake force distribution, alloy wheels; cruise control; sat-nav optional.

PERFORMANCE maximum speed 218kph (135.7mph); 35.3kph (21.9mph) @ 1000rpm; 0-100kph (62mph) 8.8sec; fuel consumption 8.2l/100km (34.4mpg).
1.8: 1305kg (2877lb); 80.5mm x 88.2mm; 1796cc; 92kW (123.3bhp) @ 5600rpm; 51.2kW (68.6bhp)/l; 170Nm (125.4lbft) @ 3800rpm; Z18XE engine 2 belt-driven ohc; final drive 3.74:1; 210kph (130.8mph); 33.9kph (21.1mph) @ 1000rpm;

9.5sec; 7.8l/100km (36.2mpg).

2.0 Turbo: 1260kg (2777.7lb); 86mm x 86mm; 1998cc; compr 8.8:1; 140kW (187.7bhp) @ 5400rpm; 70kW (93.8bhp)/l; 250Nm (184.4lbft) @ 1950rpm; Z20LET engine; Motronic management; turbocharger, intercooler; Traction Control; final drive 3.63:1; 30.8cm (12.1in) dia brake discs; 245kph (152.6mph); 39.3kph (24.4mph) @ 1000rpm; 7.5sec; 8.9l/100km (31.7mpg).

1.7 CDTI 80PS: 1260kg (2777.7lb); Estate 1315kg (2899lb); 79mm x 86mm; 1686cc; compr 18.4:1; 59kW (79.1bhp) @ 4400rpm; 35kW (46.9bhp)/l; 170Nm (125.4lbft) @ 1800rpm; 1/1.8bar turbo; final drive 3.74:1; discs 28cm (11in) and 26.4cm (10.3in); 168kph (104.6mph); 41kph (25.5mph) @ 1000rpm; 15sec; 5.1l/100km (55.3mpg)

PRICE 1.8 £14,970; 2.2 £16,470; Convertible £18,815; 2.0 Turbo £18,815.

2003 Meriva 1.6, 1.8, 1.7CDTi turbodiesel

There were elements of Corsa, Astra, and Vectra in the versatile one-box Meriva. Looking a bit like the bigger seven seat Zafira, its wheelbase was not far short, it was just as tall, yet it had the manoeuvrability of an Astra. It not only looked like Zafira, it also had FlexSpace with the option of three passengers in the back or executive-style comfort for two. The rear seat was in effect three, of which the middle one folded flat, and the two outsides moved fore and aft by 20cm (7.8in) or sideways by 7cm (2.7in) for more shoulder room. The interior could be altered from five seats to one without taking any out but just folding them flat. A front bulkhead well forward and extending the windscreen into the roof gained space. There were three trim levels, Life (ABS, electric windows, airbags), Enjoy (air conditioning, Twin Audio), and Design (alloy wheels, black door pillars, tinted glass, CD player leather steering wheel). Meriva had the choice of two 1.6litre petrol (8-valve and 16-valve), 1.8 petrol and 1.7 turbodiesel and its maintenance schedule meant that service was required only once a year, or at 20,000 miles. Increasing demand for security brought an electronic engine deadlock immobiliser, and code protection for audio equipment. Meriva was built by General Motors Europe at Zaragoza, Spain and in Brazil where it was the Chevrolet Meriva.

INTRODUCTION Concept M Geneva 2002, Paris, Birmingham 2002, 1.6 Geneva 2003; 1.8 16v and diesel autumn 2003.

BODY Saloon MPV; 5-doors, 5-seats; weight, 1.6 1275kg (2810.8lb), 1.6 16v 1300kg (2865.9lb) 1.8 1305kg (2877lb), diesel 1320kg (2910lb).

ENGINE 4-cylinders, in-line; front; transverse; 79mm x 81.5mm; 1598cc; compr 9.6:1; 64kW (85.8bhp) @ 5400rpm; 40kW (53.6bhp)/l; 138Nm (101.8lbft) @ rpm.
16v 1598cc compr 10.5:1; 74kW (99.2bhp) @6000rpm; 46.3kW (62bhp)/l; 150Nm (110.6lbft) @ 3600rpm.
1.8 80.5mm x 88.2mm; 1796cc; 92kW (123.3bhp) @ 5600rpm; 51.2kW (68.6bhp)/l; 170Nm (125.4lbft) @3800rpm.
Turbodiesel 79mm x 86mm; 1686cc; compr 18.4:1; 55kW (73.7bhp) @ 4400rpm; 32.6kW (43.7bhp)/l; 165Nm (121.7lbft) @ 1800rpm – later 74kW (99.2bhp), 240Nm (177lbft) @2300rpm

ENGINE STRUCTURE Z16SE: 8-valve; belt-driven ohc; Z16XE 16-valve; 2 belt driven ohc; aluminium cylinder head, block; electronic fuel injection, engine management; 5-bearing crankshaft. 1.8 Z18XE1. Turbodiesel Y17DT 2 ohc; Bosch injection; 0.9bar turbo, intercooler.

TRANSMISSION front wheel drive; hydraulic sdp clutch; 5-speed gearbox; Easytronic option on 1.8 and diesel; final drive 3.49:1, 1.6 16v, 1.8 and diesel, 3.94:1.

CHASSIS steel monocoque with sub-frames; MacPherson strut independent front suspension; anti roll bar; rear suspension torsion beam axle, transverse arms, coil springs; anti roll bar; telescopic dampers; hydraulic servo disc brakes, front 28.8cm (11.3in) dia ventilated, rear 28.6cm (11.3in), dual circuit, Bosch ABS; electro-hydraulic PAS; 53l (11.6gal) fuel tank; 175/70 R14 tyres, 6J rims.

DIMENSIONS wheelbase 263cm (103.5in); track front 145cm (57in) rear 146.5cm (57.6in); length 404cm

(159in); width 169.5cm (66.7in); height 162cm (63.7in); ground clearance 15cm (5.9in); turning circle 10.3m (33.7ft).

EQUIPMENT Twin Audio radio or CD independent in front or back with headphones, optional Autovision with DVD or games console for rear passengers, Travel Assistant with armrest and cup holders; 1.8 optional traction control.

PERFORMANCE maximum speed 170kph (105.8mph); 175kph (109mph); 192kph (119.5mph); 34.1kph (21.2mph) @ 1000rpm; 0-100kph (62mph) 14.5sec; 13.3sec; 11.3sec; fuel consumption 8.1/100km (34.8mpg); 7.8l/100km (36.2mpg); 8.5l/100km (33.2mpg); 5l/100km (56.5mpg).

PRICE 1.4 16v Expression £9,995; 1.6 Life £12,845, Club £13,395, Design £14,300; 1.7CDTi £13,470.

329

2003 Signum 4-cylinder 1.8 16v, 2.2 16v, 2.0 turbo

Vauxhall claimed the arrival of Signum invented a new sector of the market, in effect replacing the much-admired Omega, which ceased production soon afterwards. Premium buyers found themselves with a different shape of car. Signum was two-box rather than three like the Omega, with a wheelbase 13cm (5.1in) longer than the Vectra it was developed from, using aluminium components in the suspension. By no means languorous at 463.6cm (15.2ft) it had a short rear overhang with, as Martin Smith Executive Design Director said, "… dimensions entirely different from either the saloon or hatchback Vectra." Key features were domed rear window and wide C-pillars directly over the rear wheels. Like the smaller Zafira, Signum had the ingenious FlexSpace interior allowing variations in seating to meet executive or family requirements. Three new Ecotec engines included Vauxhall's first 2.2litre direct injection petrol, and an aluminium 2.0 turbo. Adaptive lighting shone the headlamp beams through 30 degrees on corners, and the new 6-speed manual gearbox with a two-section aluminium casing weighed only 50kg (110.2lb). Interactive Driving System (IDS), as on Vectra, co-ordinated functions with ABS, Cornering Brake Control (CBC) Electronic Brake Force Distribution (EBD) and TC Plus traction control and Electronic Stability Program (ESP).

INTRODUCTION Geneva 2003, on sale summer 2003.
BODY Saloon; 4-doors, 4/5-seats; weight 1.8 1405kg (3097.4lb); 2.2 and 2.0 turbo 1485kg (3273.8lb).
ENGINE 4-cylinders, in-line; front; transverse; 80.5mm x 88.2mm; 1796cc; compr 10.5:1; 90kW (120.6bhp) @ 6000rpm; 50.1kW (67.1bhp)/l; 167Nm (123.2lbft) @ 3800rpm. 2.2 86mm x 94.6mm; 2198cc; compr 12:1; 114kW (152.8bhp) @ 5600rpm; 51.9kW (69.5bhp)/l; 220Nm (162.3lbft) @ 3800rpm. 2.0t 86mm x 86mm; 1988cc; compr 9.5:1; 129kW (172.9bhp) @5500rpm; 64.9kW (87bhp)/l; 265Nm (195.5lbft) 2500rpm.
ENGINE STRUCTURE Z18XE 16valve; 2 belt driven overhead camshafts; aluminium cylinder head; electronic fuel injection; 5-bearing crankshaft. 2.2 Z22YH; chain driven camshafts, aluminium head and block; 2.0t turbocharger 0.7bar, intercooler.
TRANSMISSION front wheel drive; hydraulic sdp clutch; 5-speed gearbox; automatic optional; final drive 3.94 auto 4.97:1. 2.2 Getrag gearbox; 4.17:1, Aisin-Warner 5-speed auto 2.6:1. turbo, Opel 6-speed gearbox; 3.91:1.
CHASSIS steel monocoque; MacPherson strut independent front suspension; hydroformed suspension subframe and four-link rear axle; anti roll bars front and rear; telescopic dampers; hydraulic servo disc brakes, front ventilated 28.5cm (11.2in), rear 27.8cm (10.9in), ABS; electro-hydraulic PAS; 60l (13.1gal) fuel tank; 215/55 R16, 225/50 R17, 225/45 R17, 225/45 R18 tyres 6.5, 7, 7.5J rims.
DIMENSIONS wheelbase 283cm (111.4in); track front 153.5cm (60.4in) rear 152.5cm (60in); length 463.5cm (182.4in); width 179.8cm (70.7in); height 146cm (57.4in); turning circle 11.2m (36.7ft).
EQUIPMENT Twin Audio, AFL lighting, air conditioning, electric windows front and rear. Cruise control, rain-sensitive wipers.

PERFORMANCE maximum speed 197kph (122.7mph); 211kph (131.4mph); 230kph (143.2mph). 38.8kph (24.1mph), 39.1kph (24.3mph), 38.6kph (24mph) @ 1000rpm; 0-100kph (62mph) 12.2, 9.8, 9.1sec; fuel consumption 8.3l/100km (34mpg), 9.56l/100km (29.5mpg), 9.43l/100km (29.9mpg). PRICE Elegance 2.2 £17,995, Turbo £18,550. Elite 2.2 £21,350 Turbo £21,850. Design 2.2 £18,595, Turbo £19,095

2003 Signum V6 petrol; 2.2 and 3.0 V6 diesels

Signum was worthy rather than a landmark car. It came with a choice of seven engines, of which three were completely new including the V6 3.0 CDTi common rail turbo-diesel with its compact light 6-speed gearbox. Three years since its launch it underwent a refreshment, although *Autocar* still called it, "… a curious hatchback/estate that wants us to think it's a mass-market limousine". It gained some of the same chassis and front-end improvements as Vectra. The Vauxhall 'V' in the grille became more prominent, together with bigger diamond-shaped lights and a deeper, sculpted bumper. There were welcome adjustments to ride and handling although the only components changed were the suspension bushes. The car felt more taut, yet critics took the view that the smaller-engined ones were better than the V6s. It was fine on motorways but fidgety on bumpy roads. Improvements to meet Euro 4 regulations added some 5kW (6.7bhp) to the V6 diesel and made it smoother. Unlike smaller diesels the V6 had responded slowly to the turbocharger, pulling away from low revs with what the testers called "a particularly linear throttle response." Satellite navigation became standard. Vauxhall made an effort to reduce ownership costs, with the flexible service indicator but unfortunately low residuals were a persistent difficulty.

INTRODUCTION Geneva 2003, on sale summer 2003.
BODY Saloon; 4-doors, 4/5-seats; weight 3.2 1536kg (3386.2lb); 2.2 1535kg (3384lb) 3.0 1595kg (3516.3lb).
ENGINE Petrol V6, 54deg front; transverse; 87.5mm x 88mm; 3176cc; compr 10:1; 155kW (207.8bhp) @ 6200rpm; 48.8kW (65.4bhp)/l; 300Nm (221.3lbft) @ 4000rpm. 2.2 84mm x 98mm; 2171cc; compr 18.5; 92kW (123.3bhp) @ 4000rpm; 42.4kW (56.8bhp)/l; 280Nm (206.5lbft) @ 1500rpm. Diesel V6, 3.0 66deg; 87.5mm x 82mm; 2962cc; compr 18:1; 129kW (172.9bhp) @ 4000rpm; 43.6kW (58.4bhp)/l; 350Nm (258lbft) 1800rpm.
ENGINE STRUCTURE Z32SE 4-valves @ 39deg; 2x2 overhead camshafts; aluminium cylinder heads; electronic fuel injection; 4-bearing crankshaft. 2.2 Y22DTR; chain driven overhead camshaft, 4-valves; aluminium head and block; turbocharger, intercooler. 3.0 V6; 4-

valves; 2x2 belt-driven ohc aluminium heads and block; Garrett turbocharger, intercooler
TRANSMISSION front wheel drive; hydraulic sdp clutch; 5-speed gearbox; automatic optional; final drive 4.05 auto 2.44:1. 2.2 Saab gearbox; 3.61:1, Aisin-Warner 5-speed auto 2.44:1. 3.0 Opel 6-speed gearbox; 3.91:1.
CHASSIS steel monocoque; MacPherson strut independent front suspension; hydroformed suspension subframe and four-link rear axle; anti roll bars front and rear; telescopic dampers; hydraulic servo disc brakes, front ventilated 28.5cm (11.2in), rear 27.8cm (10.9in), ABS; electro-hydraulic PAS; 60l (13.1gal) fuel tank; 215/55 R16, 225/50 R17, 225/45 R17, 225/45 R18 tyres 6.5, 7, 7.5J rims.
DIMENSIONS wheelbase 283cm (111.4in); track front 153.5cm (60.4in) rear 152.5cm (60in); length 463.5cm (182.4in); width 179.8cm (70.7in); height 146cm (57.4in); turning circle 11.2m (36.7ft).

EQUIPMENT Twin Audio, AFL lighting, air conditioning, electric windows front and rear. Cruise control, rain-sensitive wipers.

PERFORMANCE maximum speed 237kph (147.6mph); 200kph (124.5mph); 221kph (137.6mph). V6s 38.8kph (24.1mph); 2.2 46.6kph (29mph) @ 1000rpm; 0-100kph (62mph) 7.5; 11; 9.4sec; fuel consumption 10.7l/100km (26.4mpg); 5.9l/100km (47.8mpg) 7.8l/100km (36.2mpg).

PRICE Elegance 2.0DTi £18,350, 2.2DTi £18,900, Elite 3.2i £22,850, 3.0CDTi £25,600, Design 2.2DTi £19,445, 3.0CDTi £23,995

Right: Later Signum Exclusiv came with 1.8 (£17,995), 2.2 (£18,595), 1.9 CDTi (£19,995 or £20,495 5-door).

2003 VXR220

The 1998cc Astra 2.0 turbocharged engine ahead of the rear axle line, provided swifter acceleration for Vauxhall's responsive sports car. Based on the VX220, VXR220 had a power upgrade to 220PS, thanks to a free-flow air filter, a hybrid turbo and a reprogrammed ECU. It required more cooling capacity, changes to the exhaust, a turbo heat shield and undertray, with minor changes to the VX220 chassis on account of the additional power. Despite the success of the aluminium 2-seater the model took time to cease being regarded as a Lotus clone and was sold only through a network of specialist Vauxhall dealers. *Car* magazine voted it Performance Car of the Year for 2003, judging it, "a well designed, well engineered driver's car that is guaranteed to spark a warm glow of anticipation every time you reach for the keys." *Car* took the view that it not only had the best chassis, best steering, and best brakes at the price, but also the best and most sensational full-stop braking. More noticeable were wider air intakes on the sides of the composite body and extra spoilers. Furnishings became a little less severe and work on NVH made the car feel less harsh. There was even the option of CD player and satellite navigation.

INTRODUCTION 2003.
BODY roadster; 2-doors, 2-seats; weight 930kg (2050.2lb).
ENGINE 4-cylinders, in-line; mid; transverse 7deg 50min inclination forward; 86mm x 86mm; 1998cc; compr 8.8:1; 147kW (197.1bhp) @ 5500rpm; 73.9kW (99bhp)/l; 250Nm (184.4lbft) @1950rpm. Optional 164kW (220bhp) @ 5800rpm; 298.4Nm (221lbft) @ 4800rpm.
ENGINE STRUCTURE 4-valves; 2 chain-driven overhead camshafts; aluminium cylinder head, block; Simtec electronic engine management; 5-bearing crankshaft. Turbo 2 belt-driven ohc; Motronic ME155 sequential multi-point fuel injection; aluminium cylinder head iron block; turbocharger 0.85bar, intercooler.
TRANSMISSION rear wheel drive; hydraulic sdp clutch; 5-speed gearbox; final drive 3.95:1.
CHASSIS Aluminium chassis; double wishbone independent suspension, coil over dampers, subframe at rear; front anti roll bar;

hydraulic servo ventilated and cross-drilled 28.8cm (11.3in) disc brakes; ABS; PAS; 38L (8.3gal) fuel tank; alloy wheels, Yokohama A048R tyres, front 195/45R16, rear 225/35R17s.
DIMENSIONS wheelbase 233cm (91.7in); track front 145cm (57in) rear 148.8cm (58.5in); length 378.6cm (149in); width 170.8cm (67.2in); height 111.7cm (43.9in); turning circle 10.6m (34.7ft).
EQUIPMENT rollover bar, Speedline 5-spoke alloy wheels, driver's airbag, leather covered Momo steering wheel, optional central locking, body-coloured hardtop, sport seats upholstered with Alcantara, carbon fibre-effect leather trim.
PERFORMANCE
max speed 243kph (151.3mph), 249.4kph (155mph) 36kph (22.4mph) @ 1000rpm; 0-100kph (62mph) 4.7sec, 4.2sec; fuel consumption (33.3mpg).
PRICE £26,495, £29,995

2003-2004 Monaro and 2005-2006 VXR

When it was launched in 1968, Monaro was the sporting flagship of General Motors Holden in Australia. By the 21st century it could trace its ancestry through the Omega and the Holden VZ Commodore, and was selling in the United States as the Pontiac GTO. In 2001 it was relaunched, and brought to the United Kingdom in the spring of 2004 as, "…a true rear wheel drive musclecar for enthusiasts". Sales at first were limited to 300 per year. The 5.7litre engine developed 244.5kW (328bhp) and 465.3Nm (347lbft) of torque and besides a comprehensive specification that included leather upholstery, eight-way electric seats and alloy wheels, it had traction control and a top speed of 257kph (160mph). It was 20 per cent cheaper than a Mercedes-Benz CLK 320, and 40 per cent of a BMW 6-series. In March 2005 a new induction system, free-flowing exhaust, reprofiled cams and new engine management increased power and torque to match sportier suspension. Visual changes included two bonnet air scoops, a bigger air dam and the edition sold out within three months. In December 2004 it was promised that for 2005 Monaro would have the option of the 6.0 Corvette LS2 engine and drive train, making it the fastest Vauxhall ever. New 10-spoke 19in alloy wheels showed off grooved brake discs and VXR-branded callipers.

INTRODUCTION 2004 produced to 2006.
Specifications: 2004 5.7 and 2005 6.0
BODY Coupe; 2-doors, 4-seats; weight 1690kg (3725.7lb).
ENGINE 8-cylinders, 90deg V; front; 99mm x 92mm; 5665cc; compr 10.1:1; 260kW (348.6bhp) @ 5600rpm; 45.9kW (61.5bhp)/l; 500Nm (368.8lbft) @ 4000rpm. From 2006, 101.6mm x 92mm; 5967cc; compr 10.4:1; 420PS 270kW (362.1bhp) @ 5700rpm; 45.9kW (61.5bhp)/l; 550Nm (40.7lbft) @ 4400rpm.
ENGINE STRUCTURE 2-valves; pushrod ohv crossflow; central camshaft; aluminium cylinder head, block; sequential fuel injection, distributorless ignition with coil-per-cylinder, twin knock sensors; 4-bearing crankshaft.
TRANSMISSION rear wheel drive; hydraulic sdp clutch; 6-speed gearbox; limited slip diff, traction control; final drive 3.46:1.
CHASSIS steel monocoque; MacPherson strut independent front suspension; anti roll bar; rear suspension independent control-link, coil springs; anti roll bar; telescopic dampers, gas pressure at rear; hydraulic servo ventilated disc brakes, front 29.6cm (11.6in) dia, rear 28.6cm (11.2in) dia, finned callipers; ABS; PAS; 75l (16.4gal) fuel tank; 235/40 R18 Bridgestone Potenza RE040 tyres.
DIMENSIONS wheelbase 278.8cm (109.7in); track front 155.9cm (61.3in) rear 157.7cm (62in); length 478.9cm (188.5in); width 184.1cm (72.4in); height 139.7cm (54.9in); ground clearance 12.5cm (4.9in); turning circle 11m (36ft).
EQUIPMENT 5-spoke alloy wheels, 6-disc CD, cruise control, electric windows and sunroof, airbags, steel spacesaver spare wheel.
PERFORMANCE maximum speed 240kph (149.4mph); 0-100kph (62mph) 6sec; fuel consumption 14.4l/100km (19.6mpg).
PRICE £28,650.

Ten-spoke alloys and bonnet air scoops identified the later 6.0 Monaro *(above)* from the original Australian muscle car. The bigger engine *(right)* needed 6.3cm (2.5in) exhaust tailpipes.

337

2004 Astra 1.4 and 1.6, 1.8 and 2.0 turbo

By the fifth generation over 2 million Astras had been sold in the UK. A 5-door hatchback arrived in May, 5-door estate in the autumn, and 3-door hatchback in the spring of 2005. The segment accounted for nearly a quarter of the entire European car market. Among the new technologies was adaptive IDS-plus suspension with Continuous Damping Control (CDC), and a network integrating individual systems such as Electronic Stability Program (ESP), Traction Control (TC) and ABS. IDS-plus had a sports switch to provide firmer handling. A further refinement was the Adaptive Forward Lighting (AFL) already on the Vectra Estate. Electro-hydraulic power steering (EHPS) was map-controlled, which meant that the level of power assistance was determined by speed, and how fast the driver turned the steering wheel. Astras with sport suspension got a more direct steering ratio of 14:1 instead of 15:1. Six engines were available, all Euro 4 compliant, among them new Twinport 1.6 petrol. This had the option of Easytronic, with steering wheel-mounted controls, and the 2.0 Turbo a 6-speed manual gearbox. Martin Smith, then GM Europe's design chief, was responsible for the Astra's body shape and luggage space of 350litres (12.4cuft) with all the seats in place or 1270litres (44.8cuft) with them folded. Service for petrol engined cars two years or 20,000 miles.

INTRODUCTION 1 May 2004, 5-door.
Specification 1.4 Twinport Ecotec: variations for 1.6, 1.8, 2.0 turbo.
BODY Saloon; 3/5-doors, 5-seats; weight 1155kg (2546.3lb).
ENGINE 4-cylinders, in-line; front; transverse; 73.4mm x 80.6mm; 1364cc; compr 10:1; 66kW (88.5bhp) @ 5600rpm; 48.4kW (64.9bhp)/l; 125Nm (92.2lbft) @ 4000rpm .
ENGINE STRUCTURE 4-valves; 2 chain-driven ohc; aluminium cylinder head; electronic fuel injection; 5-bearing crankshaft.
TRANSMISSION front wheel drive; hydraulic sdp clutch; 5-speed gearbox; final drive 4.18:1.
CHASSIS steel monocoque; MacPherson strut independent front suspension; anti roll bars; rear suspension torsion beam axle; telescopic dampers; hydraulic servo brakes, front 28cm (11in) dia ventilated disc, rear 24cm (9.4in) dia discs, ABS; EHPS; 52l (11.4gal) fuel tank; tyres 195/65 R15, 205/55 R16,

215/45 R17, 6.6, 7J rims.
DIMENSIONS wheelbase 261.5cm (102.9in); track 149cm (58.6in); length 425cm (167.3in); width 175.5cm (69in); height 146cm (57.4in); ground clearance 13cm (5.1in); turning circle 11.2m (36.7ft).
EQUIPMENT Expression, Life, Club, Design, Elite, Sxi, Sri trims; remote locking. Airbags. Electric front windows, radio/CD player standard.
PERFORMANCE maximum speed 178kph (110.8mph); 31.2kph (19.4mph) @ 1000rpm; 0-100kph (62mph) 13.7sec; fuel consumption (6.3l/100km (44.8mpg).
1.6 Twinport: 1190kg (2623.4lb); 79mm x 81.5mm; 1598cc; compr 10.5:1; 77kW (103.2bhp) @ 6000rpm; 48.2kW (64.6bhp)/l; 150Nm (110.6lbft) @3900rpm. Belt-driven ohc; final drive 3.94:1; Easytronic option; 185kph (115.2mph); 33kph (20.5mph) @ 1000rpm; 12.3sec; 6.6l/100km (42.8mpg).
1.8: 1200kg (2645.5lb); 80.5mm x

338

88.2mm; 1796cc; 92kW (123.3bhp) @ 5600rpm; 51.2kW (68.6bhp)/l; 170Nm (125.4lbft)/l @ 3800rpm; final drive 3.94:1; 4-speed auto 4.12:1; front discs 28cm (11in), rear 26.4cm (10.3in); 198kph (123.3mph); 10.9sec; 7.8l/100km (36.2mpg).

2.0 turbo: 1310kg (2888lb); 86mm x 86mm; 1998cc; compr 8.8:1; 125kW (167.6bhp) @ 5200rpm; 62.6kW (83.9bhp)/l; 250Nm (184.4lbft)/l @ 1950rpm; turbocharger 0.85bar; intercooler; 6-speed gearbox; front discs 30.8cm (12.1in); rear 26.4cm (10.3in); tyres 225/45 R18; 217kph (135.1mph); 47.5kph (29.5mph) @ 1000rpm; 8.7sec; 9.1l/100km (31mpg).

PRICE £10,995 to £17,645

2004 Astra 1.4, 1.3 and 1.9 CDTi

Two 1.7litre turbodiesels were available for Astra on launch, one of 80PS and one of 100PS, followed by a more powerful 1.9, promising an even livelier turn of speed with a choice of 120PS or 150PS. The Astra Estate was first shown at the Madrid Motor Show in May and went on sale in the autumn, the 270cm (106.2in) wheelbase against the hatchback's 261.5cm (102.9in) providing a load space of 505 litres (17.8cuft) under the luggage cover. With the rear bench seat flat it was 1570 litres (55.4cuft). Overall length of the estate was 451cm (177.5in), 26cm (10.2in) longer than the hatchbacks. The new 90PS diesel (illustrated) brought the available engine options for Astra to nine. The first Vauxhall with communication, entertainment, navigation, maintenance and climate control accessed by means of a screen, the Astra's DAB digital radio was claimed as a first in the sales segment. Security was enhanced with remote control locking standardised and Auto-Lock, which re-locked the vehicle five minutes after the doors were unlocked and not re-opened. Speedlock secured the doors whenever the driver exceeded 7mph to resist attempts at car-jacking. A further option was keyless entry and start, which unlocked the doors as the driver approached, and locked them again on leaving.

INTRODUCTION 1 May and September 2004.
Specification 1.4 CDTI 80PS, variations for 90PS and 100PS, 1.9CDTi
BODY Saloon, Estate; 3/5-doors, 5-seats; weight 1260kg (2777.7lb), petrol estate 1200kg (2645.5lb), diesel estate 1315kg (2899lb).
ENGINE 4-cylinders, in-line; front; transverse; 79mm x 86mm; 1364cc; compr 18.4:1; 59kW (79.1bhp) @ 4400rpm; 35kW (46.9bhp)/l; 170Nm (125.4lbft) @ 1800rpm .
ENGINE STRUCTURE 4-valves; 2 belt-driven ohc; aluminium cylinder head; electronic common rail fuel injection; turbocharger 1.18bar; intercooler; 5-bearing crankshaft.
TRANSMISSION front wheel drive; hydraulic sdp clutch; 5-speed gearbox; final drive 3.74:1.
CHASSIS steel monocoque; MacPherson strut independent front suspension; anti roll bars; rear suspension torsion beam axle; telescopic dampers; hydraulic servo brakes, front 28cm (11in) dia ventilated disc, rear 26.4cm (10.3in) dia discs, ABS; EHPS; 52l (11.4gal) fuel tank; tyres 195/65 R15, 205/55 R16, 215/45 R17, 6.6, 7J rims.
DIMENSIONS wheelbase 261.5cm (102.9in); track 149cm (58.6in); length 425cm (167.3in); width 175.5cm (69in); height 146cm (57.4in); ground clearance 13cm (5.1in); turning circle 11.2m (36.7ft).
EQUIPMENT Expression, Life, Club, Design, Elite, Sxi, Sri trims; remote locking. Airbags. Electric front windows, radio/CD player rain-sensing wipers standard.
PERFORMANCE maximum speed 168kph (104.6mph); 41kph (25.5mph) @ 1000rpm; 0-100kph (62mph) 15sec; fuel consumption 4.9l/100km (57.6mpg).
100PS: 74kW (99.2bhp) @ 4400rpm; 43.9kW (58.8bhp)/l; 240Nm (177lbft) @ 2300rpm; final drive 3.95:1; 6-speed 3.65:1; 181kph (112.7mph); 12.3sec; 56.3mpg (5l/100km).
1.3CDTi 90PS: 1255kg (2766.7lb); 69.6mm x 82mm; 1248cc; compr 18:1; 66kW (88.5bhp) @ 4000rpm;

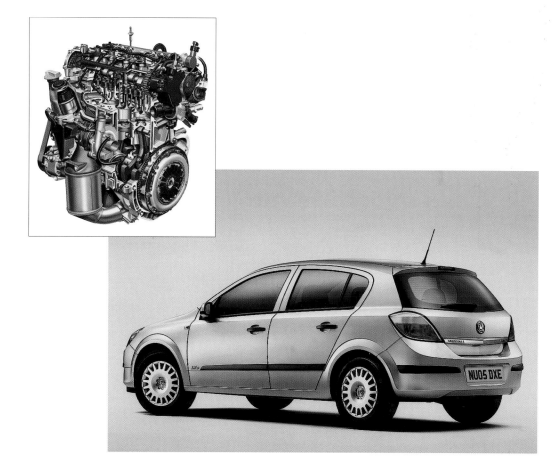

52.9kW (70.9bhp)/l; 200Nm (147.5lbft) @ 1750rpm; 2 chain-driven ohc; turbocharger; 6-speed; final drive 3.72; 172kph (107.1mph); 38kph (23.6mph) @ 1000rpm; 13.7sec; 5l/100km (56.5mpg)

1.9 CDTi 120PS: 1320kg (2910lb), Estate 1375kg (3031.3lb); 82mm x 90.4mm; 1910cc; compr 17.5:1; 88kW (118bhp) @ 3250rpm; 46kW (61.6bhp)/l; 280Nm (205.5lbft) @ 1750rpm; 6-speed gearbox; final drive 3.65:1; 30.8cm (12.1in) front discs, 26.4cm (10.3in) rear; 191kph (118.9mph); 10.5sec;

1.9CDTi 150PS: 110kW (147.5bhp) @ 4000rpm; 57.6kW (77.2bhp)/l; 320Nm (236lbft) @ 2000rpm; 208kph (129.5mph); 8.9sec; 9.1l/100km (31mpg)

PRICE 1.7CDTi Life Estate £14,595; Club £15,945; 1.9 CDTi Design £18,695; SXi £16,445

2004 Vectra Estate 1.8 16v, 2.2 Direct 16v, 3.0 V6 CDTi

Completing the Vectra range, the Estate claimed the biggest luggage area in the class, had the FlexOrganiser for tailor-made cargo compartments, a Signum wheelbase and a choice of seven engines, four petrol and three diesel. The estate also had a retractable towbar and optional power tailgate. Between 530litres (18.7cuft) and 1850 litres (65.3cuft) of cargo meant the Vectra offered more than the Omega or its rival Ford Mondeo. FlexOrganiser had upper and lower parallel rails on each side of the load space, with dividers, nets, poles or hooks to tidy it up for supermarket shopping or recreational kit. The power tailgate operated from the key-fob or a button inside the cabin, and the tow-bar stowed out of sight horizontally behind the back bumper. Vectra Estates had 5 or 6-speed manual gearboxes, Continuously Variable Transmission (CVT), or fully automatic. The front suspension and four link rear axle now used aluminium components. The 3.0 V6 CDTi, and the 2.2 direct injection petrol engines figured in a new version of the Signum besides the Vectra. In the SRi and Elite, the diesel V6 had an aluminium head and block. From the spring of 2004 the 1.9CDTi was Vauxhall's first diesel with a maintenance free particulate filter, requiring no additives and complying with Euro IV emissions legislation.

INTRODUCTION on sale November 2003.
Specification 1.8
BODY Estate; 5-doors, 5-seats; weight 1415kg (3119.5lb).
ENGINE 4-cylinders, in-line; front; transverse; 80.5mm x 88.2mm; 1796cc; compr 10.5:1; 90kW (120.6bhp) @ 6000rpm; 50.1kW (67.1bhp)/l; 167Nm (123.2lbft) @ 3800rpm .
ENGINE STRUCTURE Ecotec, 4-valves; 2 belt-driven overhead camshafts; aluminium cylinder head; electronic injection, ignition; 5-bearing crankshaft.
TRANSMISSION front wheel drive; sdp clutch; 5-speed gearbox; final drive 3.74:1; CVT 4.97:1.
CHASSIS steel monocoque with sub-frames; MacPherson strut independent front suspension; anti roll bar; rear suspension torsion beam axle, transverse arms, coil springs; anti roll bar; telescopic dampers; hydraulic servo disc brakes, front 28.5cm (11.2in) dia ventilated, rear 27.8cm (10.9in),

ABS; electro-hydraulic PAS; 61l (13.4gal) fuel tank; 195/65 R15 tyres, 6.5J rims.
DIMENSIONS wheelbase 283cm (111.4in); track front 153.5cm (60.4in) rear 152.5cm (60in); length 482cm (189.7in); width 179.5cm (70.6in); height 150cm (59in); turning circle 11.9m (39ft).
EQUIPMENT air conditioning; electric front windows; airbags, curtain airbags; CD player standard, ESP on V6s.
PERFORMANCE maximum speed 199kph (123.9mph); 38.8kph (24.1mph) @ 1000rpm; 0-100kph (62mph) 12.1sec; fuel consumption 8.3l/100km (34mpg).
2.2: 1460kg (3218.7lb); 86mm x 94.6mm; 2198cc; compr 10.0:1; 108kW (144.8bhp) @ 5800rpm; 49.1kW (65.8bhp)/l; 203Nm (149.7lbft) @ 4000rpm; Z22XE, chain-driven ohc; aluminium head and block; final drive 3.95:1; 5-speed auto 2.6:1; 215/55 R 16 tyres; auto 210kph (130.8mph); 10.8sec.
3.0 V6 CDTi: 1675kg (3692.7lb);

66deg V6; 87.5mm x 82mm; 2958cc; compr 18.5:1; 130kW (174.3bhp) @ 4000rpm; 43.9kW (58.8bhp)/l; 370Nm (272.9lbft) @ 1900rpm; 2x2 belt-driven ohc; aluminium heads and block; 4-bearing crankshaft; Garrett turbo, intercooler; 6-speed gearbox 3.91:1 final drive, 5-speed Aisin-Warner automatic 2.23:1; 222kph (138.2mph); 9.8sec; 7.7l/100km (36.6mpg)

PRICE Estate 1.8 LS £16,045; Club 2.0DTi £16,945; SXi 2.0 Turbo £17,995; Elegance 2.2 DTi £18,995; Elite 3.0CDTi £25,100.

2005 Tigra Twin Top

The first hint of entry into the market for stylish metal-topped convertibles came with confirmation in January 2004, that the Tigra title of 1994-2000 (qv) would be reinstated for a prototype at the Geneva Motor Show in March. Produced in France by the coachbuilder Groupe Henri Heuliez SA the new Tigra had an electro-hydraulic retractable steel roof that folded into a compartment between the boot and the seats. The little car proved so popular that it went on sale in South Africa as an Opel, and in Australia as a Holden, but only with the 1.8 litre petrol engine. In Britain it also became available with the Corsa's 1.3litre turbocharged diesel, giving company car drivers an opportunity for an economical roadster. Its Co2 emissions of only 124gm/km fell into the lowest tax band for conventionally engined cars. With an annual mileage of 12,000, business drivers could save up to £450 under government taxation. Tigra also signified Vauxhall's policy of tackling niche markets, hitherto neglected owing to their small volumes, by ringing the changes with available componentry to produce a diversity of products. Managing director Kevin Wale said Tigra played an important part in Vauxhall's pursuit of niche markets. Twenty per cent of its product portfolio would henceforth be aimed at speciality buyers.

INTRODUCTION Geneva 2004, on sale spring 2005.

BODY roadster; 2-doors; 2-seats; weight 1165kg (2568.3lb); 1.8 and turbodiesel, 1165kg (2568.3lb).

ENGINE 4-cylinders, in-line; front; transverse; 73.4mm x 80.6mm; 1364cc; compr 10.5:1; 66kW (88.5bhp) @ 5600rpm; 48.8kW (65.4bhp)/l; 125Nm (92.2lbft) @ 4000rpm. 1.8 80.5mm x 88.2mm; 1796cc; compr 10.5:1; 92kW (123.3bhp) @ 6000rpm; 51.2kW (68.6bhp)/l; 165Nm (121lbft) @ 4600rpm. Turbodiesel 69.6mm x 82mm; 1248cc; compr 18:1; 51kW (68.3bhp) @ 4000rpm; 40.9kW (54.8bhp)/l; 170Nm (125.3lbft) @ 1750rpm.

ENGINE STRUCTURE Twinport, 4-valves; 2 chain-driven ohc; aluminium cylinder head; electronic fuel injection; 5-bearing crankshaft. Ecotec belt-driven camshafts 1.3CTDi common rail injection, turbocharger, intercooler

TRANSMISSION front wheel drive; hydraulic sdp clutch; 5-speed gearbox; final drive 3.74:1, 5-speed Easytronic 3.94:1. CDTi final drive 3.55:1

CHASSIS steel monocoque with front subframe; MacPherson strut independent front suspension; anti roll bars; rear suspension torsion beam axle; telescopic dampers; hydraulic servo brakes, front 26cm (10.2in) dia ventilated disc, rear drums, 1.8 24cm (9.4in) discs, ABS; EHPS; 45l (9.8gal) fuel tank; tyres 185/60 R15, 6.5J rims.

DIMENSIONS wheelbase 249cm (98in); track front 143cm (56.2in) rear 142cm (55.9in); length 392cm (154.3in); width 168.5cm (66.3in); height 136.5cm (53.7in); ground clearance 14cm (5.5in); turning circle 10.5m (34.4ft).

EQUIPMENT air conditioning, 5-spoke alloy wheels, CD30 stereo, alloy trimmed pedals, ultrasonic security alarm.

PERFORMANCE maximum speed 180kph (112.1mph), 1.8 204kph (127mph), CDTi 167kph (104mph); 32kph (19.9mph), CDTi 39.5kph

(24.6mph) @ 1000rpm; 0-100kph (62mph) 12.4sec, 9.4sec, 15.5sec; fuel consumption 6.4l/ 100km (44.1mpg), 8.1l/100km (34.8mpg), 4.76l/100km (59.3mpg).
PRICE 1.4 Exclusiv £14,702; 1.8 Sport £15,507; CDTi £14,692.

2005 Astra Sport Hatch

Despite its exclusive style the Sport Hatch was carefully priced no more than a 5-door Astra. Vauxhall was convinced that 3-door buyers preferred something lower and racier than a simple saloon. The Sport Hatch was 3.2cm (1.2in) lower, and although its resemblance to the rest of the range was obvious, the only body panels common to the 5-door were the bonnet and front wings. Four petrol engines were available, Twinport 1.4 and 1.6, a 125PS 1.8, and a 2.0 Turbo. There were also three common rail Euro IV compliant diesels. Every Sports Hatch had the option of the Panoramic windscreen, a 1.5m (4.9ft) sweep of glass to the middle of the roof without bars or pillars, giving the appearance of an aircraft canopy. In the event not many buyers took it up, but it did provide a talking point, and helped establish the model's credentials. Crash testing showed that the Panoramic wind-screen did not compromise safety. The 2.0 petrol and both 1.9 diesels had 6-speed gearboxes as standard, a clutchless Easytronic robot gearbox was available on the 1.6, and conventional automatic on the 1.8. Suspension was lower and firmer than the 5-door and there were SXi, Design, and SRi trim options, the upper offering an exterior styling pack with spoilers and skirts.

INTRODUCTION GTC Concept Geneva 2003, on sale April 2005. Specification 1.4
BODY Coupe; 3-doors, 5-seats; weight 1155kg (2546.3lb).
ENGINE 4-cylinders, in-line; front; transverse; 73.4mm x 80.6mm; 1364cc; compr 10.5:1; 66kW (88.5bhp) @ 5600 rpm; 48.4kW (64.9bhp)/l; 125Nm (92.2lbft) @ 4000rpm .
ENGINE STRUCTURE Twinport, 4-valves; 2 chain-driven ohc; aluminium cylinder head; electronic fuel injection; 5-bearing crankshaft.
TRANSMISSION front wheel drive; hydraulic sdp clutch; 5-speed gearbox; Easytronic option; final drive 4.18:1.
CHASSIS steel monocoque with front subframe; MacPherson strut independent front suspension; anti roll bars; rear suspension torsion beam axle; telescopic dampers; hydraulic servo brakes, front 28cm (11in) dia ventilated disc, rear 24cm (9.4in) discs, ABS; EHPS; 52l (11.4gal) fuel tank; tyres 195/65 R15, 205/55 R16, 215/45 R17; 6.5J or 7J rims.
DIMENSIONS wheelbase 261.5cm (102.9in); track 149cm (58.6in); length 425cm (167.3in); width 175.5cm (69in); height 146cm (57.4in); ground clearance 13cm (5.1in); turning circle 10.6m (34.7ft).
EQUIPMENT air conditioning, CD player, six airbags standard, satellite navigation, DAB digital radio, MP3 compatible disc readers, optional, ESP-plus stability control, Panoramic roof £850.
PERFORMANCE max speed 180kph (112.1mph); 31.2kph (19.4mph) @ 1000rpm; 0-100kph (62mph) 13.6sec; fuel consumption 6.6l/100km (42.8mpg). 1.6 Twinport: 1190kg (2623.4lb); 79mm x 81.5mm; 1598cc; compr 10.5:1; 77kW (103.2bhp) @ 6000rpm; 48.2kW (64.6bhp)/l; 150Nm (110.6lbft) @3900rpm. Belt-driven ohc; final drive 3.94:1; Easytronic option; 185kph (115.2mph); 33kph (20.5mph) @ 1000rpm; 12.3sec; 6.6l/100km (42.8mpg).

1.8: 1200kg (2645.5lb); 80.5mm x 88.2mm; 1796cc; 92kW (123.3bhp) @ 5600rpm; 51.2kW (68.6bhp)/l; 170Nm (125.4lbft)/l @ 3800rpm; final drive 3.94:1; 4-speed auto 4.12:1; front discs 28cm (11in), rear 26.4cm (10.3in); 198kph (123.3mph); 10.9sec; 7.8l/100km (36.2mpg).

2.0 turbo 240PS: 1310kg (2888lb); 86mm x 86mm; 1998cc; compr 8.8:1; 176kW (236bhp) @ 5600rpm; 88.6kW (118.8bhp)/l; 320Nm (236lbft)/l @ 2400; turbocharger 0.85bar; intercooler; 6-speed gearbox; final drive 3.83:1; front discs 32.1cm (12.6in); rear 27.8cm (10.9in); tyres 225/40 R18; 244kph (151.9mph); 47.5kph (29.5mph) @ 1000rpm; 6.2sec; 9.7l/100km (29.1mpg)

1.9CDTi 150PS: 110kW (147.5bhp) @ 4000rpm; 57.6kW (77.2bhp)/l; 320Nm (236lbft) @ 2000rpm; 208kph (129.5mph); 8.9sec; 9.1l/100km (31mpg)

PRICE 1.4 SXi £13,795, 2.0i Turbo 170PS Design £17,945, 150PS SRi 1.9CDTi £17,495, 1.8SRi with exterior pack £16,145.

2005 Zafira

There was no need to change the format for the second generation Zafira, beyond making it 15cm (5.9in) longer and 3.4cm (1.3in) wider. This gave a bit more room, otherwise there were few alterations. A Panorama roof was offered, as well as the lightweight 1.8 litre 140PS engine with 14 per cent more power using four per cent less fuel. This had DCVCP, or double continuous variable cam phasing, which twisted the intake and exhaust cams relative to the crankshaft, in response to a hydraulic vane-type phaser, loosely following Pomeroy's principles of 90 years before. The hollow frame cylinder block was 20 per cent lighter. Seven engine (1.6, 1.8, 2.2, 2.0 Turbo, three 1.9CDTi) and five trim choices kept up the momentum for a car that had sold 1.4 million, 15 per cent of which were in the UK. Unusually, in its sixth season, sales had risen steadily every year, despite competition from newer multi purpose vehicles. There were new large air inlets in the front bumper, hi-tech-looking headlamps with the option of Adaptive Forward Lighting, and innovative tail lights. Inside, the gearshift lever was higher, making space for a U-shaped handbrake in the central console. A good deal of Zafira's success stemmed from Flex7 seating, with a third row of seats that could be completely folded down and stowed away. Luggage space gained 20litres (0.7cuft).

INTRODUCTION Geneva Motor Show 2005, on sale July.
Specification 1.8
BODY Saloon; 5-doors, 5/7-seats; weight 1430kg (3152.5lb).
ENGINE 4-cylinders, in-line; front; transverse; 80.5mm x 88.2mm; 1796cc; compr 10.5:1; 103kW (138.1bhp) @ 6000rpm; 57.3kW (76.8bhp)/l; 175Nm (129lbft) @ 3800rpm.
ENGINE STRUCTURE Ecotec VVT, 4-valves; 2 belt-driven overhead camshafts; aluminium cylinder head; electronic fuel injection, ignition; 5-bearing crankshaft.
TRANSMISSION front wheel drive; hydraulic sdp clutch; 5-speed gearbox; final drive 3.94:1, Easytronic 4.19:1.
CHASSIS integral steel structure; independent front suspension by MacPherson struts; anti roll bar; rear suspension torsion tube, compound links, coil springs; anti roll bar; telescopic dampers; hydraulic servo ventilated disc brakes, front 28cm (11in), 30.8cm (12.1in) dia, rear 26.4cm (10.3in) dia, dual circuit, ABS; EPAS; 58l (12.7gal) fuel tank; 205/55 R16 tyres 6.5J rims.
DIMENSIONS wheelbase 270.5cm (106.4in); track front 149cm (58.6in) rear 151cm (59.4in); length 447cm (175.9in); width 180cm (70.8in); height 163.5cm (64.3in); ground clearance 15cm (5.9in); turning circle 10.9m (35.7ft).
EQUIPMENT side airbags, roof rails, trip computer, optional cruise control, electronic climate control.
PERFORMANCE maximum speed 197kph (122.7mph); 33kph (20.5mph) @ 1000rpm; 0-100kph (62mph) 11.5sec; fuel consumption 7.96l/100km (35.4mpg). 2.2 150PS: 1500kg (3306.9lb); 86mm x 94.6mm; 2198cc; compr 10:1; 110kW (147.5bhp) @ 5600rpm; 50kW (67bhp)/l; 215Nm (291lbft) @ 4000rpm; 2.2 Directotec 2 chain-driven ohc; aluminium head and block; 6-speed gearbox; final drive 3.83:1; automatic 2.81:1; 200kph (124.5mph); 41kph (25.5mph) @ 1000rpm; 10.6sec; 8.9l/100km (31.7mpg).

2.0 Turbo 200PS (VXR 240PS): 86mm x 86mm; 1998cc; compr 8.8:1; 147kW (197.1bhp) @ 5400rpm; (VXR 176kW (236bhp)); 73.6kW (98.6bhp)/l; 262Nm (193.25lbft) @ 4200rpm; turbo-charger 0.85bar, intercooler; 6-speed; final drive 3.94:1; 30.8cm (12.1in) discs (VXR 32.1cm (12.6in) and 26.4cm (10.3in)); 225/40 R18 tyres, 7.5J rims; 225kph (140.1mph); 40kph (24.9mph) @ 1000rpm; 9sec; 10l/100km (28.2mpg); VXR 231kph (143.8mph); 7.8sec.

1.9CDTi 150PS: 1555kg (3428.1lb); 82mm x 90.4mm; 1910cc; compr 17.5:1; 110kW (147.5bhp) @ 4000rpm; 57.6kW (77.2bhp)/l; 320Nm (236lbft) @ 2000rpm; 6-speed final drive 3.83; 6-speed automatic 2.77:1; 202kph (125.8mph); 49.5kph (30.8mph) @ 1000rpm; 10.4sec; 6.4l/100km (44.1mpg)

PRICE 1.6i Expression £12,995, 2.2i Direct £16,8451.9CDTi Club Euro IV £18,095, 2.0 Turbo £19,995.

349

2005 Astra VXR

Back in 1961 VX 4/90 was a Victor FB (qv) with high gearing, an aluminium cylinder head, two Zenith carburettors and disc brakes. Yet it brought Vauxhall a sporting pedigree it had not had since the 1920s. VX had probably been a trendy term for *VauXhall*, the 4 was for the cylinders, the 90 implied horse power although it wasn't, but the top speed was about 90mph. Like everybody else Vauxhall sought a distinctive brand title indicating performance options and premium prices. VXRacing team Astras were busy winning five British Touring Car Championships so VXR was applied to models, "with racing DNA". Chassis tuning was done in conjunction with Lotus Engineering, and Luton declared that its set-up was uniquely tailored for British roads, and not some Euro-compromise. Developed from the Sport Hatch, an HPC concept car was shown at Paris in 2004, the production version distinguished by flared wheelarches, suspension lowered by 1.5cm (.5in), and a distinctive styling kit set it apart from run-of-the-mill Astras. A deep air dam, extended side sills, tailgate roof spoiler and centre-exit trapezoidal exhaust left no doubt. As a final flourish, like all classic speedsters it sported huge ventilated brake discs, Arden blue callipers, ultra low-profile tyres, and the obligatory Recaro seats to hold the driver in place for fast cornering.

INTRODUCTION September 2005.
Specification 240PS VXR
BODY Coupe; 3-doors, 5-seats; weight 1310kg (2888lb).
ENGINE 4-cylinders, in-line; front; transverse; 86mm x 86mm; 1998cc; compr 8.8:1; 176kW (236bhp) @ 5600 rpm; 88.6kW (118.8bhp)/l; 320Nm (236lbft) @ 2400rpm .
ENGINE STRUCTURE 2.0 Turbo, 4-valves; 2 belt-driven ohc; aluminium cylinder head; electronic fuel injection; 5-bearing crankshaft; turbocharger 0.85bar; intercooler.
TRANSMISSION front wheel drive; hydraulic sdp clutch; 6-speed gearbox; final drive 3.83:1.
CHASSIS steel monocoque with front subframe; MacPherson strut independent front suspension; anti roll bars; rear suspension torsion beam axle; telescopic dampers; hydraulic servo ventilated disc brakes, front 32.1cm (12.6in) dia, rear 27.8cm (10.9in), ABS; EHPS; 52l (11.4gal) fuel tank; tyres 225/40 R 18, 8J rims.

DIMENSIONS wheelbase 261.5cm (102.9in); track 149cm (58.6in); length 425cm (167.3in); width 175.5cm (69in); height 146cm (57.4in); ground clearance 13cm (5.1in); turning circle 10.6m (34.7ft).
EQUIPMENT leather pack £1000; electronic climate control £250; cruise control £200; adaptive forward lighting, bi-Xenon headlights £750; 19in alloy wheels £500; parking sensor £350; CD70 stereo, sat-nav, etc £1250.
PERFORMANCE maximum speed 244kph (152mph); 47.5kph (29.5mph) @ 1000rpm; 0-100kph (62mph) 6.2sec; fuel consumption 9.7l/100km (29.1mpg).
PRICE £18,995

2005 Zafira VXR

Putting the turbo-charged Astra VXR engine into the 7-seat Zafira, resulted in an MPV with the speed of a hot hatchback. IDS-plus technology and continuously damped suspension provided agreeable handling when laden, although the stiffened springing left it with a harsher ride. It gained the VXR honeycomb grille, bigger front bumper, deeper sill extensions a spoiler on top of the tailgate and brandished twin exhausts. Recaro seats were two-tone leather and fabric, and the ingenious Flex7 seating was retained. Welcomed by keen drivers with large families, it extended niche marketing to new boundaries and cornered flatter than some other MPVs. *Autocar* thought: "The packaging …typically clever – plenty of oddment space, the same trick seating arrangement as on the bread-and-butter models. Indeed, there's precious little to indicate that you're sitting in something special – a touch of aluminium on the dash, a bit of VXR branding and a 'Sport' button that weights up the steering and improves the already-impressive throttle response." The Panorama glass roof was still an option, but a more steeply-angled windscreen gave better views from the front three-quarter windows for cornering. In 2005 it cost £220 more than the standard Zafira, and in 2007 *What Car?* named the entire range best used car buy in the MPV sector.

INTRODUCTION Shown Geneva, on sale October 2005.
BODY Saloon; 5-doors, 5/7-seats; weight 1535kg (3384lb).
ENGINE 4-cylinders, in-line; front; transverse; 86mm x 86mm; 1998cc; compr 8.8:1; 176kW (236bhp) @ 6000rpm; 88kW (118bhp)/l; 320Nm (433.8lbft) @ 4200rpm .
ENGINE STRUCTURE 2.0 Turbo 4-valves; 2 belt-driven overhead camshafts; aluminium cylinder head; electronic fuel injection, ignition; 5-bearing crankshaft; turbocharger 0.85bar; intercooler.
TRANSMISSION front wheel drive; hydraulic sdp clutch; 5-speed gearbox; automatic; final drive 3.94:1.
CHASSIS integral steel structure; independent front suspension by MacPherson struts; anti roll bar; rear suspension torsion tube, compound links, coil springs; anti roll bar; telescopic dampers; hydraulic servo ventilated disc brakes, front 30.8cm (12.1in) dia, rear 26.4cm (10.3in) dia, ABS; EPAS; 58l (12.7gal) fuel tank;

205/55 R16 tyres 6.5/7.5J rims.
DIMENSIONS wheelbase 270.5cm (106.4in); track front 149cm (58.6in) rear 151cm (59.4in); length 447cm (175.9in); width 180cm (70.8in); height 163.5cm (64.3in); ground clearance 15cm (5.9in); turning circle 10.9m (35.7ft).
EQUIPMENT electronic climate control £250; Bluetooth compatible mobile phone £300; parking sensors £350; 19in alloy wheels £500.
PERFORMANCE maximum speed 231kph (143.8mph); 40kph (24.9mph) @ 1000rpm; 0-100kph (62mph) 7.8sec; fuel consumption 10l/100km (28.2mpg).
PRICE £22,145

Everything forward of the windscreen was new, the Vauxhall identity emphasised by the Astra-style bold V grille, and a new 2.8litre turbocharged V6 with 6-speed automatic gearbox appeared at the top of the range. Pierluigi Collina, the international football referee, endorsed a novel promotional campaign for both restyled Vectra and Signum. He awarded the penalty, from which David Beckham scored, taking England to a win during the FIFA 2002 World Cup. Collina summed it up: "The Vectra and Signum's driving dynamics enable a split-second judgement in every situation – just like a referee on a football pitch." Changes to the interior were new materials, a soft-touch facia, and a vaguely retro instrument panel. UK chassis engineers improved steering feel and control, tuning Vectra for British roads and more than 7,000 orders were taken before it went on sale on 1 October. More than half were for the 1.9CDTi. In March 2007 for the second year in a row *What Car?* Nominated the Vectra 1.9CDTi Exclusiv its best estate car buy between £15,000 and £35,000: "It doesn't have the badge cachet of some of its rivals but none can surpass its combination of space, practicality, and ease of use." At £17,230 with a 530l (18.7cuft) boot, "…the Vectra is comfortable, good to drive, and refined … it makes a seriously compelling case."

INTRODUCTION July 2005. Specification 1.8
BODY Saloon; 5-doors, 5-seats; weight 1320kg (2910lb).
ENGINE 4-cylinders, in-line; front; transverse; 80.5mm x 88.2mm; 1796cc; compr 10.5:1; 90kW (120.6bhp) @ 6000rpm; 50.1kW (67.1bhp)/l; 167Nm (123.2lbft) @ 3800rpm.
ENGINE STRUCTURE Ecotec, 4-valves; 2 belt-driven overhead camshafts; aluminium cylinder head; electronic injection, ignition; 5-bearing crankshaft.
TRANSMISSION front wheel drive; sdp clutch; 5-speed gearbox; final drive 3.74:1.
CHASSIS steel monocoque with sub-frames; MacPherson strut independent front suspension; anti roll bar; rear suspension torsion beam axle, transverse arms, coil springs; anti roll bar; telescopic dampers; hydraulic servo disc brakes, front 28.5cm (11.2in) dia ventilated, rear 27.8cm (10.9in), ABS; electro-hydraulic PAS; 61l

(13.4gal) fuel tank; 195/65 R15 tyres; 6.5J rims.
DIMENSIONS wheelbase 270cm (106.2in); track front 153.5cm (60.4in) rear 152.5cm (60in); length 461cm (181.4in); width 180cm (70.8in); height 146cm (57.4in); turning circle 11.5m (37.7ft).
EQUIPMENT air conditioning; electric front windows; airbags, curtain airbags; CD player standard, ESP on V6s.
PERFORMANCE maximum speed 205kph (127.6mph); 38.8kph (24.1mph) @ 1000rpm; 0-100kph (62mph) 11.2sec; fuel consumption 8l/100km (35.3mpg)
2.2: 1360kg (2998.2lb); 86mm x 94.6mm; 2198cc; compr 10.0:1; 108kW (144.8bhp) @ 5800rpm; 49.1kW (65.8bhp)/l; 203Nm (149.7lbft) @ 4000rpm; Z22XE, chain-driven ohc; aluminium head and block; final drive 3.65:1; 5-speed auto 2.6:1; 215/55 R 16 tyres; auto 218kph (135.7mph); 9.6sec.
1.9 CDTi 120PS: 1435kg (3163.6lb); 4-cylinders; 2-valves in parallel;

82mm x 90.4mm; 1910cc; compr 18:1; 88kW (118bhp) @ 3500rpm; 46kW (61.6bhp)/l; 280Nm (206.5lbft) @ 2000rpm. 150PS, 4-valves; compr 17.5:1; 110kW (147.5bhp) @ 4000rpm; 57.6kW (77.2bhp)/l; 320Nm (236lbft) @ 2000rpm; 6-sped gearbox final drive 3.55:1; 150PS 6-speed automatic 2.67:1; 200kph (124.5mph); 11.5sec; 5.9l/100km (47.8mpg); 150PS 217kph (135.1mph); 9.8sec; 6l/100km (47mpg).

2.8 Turbo 230PS: 1490kg (3284.8lb); 60deg V6; 89mm x 74.6mm; 2792cc; compr 9.5:1; 169kW (226.6bhp) @ 5500rpm; 60.5kW (81.1bhp)/l; 330Nm (243lbft) @ 1800rpm; 2x2 chain-driven ohc; aluminium block and heads; 4-bearing crankshaft; 6-speed manual 3.55:1 final drive; auto 3.2:1; 250kph (155.7mph); 7.3sec; 11l/100km (25.6mpg)

PRICE Estate 1.8 Club £16,822; 1.9 CDTi Exclusive £15,577; 2.0 Turbo SRi £18,392; 2.8i V6 Turbo Design £22,822; Elite 3.0CDTi £24,737.

Right: Sensibly well proportioned, Vectra sales built up before its introduction, following promotion by international whistleblower *(above)* Pierluigi Collina.

2005 Vectra VXR

Both Vectras came in for VXR treatment, Vauxhall claiming they were the fastest 5-door hatchback and estate car on the market. Chassis tuning was taken a stage further to deal with the power, with Vectra and Zafira VXR first with a new generation of electronic damping control using two processors. Aimed at reducing body roll IDS-Plus2's software was claimed to optimise pitch, roll, and turn-in to exploit the generous power. This was the first application of the aluminium V6 with variable valve timing and twin-scroll turbocharger, which aimed to achieve a smooth flow of power with little turbo lag. Development went on so that by 2007 it was producing 280PS and 355Nm (261.8lbft) with a redesigned induction system and retuned software. This brought the 0-60 time down to 6.1sec for the hatchback and 6.3 for the estate. A switch on the facia operated a Sport setting for the suspension. Downside was heavier fuel consumption and something of a struggle for the front wheels to keep a grip of the road on tight turns. More revisions to the spring and damper settings and software did not quite do the trick. "The last thing the Vectra needed was more power – its front wheels had a tough enough time with 252bhp," said *What Car?*

INTRODUCTION Frankfurt September 2005.
BODY Saloon; 5-doors, 5-seats; weight 1490kg (3284.8lb).
ENGINE front, transverse; 60deg V6; 89mm x 74.8mm; 2792cc; compr 9.5:1; 188kW (252.1bhp) @ 5500rpm; 60.5kW (81.1bhp)/l; 320Nm (236lbft) @ 1800rpm
ENGINE STRUCTURE 2x2 chain-driven ohc; aluminium block and heads; 4-bearing crank; electronic injection, ignition; 4-bearing crank, variable valve timing, twin-scroll turbocharger.
TRANSMISSION front wheel drive; sdp clutch; 6-speed manual 3.55:1 final drive; auto 3.2:1.
CHASSIS steel monocoque with sub-frames; MacPherson strut independent front suspension; anti roll bar; rear suspension torsion beam axle, transverse arms, coil springs; anti roll bar; dual-processor electronically controlled telescopic dampers; hydraulic servo ventilated disc brakes, front 34.5cm (13.5in) dia, rear 29.2cm (11.4in), ABS;

electro-hydraulic PAS; 61l (13.4gal) fuel tank; 235/40 R18 or 235/35 ZR19 tyres.
DIMENSIONS wheelbase 270cm (106.2in); track front 153.5cm (60.4in) rear 152.5cm (60in); length 461cm (181.4in); width 180cm (70.8in); height 146cm (57.4in); turning circle 11.5m (37.7ft).
EQUIPMENT Recaro seats; 18in alloy wheels; 19in optional; VXR body kit; Advanced Forward Lighting £850
PERFORMANCE maximum speed 260kph (161.9mph); 38.8kph (24.1mph) @ 1000rpm; 0-100kph (62mph) 6.7sec; fuel consumption 11l/100km (25.6mpg)
PRICE 5-door £23,995, Estate £24,995.

2006 Meriva 1.6 Twinport and 1.3CDTi

Revisions to Vauxhall's smallest MPV were a fresher appearance, with a reprofiled bumper and more prominent V-grille at the front, and dark rear lamp lenses and a chrome strip across the tailgate. There were two new engines, the 1.3-litre CDTi diesel, as used in Corsa and Tigra, appeared in Meriva for the first time, together with the petrol 1.6-litre 105PS Twinport from Astra and Zafira. With 5PS more than the outgoing Meriva 1.6, it promised to be livelier yet more economical. All versions of Merivas were provided with a halogen version of Adaptive Forward Lighting (AFL), which cost less than Xenon. Among other new features were a power release tailgate, and interior lighting activated by remote control to help find the car in the dark. Follow-me-home headlights were also standard, while mobile phones with Bluetooth interface appeared on the options list. Although only just over 4metres long Meriva gave generous storage and comfortable adaptable seating justifying its place as a good value versatile all-rounder. Merivas with Easytronic automated manual transmission had Hill Start Assist as standard. This maintained pressure in the braking system for 1.5sec after the foot brake was released, giving the driver time to select a gear and apply the accelerator without rolling back. As soon as the car started to move, braking pressure released.

INTRODUCTION February 2006. Specification 1.6
BODY Saloon MPV; 5-doors, 5-seats; weight 1300kg (2865.9lb).
ENGINE 4-cylinders, in-line; front; transverse; 79mm x 81.5mm; 1598cc; compr 10.5:1; 77kW (103.2bhp) @ 6000rpm; 48.2kW (64.6bhp)/l; 150Nm (110.6lbft) @ 3900rpm .
ENGINE STRUCTURE Twinport 1.6 Ecotec, 4-valves; 2 belt-driven overhead camshafts; aluminium cylinder head; electronic fuel injection and ignition; 5-bearing crankshaft.
TRANSMISSION front wheel drive; hydraulic sdp clutch; 5-speed gearbox; final drive 3.94:1; Easytronic 5-speed 3.94 or 4.19:1.
CHASSIS steel monocoque with sub-frames; MacPherson strut independent front suspension; anti roll bar; rear suspension torsion beam axle, transverse arms, coil springs; anti roll bar; telescopic dampers; hydraulic servo disc brakes, front 26cm (10.2in) dia

ventilated, rear 24cm (9.4in), Bosch ABS; electro-hydraulic PAS; 53l (11.6gal) fuel tank; 175/70 R14, 185/60 R15 tyres, 5.6, 6J rims.
DIMENSIONS wheelbase 263cm (103.5in); track front 145cm (57in) rear 146.5cm (57.6in); length 405cm (159.4in); width 169.5cm (66.7in); height 162.5cm (63.9in); ground clearance 15cm (5.9in); turning circle 10.5m (34.4ft).
EQUIPMENT halogen lighting; power release tailgate; optional mobile phone with Bluetooth interface.

PERFORMANCE maximum speed
181kph (112.7mph); 34.1kph
(21.2mph) @ 1000rpm; 0-100kph
(62mph) 13.3sec; fuel consumption
7l/100km (40.3mpg).
1.3CDTi: 69.6mm x 82mm; 1248cc;
compr 17.6:1; 55kW (73.7bhp) @
4000rpm; 44.1kW (59.1bhp)/l;
170Nm (125.4lbft) @ 1750rpm; 4-
valves in parallel; 2 chain-driven ohc;
aluminium head; common rail
injection; turbocharger, intercooler;
157kph (97.7mph); 41kph (25.5mph)
@ 1000rpm; 17.8sec; 5.1l/100km
(55.3mpg).
PRICE 1.3CDTi Life £13,547; 1.6
Design £13,817; 1.6 Life Easytronic
£12,437.

2006 Meriva VXR

Acclaimed as the first hot mini-MPV at the Essen Motor Show in November 2005, Vauxhall felt the VXR version of the Meriva would appeal to customers who: "liked their cars fast, fun and more than a little cheeky." It had what was known as the Sport Chassis, which was more dynamic that the standard car's. Tested at GM's high-speed test centre at Pferdsfeld, Germany, as well as on the Nürburgring, the VXR chassis was 1cm (0.4in) lower at the front and 1.5cm (0.6in) lower at the rear. Up to 50 per cent stiffer springs, dampers and bushes reduced body roll, and the electronic power steering had a quicker 16.7:1 ratio. The water cooled turbocharger on the new 180PS 1.6 litre engine was integrated with the exhaust manifold, weighed only 131kg (288.8lb) and had an overboost facility to increase torque by 15 per cent, from 230Nm (169.6lbft) to 266Nm (196,2lbft). Brought into action by opening the throttle fast, for safe overtaking, the extra torque remained available for up to 5sec. The bumpers linked the style with the VXR Astra, Zafira and Vectra models, there were VXR logos on dials, gear lever and steering wheel, also on the optional 17-inch alloy wheels, with 205/45 ZR 17 tyres. Meriva VXR nevertheless retained all the practicality of FlexSpace seating.

INTRODUCTION February 2006.
BODY Saloon MPV; 5-doors, 5-seats; weight 1350kg (2976.2lb).
ENGINE 4-cylinders, in-line; front; transverse; 79mm x 81.5mm; 1598cc; compr 8.8:1; 132kW (177bhp) @ 5500rpm; 82.6kW (110.7bhp)/l; 230Nm (169.6lbft) @ 2200rpm .
ENGINE STRUCTURE Twinport 1.6 Ecotec, 4-valves; 2 belt-driven overhead camshafts; aluminium cylinder head; electronic fuel injection and ignition; turbocharger, intercooler; 5-bearing crankshaft.
TRANSMISSION front wheel drive; hydraulic sdp clutch; 6-speed gearbox; final drive 3.94:1; Easytronic 5-speed 3.94 or 4.19:1.
CHASSIS steel monocoque with sub-frames; MacPherson strut independent front suspension; anti roll bar; rear suspension torsion beam axle, transverse arms, coil springs; anti roll bar; telescopic dampers; hydraulic servo disc brakes, front 26cm (10.2in) dia ventilated, rear 24cm (9.4in), Bosch

ABS; electro-hydraulic PAS; 53l (11.6gal) fuel tank; 175/70 R14, 185/60 R15 tyres, 5.6, 6J rims.
DIMENSIONS wheelbase 263cm (103.5in); track front 145cm (57in) rear 146.5cm (57.6in); length 405cm (159.4in); width 169.5cm (66.7in); height 162.5cm (63.9in); ground clearance 15cm (5.9in); turning circle 10.5m (34.4ft).
EQUIPMENT halogen lighting; power release tailgate; optional mobile phone with Bluetooth interface.
PERFORMANCE maximum speed 222kph (138.2mph); 34.1kph (21.2mph) @ 1000rpm; 0-100kph (62mph) 8.2sec; fuel consumption 8.1l/100km (34.8mpg).
PRICE £16,520.

Above: Easily the most powerful car in the class, according to Vauxhall, the exterior was upgraded and reprofiled. *(Right)* FlexSpace seating was retained along with VXR logos on the special Recaro seats.

2006 Astra Twin Top

The Astra Twin Top had a folding metal roof which, since its electro-hydraulic mechanism dismantled in three sections, the Vauxhall press office was unable to resist calling Three-Piece-Sweet. The overhead sections of the roof stacked on top of the back window, flat-packing themselves tidily and swiftly in the boot. Like the Astra Convertible, Bertone produced the Twin Top in Turin, where the body was stiffened underneath to compensate for the roof. Buyers had a choice of four engines 1.6 105PS, a new 1.8 of 140PS (pictured), 2.0Turbo of 170 or 200PS, and a 1.9CDTi of 150PS. When it reached production in 2006 it was cheaper than its soft-topped predecessor, even though the boot size was halved and weight increased by about 200kg (441lb). The Twin Top was also some 200kg (441lb) heavier than the 3-door hatchback on which it was based and rear seat room was not generous. One of four mid-size coupé cabriolets that appeared during the year, the Astra undercut rivals although buyers at the bottom of the scale had to do without the alloy wheels, and make do with the somewhat lethargic 1.6. *What Car?* found the Astra's "taut handling and composed ride … largely unsullied so you can push on with confidence". Twin Top gained three awards in its first season from *Auto Express*, and *Diesel Car*.

INTRODUCTION Frankfurt 2005, on sale spring 2006.
BODY Convertible 2-doors; 4-seats; weight 1400kg (3086.4lb); 2.0 Turbo, CDTi 1450kg (3196.6lb).
ENGINE 4-cylinders, in-line; front; transverse; 79mm x 81.5mm; 1598cc; compr 10.5:1; 77kW (103.2bhp) @6000rpm; 48.2kW (64.6bhp)/l; 150Nm (110.6lbft) @ 3900rpm. 1.8 80.5mm x 88.2mm; 1796cc; compr 10.5:1; 103kW (138.1bhp) @ 6300rpm; 57.3kW (76.8bhp)/l; 175Nm (129lbft) @ 3800rpm. Turbo 86mm x 86mm; 1998cc; compr 8.8:1; 125kW (167.6bhp) @ 5200rpm; 250Nm (184.4lbft) @ 1950rpm. CDTi 82mm x 90.4mm; 1910cc; compr 17.5:1; 110kW (147.5bhp) @ 4000rpm; 320Nm (236lbft) @ 2000rpm. Option 147kW (197.1bhp) @ 5400rpm; 262Nm (193.35lbft) @ 4200rpm.
ENGINE STRUCTURE Twinport, Ecotec 4-valves; 2 belt-driven ohc; aluminium cylinder head; electronic fuel injection; 5-bearing crankshaft.

CTDi common rail injection. Turbo 0.85bar, intercooler
TRANSMISSION front wheel drive; hydraulic sdp clutch; 5-speed gearbox; Turbo 6-speed; final drive 3.94:1; 1.8 auto 4.12:1; CDTi 3.65:1.
CHASSIS steel monocoque with front subframe; MacPherson strut independent front suspension; anti roll bars; rear suspension torsion beam axle; telescopic dampers; hydraulic servo disc brakes, front 28cm (11in) dia ventilated, rear 24cm (9.4in), 1.8 and Turbo 30.8cm (12.1in) and 26.4cm (10.3in); 52l (11.4gal) fuel tank; tyres 195/65 R16, 205/55 R16, 215/45 R17, 6.5 or 7J rims.
DIMENSIONS wheelbase 261.5cm (102.9in); track 149cm (58.6in); length 447.5cm (176.1in); width 183cm (72in); height 141.5cm (55.7in); ground clearance 13cm (5.1in) turning circle 11m (36ft).
EQUIPMENT air conditioning, 5-spoke alloy wheels, CD30 stereo, alloy trimmed pedals, ultrasonic security alarm.

PERFORMANCE maximum speed
186kph (115.8mph); 1.8, 209kph
(130.1mph); Turbo 224kph
(139.5mph); CDTi 213kph
(132.6mph); 0-100kph (62mph)
14.1sec, 11.4sec, 9.5sec, 10.2sec.
PRICE 1.6 £16,807, 1.8 Design
£18,807, CDTi Design £20,522.

**First Vauxhall to match the
140PS 1.8 engine** *(above)* **to an
automatic gearbox, the Twin
Top was available with pop-up
roll over bars.**

2006 Corsa 3-door and 5-door

The new Corsa made its debut at the first British International Motor Show in Docklands, London in the summer of 2006. With the front altered to conform with the Vauxhall family resemblance, and coupé styling, it was up-to-the-minute as ever and buyers were made a tempting offer on the 1.2 5-door at £945 less than its predecessor. Longer wheelbase and wider track provided more room inside; the 5-door Corsa was 18.3cm (7.2in) longer, 6.1cm (2.4in) wider and 5.2cm (2in) taller. The different appearance was designed to tempt younger, sportier buyers to the 3-door. Design chief Bryan Nesbitt said the two versions were tailor-made for different types of customer. Six engines were available, four petrol from the 1.0 3-cylinder 60PS, to 1.8litre, and two common rail diesels, one the 1.3 CDTi of 70/90PS, and the other a new 1.7litre of 125PS. There were six trim levels for the 3-door and 5-door range, Expression (a 3-door only), Life, Active, Design, SXi and SRi. Easytronic automated manual transmission was available on 1.0 and 1.2. Encouraged by the success of the versatile seating systems on larger Vauxhalls the Corsa had Dual Floor in which the load section could be set at different heights and Flex-Fix, an integral carrier that pulled out from the back bumper and could carry two bicycles.

INTRODUCTION on sale Oct 2006
Specification 1.2 Twinport.
BODY Saloon; 3/5-doors, 5-seats; weight 1055kg (2325.8lb)/1085kg (2391.9lb).
ENGINE 4-cylinders, in-line; front; transverse; 73.4mm x 72.6mm; 1229cc; compr 10.5:1; 59kW (79.1bhp) @ 5600rpm; 48kW (64.3bhp)/l; 110Nm (81.1lbft) @ 4000rpm .
ENGINE STRUCTURE 4-valves; 2 chain-driven ohc; al cylinder head; electronic fuel injection, engine management; 5-bearing crankshaft.
TRANSMISSION front wheel drive; hydraulic sdp clutch; 5-speed gearbox; final drive 4.29:1 Easytronic option; final drive 4.18:1.
CHASSIS integral steel structure, ifs by MacPherson struts; rear suspension torsion beam axle; coil springs, dampers, anti-roll bar; hydraulic servo disc brakes front ventilated 26cm (10.2in), rear drum; ABS and EBA; electric PAS; 45l (9.8gal) fuel tank; 185/70 R14 tyres, 185/65 R15, 195/55 R16, 214/45 R17 5.5J/6/7 rims.
DIMENSIONS wheelbase 261cm (102.7in); track front 148.5cm (58.4in) rear 148cm (58.2in); length 400cm (157.4in); width 171.5cm (67.5in), 5-door 174cm (68.5in); height 149cm (58.6in); ground clearance 14cm (5.5in); turning circle 10.4m (34.1ft).
EQUIPMENT CD sound system, electric door mirrors, Club side and curtain airbags, MP3 compatible audio; SXi heated mirrors, 16in alloy wheels, chrome tailpipe; Design automatic lighting control, rain sensing wipers, a/c, chrome dials.
PERFORMANCE maximum speed 168kph (104.6mph); 29.6kph (18.4mph) @ 1000rpm; 0-100kph (62mph) 13.9sec; fuel consumption 6.1l/100km (46.3mpg).
1.4: 1080kg (2380.9lb)/1120kg (2469.1lb); 73.4mm x 80.6mm; 1363cc; 66kW (88.5bhp) @ 5600rpm; 48.4kW (64.9bhp)/l; 125Nm (92.2lbft) @ 4000rpm; 5-speed final drive 4.18:1; 4-speed

automatic 4.12:1; 173kph (107.7mph);
12.4sec; 6.16l/100km (45.8mpg);
automatic 166kph (103.4mph);
14.8sec; 7.06l/100km (40mpg).
1.3 CDTi 70PS: 1130kg (2491.2lb);
69.6mm x 82mm; 1248cc; compr
18:1; 51kW (68.4bhp) @ 4000rpm;
40.9kW (54.8bhp)/l; 170Nm
(125.4lbft) @ 1750rpm (90PS: 66kW
(88.5bhp); 53kW (71.1bhp)/l;
200Nm (147.5lbft); turbocharger,
intercooler); 3.74:1 final drive (90PS
6-speed 3.72:1); 165kph (102.8mph);
14.5sec; 4.76l/100km (59.3mpg);
(90PS: 172kph (107.1mph); 12.7sec)
1.7CDTi 125PS: 1205kg (2656.5lb);
79mm x 86mm; 1686cc; 92kW
(123.4bhp) @ 4000rpm; 54.6kW
(73.2bhp)/l; 280Nm (206.5lbft) @
2300rpm; 2 belt-driven ohc; turbo
1.8bar; final drive 3.35:1; disc brakes
28cm (11in) front ventilated; 26.4cm
(10.4in) rear; 190kph (118.4mph);
9.9sec; 5l/100km (56.5mpg)
PRICE 1.0i 12v Active 3-door £9352;
1.2 Life 5-dor £10,122; 1.3 CDTi
Active Easytronic £11.342, 1,3 CDTi
SXi £12,107, 1.8 SXi 5-door £12,460.

2007 Antara

Similar to the Chevrolet Captiva, produced in South Korea, the Antara GTC (Gran Turismo Crossover) was announced at the Frankfurt Motor Show in 2005, where it gained *Autocar's* Concept Car of the Year award. It reached market in the closing months of 2006, nominally an SUV (Sports Utility Vehicle) that crossed over into off-road territory with Electronic Stability Programme (ESP), intelligent four wheel drive and hill descent control. Antara operated in front wheel drive for economy, automatically switching into four-wheel drive when ESP electronics was instructed to by an electro-hydraulic differential. There were three levels of trim, E with air conditioning, ultrasonic alarm, silver-coloured roof rails, 17in alloy wheels, CD and MP3 compatibility; S 18in alloys, climate control, heated seats, self-levelling suspension and chrome detailing; SE all these plus satellite navigation, leather upholstery, parking sensors and tyre pressure monitoring. The £475 Flex-Fix carrier took two bikes, without roof bar systems or tailgate frames. The entry-level 2.4-litre 140PS 4-cylinder petrol had two overhead camshafts, a Lanchester-type balancer shaft, and a manual gearbox. The 150PS 2.0-litre common-rail turbo-diesel (CDTi) had an automatic option. Within months it was joined by a 127 PS, also with a maintenance-free diesel particulate filter.

INTRODUCTION Paris Motor Show 2007.
Specification 2.4 140PS
BODY Saloon; 5-doors, 5-seats; weight 1730kg (3813.96lb).
ENGINE 4-cylinders, in-line; front; transverse; 87.5mm x 100mm; 2405cc; compr 9.6:1; 103kW (138.1bhp) @ 5200rpm; 42.8kW (bhp)/l; 220Nm (162.3lbft) @ rpm .
ENGINE STRUCTURE 4-valves; 2 belt-driven overhead camshafts; aluminium cylinder head; electronic Siemens EMS fuel injection, ignition; 5-bearing crankshaft.
TRANSMISSION front wheel drive, ESP controlled 4WD; hydraulic sdp clutch; 5-speed gearbox, final drive 4.36:1; 5-speed automatic; final drive 2.06:1.
CHASSIS steel monocoque with sub-frames; MacPherson strut independent front suspension; anti roll bar; rear suspension torsion beam axle, four transverse arms, coil springs; anti roll bar; telescopic dampers; hydraulic servo ventilated disc brakes, front 29.6cm (11.7in)

dia, rear 30.3cm (11.9in), ABS; speed-dependent PAS; 65l (14.3gal) fuel tank; 205/70 R16, 235/60 R17, 235/55 R18 tyres; 6.5/7 rims.
DIMENSIONS wheelbase 270.5cm (106.5in); track front 156cm (61.4in) rear 157cm (61.8in); length 457.5cm (180.1in); width 185cm (72.8in); height 170.5cm (67.1in); ground clearance 20cm (7.9in); turning circle 12.8m (42ft).
EQUIPMENT steering wheel mounted radio controls, rain-sensitive wipers, heat-reflective windscreen on S; electric folding mirrors, Bluetooth phone, xenon headlamps on SE.
PERFORMANCE maximum speed 175kph (109mph); 0-100kph (62mph) 11.9sec; fuel consumption 10.06l/100km (28.1mpg).
PRICE E 2.4 manual £19,850; 2.0CDTi automatic £22,395; S 2.0 CDTi automatic £23,995; SE manual £26,295.

2007 Corsa VXR

The VXR version of the Corsa was only available with three doors, and the style cue was triangular. Mirrors, front foglamp surround, and centre exhaust tailpipe were all distinctively three-sided. Identifiable by racy bumpers, side skirts and a roof spoiler, mesh grille and blue brake callipers, the VXR looked the part. Shell-backed seats, drilled aluminium pedals, piano black trim and VXR detailing including a competition-style flat-bottomed steering wheel made aspiring racing drivers feel at home. According to *Autocar* Corsa VXR scored well because, apparently unlike other VXRs, the Corsa's upgrading was planned from the beginning. Ride height was 1.9cm lower at the back, 1.2cm at the front, with stiffer springs and dampers, the anti-roll bar was 25 per cent stronger, brakes bigger and the ESP re-calibrated. The result was well balanced and exciting handling coupled with, unusually for a small hot hatchback, "a comfortable grown-up ride quality over just about any road surface." In September the SRi badge was brought back for drivers who did not require all the speed of the VXR, but liked its style and sharp driving. Available with five doors petrol versions had a detuned 150PS version of the turbo VXR, giving 0-60mph in 7.6sec and a top speed of 209kph (130mph). There was also a 125PS 4.8l/100km (58.9mpg) diesel.

INTRODUCTION on sale March 2007

BODY Saloon; 3-doors, 5-seats; weight 1350kg (2976.2lb).

ENGINE 4-cylinders, in-line; front; transverse; 79mm x 81.5mm; 1598cc; compr 8.8:1; 141kW (189bhp) @ 5500rpm; 88.2kW (118.2bhp)/l; 230Nm (169.61lbft) @ 2200rpm, 260Nm (191.8lbft) with overboost .

ENGINE STRUCTURE 4-valves; 2 belt-driven overhead camshafts; aluminium cylinder head; electronic fuel injection, engine management; 5-bearing crankshaft, turbocharger, intercooler.

TRANSMISSION front wheel drive; hydraulic sdp clutch; 6-speed gearbox; final drive 3.94:1.

CHASSIS integral steel structure, ifs by MacPherson struts; rear suspension torsion beam axle; coil springs, dampers, anti-roll bar; hydraulic servo ventilated disc brakes front 30.8cm (12.1in), rear 26.4cm (10.3in); ABS and EBA; electric PAS; 45l (9.8gal) fuel tank;

215/45 R17, 225/40 R18 tyres 7 J rims.

DIMENSIONS wheelbase 261cm (102.7in); track front 148.5cm (58.4in) rear 148cm (58.2in); length 400cm (157.4in); width 171.5cm (67.5in), 5-door 174cm (68.5in); height 149cm (58.6in); ground clearance 14cm (5.5in); turning circle 10.4m (34.1ft).

EQUIPMENT Recaro seats; CD sound system, electric door mirrors, side and curtain airbags, MP3 compatible audio; heated mirrors, chrome tailpipe; automatic lighting control, rain sensing wipers, air-conditioning, chrome dials.

PERFORMANCE maximum speed 225kph (140.1mph); 0-100kph (62mph) 6.8sec; fuel consumption 7.9l/100km (35.7mpg).

PRICE £16,495

Above: Triangular exhaust tailpipe, sweeping side skirts and an angular roof spoiler gave the little Corsa a muscular appearance. *(Right)* Mesh front grille echoed radiator stone-guards of pioneering race days on unmade tracks.

2007 Astra

The main changes for the new year were two new engines that had improved economy and exhaust emissions, as well as more speed. The 1.6 Twinport was replaced by an Ecotec unit with 10PS more than before, for Sport Hatch, 5-door, Twin Top and Estate, most of which also gained the new 1.6litre turbocharged engine replacing the 170PS 2.0litre. The freshening-up provided the Astra with new front and rear lights, front bumper, extra chrome detailing on the grille and the option of piano black or matt chrome interior. Sport Hatch Astras gained a honeycomb style grille and there were four petrol options, three diesels, and the VXR with 237PS as well as individual styling, trim, and chassis. The Astra was a well-balanced car, the suspension of the less-sporty ones supple and the ride agreeable. Yet against rivals from say Audi, Volvo or VW depreciation of Vauxhall's mid-range car was sometimes heavy; *What Car?* found the Sport Hatch worth only 36 per cent of its list price after three years against 47 to 50 per cent for others. On the credit side it found the Astra well priced, stylish, and powerful, "eager at town speeds and by the time you shift up into fifth noticeably urgent." Road noise was reduced in Astras against rivals but diesel commotion remained.

INTRODUCTION January 2007 Specification 1.6 Twinport.
BODY Saloon; 5-doors, 5-seats; weight 1190kg (2623.47lb); estate 1250kg (2755.75lb).
ENGINE 4-cylinders, in-line; front; transverse; 79mm x 81.5mm; 1598cc; compr 10.5:1; 85kW (113.98bhp) @ 6000rpm; 48.2kW (64.64bhp)/l; 155Nm (114lbft) @ 3900rpm .
ENGINE STRUCTURE Twinport Ecotec, 4-valves; 2 belt-driven overhead camshafts, aluminium cylinder head; electronic fuel injection, ignition; 5-bearing crankshaft.
TRANSMISSION front wheel drive; sdp clutch; 5-speed gearbox; final drive 3.94:1; 5-speed Easytronic option.
CHASSIS steel monocoque with front subframe; MacPherson strut independent front suspension; anti roll bars; rear suspension torsion beam axle; telescopic dampers; hydraulic servo disc brakes, front 28cm (11in) dia ventilated, rear 24cm

(9.4in); 52l (11.4gal) fuel tank; tyres 195/65 R16, 205/55 R16, 215/45 R17, 6.5 or 7J rims.
DIMENSIONS wheelbase 261.5cm (102.9in); estate 270cm (106.3in); track 149cm (58.7in); length 425cm (167.3in); estate 451.5cm (177.8in); width 175.5cm (69.1in); estate 179cm (70.5in); height 146cm (57.5in); estate 150cm (59.1in); ground clearance 13cm (5.1in); turning circle 11m (36.1ft).
EQUIPMENT air conditioning, alloy wheels, airbags, SRi stability control.
1.6 Turbo: 1350kg (2976.2lb); 79mm x 81.5mm; 1598cc; compr 8.8:1; 132kW (177bhp) @ 5500rpm; 82.6kW (110.8bhp)/l; 230Nm (169.6lbft) @ 1980rpm; turbocharger, intercooler; 6-speed gearbox; 3.94:1 final drive; 221kph (137.7mph); 8.3sec; 8l/100km (35.3mpg).
1.6 Turbo180PS: 1350kg (2976.2lb); 79mm x 81.5mm; 1598cc; compr 8.8:1; 132kW (177bhp) @ 5500rpm; 82.6kW (110.8bhp)/l; 230Nm

(169.6lbft) @ 1980rpm; 6-speed final drive 3.94:1; 221kph (137.7mph); 8.3sec; 8l/100km (35.3mpg).

VXR 2.0 240PS: 1310kg (2888lb); estate 1350kg (2976.2lb); 86mm x 86mm; 1998cc; 177kW (237.4bhp) @ 5600rpm; 88.6kW (118.8bhp)/l 320Nm (236lbft) @ 2400rpm; 0.85bar turbo; 6-speed 3.83:1 final drive; 32.1cm (12.6in) and 27.8cm (10.9in) discs; 225/40 R18 tyres 8J rims; 244kph (152mph); 47.5kph (29.6mph) @ 1000rpm; 6.4sec; 9.73l/100km (29mpg).

PERFORMANCE maximum speed 187kph (116.5mph); 33kph (20.6mph) @ 1000rpm; 0-100kph (62mph) 12.2sec; fuel consumption 6.9l/100km (40.9mpg).

PRICE 1.6 Life 5 door £13,515; 1.6 Turbo SRi Sport Hatch £18,200 1.9CDTi Design £18,275; VXR £19,120.

2007 VXR8

GM Europe had no equivalent of the Australian-built Vauxhall VXR8, effectively a replacement for the Monaro, with the same 6.0litre 420PS V8 producing even more power. A 4-door saloon based on the Holden Clubsport R8, it was more practical than a Monaro, with electronic driver aids such as a stability system and traction control that could be turned off by drivers on a track day. VXR8 was the first in the Holden series of Vauxhall's high-performers to have the option of an automatic transmission. To offer sporting drivers total control this had a manual over-ride, and a sport setting to make the make the most of the strong performance. The automatic was claimed to be only half a second slower to 60mph than the manual. Stopping power was commensurate; Vauxhall said it would come to a standstill from 60mph faster than a Lamborghini Murcielago or a BMW M5. Monaro was not completely played out following the VXR8's arrival however. The limited edition VXR500 with a positive displacement supercharger produced 500PS and 677Nm, reached 60mph in less than 5sec and had a top speed of 180mph. A number of the special conversions was available at £35,995, claimed to be half the price of any other 500PS coupe, from dealer Greens Vauxhall.

INTRODUCTION July 2007.
BODY Saloon; 4-doors, 5-seats; weight 1805kg (3979.3lb).
ENGINE 8-cylinders, 90deg V; front; 101.6mm x 92mm; 5967cc; compr 10.4:1; 309kW (414.4bhp) @ 5700rpm; 51.8kW (69.5bhp)/l; 550Nm (405.7lbft) @ 4400rpm.
ENGINE STRUCTURE Gen III (L98) 2-valves; pushrod ohv crossflow; central camshaft; aluminium cylinder head, block; sequential fuel injection, distributorless ignition with coil-per-cylinder, twin knock sensors; 5-bearing crankshaft.
TRANSMISSION rear wheel drive; hydraulic sdp clutch; 6-speed gearbox; limited slip diff, traction control; final drive 3.45:1; 6-speed automatic; final drive 2.92:1.
CHASSIS steel monocoque; MacPherson strut independent front suspension; anti roll bar; rear suspension independent controllink, coil springs; anti roll bar; telescopic dampers, gas presssure at rear; hydraulic servo ventilated disc brakes, front 36.5cm (14.4in) dia, rear 28.6cm (11.3in) dia, finned callipers; ABS; PAS; 73l (16.1gal) fuel tank; 245/45 R18, 245/40 R19 tyres, Felgen 7/8J rims.
DIMENSIONS wheelbase 291.5cm (114.8in); track front 160cm (63in) rear 162cm (63.8in); length 489.5cm (192.7in); width 190cm (74.8in); height 147.5cm (58.1in); ground clearance 11.5cm (4.5in); turning circle 11.5m (37.7ft).
EQUIPMENT climate control, leather trim, automatic £1,400, satellite navigation, 20in wheels.
PERFORMANCE maximum speed 240kph (149.5mph); 0-100kph (62mph) 4.9sec; fuel consumption 12l/100km (23.5mpg).
PRICE £34,995.

Vauxhall Chronology: 1857 to the 21st century

1857 Alexander Wilson produces marine engines at Vauxhall Iron Works.

1894 Wilson leaves Vauxhall

1903 First Vauxhall car

1904 Glasgow-London reliability trial; success of 6hp Vauxhall.

1905 Car factory moves to Luton. First 4-cylinder model, the 18 hp.

1906 Bonnet flutes appear on Vauxhall cars.

1907 Formation of Vauxhall Motors Limited.

1908 Vauxhall wins 2000-mile RAC Trial.

1909 A 20 hp achieves speed and distance records at Brooklands. Vauxhall wins O'Gorman trophy at Brooklands

1910 Vauxhall enters three 20hp cars in Prince Henry of Prussia trial. A Vauxhall becomes first 20hp car to exceed 100mph. Vauxhall wins second O'Gorman Trophy

1911 Vauxhall wins third O'Gorman Trophy and a 16hp completes the Russian Reliability Trial. Modified 16hp Vauxhall takes four world speed records. New 20hp C-type (Prince Henry).

1912 Vauxhall works team takes part in French Coupe de l'Auto race.

1913 E-type 4½-litre – later known as the 30-98 - sets new hill-climb record at Shelsley Walsh.

1914 In May a 30-98 E-type finishes second in Russian Grand Prix. GP Vauxhalls compete in Isle of Man TT race and French Grand Prix.

1914–1918 Nearly 2000 25hp D-types produced as Army staff cars.

1922 The 25hp D-type becomes the 23hp OD (23/60 model). Three special TT racers built.

1924 Vauxhall Motors withdraws from motor sport.

1925 Vauxhall Motors becomes wholly owned subsidiary of General Motors.

1927 Production of R-type 20/60 begins.

1929 Replacement of R-type with T-type 20/60.

1930 1931MY Cadet 17 and 26hp models launched together with T80 6-cylinder chassis.

1931 First Bedfords; 2-ton trucks (WHG and WLG) and two bus chassis (WHB and WLB)

1932 Bedfords account for half British commercial vehicle exports. Introduction of 30cwt Bedford (WS) and 12 cwt vans. Cadet VY/VX first with synchromesh.

1933 Vauxhall Light Six (ASY and ASX) 12 and 14hp models launched. Also BY and BX 20hp and 26hp 6-cylinder models. 3-ton Bedford trucks (WT) and 8cwt vans (ASY, ASX) introduced.

1935 Light Six replaced by DY and DX; first British cars with independent front suspension. 26-seater bus chassis (WTB) joins Bedford range.

1936 Introduction of 1937 MY 25hp GY and GL.

1937 H-type – first integral-construction British car. First production car with independent front suspension.

1938 12hp I-type, also 14 hp J-type. Bedford introduces 5/6cwt van (HC).

1939 Introduction of 10/12cwt Bedford van (JC) and OB coach.

1939–1945 War production includes 250,00 Bedford trucks and 5640 Churchill tanks.

1946 Car production resumes – H, I, and J-types. K, M, and O Bedford models in production. 5-ton trucks and tractor unit for articulated vehicles; OB 26-seater coach chassis.

1947 Bedford first British manufacturer to make 500,000 trucks

1948 L-type Wyvern and Velox. Factory expansion at Luton costs £14 million.

1950 'Big Bedford' S-type 7-ton truck and 10-ton tractor unit – Bedford's first forward-control civilian models. 32/40-seater bus chassis (SB).

1951 E-type Wyvern and Velox.

1952 Bedford 10/12cwt CA van first British non-car derived light van. R-type first 4 x 4 civilian truck.

1953 Vauxhall Jubilee. Millionth vehicle. New Bedford A-type Middleweights replace K, M and O.

1954 £36 million plant-expansion project; E-type Cresta.

1955 Bedford production increased by transfer of trucks from Luton to Dunstable. 64,773 Bedfords is more in one year than any other British make.

1957 First Victor, 1½-litre F-type saloons. PA 6-cylinder models replace E-type. Two new 6-ton Bedford C and D trucks, normal and forward control. First Bedford-built diesels.

1958 Victor first factory-built Vauxhall estate. The 1,000,000th Bedford is made. TJ normal-control models introduced.

1959 Vauxhall Motors produces 2–millionth vehicle. Expansion announced at Ellesmere Port, Cheshire

1960 Bedford TK trucks and tractor units. Bedfords output exceeds 100,000 a year.

1961 Vauxhall FB Victor. Bedford VAS 30-seater coach chassis.

1962 PB 6-cylinder Vauxhalls. VAL twin-steer Bedford coach chassis for 52/55-seaters.

1963 HA Viva 1-litre saloon. First production at Ellesmere Port

1964 Victor 101 (FC series), 3.3-litre engine for

PB Velox/Cresta. Bedford 6cwt and 8cwt Bedford HA vans. Ellesmere Port opens with HA Viva.

1965 PC 6-cylinder cars and 250,000th Viva. VAM 45-seat coach chassis.

1966 HB Viva at Ellesmere Port. KM heavy trucks take Bedford into the 22/24-ton class.

1967 FD Victor , British Car of the Year.

1968 Ventora variant; three new FD Victor estates. HB Viva 4-door. Work starts on Millbrook proving ground. KM 6 x 2.

1969 2,000,000th Bedford – 1,500,000 of them trucks. CF van.

1970 HC Viva. Bedford M-type 4 x 4 truck and first underfloor engine coach chassis (YRQ)

1971 Millionth Viva. Firenza coupe. Dealer Team Vauxhall formed. Bedford KM expands with 6 x 4 models.

1972 FE 1800 and 2300 Victors.

1973 Magnum 1800 and 2300.

1974 First phase of Bedford TM premium trucks and tractor units (Detroit Diesel 6V-71 models)

1975 Chevette hatchback. Cavalier saloons and coupe. Phase 2 Bedford TMs (500 engine). Bedford's 500 engine for TK, KM and coach chassis. 140in wheelbase added to CF.

1976 Replacement of FE series VX. Five saloons

and estate added to Chevette. Phase 3 Bedford TMs introduced (Detroit Diesel 8V-71). JJL Midi Bus. Van range widened with Chevanne. GM diesel engine for CF.

1977 Cavalier begins at Luton.

1978 Vauxhall 75th anniversary. Equus Concept sports car shown. 1,000,000th Bedford van. 2,000,000th Bedford truck – over 500,000 of them TKs. Record totals for British truck make and British truck model.

1979 Astra front-wheel-drive for MY 1980. GM Trucks Dortmund markets Bedfords in Germany. TM 'Long Haul' concept vehicle.

1980 Vauxhall Viceroy. Bedford TL trucks, KB 25 pick-up and YNT turbocharged coach chassis.

1981 J-series Cavalier. Bedford's 50th anniversary. TL Aero concept truck. First Astras at Ellesmere Port.

1982 Diesel option for Astra and Cavalier; Cavalier 2-door convertible. ½ millionth Bedford TJ truck since 1958. 1½ millionth Bedford exported. Astra van in Bedford range.

1983 Nova and Astra GTE launched. Three year £70 million expansion of Bedford production. Bedford made part of GM Overseas Vehicle Corporation.

1984 GM £100 million investment in Vauxhall facilities. Mark 2 Astra. Bedford CF electric van; CF2 van; Astra van and 1-tonne Midi van.

1985 £90 million paint shop at Luton. Astra 4 x 4 rally car; ½ millionth Cavalier sold in UK. New Bedford van plant at Luton; Astramax van and Rascal ½-ton micro-van.

1986 Bedford YMPS coach chassis. Truck production phased out. GM Europe established.

1987 New paint shop in operation at Luton. Carlton voted 'Car of the Year'.

1988 Vauxhall-Lotus racing car. Cavalier sales pass 1 million with Cavalier III. Vauxhall Motors net profit £152 million.

1989 Cavalier 4 x 4 and Lotus-Carlton. Astra range 32 models. £50 million modernisation of Luton plant as Vauxhall and Opel make 1.5 million cars a year and achieve record increased market share. UK sales up 15 per cent to 349,000 cars.

1990 Griffin House, named after heraldic corporate logo, new headquarters in Luton. MasterFit servicing and Network Q used car programmes inaugurated. Vauxhall starts first major export initiative for 15 years

1991 Frontera; Vauxhall enters SUV market

1992 Scamp concept recreational pick-up. Network Q introduced. ECOTEC £193million V6 engine plant opens

1993 Queen's Award for Export Achievement; Investors in People Award

1995 Maxx concept car. Vauxhall 90 years in Luton; £3million recreational facility. 100,000 V6 engines made at Ellesmere Port

1997 CTC (City Trekking Concept) shown. Luton 22 May 250,000th Vectra. Bio-fuel Combo van

1998 Ellesmere Port makes 250,000th V6 engine. 3-shift working for new Astra. Frontera built at IBC Luton plant following £100m refurbishment. Frontera sets record driving round the world in 21days 2hours 14minutes.

1999 Movano medium van; Ellesmere Port makes 3 millionth car; £5m engineering centre for light commercial and recreational vehicles established at Millbrook

2000 Manufacturing restructure; Luton to cease production of cars. Aliminium Ecotec engine. New engineering centre at Millbrook opens. Vauxhall's Sustainability Report UK's first with social,economic, and environmental data equally.

2001 GM-Fiat joint venture. Vivaro medium van. Kevin Wale MD. Vauxhall wins BTC

2002 Luton's last car 7,415,045th. Vauxhall Motors produces 131,390 vehicles with workforce of 5,500. Network Q sells its millionth, half millionth Vectra sold in UK. Second BTC. GM Daewoo integrated

2003 Century in Motion celebrations. Recreation of 1000-mile Trial. 3000 Dualfuel sales. Third BTC

2004 VXR performance brand introduced, inspired by VX Racing BTC success. Trixx concept car at Geneva Motor Show. Millionth Corsa in UK. Fourth BTC

2005 Three month million mile programme results in 17,395 test drives makes Vauxhall Britain's best selling car brand in April. Ellesmere Port's 4 millionth Astra. Commercial vehicle sales rise by 32 per cent

2006 Corsavan concept at Paris Motor Show. HydroGen 3 fuel cell Zafira does 9696km (6025mile) reliability run

2007 GTC Concept at Geneva Motor Show Ellesmere Port nominated along with Bochum Germany, Tröllhattan Sweden, and Gliwice Poland in £2billion investment plan to build Astra.

Bibliography

The Motoring Encyclopedia, Waverley & Amalgamated 1934 & 1938
Classic Car Profiles, ed Anthony Harding, Profile Publications 1967
A History of Vauxhall, Vauxhall Public Relations Department 1980
Motor Makers in Ireland, John Moore, Blackstaff 1985, Lagan 1995
The Griffin Story, Vauxhall Public Affairs Department 1990
Vauxhall The Postwar Years, Trevor Alder 1991
The Vauxhall, Peter Hull, Shire Publications 1992
Vauxhall 30-98, Nic Portway, New Wensum Publishing 1995
Vauxhall, Stuart Fergus Broatch Sutton Publishing Ltd 1997
Vauxhalls of the 1930s, Motoring Portfolio, compiled Colin Pitt
Pre-War Vauxhall, Vol 1, Transport Source Books
Vauxhalls of the 1940s and 1950s, Transport Source Books
Cars in the UK, 1945-1995 Vols 1 and 2 Graham Robson MRP 1996
A-Z of British Coachbuilders 1919-1960, Nick Walker Bay View Books 1997
Vauxhall, A Century in Motion 1903-2003, David Burgess-Wise, CWP 2003
Vauxhall Cars 1903-1918, Nic Portway, New Wensum Publishing 2006

Among the sources used in research were the author's collections of the Swiss annual *Automobil Revue/Revue Automobile* published by Hallwag and Espace Media, *Automobile Year* published by Editions J-R Piccard, and also of *The Motor*, The *Autocar, Autosport, Motor Sport, Classic Car, Classic & Sportscar, The Automobile, Automobile Quarterly, Veteran & Vintage* and *Brooklands Books* Compilations to all of whose proprietors motoring historians owe continuing thanks.

Acknowledgements

The publishers would like to thank Nick Reilly, former chairman and chief executive, and Vauxhall Motors Ltd for helping to make the first Vauxhall File possible, and Vauxhall staff, in particular Tony Spalding and Andrew Andersz for help and encouragement, and Dennis Shearer for photographic research. *Vauxhall File 2* was made possible with support from Denis Chick. Thanks are also due to former incumbents at the Vauxhall press office with whom we have dealt over many years including Michael Marr, Derek Goatman, Ken Moyes, Dick Herdegan, Tom Dobbyn, and many more whose enthusiastic promotion of Vauxhall cars contributed to our knowledge and experience. Special mention must be made of the late Gwyn Hughes of *The Vauxhall Motorist* and his revisions of the Vauxhall histories produced by the Public Affairs department.

Probably no individual knows the early history of Vauxhall as well as Nic Portway, author of the definitive book on the 30-98, who kindly read, added to, and revised the manuscript dealing with the years up to the General Motors takeover. Our photographic research was based on Vauxhall's archives, the National Motor Museum with thanks to Jonathan Day, and Nic Portway's extensive collection of hitherto unpublished pictures.

David Fletcher at the Bovingdon Tank Museum provided information on the Churchill tank and as with all Dove Publishing books, our thanks are due to print consultant David Bann, directors Mike Roberts and Ruth Dymock, and designer Andrew Barron.

Index

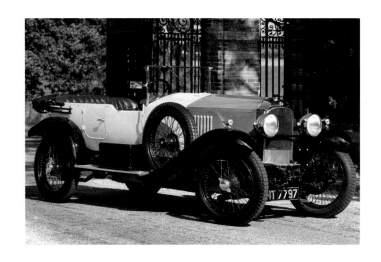